INSURGENT NATIONS

T0386567

/ AFRICAN
/ ARGUMENTS

African Arguments is a series of short books about contemporary Africa and the critical issues and debates surrounding the continent. The books are scholarly and engaged, substantive and topical. They focus on questions of justice, rights and citizenship; politics, protests and revolutions; the environment, land, oil and other resources; health and disease; economy: growth, aid, taxation, debt and capital flight; and both Africa's international relations and country case studies.

Managing Editor, Stephanie Kitchen

Series editors

Adam Branch
Eyob Gebremariam
Ebenezer Obadare
Portia Roelofs
Jon Schubert
Nicholas Westcott
Nanjala Nyabola

PAULA CRISTINA ROQUE

Insurgent Nations

Rebel Rule in Angola and South Sudan

HURST & COMPANY, LONDON

Published in collaboration with the International African Institute.
First published in the United Kingdom in 2024 by
C. Hurst & Co. (Publishers) Ltd.,
New Wing, Somerset House, Strand, London WC2R 1LA

A Cataloguing-in-Publication data record for this book
is available from the British Library.

ISBN: 9781787389434

www.hurstpublishers.com

CONTENTS

ACKNOWLEDGEMENTS

A book that started as a DPhil thesis carries with it many transformations but also many debts of gratitude. From a very young age, I was read into the world of rebel governance and insurgency in Angola because of my family and their links to Angolan liberation. We had supporters and active members from all three liberation movements: UNITA (União Nacional para a Independência Total de Angola), MPLA (Movimento Popular para a Libertação de Angola) and FNLA (Frente Nacional para a Libertação de Angola). Until the 1992 elections, I was convinced that both the MPLA and UNITA had the capacity to win the war and run a state based on the version of Angola they envisioned. It would take another 20 years, when I was finally able to visit UNITA's ruined rebel capital of Jamba in 2012, before I understood fully that these two visions had been so radically different with deep resonance in current politics and society.

I am indebted to all the UNITA and SPLM/A politicians and military commanders who over the years have trusted me with their stories. While I had lived Angola's war in a very personal way, the privilege of working on South Sudan began only in 2008 when the SPLM/A was already governing an autonomous entity. I began to question what factors allowed some groups to govern and others to falter. I began to closely engage with the SPLM/A's leadership on several occasions, including a scenarios exercise in preparation for the transition to independence. In 2011, I had the honour of witnessing first-hand the hope, dignity and unity demonstrated by the millions of South Sudanese when they voted for self-determination. I was there to celebrate the declaration of independence. Unfortunately, I was also witness to the nation's descent into chaos in 2013, and again in 2016.

Obtaining the permissions required to reach both Jamba and New Site was complex, but for different reasons. For UNITA's capital Jamba, matters were complicated by the sensitivities of allowing a civilian into the military area of the defeated enemy, in an atmosphere where historical denial and revisionism was a post-conflict strategy by the victors. Permission had to be granted by the Chief of General Staff of the Angolan Armed Forces, and the mission had to be conceived as a military mission, with introduction letters and requests for passage and logistical support from all the military units across the eight provinces I crossed in Angola. Thank you to General Geraldo Sachipengo Nunda for giving me the military clearance and mission support to visit Jamba. You took time out of your busy schedule to help me, and for that I am truly grateful. The Angolan Armed Forces were a pillar of support for me. Reaching Jamba also required passing into Namibia, as entire areas in the province of Kuando Kubango were left mined and destroyed, perhaps as a deterrent for those trying to see what Jamba was. Thank you, Colonel Agnaldo, Sargent Nelson and Captain Zenobio for being my travel companions. Thank you, Isaias Samakuva and Liberty Chiaka, for encouraging people to talk to me about all aspects of UNITA's history, even the taboos and dark episodes. Your time and teachings were invaluable. In Angola, I owe my gratitude to General Peregrino Chindondo Wambu and Lola who inspired, supported and provided me always with logistical solutions for travelling across the eight provinces. Over the years, General Gato, Abel Chivukuvuku, Horacio Njunjuvili, Ernesto Mulato, Adalberto da Costa Junior, Carlos Morgado, General Numa, General Chiwale, among many others, taught me so much about UNITA and Angolan politics. I am also grateful to Savimbi's mapmaker, Colonel José Kungo, for drawing from memory the layout of Jamba.

Travelling to the SPLM/A's leadership headquarters in New Site was also a complicated affair, given the sensitive nature of entering military training grounds in a country that, despite having attained independence from Khartoum, was still on full operational readiness for war. It was necessary to obtain permission from the Ministry of National Security and the former Chief of General Staff of the SPLA. Thank you, Lima Lima and General Oyay Deng Ajak, for getting me that military clearance. Batali, I was so lucky to have you as a travel companion on the difficult and dangerous journeys. A letter was prepared giving me full access and free passage to New Site, and upon reaching the closest town, Kapoeta, we were instructed to take an armed officer to show us the way and protect us from armed Toposa groups. I am so grateful to John Gai Yoh and Mary, Killa Janda, Aleu Garang, Pagan Amum, Edward Lino, Luka Biong Deng, Gen Majak D'Agoot, Kosti Manibe, Gabriel Deng, Atem Yaak Atem, Alfred Lukoji, Atiff Kiir, Lual Deng, James Okuk, James Wanni Igga and Emmanuel Bamia for all your advice, support and wisdom during my research in South Sudan. The many difficult, days-long drives to Yambio from Juba were made possible by the safe driving of Mathew and Kennedy. The year 2021 was one of great loss. In South Sudan, I was taken in, guided and protected by Canon Clement Janda. Uncle Clement had the political foresight of a leader who had survived many trials and tribulations. His sacrifice and dedication to the liberation of his people was extraordinary. I also had the great privilege of working with Ambassador Nicholas Bwakira, who remains one of the most exceptional and kindest diplomats I have ever encountered. Their departures are huge losses for their families and friends, but also for Africa, which has lost two wise men and living libraries.

While researching in Angola and South Sudan, I encountered many difficulties. In Yambio, I came close to death with a gall bladder infection and pneumonia that could only be treated in South Africa—a 12-hour drive to Juba and then two flights away. Experiencing the basic healthcare system in South Sudan and talking to the only doctor in Juba who had a functioning ultrasound machine, I came to better understand the difficulties of building a state without infrastructure, human capital and logistics. I am grateful to all those who helped. Thank you, Paru Sankar and Uncle Clement Janda, for looking out for me in Juba. Thank you, Moretlo Molefi, Carole Chiloane and Philemon Ndlovu, for keeping me safe and taking me to the hospital.

Several friends helped in the hardest moments of writing the doctoral thesis. Sean Cleary, always a mentor, your comments were frank and wonderful. Thank you, Patrycja Stys, Will Jones, Shane MacGiollabhui and Douglas Johnson, for your feedback and invaluable advice. Thank you, Raufu Mustapha, for being my friend and supervisor. You left a huge vacuum in Oxford and are very missed. I am truly grateful to Ricardo Soares de Oliveira, not only for being a friend but for stepping in to help me.

This book is dedicated to my mother, Fatima Moura Roque, and my children, Santiago, Balthazar and Sophia.

LIST OF ABBREVIATIONS

ARCISS	Agreement for the Resolution of the Conflict in South Sudan
AU	African Union
BRINDE	*Brigada National de Defesa do Estado* (Brigade for the State's National Defence)
CANS	Civil Authority for a New Sudan
CCSS	Coordination Council of South Sudan
CDRF	County Development Revolving Fund
CEKK	*Centro de Formação Comandante Kapese Kafundanga* (Commander Kapese Kafundanga Leadership School)
CENFIN	*Centro de Formação Integral da Juventude* (Centre for the Formation of the Youth)
CMA	Civil–Military Administrator
CNE	*Comissão Nacional Eleitoral* (National Electoral Commission)
COPE	*Commando Operacional Estratégico* (Strategic Operational Command)
CPA	Comprehensive Peace Agreement
DDR	disarmament, demobilisation and reintegration

DIVITAC	*Divisão de Transmissões do Alto Commandante* (Transmissions Division of the Commander in Chief)
DRC	Democratic Republic of the Congo
ETAPE	*Escola Técnica de Agricultura e Pecuária* (Technical School for Agriculture and Livestock)
FAA	Angolan Armed Forces
FALA	*Forças Armadas de Libertação de Angola* (Armed Forces for the Liberation of Angola)
FAO	Food and Agriculture Organization
FAPLA	*Forças Armadas Populares de Libertação de Angola* (Popular Armed Forces for the Liberation of Angola)
FNLA	*Frente Nacional para a Libertação de Angola* (National Front for the Liberation of Angola)
GFSCC	General Field Staff Command Council of the SPLM/A
GITOP	*Gabinete de Intercepção Técnico e Operacional* (Office of Operational and Technical Interception)
GNU	Government of National Unity
GOSS	Government of South Sudan
IDEAS	Institute of Development Environment and Agricultural Studies
IDP	internally displaced person
INGO	International Non-Governmental Organisation
IPCS	Institute for the Promotion of Civil Society
JURA	*Juventude Revolucionária de Angola* (UNITA's Youth League)
KUPA	Kwatcha UNITA Press
LIMA	*Liga da Mulher Angolana* (UNITA's Women's League)

MIRNA	*Ministério dos Recursos Naturais* (Ministry of Natural Resources)
MoU	memorandum of understanding
MPLA	*Movimento Popular para a Libertação de Angola* (Popular Movement for the Liberation of Angola)
MRDA	Mundri Relief and Development Association
MSF	*Médecins Sans Frontières*
NAPEC	National Political and Executive Committee of the SPLM/A
NCP	National Congress Party
NEC	National Executive Council of the SPLM/A
NHA	National Health Authority
NIF	National Islamic Front
NILEPET	National Petroleum Corporation
NLC	National Liberation Council of the SPLM/A
NSCC	New Sudan Council of Churches
OFICENGUE	*Oficina de Guerra* (Central Workshop of War Material)
OLS	Operation Lifeline Sudan
PHC	primary healthcare
PMHC	Politico–Military High Command of the SPLM/A
QG	*Quartel General* (general headquarters)
REOP	*Repartição de Obras Publicas* (Public Works Department)
RM	UNITA Military Region
SADF	South African Defence Force
SALTE	*Serviço de Água e Electricidade* (Water and Electricity Service)
SINGO	Indigenous NGO in South Sudan
SMC	Sudan Medical Care

LIST OF ABBREVIATIONS

SPLM/A	Sudan People's Liberation Movement/Army
SPLM-Nasir	Sudan People's Liberation Movement – Nasir faction
SRRA	Sudan Relief and Rehabilitation Association
SSG	*Serviço de Segurança Geral* (General Security Service)
STAR programme	Sudan Transitional Assistance Rehabilitation programme
TREC	Timber Resources Evaluation Committee
UN	United Nations
UNITA	*União Nacional para a Independência Total de Angola* (National Union for the Total Independence of Angola)
UNSC	United Nations Security Council
UPA	*União das Populações de Angola*
VORGAN	*Voz da Resistência do Galo Negro* (Voice of Resistance of the Black Cockerel)
WES	Western Equatoria State
WFP	World Food Programme
YAFA	Yambio Farmers Association

LIST OF TABLES AND FIGURES

INTRODUCTION

In the house of the 'enemy', not all is draped with vengeance, chaos and violence; you can find much familiarity, structure and intricacy. Travelling to the rear bases of two of Africa's most emblematic, resilient and complex insurgencies revealed many of the contradictions of war, state-building, social engineering and the game of perceptions and legitimacy. The trips always began with bureaucratic processes of seeking permission and justifying the visit. Military commanders, intelligence chiefs and their advisors were made privy to the details of field research trips seeking to understand a portion of history. They followed with military armed escorts in Toyota pick-ups across sparsely populated areas, some heavily mined, others ridden with tribal militia guarding against cattle rustling. The destinations were Jamba—the capital of the União Nacional para a Independência Total de Angola (UNITA)— at the south-easternmost tip of Angola that bordered Zambia and Namibia, and the mountainous base of New Site of the Sudan People's Liberation Movement/Army (SPLM/A) in South Sudan. Destinations also included Yambio, the first county liberated by the SPLM/A, bordering the Democratic Republic of the Congo (DRC) and the Central African Republic (CAR).

The Republic of the Free Lands of Angola and the New Sudan, UNITA and the SPLM/A's political and territorial orders housed the imaginings of a future state and nation, grounded administrative exercises in local realities and simultaneously revealed the most

1

hopeful and reformist—and draconian and expedient—features of parallel statehood. They denied the governments of Sudan and Angola the ability to extend administrative control over their countries and reap the full benefits of sovereignty. As with every war, each society and each rebel movement were transitory and ever-changing ecosystems. Structured according to differing principles, institutions, relationships and priorities, the parallel states of the SPLM/A in Yambio and UNITA in Jamba were both aimed at military and logistical survival, political renewal and social embeddedness. Visiting several towns that comprised these alternative political orders in 2012 revealed a temporal deferment of finality: both nations remained in waiting, both states failed to protect their people and history would record the abuses and terror, not so much the successes. They would forever remain incomplete reformist projects. The history of rebel governance in both countries was as much an inherent property as it was an external threat. The threat was to the unfulfilled possibilities and remaining expectations that peace and political transition had failed to deliver 20 years after the wars had ended.

But this story begins many years before.

On 22 February 2002, Angola awoke to the news that would end the civil war: the leader of UNITA, Jonas Malheiro Savimbi, had been killed. Reactions were varied in Luanda. Many celebrated, others remained calm but several from different political organisations and opposition parties understood that the main source of resistance to the governing Movimento Popular para a Libertação de Angola (MPLA) had been extinguished. The mood across the country was sombre despite the renewed hope for a durable peace. Reactions in the countryside were very different, as over four million people were affected by years of scorched-earth policies resulting in a deepening and underreported humanitarian crisis. The leader, once admired for his resilience and vision for Angola, died a brutal warlord who had killed, maimed and purged many of his own during the last decade of the war. Rapidly the mythology of how he had died gave rise to several versions of how this seemingly invincible warrior had finally been eliminated. In the accounts of several survivors and political supporters, he was executed after being tracked down by

2

government troops in the province of Moxico, his body riddled with bullets. Others believe he took his own life with his personal ivory-crafted revolver, accepting his fate but not allowing himself to be captured. Twenty years later, the truth of what happened remains contested. Yet his death was both expected and wrapped in betrayal, revenge and a collective effort to hunt down a man who epitomised a struggle against a government that for many remained illegitimate.

On 4 April 2002, UNITA and the government of Angola signed the Luena Peace Accords. The preceding three decades of conflict had seen the deaths of 1 million Angolans, the displacement of 4.1 million, the fleeing of 450,000 to neighbouring countries, the maiming of 100,000 and the all-encompassing militarisation of society. The war had also ravaged the country's political and social institutions, leaving severe physical, social and psychological scars on the population. It had been a war over identity, perceptions of enmity solidified through fear, of two opposing leaders fed by unmeasured ambition and unhindered access to natural resources. It was also a war between differing versions of two societies and two states, fuelled by Cold War rivalry. When it ended, the country emerged fractured and stratified.

At the same time across the continent, on 20 July 2002, the SPLM/A's leader, John Garang de Mabior, was preparing to sign the Machakos Protocol with the government of Sudan. The war continued to rage, but principles for peace were slowly building confidence in a new political reality. After years of negotiations and sustained international pressure, the National Congress Party (NCP) and the SPLM/A signed the Comprehensive Peace Agreement (CPA) on 9 January 2005. It included a 6-year road map to initiate political transformation and address economic marginalisation and mismanaged diversity through power-sharing and wealth-sharing provisions. Although the CPA aimed at restructuring the centre of power in Khartoum with a Government of National Unity (GNU), the country would function as two separate entities, creating the autonomous Government of South Sudan (GOSS). An ambitious reform programme for the state, the CPA was an agreement that reflected the two default negotiating positions of regime survival for Khartoum, and achieving independence for the SPLM/A. Two million had died of war, famine and disease in the two decades of conflict, with four million being displaced from their homes, both across borders and within Sudan. A brutal civil war that had torn apart the social fabric of the country, fed by ethnic militarisation and contestation, it bred a sense of collective victimisation for some, continued marginalisation for others and sustained polarising visions of the state, society and nation.

On 30 July 2005, Sudan received the news that First Vice President John Garang had been killed in a helicopter crash. After returning from a meeting with Ugandan President Yoweri Museveni, Garang and thirteen others had crashed into the Zulia Mountains aboard an MI-172 Ugandan presidential aircraft. He had survived decades of war only to perish three weeks after taking office. Protests erupted all over the country when news of his death broke, threatening to destabilise the government in Khartoum and reignite the war. Many understood that the only leader capable of steering a structural reform programme for the country had died too early. Others saw his death as an opportunity to recalibrate strategic alliances that would lead them into war again. Several observers and cadres hoped that this would become an opportunity to renew a political movement that was deeply attached to the traits of its founding leader, and calls for democratisation were mounting from within. For the southerners, the death of Garang left the country rudderless and without a vision for the future. The SPLM/A leadership retreated into a crisis meeting, haunted by the presumed assassination of their iconic leader, whose stature was uniquely placed to unite a fragmented group of militias, interests and competing visions for the South.

Savimbi died in retreat, outgunned and outmanoeuvred, while Garang died in office. Neither lived to witness the transformation of their experience of wartime state building into a process of reconstructing the state during peacetime. The political orders of the liberated areas of the SPLM/A and UNITA fizzled away into irrelevance in a post-war landscape dominated by other economic and party interests. UNITA lost the war, but the Free Lands remained a testament to their great contribution to the liberation of the marginalised. As an unarmed political party, navigating the obstacles of a securitised state and a manipulated illiberal democracy, UNITA initially struggled to reinvent itself and capitalise on the glaring mistakes of the ruling MPLA. The SPLM/A were wholly unprepared for independence when they eventually won it, divided and driven by personalised strategies for power and economic benefit. Political warlords managed their ministries and regions like fiefdoms, many of them amassing fortunes and private militias. Two years later, these leaders would fight each other in a brutal civil war that would drag the people of South Sudan into self-perpetuating cycles of famine, factionalism and ethnic animosity.

Had Savimbi and Garang lived, and had they been able to redefine the post-war setting, there is no guarantee that the 'states' and insurgent 'nations' they presided over would have transitioned into peacetime collective entities and institutions. Perhaps the transposing of lessons and structures would prove an unrealistic feat, contested by elites and civil servants, or perhaps it would not produce the semblance of functionality that existed in smaller, more controllable scales. However, both leaders and their liberation movements did, in very different ways and living very distinct experiences, learn to govern civilian populations with authority and not just coercion. Structures that mimicked a state project were erected, other structures emerged that were suited to overcome specific challenges and still others were built to contrast with the structures of 'oppression' of the enemy state. As a result of these parallel states, the governments of Angola and Sudan were denied the ability to exercise the prerogatives of statehood in several parts of their countries. Each parallel state was an exercise in political and symbolic expediency, transactional politics and military strategy, but they were also projects of an envisaged future which aimed to alter state–society and society–society relations. They both attempted to found an insurgent nation where civilians, soldiers, cadres, intellectuals and chiefs would join their reformist political orders. Nothing about these rebel parallel states was simple or straightforward, and to attempt to explain their contours requires a deeper understanding of the liberation movements themselves.

Nowadays, Angola and South Sudan suffer from exclusionary policies, severe economic mismanagement, corruption and a population that contests the legitimacy of different political parties, and they are in varying degrees failed states. Several things explain how we came to this state of affairs. Answers lie in the historical trajectory of their wars and the way peace was achieved/negotiated, but also in the internal characteristics, the behavioural DNA and the choices made by the political entities that drove solutions by design or default.

Insurgent Nations examines portions of the history of Angola and Sudan when, over a period of 12 years—1979–91 for UNITA and 1990–2002 for the SPLM/A—these countries had two opposing 'states' with competing conceptions of society, history and national identity. This book describes in detail the 'nations', 'states' and 'societies' that were forged by the ideology, sub-nationalist concerns and experienced interactions of these two movements. UNITA and the SPLM/A's parallel states and the way they staged their liberations challenged the governments in Luanda and Khartoum on many levels. The conflicts transitioned from being theatres of insurgent and counterinsurgent warfare to theatres of political legitimacy and symbolic sovereignty. The presence of parallel states broadened the areas for intervention to align with changing political, military, social and economic conditions. It tilted the balance of legitimacy and perceptions of powers that went beyond the battlefield and into the political and social realms. It was because of the parallel states that both movements managed to introduce a level of protractability to their wars requiring multifaceted responses, not just military ones. The parallel states became the movements' main tools for surviving a certain period of their wars and ultimately reaching peace negotiations, but they were also expressions of political orders reflecting the convictions, fears, strengths and weaknesses of the two movements and their supporters.

This study on rebel political orders, and the degree of governance insurgent movements can install in their liberated areas, seeks to understand how force transformed into authority under the rule of two military organisations fighting asymmetrical wars in highly divided societies. Huntington (1968) made the critical point that 'the most important political distinction among countries concerns not their form of government but their degree of government'. His concern was to show that whatever the political system, its politics had to embody 'consensus, community, legitimacy, organisation, effectiveness, and stability' (Huntington 1968: 1). Both UNITA and the SPLM/A sought to correct the perceived failings of the first liberations of their countries and subsequent nation and state-building projects in the name of those excluded from these projects. Their reformist wars occurred in a post-independence setting, triggering further wars of liberation. Yet the degree of rebel government in South Sudan was vastly different from the degree of rebel government in Angola. The legitimacy of these political projects also differed. In areas liberated by UNITA, the civilian population experienced a centrally controlled, bureaucratic and rigid state, steeped in ideology, indoctrination and self-justification. In the Free Lands of Angola, a shared vision of public interest was forged through deep political work and the strength of institutions, with lives and livelihoods embedded in a UNITA state. In areas liberated by the SPLM/A, the civilian population experienced a disorganised, ineffective, experimental and unregulated state that outsourced services. In the New Sudan—the SPLM/A's parallel state—institutions existed to manage social conflict and order efforts to match those of the SPLM/A, while they were unable to structure a core legitimising force of service delivery that remained under the control of the humanitarian community.

The degrees of government in each of these parallel states reflected the level of institutionalisation and the creation of a political community. While one parallel state provided greater degrees of government than the other, they both produced parallel societies that served to empower the idea of contested sovereignty in each country. The SPLM/A managed through little direct interference to create political institutions meant to moderate and redirect social power so that communities accepted the movement and joined the liberation. In the context of a fragmented and vastly diverse South Sudan, the SPLM/A governed by ensuring rural peace and by not imposing a system of government that altered the forms of existing authority (chiefs) but rather introduced layers of political organisation that would link these diverse groups to the overall liberation. The parallel society in SPLM/A areas entrenched local power and a commitment to rid communities from Arab oppression. Yet it had little allegiance to a political collective that wasn't just territorially circumscribed but pacified by an integrative nationalism linking devotion to the land with an imagined future and common fate. Instead South Sudan had many nations, many divisions, few political communities and no public sphere that served all needs, values and interests. UNITA's intrusive and strict system of government reordered society and created a political community that united some but divided others in the context of a heterogenous society that had experienced little social conflict compared with South Sudan. The parallel society in UNITA areas was instrumentalised to convince people of its authenticity and its standing against an 'un-African' enemy that oppressed and denied the attributes that UNITA valued. At the same time, different social forces were allowed space to manage their affairs if they conformed with UNITA's political vision, which invariably altered the way people thought of themselves and their national identity. Because the institutions of the Free Lands of Angola existed outside their social groupings, they required greater institutionalisation and became insulated against pressures for change. In this way, UNITA's political order balanced different organisational imperatives, which included subordination, coherence, complexity and rigidity, while the SPLM/A balanced the organisational imperatives of autonomy, incoherence, simplicity and adaptability.

The Republic of the Free Lands of Angola—UNITA's parallel state—was a centrally controlled and totalitarian project, built from the top down, that embodied Savimbi's personalised rule. It was aimed at securing UNITA's legitimacy in representing a constituency in need of 'liberation'. It was a centrally controlled and authoritarian exercise of 'stateness' based on a utopian projection of a new society and reconfigured state–society relations. All three branches of the movement—administration, party and military—worked within defined and regulated objectives that were self-reinforcing and complementary. All aspects of civilian and military life were embedded within a deeply intrusive political and propaganda setting. UNITA's parallel state reflected its politicised focus of formulating a new order that indoctrinated, educated and conditioned cadres and civilians to believe they could take the reins of power. UNITA's state relied on self-sufficiency drives to manage service delivery and was an exercise in the division of labour, power and coordination at all levels. The New Sudan was decentralised and minimalist, built from the bottom up and embodied pragmatism and local power, while it was tenuously attached to the central leadership through the nationalist vision of a reformed and free state. It was a political and administrative project that followed loose regulations and was built on institutions that fell outside the direct control of the rebels, i.e. the structures of traditional authorities and the development programmes of NGOs. Moreover, it was a strategy to incorporate existing systems of authority into a roughly defined governing approach aiming to politically unify a diverse nation. Broad principles of emancipation delineated the political programme and were locally implemented without coordinated central control. Ineffective party structures failed to curb the overriding power of the military arm at behavioural, functional and command levels. The movement never shed its militarism, which neutered its capacity to create political structures, programmes and collective leadership.

These parallel states were meant to create the physical conditions necessary to operate a rebellion, but they were also meant to deliver several tangibles (services, order, justice) and intangibles (reimagined normality, participating in developing a new future, new definitions of citizenship and representation). All the intangibles were there to counter the nefarious effects of war and chaos, which had changed the social fabric of these communities in various reinforcing ways. They were also there to allow the movements to entrench their influence in defining the political communities and social orders, by acting as a government, and becoming the source of representation of different communities. These rebel movements built parallel states with two objectives: to help sustain their war efforts and to build a 'nation' of supporters in order to legitimise their parallel political project. Securing such a support base was a key element of the parallel state, as defined by nationalist political programmes that aimed to reform the state through the emancipation of the 'people' they claimed to represent. What they aimed to achieve and managed to achieve were two different things. The political orders produced in the Free Lands of Angola and the New Sudan were sustained by diverse and opposing forces—of centralised and uncentralised control, of instrumentalised systems of authority, of contractarian and relational dynamics—but, ultimately, they were exercises in survival, resilience and adaptation.

To understand the dynamics and strategies that led both movements to govern territory and civilians, this book studies these two movements through the prism of rebel agency as an organising tool for the comparison. Rebel agency is captured by four strategic internal areas: the characteristics and structures of their leadership, the ideology and political programmes they used, their organisational complexity and linkages, and their defined approach to civilians. I call this the rebel-system, which uses the study of territorial and civilian governance to refract meaning, context and nuance in order to help explain choices and strategies that impacted how movements function, why they survived and why they failed. The establishment of the parallel states and the forms they took were a direct result of how leadership, ideology, organisation and approach to civilians were aligned into a broader strategy to defeat the enemy on multiple fronts. The rebel-system builds a theory of operation for each of the cases by highlighting 1) how insurgencies react to critical junctures, 2) what accounts for their survival and 3) what kind of parallel state they end up with. As a result, the study of rebel governance moves beyond the description of rebel structures and institutions, defining the characteristics of these rebel movements which enabled their willingness and ability to govern civilian populations in parallel states. It opens a new line of inquiry on how to understand insurgencies that govern territory, and what their strategies and internal characteristics reveal about the pathways of war on which they embarked. It offers a unique insight into the internal functioning of two of Africa's most resilient liberation movements, which later collapsed as organisations in new eras of war and peace. This book explains why these movements experienced these multi-layered defeats at distinct stages of their history.

The rebel-system analysis

Every insurgency has a leadership structure, an ideology and political programme, a form of organisation and some defined approach to civilians. Understanding how these four elements shift and adapt over time reveals the main drivers of strategy at distinct junctures. These elements are interconnected and therefore can be studied as a system. Analysing an insurgency as a system allows for models of interaction that bring varied elements into coherent and reinforcing relationships. In the rebel-system, three areas of analysis intersect: 1) the study of the internal dynamics and characteristics of insurgencies, 2) the study of critical junctures that push these insurgencies into taking different directions and 3) the study of strategies that governed civilian constituencies and held territory. Frameworks serve the purpose of placing 'facts in some ordered relationship, and thus mak[ing] it possible to compare political processes between polities, without wrenching them from the context which gives them meaning' (Clapham 1976: 2). This analytical framework does not attempt to provide an explanation of war, or a holistic understanding of insurgency. It aims merely to overcome a monocausal explanation of how and why UNITA and the SPLM/A built their parallel states. Both began their state-building projects during moments of severe psychological and military defeat, under the duress of limited resources, and beleaguered by rivals that denied their identities and the level of legitimacy they sought. Yet UNITA and the SPLM/A built very different states, struggling in certain areas and flourishing in others because of distinct dynamics. The rebel-system analysis seeks to explain these differences.

Insurgencies suffer different forms of rebel-system mutation and alteration over time that push them into compromise and strategic re-adaptation. The rebel-system helps to reveal the factors explaining the survival of these insurgencies as well as how they transformed, in contrast to approaches which just assume some set of factors of rebel characteristics in advance. I claim that an analysis of the internal elements (leadership, ideology, organization, and approach to civilians) of territory-governing and state-building insurgencies facilitates a better understanding of these movements, in that it assesses their choices and policies in areas where they had the power to make strategic adjustments. External elements do not always allow rebels that level of power and control. Internal elements are agentic and traceable, showing how rebel movements progress by way of decisions made within their leadership and shifts resulting from new challenges. In contrast, 'external' elements—like accessibility to resources, external support and patrons, government responses, type and duration of war, social cleavages and ethnic relations—arguably fall outside movements' direct ability to control and direct. The understanding is that external factors would impact only as far as the movement was able to manage and strategically align its internal factors. As the internal elements shift in form and structure throughout the war, so did the governing strategies in the liberated areas.

External elements are, however, crucial in both these wars, and the access to resources from aid operations for the SPLM/A and diamonds for UNITA—as well as the vast training support and armament provided to both by external patrons—was critical for their success. Needless to say, internal elements are at times deeply impacted by external elements, and both are in one way or another interconnected. However, the focus of this book is on agency and the paths of war or peace taken by insurgent movements. It seeks to understand the SPLM/A and UNITA within the context of their capacity to instrumentalise, manage and operationalise the many external factors through alignment and strategic adaptation of their internal factors.

In the analysis on progression and regression, two events impacted the paths taken by state-building rebel movements: the launching of the rebellion and extant conditions at the time, and the subsequent critical junctures. Critical junctures are moments in political life that lead transitions to 'establish certain directions of change and foreclose others in a way that shapes politics for years to come' (Collier and Collier 2002: 17–31). The critical junctures I have selected for the SPLM/A and UNITA are not taken from my own subjective understanding of the rebellions, but rather are well-documented—internally by the rebellions themselves as well as externally by supporters, observers, diplomats, academics and allies—as moments where critical shifts occurred that changed the capacity, form, willingness and strategy of these two movements. The critical junctures analysed reveal the strengths and deficiencies of the four internal areas. The critical junctures (1991 for the SPLM/A and 1976 for UNITA) that led to the creation of the parallel states revealed that governance could emerge even when rebel movements were at their weakest points and facing near defeat. For UNITA, this occurred after The Long March which followed the 1976 military defeat from Cuban- and Soviet-backed MPLA forces, and for the SPLM/A it came after the loss of its rear base in Ethiopia and the factional splintering of the movement in 1991. These critical moments led to the redefinition of existing governing strategies towards greater inclusion of civilians and the creation of new systems of order to manage them. The parallel state was greatly influenced by the form of the critical juncture and the threats it faced which was not replicated in subsequent critical junctures that resulted in the dismantling of the parallel state as new threats and opportunities arose.

The parallel states and symbolic sovereignty of UNITA and the SPLM/A reveal the many ways governance can occur during wartime. Each was a factor of the prevailing circumstances and elements of uncertainty of their wars, and each balanced differently the elements of consent, authority and repression. The amount of authority generated, and the amount of coercion exercised, varied because of all the dynamics surrounding leadership, ideology and organisation. Coercion was linked to the level of transformation and adaptability pursued. Both movements aimed to transform the state and society in very deep ways, yet their experiences showed that persuasion had to play a part in the governance of civilians. In this way, coercion and authority coexisted, with other factors serving to counterbalance the more disreputable aspects of insurgent governance, some of them more tangible while others were merely symbolic. Both insurgent movements made alliances at the grassroots levels in order to govern with consent and extend structures of authority. Traditional authorities from different communities were given prominent roles in their strategies towards civilians. The movements did this for pragmatic reasons, namely to fortify their territorial control and avoid internal clashes within the parallel state that could weaken their grip on power and threaten their ability to govern. The levels of consent and legitimacy varied for each movement but were pillared on similar dynamics, dependent on the ability to provide security and some degree of predictability. Yet for the SPLM/A the provision of justice was a major factor, while for UNITA it was the provision of services, training and rhetoric that allowed them to govern diverse populations.

Leadership played a vital role in this imagining of public order and was the driving force behind the structure of the state, its central and localised forms and the different conduits for civilian organisation. The founding leaders of both movements were the source of political power and military strategy, both viewing themselves as 'presidents' of their people. The Republic of Free Angola was not meant to operate fully without Savimbi, who conceived it and provided the vision for its existence, and who also personalised it by naming squares, neighbourhoods and structures with meaningful dates, mentors and symbols. For the SPLM/A, local leadership was vitally important, as was the role played by Garang albeit as a remote leader.

Governing during moments of extreme chaos and destruction— as was the case with highly divisive and complex wars such as the ones experienced in Angola and Sudan—required diligent linkages between civilians and the leadership. Tiered leadership structures differed according to the capacity of the organisation. While the SPLM/A used traditional authorities for these purposes, UNITA used structures of democratic centralism and party control, as well as cultivating relationships with local chiefs, to create the necessary proximity with civilians. Yet both movements localised political structures to help perpetuate and extend their grip on populations. Structures that utilised legitimate interlocutors (SPLM/A) at the local level, but that were detached from interactions or linkages (political, organisational, symbolic, ideological) with the central leader, saw the parallel state develop differently. This became a lost transformational opportunity for the SPLM/A. It was an organisational but also societal issue that created layers of separation between Garang and the people he liberated in different localities. Local leaders began to appropriate the appeals of loyalty and even diffuse the need to be linked to the central command, resulting in a vacuum that would later cause problems for the longevity and legacy of the movement. For UNITA, the presence of Savimbi was overpowering and symbolic—aimed at attracting followers through charismatic appeals and declarations of the righteousness of the leader—with different forms of linkages experienced through organisational strategies and command structures. UNITA's leaders had sufficient centralised control and bureaucratic capacity in the mid-level cadres and commanders that they were able to effectively decentralise operations to committed and loyal lower-level leaders and cadres.

In terms of ideology, both movements managed to organise and channel the interests of a large segment of their people. Leaders and ideologues attempted to align their quest for power and permanence with certain popular aspirations, which in turn provided them with a way to connect with and redefine both social identities and societies as a whole. The degree of governance, as Huntington argued, was as important as the degree of constituent support garnered through ideological structure and identification. When governance was too intrusive in implementing systems of governance and livelihood strategies, or when ideology took on strict doctrinal forms, it antagonised over time different segments of the very constituent group the movements were appealing to and attempting to govern. On the other hand, when movements engaged ideologically with principles of governance and societal transformation that did not resonate with their natural constituents, yet were supported due to nationalist fervour for freedom, a deep dissonance occurred between how populations were governed and experimental ways in which the movements sought to alter how they operated. Simply put: too much ideology or too little failed to bring movements into adapting to different stages of war, and it certainly failed them when it came to transitioning into peace. Populations could be won and lost over the degree of ideology and the strategies imposed to delivered it.

The strength of nationalist rhetoric and capacity to maintain engaged constituents and civilians played a huge role in the form of the parallel state. In the case of the SPLM/A, the natural groupings among southern Sudanese allowed the movement to experiment with systems of governance that had little ideological grounding within the broader population. The policy of unity (rather than secession) of the New Sudan did not result in sustained mobilisation and integration of diverse constituents. Strong group cohesion (in the form of a popularly driven and integrative nationalism) capable of uniting different segments of the population across class, economic status, levels of education and tribes overpowered the ideological experimentation of governance. However this was masked by the collective and visceral desire for freedom from northern oppression and cultural assimilation. This gave the SPLM/A a false sense of support for its political projects, which would later result in the movement's unravelling in 2013. UNITA, which also had natural constituents to uphold and could take forward forms of nationalist and ideological fervour in the form of the disenfranchised and politically marginal group—the Ovimbundu—employed such strict ideological and doctrinal discipline that it narrowed the forms of participation to allow for broader appeals. It mobilised some to the end but ostraciseed others, causing irreparable damage. In this way the political programme had to be sufficiently strong to maintain coherence and unity in the liberated areas, but it also needed to be aligned with popular aspirations. If the new society and state proposed was not aligned to the needs and values of the civilian population, it struggled to take root. Ironically, the SPLM/A succeeded in this way despite having a weak ideological basis because governance was localised. UNITA attempted to alter society in very profound ways, which resulted in some societal disengagement.

Organisationally both insurgencies operated using the triads of administration, military and party branches. The movements depended on the strength of at least one organ to sustain state-building momentum and infuse their liberation with legitimacy, purpose and structure. In both cases it was their rapid and impressive military successes and military prowess, as well as the capacity of their armies to defeat conventional forces in asymmetrical terrains and battles, that provided these movements with support both internally and externally. Their ability to conquer and hold territory through military means gave them the ideological platform to run the parallel state. Their military organs were robust and functioned under tight command structures; they incorporated different fighting forces and were versatile enough to engage in combat on different fronts. The political organs would supplement these efforts, but not all succeeded in creating reinforcing dynamics among their triads. The SPLM/A's military commanders and senior political cadres shared control and responsibilities over the military, party and administration levels, but only the military was fully operational, as the political structures were underdeveloped and understaffed, and the administrative structures under-resourced. In contrast, UNITA carefully separated their leadership among their triad and closely coordinated their operations in reinforcing ways because of the procedures, regulations and bureaucracy they put in place. In addition to these, UNITA sustained a large propaganda and communications operation that could arguably be analysed as its fourth organisational branch.

A movement's capacity to secure a form of social contract with populations through the delivery of services, order and justice was dependent and influenced by these organisational and administrative shortcomings and strengths. The SPLM/A delivered order and justice at different stages of its governance but failed to effectively provide services which remained outsourced to the international community. UNITA did not set up courts or operate a far-reaching judiciary, like the SPLM/A, but opted instead to mediate disputes among communities and police citizens to avoid dissent and enemy infiltration. Structures for control and enforcement of procedures that provided political direction were crucial, and this is how UNITA managed to create a functioning society and state that was linked to utopian ideals. UNITA focused on training cadres in order to create the human capital and infrastructure necessary to aid with their service delivery strategy. It specifically sought to develop leadership schools and widespread training programmes for all its civilians, cadres and fighters in the liberated areas. It sent its most talented members to study abroad and upon returning to then implement their training in the parallel state. Both movements understood the power of education as an indoctrination tool, but this power was supplemented by the effectiveness of the political training of civilians, the embeddedness of political commissars and the coherence of the vision for the new state and new society, which the SPLM/A failed at. Regulating the behaviour of combatants became just as important as setting the parameters for interaction and horizontal relationships among civilians. By administering norms and quotidian practices of reciprocity, agency and cooperation, these movements linked civilians to their states. Both movements used their creation of alternative political orders to incorporate (but not always managing to implement) doctrines of fair treatment, merit, hard work and dedication as well as respect for customs. These dynamics of the parallel state were meant to foster bonds between citizens and their societies and new political orders.

A note on terminology is necessary. This book will use in an interchangeable way the terms 'rebel movement' and 'insurgency'. When referring to traits of reform rebellions as described in the next chapter it will specify as much, but when referring to broader characteristics and angles of analysis relevant to other groups that govern territory it will use the terms 'insurgency' or 'territory-governing rebels'. Insurgency is defined as 'a popular movement that seeks to overthrow the status quo through subversion, political activity, insurrection, armed conflict, and terrorism' (Kilcullen 2004: 603). Territory-governing insurgencies amalgamate a large variety of insurgencies that vary in strategy, ideology, theatre of operations, organisation and tactics. The term does not attempt to define a generic type of insurgency but rather identifies them as a phenomenon that needs to be understood for its resurgence within a wide diversity of forms. They are particularly challenging to the governments which want to defeat them, and the conflicts they are involved in are protractible and long affairs. This book also refers to 'parallel states', not with the intent of describing and focusing on the 'state'-like features of governance in areas liberated by rebels, but rather to suggest a wider exercise of institution-building, social engineering and creating symbolism of counter-sovereignty. The title of this book focuses on the 'nations' aspect of rebel rule, which is a more encompassing expression of this parallel state but also of the society that inhabited and influenced it. The wartime experiences of these insurgent nations existing under the rule of two violent organisations became examples of alternative ways of finding normalisation during conflict, and of balancing the rejection of domination while welcoming the promise of liberation.

This study also makes use of the historically charged term 'tribe'. 'Tribe' has been used in very derogatory ways to represent communities governed by primeval affiliations. In Southern Africa in particular the term is problematic, more so than in East Africa where it is widely used without any derogative connotation. 'Tribe' is used in East Africa as an 'indigenous term for something that can be of immense importance', among many others including 'ethnicity' as well as other regional/linguistic classifications and categorisations that must be locally understood (Allen 1994).[1] Throughout my research, and while conducting interviews for the SPLM/A case study, I encountered leaders and communities who used this term themselves. Indeed, it was so widely used throughout South Sudan that I decided to keep the term in the research as part of the discourse of those interviewed. In contrast, the use of 'tribe' in the Angolan case study would not only have been inappropriate and offensive, but it would have meant something entirely different from the term used in the previous context. The MPLA's portrayal of UNITA as a 'tribalistic' movement was meant to degrade its image and focus on the backwardness of both its leaders and the people it represented; the use of the term 'tribe' carried its own historical weight because of the war. Lastly, I have characterised the SPLM/A's system of governance as 'decentralised', when in reality decentralisation can only occur when there is a capacity to centralise. The SPLM/A centralised leadership but little else, as it ran a very loose and ill-defined parallel state where power was devolved to the local level by default. It is therefore important to note that the usage of 'decentralisation' here departs from the standard social science understanding.

This book does not attempt to build a broader theory of rebel governance across cases and within any subset of insurgencies. I purposefully avoid broader conclusions in this book in order to avoid reductionism, the obfuscation of crucial nuance and other errors. Typologies tend to fall short, as groups rarely fall squarely into one category and in fact shift in form and nature during prolonged wars as their fortunes vary. Single-cause explanations of what made rebel movements successful in building wartime states encounter difficulties when applied to other cases. In fact, any focus on a key variant of rebellion and war will in my view fail to address the complexity of the origins, motivations, development, critical junctures (loss and successes) and transformations of insurgencies. Lumping phenomena together can inaccurately make them seem to share more similarities than they do. What this book ultimately strives to do is tell the stories of two eras of war and governance in Angola and Sudan.

Research was conducted between 2012–13 over a period of 10 months in South Sudan and Angola. For the SPLM/A case study, 104 interviews were conducted in Yambio (Western Equatoria State), Juba and Yei (Central Equatoria state), and in Torit, New Site, Chukudum and Kapoeta (Eastern Equatoria state). For the UNITA case-study, 80 interviews were conducted in Jamba (province of Kuando Kubango); Luanda; the cities of Huambo, Bailundu and Katchiungu (Huambo province); and in Kuito and Andulo (Bie Province). At the time the research took place, Jamba and Yambio no longer played any specific role in the political arena of both movements-turned-parties, so I had to track down leaders and cadres who could explain the operations of the parallel state in these two areas. Long interviews with the top leadership of both movements provided invaluable information. But the utility of talking to lower-level cadres, civilians and intellectuals cannot be overestimated. I chose to keep my interviews anonymous, as some asked not to be named directly or to have anything attributed to them. A few asked for confidentiality and stated that they were giving me 'background' information. Given the current sensitivities with the war in South Sudan and the levels of political intolerance in Angola, I have chosen to respect their wishes for confidentiality. I also used interviews conducted several years earlier (in Angola from 2004–19 and in South Sudan from 2008–17), as they corroborated conclusions drawn from the contemporary interviews and also provided an important sense of continuity in both narrative and memory.

Rebel governance: The debate and expansion

Before proceeding, it is useful to locate this study within the existing literature and the important work that precedes it. Over the last 15 years, the study of rebel governance has become part of the lexicon of studies on war, peace and insurgency. Rebel political orders and their governance projects took many forms. Rebel governance could be a political strategy of rebellion by which insurgents build relations with civilians during wartime (Huang 2012) or it could be a 'set of actions insurgents engage[d] in to regulate the social, political, and economic life of non-combatants during war' (Arjona et al. 2015: 3). A rebel government exists when an insurgency controls territory, establishes institutions inside and outside the military and sets the formal and informal rules that define the hierarchy of power (Weinstein 2007). The emerging governance system includes structures that provide public goods as well as the practices of rule adopted by rebels (Mampilly 2011). This book assesses governance in broad terms as consisting of both structures (institutions and actor constellations) and processes (modes of social coordination, rulemaking and provision of collective goods) (Borzel and Risse 2010). It looks at the distinction between authority and control, the first being the right to make rules and the second the capability of enforcing them (Thomson 1995). Authority here refers to the social frame whereby civilians are subjected to the operation of a system of meaning, significance, power and institutionalisation (Latham 2003). Elements of these parallel 'states' were aimed at producing what Mampilly (2008) called 'anti-states' of new social and political orders, where rebel groups built governing institutions as an 'opportunity to examine the potential and limitations of the *non-state*'. In zones of 'limited' statehood and during conflict, new opportunities could arise potentially containing the 'germs of new political orders' (Raeymaekers et al. 2008: 10). Unrecognised states (Pegg 1998; Geldenhuys 2009; Bahcheli et al. 2004; Kingston and Spears 2004) became described as 'nations in waiting' locally imbued with their own standards and features of governance, operating in a precarious limbo of fragile peace yet lacking international recognition.

While the conceptual, comparative and analytical elements of this literature are pioneering—in particular the work of Kasfir (2005), Mampilly (2008), Weinstein (2007), Wickham-Crowley (1987), and Arjona (2016)—they have two fundamental omissions. First, they lack operational details about the rebel states themselves, including few examples of how institutions and different sectors functioned and were interlinked. This may be a result of the parallel states under study no longer existing, but the more complex projects always leave behind historical traces found in propaganda, journalistic descriptions, people's memories and the recollections of diplomats and humanitarians. Second, these pioneering studies pay little attention to the agentic characteristics of rebels as reflected in their rebel states, linking an understanding of differentiation of institutional strategies to rebel characteristics. This book attempts to provide some answers in these two areas. This study agrees with Péclard and Mechoulan's (2015) assertion that focusing on the state itself can lead to an oversimplification and normative dichotomy between rebel organisations associated with embryonic state structures and warlords who aren't state builders. Rather, the focus around rebel structures is less about state formation and more about the 'formation of a political order outside and against the state' (Mampilly 2011: 36). Alone, the understanding of rebel rule provides us with incomplete answers as to why, how and with what tools insurgents build parallel political and territorial orders. Understanding how rebel strategy, internal shifts over time and moments of critical change all impact the world of parallel nation and statehood helps situate several answers to these questions.

The question of why insurgencies are motivated to govern territories and civilians has been partially asked and answered in the literature. Insurgencies provided governance in order to strengthen their organisations and better prepare them to contest the state. Insurgents built 'states' and governed civilians when they believed it would help them win the war (Kasfir 2005). When movements believed that a war would be a short affair, their impetus to build social and political structures was often limited, as their focus prioritised full military campaigns to defeat the existing order. Rebels with long-term horizons were more inclined to create political and social orders and govern civilians. Reliance on civilians for economic support was so fundamental for some insurgencies that they built parallel states to better control the material and political resources they required (Huang 2016). Rebels secured a social contract with civilians to more easily monitor them, making civilian obedience and support more probable (Arjona 2016).

22

Some studies gave more emphasis to resources (aid, external assistance, natural resources, protection or ransom payments) and the impact of these on governance. Weinstein (2007) claimed that resource-rich rebels, who had access to immediate resources and the ability to pay fighters, were more violent, undisciplined, led by short-term goals and abusive towards civilians. Resource-poor rebels, on the other hand, were more likely to cultivate social endowments, mobilise interpersonal networks (which built stronger relationships with civilians and recruits) and allow for civilian participation. This argument is disproven in this book. UNITA (resource-rich) provided far more social and economic benefits to civilians, mobilising kin and chiefs, while the SPLM/A (resource-poor) was just as violent and far more undisciplined. More importantly, UNITA and SPLM/A were many things at the same time, none of which can be captured with a simple dichotomy. Beyond the motivations and timing of governance, the many objectives of parallel states were to secure the information (Kalyvas 2006), resources and support (food, shelter, and labour) necessary to carry out military operations (Lidow 2016; Mampilly 2011; Weinstein 2006; Arjona 2016).

Most scholars agreed that force and coercion alone were ineffective in securing civilian support and loyalty; an element of legitimacy and authority had to be present for the long-term survival of the governing order. Some policies of rebel governance ostracised civilians and increased their resistance (Arjona 2016), while others were a fundamental part of the rebels' legitimation strategies (Kasfir et al. 2017). Ultimately, rebel governance was a mix of material and symbolic resources. Yet in none of these important studies does the element of rebel strategy factor into the explanation and assessment of their motivations. Strategy is a cross-pollination of capacity, motivation, ideology and leadership. The difference between motivation and strategy is also temporal: strategy has a longer-term view of a desired outcome. Strategy also explains variance.

Accounting for the variance in rebel governance has factored greatly in the literature. From the levels of civilian support and the role attributed to civilians (Kasfir 2005) to the effectiveness of institutions (Mampilly 2011) and their institutional arrangements (Mampilly and Stewart 2021), studies have looked at local–

structural conditions that may have either hindered or facilitated rebel rule. Political institutions were determinant in the capacity of insurgencies to govern their liberated areas and civilians. Movements that closely followed the tenets of guerrilla warfare as defined by Mao Tse Tung understood the importance of political structures, as an interface with civilian populations, in the overall strategy of a people's war. These could take a variety of forms, from political party structures to civilian feedback forums, elected committees, local governing bodies or pseudo-parliaments (Cunningham et al. 2021). They set agendas, administered affairs, devised policies and provided a form of collective leadership. These institutions also aimed to reorganise political life, secure compliant and ideologically integrated constituents and act as mechanisms for bureaucratic operations.

Typologies of political institutions and organisational structures were employed to explain differentiation but also aimed at providing identifiers for future rebel governance. According to Mampilly and Stewart (2021), political institutions varied over a set of four key dimensions: the level of power-sharing, the depth of integration, the extent of innovation and the degree of inclusion. Governing institutions and programmes could also vary across two dimensions: 'extensiveness' which referred to the distribution of governance in civilian terms and efforts to govern those that were unsupportive, and 'intensiveness' whereby governance could range from less intensive (provision of food, courts, healthcare) to very intensive (change in gender roles, land redistribution and new political institutions) (Stewart 2021). Furlan (2020) described seven dimensions of governance, namely: if there was universal inclusivity or discrimination; if civilians were participants or subjects; if compliance was generated through coercion or persuasion; the inclusion of other actors; the maintenance or innovation of institutions; levels of bureaucratisation; and levels of hierarchical style. Variance was therefore a combination of external and internal elements in explaining rebel choices and strategies. However, in this literature, internal agentic elements were never clearly linked to explaining variance or the complexity of contradictions, failings and successes of rebel rule. While some work has begun to emerge joining the analysis of internal characteristics and governance outcome, a lot more needs to be done. Stewart (2020) used quantitative evidence to claim that governance had little or no relationship with rebel strength or military capacity. Keister and Slantchev looked at the effect ideology had on governance, ranging from having a 'direct effect on civilian support, an indirect effect through its impact on the effectiveness of service provision to coercion, and another effect on the rebels' value of ruling' (2014: 21). The move towards a more multifaceted and pluralistic approach to insurgency and its governance will bring insights that have otherwise remained unconnected. This allows for an exercise of predictability of outcomes and on postwar developments.

Nothing about this book implies a paradigm shift in the study of rebel governance, especially because context and variation within the wide array of governing insurgencies advises against it. What this study does attempt is to give a nuanced and detailed account of the governing strategies of the SPLM/A and UNITA, using the perspective of rebel agency across time and during moments of critical shifts.

Book structure

The chapters that follow recount portions of the history of these two movements and their wars. This book does not provide a comprehensive history of either movement, nor does it provide a complete history of these wars, but it will introduce new information that is unique to each case. Chapter 1 explains the motivation behind the choice of using UNITA and the SPLM/A movements as case studies for this comparison and explains the choice of liberated areas. Both movements governed various and unconnected liberated areas with differing strategies and outcomes. The chapter also briefly introduces the historical context in which they emerged.

Chapter 2 traces the progression and stages of SPLM/A governance that occurred in Yambio, as it became the first county of the liberated South in 1990 until the signing of the first CPA protocol in 2002. It describes the progression of institutions—from the Civil–Military Administrator (CMA) to the Civil Authority for a New Sudan (CANS)—that allowed for the SPLM/A to gain the acceptance of the population and 'its right to rule'. A highly militarised system (the CMA system) was combined with the old traditional order of chiefs and a rehabilitation of indirect rule to secure the liberated area without the need to create legitimacy or rule through persuasion. After the critical juncture of 1991, a new approach to governance emerged that repackaged the ideological message, defined the political programme, increased power at the local levels and created the space for civil society and the population to engage in entrepreneurial activities and determine their relations with the New Sudan state. NGOs and relief agencies were instrumentalised to become the service providers for the SPLM/A. Chiefs were empowered to continue providing justice and were crucial in maintaining rural peace and social harmony. However, a militarised movement remained organised and defined at the leadership levels around the strength of the military. The party–state that functioned at the local levels was relatively detached from the central command levels, which later led to the post-conflict peacebuilding exercise facing severe challenges.

Chapter 3 traces UNITA's centralised strategy that produced a state alternative and staged a propaganda and acculturation war aimed at delegitimising the MPLA's post-independence state. The movement altered its strategy to govern civilians after the critical juncture of 1976. What had earlier operated as autonomous bases, run by guerrilla commanders and *sobas*, and relied on self-sufficiency drives to provide services became a centrally controlled and bureaucratised endeavour. The first governing strategy of the 1960s was pillared on three principles: the respect for ethnic custom, a developed agricultural system and the organisation of community institutions. After the rebel capital Jamba was built, UNITA's strategy involved a far-reaching social engineering project of 'elevating' the southern into masses to become the next leaders of Angola through extensive skills training, political indoctrination and mandatory education. The world order of civilians, fighters, cadres and leaders was defined and controlled by UNITA's political machine. From 1979 to 1991, Jamba became the embodiment of UNITA's capacity to govern a state within a state. Built as a rear base and a training ground for its growing army, UNITA used Jamba to test its redefinition of society and what it meant to be 'Angolan'. The iron-like discipline surrounding the tripartite structure (party, military, administration) resulted in a political order that was both totalitarian and utopian. This inflexible and tightly controlled programme was ultimately what led UNITA to fail to adapt to changing circumstances of war in the 1990s.

Chapter 4 frames the comparison between the two cases descriptively and analytically, highlighting the similarities and differences between the movements and their parallel projects. It employs the rebel-system frame of analysis and highlights how the movements' differences in ideology, organisation, leadership and approach to civilians influenced the strategies and institutions used to project power.

Chapter 5 begins with a comparison of the critical junctures that led both movements to form parallel states in order to highlight the shift in strategy. It then proceeds to describe and analyse—refracting context and meaning from the previous critical junctures—the moments of multi-pronged shocks that led to the dismantling of the parallel state and the disarticulation of their insurgent nations. This section on subsequent critical junctures faced by UNITA (1992 and 2002) and the SPLM/A (2005 and 2013) is introduced as a continuation to this study on internal political processes, highlighting which areas experienced significant shifts and how the previous rebel-systems mutated and evolved. The chapter provides a lens to observe shifts in peacetime that led UNITA and the SPLM/A down very difficult paths.

The concluding chapter reflects on the nationalism and sub-nationalism created by these two insurgencies, along with their effects on Angola and South Sudan. In final remarks, it highlights how the continuity of territory-governing insurgencies in today's wars opens new lines of questioning on how to rethink the state and nations being formed in war.

1

ORIGINS, CHOICES AND EXPLANATIONS

'*Wars in every period have independent forms and independent conditions, and therefore every period must have its independent theory of war.*'

Carl von Clausewitz[1]

African liberation movements have inspired great division in the worlds of policy and scholarship. Ideological considerations, subjective understandings informed by personal experience, varying levels of embeddedness in portions of their history and exposure to their brutality and propaganda resulted in widely different descriptions of the same movements. In some cases, this divergence was a result of assessing different timeframes of the insurgency, or actions under distinct leaders. It could also depend on how some movements were considered in international circles, whether they were seen to be legitimate interlocutors for their people or whitewashing the brutality that defined their relations with the civilians they purported to represent. Portraying a group as either terrorists or liberation fighters was always a choice of subjective perspective. At different times of their liberation wars, both the SPLM/A and UNITA transitioned from being on the right side to the wrong side of history, according to whichever prism their struggles were defined through. They rallied great support but also great disdain. They were viewed as beacons of hope and simultaneously triggered despair in their countries. They fought very different wars, although both helped sustain two of Africa's longest conflicts. Both movements were examples of protracted struggles that led to parallel states emerging within wider dynamics of long and asymmetrical wars. UNITA and the SPLM/A staged 'second liberations' and developed complex responses to different threats, opportunities and critical junctures. They both ran stable parallel states for over a decade, which in turn contributed to their political and military survival, increased their support base and led to peace negotiations.

The choice to use the SPLM/A and UNITA for comparison was not an obvious one. I selected these two cases based on their two main conditions of being reform rebels and having built parallel states. 'Reform rebels' were defined in the 1990s as insurgencies that sought radical reform of the national government with the goal of creating an entirely different kind of state (Clapham 1998). They believed that a 'second liberation' (Diamond 1992) could be achieved that would redeem the failures of the first (Clapham 2007),[2] which had culminated in independence. They adapted the 'anti-colonial rhetoric of national emancipations and a new societal order' (Reno 2011: 119) to suit their post-independence wars. In this book, 'reform rebels' are defined as groups seeking a new liberation to correct failed nation- and state-building projects by proposing a new socio-political order based on the emancipation of groups who previously suffered political and economic discrimination. They propose alternative visions of the state, with a national political programme based on different sub-national concerns and motivations serving as a new nationalist call to arms. Reform rebels built parallel states as state-like entities in their liberated areas to organise civilian life, advance war strategies, build capacity and seek internal and external legitimacy. They became exercises in establishing territorial, nationalistic and symbolic hegemony. Each movement created a parallel state as a 'state within a state' that sought to create a political structure benefiting its citizenry (Kingston and Spears 2004), indicating that governance was a wider project than mere territorial control or logistical survival. Governance of a parallel state therefore encompassed a multifaceted approach to war, redefining politics and creating new social orders to sustain the war effort and the reform project. The movements' transformative goals aimed to not only create new political institutions but also bend society in different and new directions (Skocpol 1979).

I also chose these two movements due to their complexity, resilience and the many transitions they underwent over several decades. UNITA transitioned from being an anti-colonial movement in the 1960s to a post-independence reformist insurgency fighting communism in the 1970s. In the mid-1990s, it transitioned into a predatory movement devoid of political direction and lost the war, yet managed to successfully transform into a political party in peacetime. In August 2022, 20 years after the war ended, UNITA was able to challenge the MPLA government in what were the most controversial peacetime elections in Angola. The SPLM/A emerged as a post-independence movement, reformist and militaristic. It gradually transitioned into a secessionist organisation that succeeded in securing South Sudan's independence yet failed to transform into a peacetime political party. This failure pushed the movement back into war, taking many forms as it splintered multiple times, with some factions becoming more mercenary than others and most only managing to rally legitimacy at the local level of their communities, as they lacked national appeal and strength. This book could not possibility do justice to these many transformations but will over the course of the different chapters attempt to explain some of these dynamics.

In the 1980s, UNITA was considered one of Africa's most successful insurgencies, led by a charismatic leader who celebrated his African values, courting centrist and conservative Western governments while accepting support from apartheid South Africa. Savimbi represented the rural and southern populations of Angola while carefully designing reformist policies for a reimagined state and nation. UNITA's role in the United States' fight against communism in Africa was of such relevance that it became a defining pillar of President Ronald Reagan's doctrine. Together with the Mujahideen in Afghanistan and the Contras in Nicaragua, UNITA held great promise for containment policies in Africa. Less than two decades into its war, UNITA's fall from grace in the early 1990s was catalysed by the failure of the peace process. The West no longer believed in its narrative of a just war and pragmatically steered support towards its enemy, the MPLA-led government. UNITA became depicted as an efficient but ruthless organisation led by a terrorist-like leader who preyed on civilians while funding a conventional war through the sale of diamonds (Brittain 1998; Malaquias 2007).[3] In peacetime, UNITA was a residual political force for the first two decades, capable of inflicting symbolic damage to the MPLA's political project but unable to mobilise its policies inside the entrails of the securitised state. While it was unable to effectively challenge the MPLA in what were fraudulent elections, UNITA gradually built a powerful support base and built a coalition of opposition movements under the new leadership of Adalberto da Costa Junior in 2020. By 2022, UNITA ruling Angola was very much a reality.

The SPLM/A stood on the opposite side of the Cold War, supported by Marxist Ethiopia and through proxy regional engagement. It emerged almost thirty years after independence to stage a 'second liberation' following a period of democratic turnover. As a movement it rapidly mobilised nationalist southern anger and built an army bigger than most conventional armed forces in East Africa. Its mistrust of politicians, a strategy which enforced military command and control to avoid factional and ethnic politics, placed the responsibility of liberating Sudan in the hands of military commanders. The SPLM/A pillaged, destroyed and killed its way across the country even as it tried to stabilise some areas and build its support base. Like Savimbi, Garang was an impressive and charismatic man capable of mobilising the international community, capitalising on the mass humanitarian engagement in the South and rallying alliances within Sudan. The SPLM/A's fight against the National Islamic Front (NIF)[4] and the continued policies of marginalisation provided it with a just banner against 'Arab' oppression. Despite this, the SPLM/A came to be depicted as an inefficient movement, lacking political structures but successfully lobbying international aid agencies to assist its war strategies, while failing to deliver tangible benefits to civilians (Young 2003).[5] It transitioned in the 1990s into the West's partner in giving voice to the South and vying for peace.

Defying the rigid opposition to altering international borders, it negotiated the secession of the South. Two decades after it began its liberation, the SPLM/A was able to govern its own internationally recognised country, only to be plunged into a devastating civil war fuelled by ethnic animosities and personal political agendas. It lost its nationalist appeal and squandered the legitimacy it had once enjoyed with all southerners. By 2022, the SPLM/A was unrecognisable.

As movements, UNITA and the SPLM/A changed priorities, strategies and responses to civilian, political and military challenges during their conflicts and while navigating peacetime politics. While both were notoriously resilient and capable of plunging their wars into intractability, they were unique in other ways. With regards to internal characteristics (ideology, leadership, organisation and approach to civilians), these movements were more dissimilar than similar, with variations in governing strategies, institutions, and approach to civilians, facilitating a nuanced analysis. At the leadership level, UNITA and the SPLM/A were run by two controlling and charismatic leaders with different perspectives of war and who faced distinct command challenges. Garang united disparate and diverse armed groups within a military hierarchy, mistrustful of politicians and wary of arousing ethnic sentiments. He expected the SPLM/A's war to be a short one, and that military success was sufficient to mobilise marginalised communities. Garang sought more consensus by balancing different needs and interests, all the while strategically placing his commanders in a position that would not challenge his hegemony. UNITA faced a long, protracted popular war where every aspect of the liberation was steeped in politics. Savimbi chose to train and empower his commanders to become future political leaders. He pushed to create an army of cadres and skilled workers from the marginalised people he claimed to represent, creating a complex military, political and administrative structure of which he was the authority. This was both a long-term strategy but also a necessity. Ideologically, UNITA largely followed Maoist principles but combined Afro-populist and capitalist ideas to create a self-styled ideology, while the SPLM/A was broadly influenced by Marxism yet later transitioned into fusing democratic principles with traditional values in such a way as to appease external and internal audiences. UNITA defined its political programme and war strategies internally, while the SPLM/A, by virtue of being created in Ethiopia, allowed the Derg to impose certain principles and political direction (unity rather than secession) from the onset. Both movements did, however, use sub-national grievances to build a new nationalist cause to unite diverse constituencies. This sub-nationalist dimension became a political force that fragmented and divided the movements' societies, devising identities enhanced by existing and manufactured grievances that ultimately narrowed their social support base. It also failed to provide the integrative nationalism that gave these movements purpose.

Organisationally, UNITA understood the need to first develop political organs and only later build military capacity. For the SPLM/A, the political organs were nonexistent until the 1991 critical juncture, and after that they remained subservient to the military, which was the main organisational pillar. The approaches of the two movements towards civilians were also different, although they both balanced elements of persuasion and coercion. While UNITA began providing services to civilians from the onset and the SPLM/A began using relief aid from the United Nations (UN) and non-governmental organisations (NGOs) as service provisions, the internally driven model was a part of UNITA's dominance and control. By virtue of lacking the means to provide services, and in the absence of a strong political party, the SPLM/A decentralised control to chiefs and civilians. These differences will be explained and analysed in detail in the following chapters. UNITA and the SPLM/A were in this way representative of several divergent characteristics of state-building rebels.

The external elements that composed the conflict-system of the wars in Angola and Sudan—meaning their societies, the level of resources available, the actors involved, the types of war and offensive instruments—were also distinct. Both wars were long, deadly and intractable affairs, but they were fundamentally different. Angola's was a high-stakes war fed by direct involvement by superpowers and later fuelled by the use of diamonds and oil to fund conventional war campaigns. In the south of Angola, the Cuito Cuanavale battle of 1987–88 became known as Africa's World War, epitomising the high stakes of ideological victory of proxies during the Cold War. The battle was also the most significant example of Cuba's mass internationalist mission abroad, and it revealed apartheid South Africa's deep commitment to containing the spread of communism in what became Pretoria's version of Vietnam.

In Sudan, support from Ethiopia, Uganda and other allies of the SPLM/A provided comparatively fewer resources, and the SPLM/A was unable to use the country's natural resources to fund its insurgency. Neighbouring countries' involvement—arming, funding and sheltering interests on both sides—reflected their own internal political divisions over providing support for Khartoum or the rebels. The effective use of ethnic militias to hinder the ability of the South to unite behind the SPLM/A became Sudan's preferred war strategy. Social fragmentation was deeply impacted by this counterinsurgency strategy, which was not the case in Angola, where the use of mass means and men by Luanda saw the deployment of Russian and Cuban troops and technicians to directly engage UNITA. The presence of the UN and aid agencies in Angola paled in comparison to Sudan. In Sudan, the UN's Operation Lifeline became the first mass humanitarian operation to directly coordinate with the rebels in the South and recognise their position as counterparts to the government, negotiating access and security. In Angola, and for the first time in UN history, the UN deemed the rebels a threat to international security, applying a Chapter VII for the first time to a non-state entity in September 1993. Aside from imposing sanctions, the UN was utterly ineffectual in Angola. These are just a few of the many differences between these two wars and the actors involved in fighting them, whose conflict-systems were as widely divergent as their rebel-systems.

To understand the progression of governance, I selected two areas for the study that were militarily unchallenged—allowing for assured territorial control—and with a large resident population. The area chosen to study the SPLM/A's governance was a town called Yambio, while for UNITA's governance it was the rebel capital Jamba. While the choice on UNITA's part was clear, given the fact that Jamba was created as the movement's capital and rear base, during the first decade of the war the SPLM/A's rear base was in Ethiopia, and the movement never developed an administrative and political capital inside the liberated areas. In 1991, when the SPLM/A lost its Ethiopian rear base, different areas in the South took on different strategic purposes, making it difficult to determine which one was the 'real' capital and the main governing centre. The closest example of a rebel-created town in South Sudan, similar to what UNITA had created in Jamba, were the two areas the SPLM/A called 'New Site' and 'New Kush'. These rebel villages emerged after the movement splintered in 1991 and, much like Jamba, were part of a survival strategy to relocate population and the families of leaders into safer areas far from the frontlines. They were created due to defeat and despair. Yet, unlike Jamba, New Site never really developed into a full-fledged rear base. New Site and New Kush would become villages for strategic thinking, military training and leadership meetings, making them more elite exercises than examples of ruling civilian populations. They did not have the mass civilian component necessary to understand how wartime governance developed. Yambio, on the other hand, did have this component, resulting in the movement's longest stint ruling a liberated area that was never recaptured. Although the SPLM/A had different headquarters for divergent purposes at different stages of its war, its capital was in Torit before its 1991 critical juncture and in Yei after 1997. However, during the 1991–95 offensives by government forces, the SPLM/A lost almost all the territory it had conquered in the preceding years, with Yambio being one of the only liberated areas that was never recaptured.

Both areas selected for this study had to be stable enough to allow for institutions to progress and develop over different stages of the war. A key essential condition was that both movements had to exercise a degree of territorial control, given that insecurity undermined the relationship of authority between rebels and civilians (Arjona et al. 2015). Neither Yambio nor Jamba were captured when they operated as parallel states, and both were far from the most violent frontlines and contested areas, making them ideal for understanding how these movements developed their governing strategies over a period of 12 years. Both Yambio and Jamba, in differing degrees, meet the criteria for 'states-within-a state', demonstrating a set of attributes: 1) a defined territory that was effectively controlled, 2) allowed for the projection of power and monopoly of force in the territory, 3) retained the presence of a defined national identity and internal legitimacy, 4) allowed for some form of revenue generation, 5) had infrastructure and administration, including roads, airstrips, farms and even telecommunications and, finally, 6) projected diverse political objectives (Kingston and Spears 2004: 19–29). Their positioning on the margins of the state, and far from the national capitals, meant that they were also 'zones of regulatory ambiguity' (Zeller 2013),[6] which provided the territorialisation necessary to attempt to transform society and install new political orders. Their proximity to international borders also provided important logistical and economic lifelines of trade, international relief aid and external assistance.

However, the choice of liberated areas had some limitations. The areas in which each movement was able to establish a parallel state were very different in South Sudan and Angola. Each had distinct prior experience with state institutions. Yambio, which had existed in the colonial period, was an established county under Khartoum's rule, but, like other areas in the South, it had limited experience outside the basic administrative, extractive and security priorities of Khartoum. Jamba was an artificial construct, an area of savannah and bush to which a population was relocated, with no pre-existing state institutions or bureaucratic structures of administration. Comparing an artificially created rebel village with a pre-existing administrative locality that was captured by a rebel movement posed challenges. The exercise of 'stateness' in Yambio was predisposed to using existing state structures, while in Jamba UNITA had a blank slate. In Yambio, pre-existing ethnic politics meant the Azande population was inclined to defiance and rejection of the rebel state; in Jamba, the population was either compliant due to being deeply intertwined and sharing lineage with the rebel movement, or they were forcibly incorporated through kidnapping. What enabled this limitation to be overcome was that both Jamba and Yambio provided the setting for two of the longest-ruled liberated areas, where the progression of governing strategies could be assessed despite the different ways they were established. They were the only two areas that allowed these two rebel movements the tranquillity to experiment with different forms of governance and parallel institutions for over a decade.

A comprehensive account of UNITA and the SPLM/A's entire governing project has never been published. This book is not representative of all aspects of governance of these two movements. It does not focus on other liberated areas that also experienced levels of stability and consolidated rule, or those that were contested or exposed to battles to retake them. What this study does represent are key aspects of the movements' internal characteristics that were analysed with regards to the specificities of Yambio and Jamba within the timeframes studied. In this way, the analysis was not impacted or distorted by the choice of liberated area, as the focus is on progression of governance over a decade, which both Yambio and Jamba facilitated, and what this revealed about the internal workings and strategies of these insurgencies. The analysis of each of their rebel-systems is complemented by how each element was reflected in the movements' governing strategies, which are also assessed separately from them.

Anchoring each struggle in history

Each insurgency is anchored in historical circumstances. While the histories of Sudan and Angola are very different, there are several similar dynamics behind their recurring civil wars. Johnson (2003) listed these key dynamics for the wars in Sudan but these also apply to the war in Angola.[7] Both involved an exploitative relationship and inequalities in development between the centre and its peripheries. The resulting inequalities in political, economic and educational development reflected and coincided with political control and economic privilege. The narrowly based nationalist movements that emerged were exclusionary and failed to integrate all the different identities and interests into a unifying platform during the first liberation wars and post-independence. Both countries experienced the colonial power's political expediency at independence that failed to prepare adequate transitions to power, which led to authority being conferred in unrepresentative formulas. The failure to achieve national consensus and the perpetuation of 'neo-imperialist' rule after independence led to cycles of conflict and 'second liberations' in both countries. Both UNITA and the SPLM/A emerged in stratified societies where large segments of the population felt marginalised and disenfranchised. The cleavages built around ethnic, racial and cultural identities during and after the colonial period, would become salient at different times of the movements' histories. The structural fault lines of these wars were multifaceted and complex and won't be analysed here in detail. Rather, key events will be highlighted that influenced the emergence of both liberation movements.

The Sudan People's Liberation Movement/Army

The SPLM/A emerged in 1983, decades after independence was achieved in 1956 and immediately following a period of democratic rule and southern autonomy under the 1972 Addis Ababa Peace Agreement. The movement developed as a response to the failings of the Peace Agreement and the internal political wrangling of the southern elites. It was a reaction to Khartoum's policies of forced assimilation and the rise of militant Islam, as well as to the growing dissatisfaction that was creating pockets of insurrection throughout the country. In many respects, the SPLM/A fought a war over the definition of national identity, seeking to liberate all of Sudan from the personalised rule of the northern riverine elites in order to redefine power relations (Wakoson 1993).[8] What motivated the SPLM/A to act was the widespread perception of historical injustice, subjugation and marginalisation among the population.

Sudan was never a territorial and national entity that enjoyed consensus among all its diverse people and communities. Decades of joint British and Egyptian rule under the Condominium (1899–1955) left the country institutionally and culturally divided, a reflection of political and economic inequality. By administrating the North and South separately under the Closed District Ordinance (1922), Arabism and Islam were reinforced in the North, while it 'encouraged southern development along indigenous African lines and introduced Christian missionary education' (Deng 1995: 11). After independence, the political debate centred on whether the South should have a special political status in a federation, 'to dilute the domination of the North in national affairs' (Wakoson 1993: 28).

Instead, the colonial power was substituted for northern hegemony. Resentment of the Islamic–Arab cultural–imperialist project, driven by the North's political and economic domination, would lead the South to rise against Khartoum. There were also marked disparities in the regional development of the country, with the South being the most neglected. The marginalisation and inequality experienced by the southerners led to 'cultural and experiential identities' (Jok 2007) that were explained through ancestral, racial, religious and other differences. Yet many other socio-economic and political factors stood as key drivers of the wars to follow.

In 1955, the mutiny in Torit began the process of resistance, hastening independence, but a coordinated political and military opposition to Khartoum would only emerge years later. The war for self-determination in the 1960s was led by the Anyanya I movement, which would develop into a coalition of guerrilla groups initially organised along tribal lines (Johnson and Prunier 1993).[9] The war came to an end when Joseph Lagu, commander of the Anyanya and leader of what had then been renamed the Southern Sudan Liberation Movement (SSLM), and President Jaafar Nimeri signed the 1972 Addis Ababa Peace Agreement. The agreement was comprised of three parts: a ceasefire agreement; the creation of a southern regional government to guarantee autonomous rule; and numerous protocols on interim arrangements dealing with administration, resettlement, judicial matters and military affairs. New administrative structures were created to allow southerners to govern the South for the first time. The regional government, however, suffered from a lack of funds, resources, organisation and personnel, which contributed to ineffective public administration. As a result, the South remained underdeveloped, with poor infrastructure, transport and communications; weak food production; and inadequate rural and industrial development. Conflicts and discord among southern political elites exposed several contradictions that Khartoum fuelled, leading to increasing polarisation between radicals (who wanted to thwart President Gaafar Muhammad Nimeiri's encroachment into southern affairs) and reformists (who preferred to appease the central government in return for favours) (Sharif and Tvedt 1994). While the army was supposed to integrate the Anyanya soldiers, only

6,000 were absorbed. This meant the disbanding of the Anyanya and gave Khartoum control over security arrangements (Malok 2009). Throughout the 1970s and early 1980s, small groups—many made up of disaffected Anyanya soldiers—took up arms against the Addis Ababa Agreement. Some of these groups became known as Anyanya II, which would later resist being integrated under the command of the SPLM/A.

The 1972 agreement, which established the guidelines for political and administrative organs for the southern region, had been violated several times by the Nimeiri regime with its unconstitutional dismissals of the Southern Region Government and Regional Assemblies in 1980, 1981 and 1983. After a failed coup attempt in 1976 by former Prime Minster Sadiq al-Mahdi, Nimeiri began a national reconciliation policy aimed at appeasing the opposition in the North, appointing several hardline opposition leaders to important cabinet posts. Increasing discontent among Islamic northern opposition movements, which thought that too many concessions were made in the Addis Ababa agreement, led Nimeiri to recognise Sharia law as the basis for all national legislation. The imposition of Sharia law in the South furthered the unravelling of the Addis Ababa agreement, and in 1982, the country was heading back to war after a decade of peace. Nimeiri attempted to redefine the borders of the South to incorporate into northern areas resource-rich (uranium, nickel and oil) regions and the fertile lands of Renk (Scott 1985). Khartoum created a new province—Unity province—to ensure that the oil fields discovered in Bentiu in 1978 fell to the North, and placed it under the presidency with the refinery in Kosti in central Sudan. The decision to build the Jonglei Canal to irrigate northern agricultural lands, diverting the Nile waters, inflamed the situation. When the regional government in Juba rejected the redrawing of the boundaries and 'theft' of resources, Khartoum strategically reorganised the South into three smaller subregions and dissolved the regional government.

This division of the South into three regions—Equatoria, Bahr El Ghazal and Upper Nile—began a process of retribalisation in the South, which in the past had led to traditional balancing of power between major ethnic groups (Salih 1989). The fallout from

41

the social and political division of the South would reverberate into the liberation years, and the post-war years after 2005. The Equatorians were the biggest proponents of the new divides, as they were resentful of the leaders from Upper Nile and Bahr El Ghazal, and of Dinka domination. The Dinka were disappointed with the Equatorians (who had led the Anyanya movement) for colluding with the northerners to abrogate the peace agreement (Wondu 2011). The order to transfer the military battalions of Bor, Ayod, Kapoeta and Aweil, comprised of former Anyanya soldiers, to the North was the final move that led to the collapse of the Addis Ababa Peace Agreement. All these factors would influence the strategy and military programmes of the SPLM/A.

The second civil war officially began on 16 May 1983 with the mutiny of the 105th battalion in Bor of former Anyanya soldiers. This led to desertions in Malakal, Nasir, Bentiu, Aweil, Wau, Rumbek and Nzara. The SPLM/A emerged in July 1983 in Ethiopia, created from many of these guerrilla and mutineer groups under the auspices of President Menguistu Haile Mariam. This *rassemblement* led to leadership struggles that were only resolved by force, and it emphasised military discipline, centralised decision-making and control over information and intelligence (Kok 1996). The development of political structures was inhibited by these struggles and by a reaction to the conduct of the political elites of the South during the first war and the peace of the 1970s. During the Second Civil War (1983–2005),[10] the SPLM/A fought against successive regimes in Khartoum (Nimeiri, Sadiq Al-Mahdi and Omar Al-Bashir), creating a national movement that would redefine Sudan's politics. The decade of war that followed witnessed a rapid succession of military conquests as the SPLM/A took a large portion of the South. The war extended to the peripheries of the North, with fighting in Darfur, the East, Blue Nile and Southern Kordofan, with multiple grievances and shifting alliances producing 'a pattern of interlocking civil wars' (Johnson 2003: 127).

Also fighting against the SPLM/A were Anyanya II, pro-government Arab and other tribal militias—like the Murle of Pibor, the Fertit in Wau and the Mundari of Terekeke—that were armed as anti-Dinka groups, reflecting the perception of the SPLM/A as a Dinka-dominated insurgency. This counter-insurgency strategy, established under Sadiq Al-Mahdi, of waging war through surrogates allowed the government to distance itself from any involvement and also to classify the conflicts as internal tribal wars (Johnson 2003). While the SPLM/A had been recruiting from Nuer and Dinka areas from the onset, it struggled to get the same support from Equatorians. However, by 1988 the SPLM/A was consolidating territorial gains in eastern Equatoria, and by late 1990 (after the taking of Yambio) it began closing in on the regional capital Juba.

Omar Al-Bashir's coup in 1989, with the 'Revolution for National Salvation', escalated the war and intensified the 'war of visions and identities'. When the NIF seized power, it declared a state of emergency, created a Revolutionary Command Council, dissolved the parliament, banned political parties and issued a widespread crackdown on the opposition. Khartoum's 'Civilization Project', which aimed at transforming Sudan into a modern Islamic state and was brutally enforced to guarantee compliance, only exacerbated existing tensions over religion.[11] This militant Islam pushed many towards supporting the SPLM/A, including the Equatorians. The movement's main patron, Ethiopia, was undergoing its own war, which resulted in the fall of Mengistu in 1991. The SPLM/A lost its bases, its supply lines, military hardware and radio station. The numerous difficulties faced by the SPLM/A and its leadership would culminate in the 1991 split. The Nasir coup severely weakened the SPLM/A and began a process of fragmentation that would continue after independence. The decade that followed witnessed a movement that had been on the brink of defeat slowly rebuilding itself, reviving its political position and retaking territory. In the late 1990s, peace negotiations would gain momentum.

The Comprehensive Peace Agreement (CPA), signed in 2005 between Bashir's ruling National Congress Party (NCP) and the SPLM/A, formally ended the 22-year civil war. In July 2011, the South achieved independence. Two years later, in December 2013, the country would erupt again in a brutal war, now emanating from within the SPLM/A, despite attempts to secure peace with the Agreement for the Resolution of the Conflict in South Sudan (ARCISS) of August 2015 and the Revitalisation Agreement of

September 2018. Within 5 years, over 400,000 had been killed, 1.9 million internally displaced, 2.4 million forced to take refuge in neighbouring counties, over 19,000 children used as child soldiers and over 7 million in need of life-saving assistance.[12] At the root of this new civil war lay the failure of the SPLM/A as a political vehicle to contain leadership disputes, which devolved into personal, ethnic and community animosities. The SPLM/A lost the necessary legitimacy and political control to unite the South and define an inclusive nationalist programme and development path. Feeding into these dynamics was its failure to reconcile communities and elites with their violent past, the ineffective integration of political and military forces opposing the SPLM/A and the unresolved tensions of the 1991 split (Johnson 2003 [updated 2016]).

União Nacional para a Independência Total de Angola

UNITA emerged in 1966 as the third liberation movement fighting the Portuguese, five years after the struggle for independence in Angola had begun. It fought as an anti-colonial movement until 1975 and continued its resistance in the post-independence civil war (1975–2002), during which Angola witnessed intermittent years of tense peace. While UNITA fought different enemies in each liberation era, it ultimately sought to represent a particular portion of Angola's disenfranchised majority. Its cause was grounded in projecting a different nationalist ideology based on its view of what it meant to be Angolan, its hope to build a nation where all had a role, correcting the historical exclusion of key constituencies.

Portuguese colonial power configuration had a severe impact on ethnic and social regional groups, reinforcing a dualist structure that cemented divisions within Angolan society. For the first 400 years, the colonial power had controlled little of the interior of the country. Portuguese presence in Angola was arguably inefficient and under-resourced. While Luanda and the coastal areas had experienced 500 years of Portuguese rule, the central highlands and the South had experienced less than 80 years. The Portuguese would only begin conquering the Ovimbundu kingdoms and incorporating them into the colony between 1890 and 1904. These different modes of development were based on the colonial government's failure to extend its administration into the interior, which created avenues for mobilising sub-national grievances. After the wars of occupation (1845–1917), a new social model was introduced, with a Secretariat for Indigenous Affairs aimed at institutionalising racial and ethnic differences and stratifying Angolan society into *indigenas* (indigenous) and *assimilados* (assimilated). The assimilated elites (estimated to have numbered 38,000 black and 45,000 *mestiço* families) were given privileges based on their literacy, values and customs, which were denied to the indigenous population (Messiant 1998).[13] Traditional authorities were subordinated to this direct rule, and the traditional kingdoms, except the Kongo kingdom, were abolished. Despite this, by 1904 the colonial power controlled only 10% of the territory. It sought to reverse this trend under Antonio Salazar's corporatist authoritarian regime, the New State (1933–75). By the 1950s, Angola experienced several contrasting dynamics—'two parallel societies engaged in two parallel economies'—with the majority living within traditional, lineage-based communities and engaged in subsistence farming on one side, and on the other an urbanised population and industrial enterprises meant to serve the towns (Newitt 2008).[14] But it also experienced a phenomen that deeply impacted the thinking of the liberation leaders. As Péclard (2021) points out, the 'colonial state in Angola … was also exclusionary and discriminatory, leaving very few avenues for upward social mobility for Angolan "natives." It was therefore mostly at the margins of the colonial world that such mobility was possible, especially within Christian missions'. These missions, mainly from North America, triggered cultural change in rural areas from the 1880s onward (Neto 2012).

The war in Angola had many beginnings (Cramer 2006). In early 1961, a series of unplanned and uncoordinated revolts in Luanda and the northern provinces launched the liberation war. The first revolt in January 1961 in the cotton-rich area of Baixa do Kassange was fomented due to anger over land expropriation, monoculture agriculture and harsh labour conditions. The insurrection was aimed at killing white settlers and Ovimbundu migrant workers (Newitt 2008).[15] In the North, the Portuguese administration had adopted a policy of conciliation towards the local elites by allowing them a limited return to independent coffee growing. In the South, however, pushback against the growth of white settler farming and ranching by the Portuguese was treated with repression, which resulted in the fragmentation of the peasant population (Birmingham 2015). Divisions among the southern and northern communities were also attributed to the perception among the Bakongo that the Ovimbundu trade with the Portuguese was an indication of collaboration and profiting from colonialism (Andresen Guimarães 2001). These divisions and historical experiences significantly impacted the direction, strategies and identity of the three liberation movements that failed to create a united front, with the rebellion lacking a nationally broad focus (Marcum 1978).

The class distinctions formulated in the colonial period were mirrored in the differences of the nationalist parties. The Movimento Popular para a Libertação de Angola (MPLA), founded in 1961 and led by Agostinho Neto, grew out of the urban centres by left-wing elites in Luanda (the *petite bourgeoisie*) and was comprised of *mulattos* (a term used in Angola to refer to biracial people), *assimilados* and white Angolans, even though its ethnic basis was Mbundu (Cleary 2001). The Mbundu, representing 23% of the population, had already integrated Portuguese language and culture into their way of life because of sustained interaction with the colonial power (Hodges 2004). The *Frente Nacional para a Libertação de Angola*'s (FNLA) preceding organisation, the União das Populações de Angola (UPA), was founded in 1957 and comprised mainly of the Bakongo (the third-largest ethnic group occupying the north-western provinces) and was led by Holden Roberto. UNITA was founded in 1966 to give political expression to the Ovimbundu (the largest ethnic group at 37% of the population) of the central highlands and other groups in eastern Angola, emerging as a response to the shortcomings of the two other movements. By 1966, Angola had three liberation movements with three distinct versions of nationalism. None of the movements were able to successfully stage protracted military campaigns that eroded the colonial power's grip on the country before 1975. The Portuguese had engaged in a relatively effective counter-insurgency campaign of 66,000 troops supported by special forces, local militias and Katanguese gendarmes (Malyn 2008).[16] For almost a decade, the three movements spent as much time fighting each other as they did the colonialists, only barely managing to keep the war alive.

In 1974, following the revolution in Portugal that hastened independence in the colonies, all three movements began to position themselves to take over the government. Although an agreement was reached between them to prepare the transition to independence, neither the FNLA nor the MPLA was prepared to share state power, preferring instead to secure a military victory over its rivals. UNITA lacked the military and diplomatic strength of the other two movements, making it more inclined to seek a compromise and wait for elections (Messiant 1998). Although a coalition government was formed in early 1975 under the Alvor Agreement, it only lasted a few months, as the FNLA launched a military takeover of the capital and failed. Having pushed the FNLA from Luanda, the MPLA declared independence in Luanda on 11 November 1975. On the same day, UNITA and the FNLA declared independence in Huambo. Following its victory, the MPLA sought to expel the other two movements from the cities and entrench its power with Cuban and Soviet assistance. The FNLA would become a residual force, while UNITA had to withdraw from Huambo in the face of a politically stronger and militarily superior enemy. After independence, UNITA began to see the MPLA as a neo-colonialist government, extending the divisions perpetuated under the Portuguese. The liberation wars (1961–75) created divisions between Angolans, but the wars that followed between UNITA and the MPLA (1975–2002) created deeper political antagonisms and social disaggregation (Messiant 1998).[17]

The post-independence war provided a fertile basis for the involvement of international forces bent on advancing their geopolitical and strategic interests. At the height of the Cold War's impact on the region, Cuban and South African troops were present in Angola. Russia supplied the MPLA with military advice, intelligence, technology and arms, and, after the repeal of the Clark Amendment in 1985, the United States did the same for UNITA. Regional networks of logistical support also played a key role interlinking the political and security dynamics of other Southern African countries.

In 1991, some hope for a political settlement came with the Bicesse Accords, signed in Portugal. Despite professing a will to implement the agreement, both sides failed to fully commit to peace, and the war restarted after failed elections in 1992. In 1994, the Lusaka Protocol was signed, which foresaw national reconciliation and the formation of a united government, as well as another disarmament, demobilisation and reintegration (DDR) process. In April 1997, a Government of Unity and National Reconciliation (GURN) was inaugurated, but the country was physically and politically divided. UNITA's access to diamonds, and the MPLA government's access to oil revenues, enabled both sides to continue fighting. The war that ravaged the country from 1998 until 2002 was one of attrition, far more brutal than the ones that preceded it. Peace came in February 2002 when several of UNITA's top leadership, including Jonas Savimbi, were ambushed and killed. The Memorandum of Understanding signed in April provided a framework for peace, including an amnesty law, the integration of 5,000 UNITA troops into the nation's armed forces, and a timetable for the demobilisation of UNITA's remaining troops. The first post-war elections were held in August 2008, allowing the MPLA to consolidate political legitimacy by employing its stranglehold on the economy and the security apparatus. A peace without dividends was built, allowing elites to capture the economy and serving a presidency that instituted a securitised form of government to protect the MPLA's political project. The double-digit growth of Angola's GDPR from oil, that peaked in 2012, attracted flocks of foreign investors who came to enjoy the spoils while Angolans fell deeper into poverty. After 38 years in power, President Dos Santos stepped down in August 2017, paving the way for the country to either reform or unravel under the weight of its unreconciled past and divided society. His successor, João Lourenço, would embark on a highly contentious anti-corruption drive targeting the Dos Santos clan and his cronies. Lourenço would double down on the securitisation of the state, which was meant to protect the power of the presidency and subjugate alternative action and thought to the political hegemony of the MPLA. He would govern over decay and face rising disillusionment at the popular level. Actions in 2022 revealed a government deeply afraid of reform and of democracy.

Imagining the state

The states and nations envisaged by UNITA and the SPLM/A were meant to be both transformative and reformed, addressing historical injustices and creating nations that provided a space for the marginalised to take the lead. The Free Lands of Angola and the New Sudan aimed to recast their countries into states that would reflect their values and ensure the economic and political power of their constituents. Both UNITA and the SPLM/A employed elements of planned nation- and state-building as well as elements of improvisation and default positionings.

As the dynamics of their wars shifted—both internally and externally—the SPLM/A and UNITA reformulated their objectives and addressed the political and socio-economic grievances of their 'people'. During the first war, for UNITA this meant a quest for an independent state that overcame the ills of imperialism, racial and class divides, and regional marginalisation. During the second war, they sought instead a state free of foreign interference, representative of its heterogeneity and built on the principles of negritude, democracy and socialism. During the SPLM/A's first decade of war, it fought for a unitary, secular and socialist state. This transitioned during the second half of the war into a demand for self-determination, pluralism, development and democracy.

The SPLM/A, more so than UNITA, was united in its opposition to the structure of the state, but it was divided over how the state should be governed (Johnson 1998).[18] The internal debate and contradictions within the SPLM/A over whether to pursue secession or unity was at its heart a debate over how best to protect and defend the South (Johnson 1998).[19] The geographic scope of the New Sudan could and eventually would diverge from its initial unitary objective of reforming the entire Sudan, not just the South. The SPLM/A understood that it could not succeed alone and focused on liberating the five areas under its theatre of war: the three areas of the South

(Equatoria, Upper Nile and Bahr El Ghazal) and the two regions of the Blue Nile and Nuba Mountains. The rest of the country would be liberated by other strategic alliances between northern opposition movements.[20]

From 1983 until 1991, the New Sudan focused on providing national solutions to Sudan's structural inequalities. This was a pragmatic decision made by Garang and supported by the SPLM/A's main external patron, Ethiopia, based on the international and regional rejection of secessionist wars. It was also based on the need to take the fight to Khartoum so that the North would also be involved in the turmoil of rebellion rather than the war only being fought in the South. Events in 1991 forced the SPLM/A to rethink this strategy. In 1993, the SPLM/A devised its modular approach as a negotiation tool during the Abuja talks, which explained the different forms of self-determination as the movement adapted its reform process to different scenarios.[21] The SPLM/A incorporated the idea of secession of the South into its political programme, as well as its rhetoric and organisational planning. Despite these changes, the programme for reformed governance rested on key principles of a multi-ethnic and multi-cultural society, the decentralisation of power to marginalised regions and peoples, and democratic principles.

UNITA's state-building vision began within the anti-colonial struggle and the dream of an independent Angola. It advocated for a political transition where a new government would begin the task of correcting the structural deficiencies of the state perpetuated by the Portuguese. The movement's rhetoric was centred on revolution, anti-imperialism and the accommodation of Africanism. When the post-independence war began, UNITA justified its fight against the MPLA on the basis that power was held in its government by a minority party comprised of *mestiços* and *assimilados* that purposefully subjugated black Angolans and was kept in power by non-African nations (the Soviets and Cubans). The 'MPLA's vision was about popular power, centralised economy, an arbitrary state and a single party'.[22] UNITA sought to lead a peasant revolution that would empower the marginalised majority, who in turn would embrace the principles of Africanism and negritude, democracy and socialism. The state it aimed to build was premised on self-sufficiency, respect for custom and tradition, rural development, a diversified market economy and a pluralistic society.

The war strategies UNITA pursued reflected these objectives and illustrated its organisational priorities. The different stages of war also helped demonstrate the role the parallel state would play in each stage. Upon its emergence, UNITA used the teachings of Mao Tse Tung to structure its organisation, prepare the military strategy and define its relationship with the population. In October 1966, Savimbi and 11 of his commanders, later known as the 'China 12', travelled to China to receive training in guerrilla warfare. UNITA followed the tenets of Mao's guerrilla strategy very closely and staged a protracted popular war, whose aims included the creation of parallel hierarchies (parallel states). This was an incremental strategy with different stages: the political organisation phase (1966–76), the guerrilla warfare phase (1976–85) and the conventional warfare phase (1985–91). In the first phase, political cells were created to propagate the message and win popular support while guerrilla teams were deployed to attack certain targets. This stage already required that rudimentary services be provided with mutual assistance programmes to secure the support of communities and build the infrastructure for self-reliance (Potgieter 2000).[23] The second phase required UNITA to have more units operating throughout the territory in order to exhaust the enemy and isolate the population from the government. At this stage it was already governing areas and creating the basis for its parallel state by providing services and politically organising the population. The last phase, deemed the conventional warfare phase, was strategically offensive and entailed a full-fledged civil war (Potgieter 2000).[24] UNITA developed parallel hierarchies as an intrinsic part of its displacement strategy of replacing political authority in liberated areas by taking over some existing structures and creating new clandestine structures. In this last phase, UNITA had a fully operational parallel state, parallel society, parallel army and shadow government.

The SPLM/A seemed to have a less structured approach, despite the movement initially being defined as Marxist and greatly influenced by the Cuban model. The war started with armed battalions and a visceral desire for insurrection, which led many to believe it would be a short conflict. The SPLM/A's liberation phases were fundamentally different from those of UNITA. The first stage (1983–84) centred around the armed struggle and armed propaganda as a mobile system because there were no liberated areas. The second phase (1984–87) centred on taking over the native administration structures of chiefs and establishing committees to mobilise support. As more territory was being conquered, this developed into the Civil–Military Administrator (CMA) system (1988–94). The next stage was the creation of the Civil Authority for a New Sudan (CANS) with the establishment of the National Executive Council (NEC). From 1995, the Peace Through Development strategy informed the operation of the CANS,[25] which aimed to operate as a parallel government. The CANS was defined as a broad-based civil authority that institutionally separated local authority structures from the military command structures. It linked decentralised and democratic governance with development and peace. In its final stage of war, the SPLM/A was attempting to operate a parallel state, build its political party and negotiate the terms of a complex political transition.

Both movements attempted to deliver their parallel states in ways that would not fundamentally contradict their visions for a reformed state. Both succeeded in enhancing respect for customs and traditional authorities, in pursuing self-sufficiency drives and in structuring local government structures. They managed to attain the legitimacy they aspired to. Yet both failed at establishing any practice of democratic processes, despite the SPLM/A's effort to conduct controlled elections in its local structures, and UNITA closely following the principles of democratic centralism at the political level. Both movements also failed to represent all the contradictory interests of the people and groups they claimed to represent, failing to find unity in a heterogeneity they could not fully control. Neither movement fully managed to incorporate their vision and ideological principles into a reformed state in a setting of wartime governance. The following chapters will describe in detail the SPLM/A's governance experience in Yambio and UNITA's in Jamba, highlighting the contradictions, difficulties and areas of innovation.

2

THE SPLM/A'S GOVERNANCE
YAMBIO AND THE NEW SUDAN, 1990–2002

'*They get food, they get shelter, they get clean drinking water, they get healthcare services, they get social amenities, they get economic infrastructure such as roads, they get jobs and so forth. Unless we provide these essential services to our people ... then the people will prefer the government of the NIF. ... This is simple arithmetic: if the SPLM cannot deliver anything and we just shout Revolution! Revolution! and yet the cattle of the people are not vaccinated; their children are not sent to school. ... When the barest minimum essential things of life are not available, then the people will drive us into the sea, even though there is no sea they will find one.*'

John Garang[1]

'*Sudan was controlled by two authorities that did not recognize each other. ... When the duality of power and sovereign authorities appeared the SPLM/A administration became more established.*'

Pagan Amum[2]

'*Demography in the South is against the process of nation-building, where the government is a structure in name only but lower down there are communities and tribes. We cannot have a loose party or a loose state because we will fall apart.*'

Youth leader[3]

On the margins of the state and the southern tip of the Sudanese territory lay Yambio, an area characterised by long-standing political neglect and underdevelopment, yet endowed with rich agricultural land and trade routes to the neighbouring Democratic Republic of the Congo and Central African Republic. A land of the Azande, it would become the 'garden of the liberated areas', where traditional custom prevailed and the SPLM/A would learn that ruling a land with systems of authority already in place required strategies of governance and inroads of participation. The SPLM/A's wartime governance in Yambio over 12 years (1990–2002) developed from a militarised and contested rule to the constitution of a 'state' imbued with a degree of legitimacy and characterised by loose regulatory and political practices. This New Sudan state project attempted to respond to the needs of the civilian population and prepare the movement to rule in a time of peace. After years of violent misrule and governing mishaps, the SPLM/A, through the Civil Authority for a New Sudan (CANS), managed to transform force into authority in Yambio. What had been perceived as an 'occupation army' now became 'our government'. The liberation movement did this against the backdrop of a highly divided and fragmented South Sudan, as well as under the strain of multidimensional defeat in 1991. The purpose of the parallel state of the New Sudan was to ensure the military, political, logistical and symbolic survival of the SPLM/A. This chapter traces the progression and stages of governance that occurred in Yambio as it became the first county of the liberated South in 1990 until the signing of the first CPA protocol in 2002.

The SPLM/A began its liberation trajectory on a highly militarised basis, with its focus being on gaining territory and bringing down the Sudanese central government rather than on politically uniting different elites and communities as part of a larger social transformation process. The establishment of the movement in Ethiopia and the influence of the military government, the Derg, defined several of its key decisions and pathways. As a result of mass recruitment campaigns and the graduation of successive military units in Ethiopia, the SPLM/A rapidly transformed its army into a semi-conventional force. The first recruits came mainly from the Dinka areas of Jonglei and Lakes, and the Nuer areas of Nasir and

Bentiu, but as the war progressed the movement sent mobile units to new areas to further recruit among their kin and age groups (Johnson 1998).[4] The SPLM/A was credited with creating military units that had a national character, with soldiers hailing from different areas and ethnic groups, which allowed it to do three things: undercut the tendency of a factionalised army; advance into new areas and recruit locally; and provide coherence of operations across regions by building local alliances. During the 1980s, the SPLM/A managed to transform itself into a formidable force, making it one of Africa's more successful guerrilla movements capable of securing considerable territory, dealing with international relief agencies and suffering no major defeat until 1991 (Johnson and Prunier 1993).[5] In 1988–89, the SPLM/A was sending battalions to the Nuba Mountains and the Blue Nile, effectively taking the war out of the South (Johnson 1998).[6] By 1989, the movement had 70,000 troops that had graduated from Ethiopian training camps.[7] That number rose to 120,000 in 1991, almost equal in size to the Sudanese army (Bayissa 2007). From 1988 to 1991, the SPLM/A had conquered over 70% of the South's territory.

During these years, it developed a militarised system of rule in the liberated areas. Millions of southerners lived under the SPLM/A at this time (Luk 1992)[8] and faced the difficulties of having to engage with a hierarchical chain of command they had no immediate access to and a movement veered towards meeting the needs of the organisation rather than the population. Citizen consent and participation in the revolution would not factor into the military strategy of the movement in the 1980s. It initially used an anger-fuelled nationalism, resulting from the failures of the 1972 peace agreement, as a mobilisation tool instead of developing the political structures to ensure that it was creating its nation as an 'artefact of men's convictions, loyalties and solidarities' (Gellner 1983: 7). It took the SPLM/A 11 years before it understood that the tangibles of legitimacy had to be accompanied by a state-like entity that would challenge Khartoum as well as other political threats from southern nationalist movements (i.e. the SPLM/A-Nasir splinter group). As the SPLM/A began conquering territory from government forces in 1984–87, it established committees and used the chief's system to install order. As the movement became stronger and started capturing major rural areas, the system of the Civil–Military Administrator (CMA) (1988–94) was devised as the first stage of organised administration for liberated areas. A highly militarised CMA system was combined with the old traditional order of chiefs, a rehabilitation of indirect rule to initially secure the liberated areas without the need to create legitimacy or rule through persuasion. The CMA system was coercive, violent and militaristic. In 1992–94, the movement redefined the liberation struggle and transformed its approach to governance as it faced a multitude of critical junctures that began in 1991. The CANS then developed from the CMA in 1994. The New Sudan state and the CANS institutions were driven by the parallel development of the party as the state of the liberated South. By doing this, the SPLM/A also began to address the legacies of the past that had characterised the rule of Khartoum by attempting to correct horizontal and vertical inequalities. The SPLM/A's strategy of empowering the local level allowed for ownership of the parallel state by different communities. Explaining the cause and creating political spaces the movement could manage and control (Reno 2011) was a vital step before the SPLM/A could transition into an organisation driven by political rather than uniquely military priorities.

The difference between the CMA and the CANS system was significant, not least because one was rule by force while the other was rule by relative consent. A state needed to be imagined and experienced for this second liberation to truly take root and allow for a new political order to emerge. Building their project on the ashes of a failed state was not the way for the SPLM/A to secure the power bases it needed to create to win the war and secure peace. Ruling through the structures left behind by Khartoum or attempting to mirror their administration was not an option, as these were part of the structural causes of the conflict. What this progression of governance points to is the imperatives of: first, the reformulation of military calculations and strategies as political programmes and objectives, by introducing political structures to support broader aims; second, the management of internal and external perceptions as part of the SPLM/A's calculus of strength at a time when it was fragmented; third, the 'popularisation' of the liberation struggle and legitimacy of the cause, which was absent during the first decade; fourth, the creation of internal bases for resource management and production of symbolic capital after the SPLM/A lost its rear base in Ethiopia; and, finally, the coordinated use of existing systems of authority as conduits to diverse populations.

The nature and characteristics of the rebel organisation influenced how resilient the parallel state became. In the absence of strong political structures, the SPLM/A strategically opted to decentralise power to local authorities, while embedding them in a broad political framework and militarising society to ensure order. The result was a shift in state–society relations and, unexpectedly, in society–society relations. The movement outsourced the delivery of key services to relief agencies and international NGOs, instrumentalising legitimacy in this manner. The New Sudan was an example of a locally experienced parallel state that never expanded centrally beyond the imagined conceptions of its leadership, a fact that would haunt the SPLM/A during the 2005 transition and after independence. This case study also points to the interaction between authority and power and how the SPLM/A understood that administrative structures had to reflect existing systems of power. In this way, the state had to be built based on existing social systems and informal patron–client networks first using chiefs (during the CMA era) and then by mobilising and corporatising society (during the CANS era).

Yambio remained one of the most politically independent areas during the transition of 2005–11, choosing in the 2010 elections the only independent governor and non-SPLM candidate, Joseph Bakosoro, of the 10 states of the South. From 2014, Yambio became a bastion of resistance to the SPLM government in Juba, with numerous armed groups—each with their own local and national ambitions—fighting for representation, economic development and security. Continued calls for decentralised governance within the Equatoria region highlighted a disconnect with the central government in Juba. All the lessons of how wartime governance had operated—its failings and successes—would bear the same traits 24 years later. The enemies had changed, and the symbolism of war and justice had shifted, but the dynamics of governance remained a warning sign for future generations. A delicate balance had to be struck between dignity and autonomy at the local level, connection and representation at the national level, and there had to be an overarching link to a unifying political order. During the 1983–2005 war, the central command of the SPLM/A failed to effectively connect with the liberated areas—a peripheral dynamic that was explained by the absence of political structures and cadres. The movement never demilitarised the way power was structured and wielded. A sense of entitlement within its leadership created a kleptocratic elite that, when they felt challenged, responded by stirring up tribal and local anger. Ironically, the relative peace experienced in Yambio from 1990 to 2005—as years of war—became an interregnum that preceded a reality few recognised after the war restarted in 2013. When research was conducted in 2012, the testimonies of those interviewed across the Equatoria region and in Yambio spoke of a time of hope and purpose. Today their recollections are marked by pain, victimisation, violence and betrayal.

Yambio: Force and persuasion

Figure 2.1: Map of Yambio

Yambio was the capital of Western Equatoria State (WES) (see Figure 2.1),[9] bordering the states of Western Bahr El Ghazal and Lakes to the north, the Democratic Republic of the Congo (DRC) to the south, the Central African Republic (CAR) to the west and the Central Equatoria State to the east. It was home to the Azande, Balanda, Mundu, Fertit, Moru, Beli and Avokaya ethnic groups. The Azande, the dominant group in WES, claimed that they would need a great level of persuasion before rendering their obedience to any authority, the Zande paramount chief stating that 'we fought everyone that tried to dominate us: the Arabs, the British and the French'.[10] Ruled by the Avungara royal clan, the Azande kingdom operated under central and hierarchically organised systems of authority. The British considered it a threat to colonial rule and attempted to reduce the power of King Gbudwe Bazingbi (eventually killing him in 1905), but they never managed to circumvent the power of such a centrally controlled system. After independence, in 1956, riots broke out in the WES when steps were taken to install greater Northern presence. Given the deep-rooted tendency of the Zande to resist any outside authority, Western Equatoria proved a challenging area for the SPLM/A to try and rule. Interviews with chiefs, commanders and civil servants consistently pointed to the predisposition of the Zande for obedience to the law, a characteristic this community claimed was pivotal in allowing the CANS to function during the war. However, part of this obedience was grounded on the Zande accepting the rule being installed.

In the 1990s, Yambio had over 250,000 people living permanently in the county, as well as groups moving in during different stages of the war between the front and the rear.[11] The local population were originally hostile to the SPLM/A, considering the movement an occupation force for many years. As the SPLM/A moved closer into the area in 1990, the population abandoned Yambio in the wake of the movement's arrival. There was a historical explanation for this. When Khartoum carved the South into three provinces, it left the region divided not only territorially and ethnically but also psychologically. Equatoria was the main bastion of pro-Kokora (a Bari word meaning 'divide equally') sentiment and had, in the 1980s, pushed for the re-division of the South. Kokora thus became equated with deep divisions across the country. When the SPLM/A arrived in Equatoria, it was perceived as an occupying force of Dinka fighters bent on revenge against the Equatorians for having betrayed the cause of a nationalist South. 'Khartoum had waged a vigorous campaign portraying the SPLM/A as an ethnic organisation, this is why people feared the movement when it arrived.'[12] The SPLM/A also had a long record of human rights abuses and a disinterest in politically mobilising civilians to join the cause.

However, Yambio was not entirely representative of the SPLM/A's wartime governance, given the diversity of the South and the accompanying demography, ecology and security challenges, although it did provide a blueprint for other areas. Governing experiences in other regions of Greater Bahr El Ghazal and parts of Greater Upper Nile (that were partly controlled by the SPLM-Nasir and had the presence of several ethnic militias) differed and were impacted by several factors. In some areas there was relative peace, trade and a sense of normalisation, while in others the SPLM/A continued to build on its reputation as a violent movement brutalising civilians, stealing aid and failing to properly administer civilian areas. Nevertheless, the elements that drove the movement to govern civilian populations in a more participatory manner post-1991 were based on several contextual and organisational aspects that were general to the war and the SPLM/A. Many governance initiatives described in this chapter and implemented in other areas had their origins in the administrative experiment of Yambio. In fact, when the CANS was devised and began to take root in 1994, only Yambio was stable enough for the movement to implement its state project. Other areas would not experience the CANS administration until after 1997. Unless specifically stated, the description of processes, institutions and initiatives deal with what the SPLM/A achieved in Yambio.

The SPLM/A captured Yambio on 25 December 1990 as part of its Brightstar campaign that had taken the war to Equatoria. The evacuation of government forces and administration allowed the movement to enter the town peacefully, although most civilians had also evacuated to neighbouring villages or across the border to the DRC and CAR, fearful of the destruction the rebels would bring. During the first years of their campaign, the SPLM/A had announced it over the SPLA Radio (based in Ethiopia) whenever they entered different areas, partly as a means of psychological warfare but also to allow the population to take shelter. Upon arriving in Yambio, all the leading commanders of the army that had liberated Western Equatoria became part of that first experiment of administration. After liberating Yambio, Garang persuaded the Zande Brigadier Samuel AbuJohn, previously a minister in Abel Alier's regional government and a local Anyanya leader from the first civil war, to take part in the SPLM/A liberation struggle. AbuJohn was given the important role of Governor of Equatoria. Leadership was an important aspect in bringing about relative acceptance of the movement, however ethnic tensions were not eased sufficiently to allow for complete acceptance of the SPLM/A during the first four years. The Zande made an interesting distinction that the problems were not created by the SPLM/A but by the Dinka.[13] Ethnic tensions were a problem the movement would have to contend with, especially as troops were deployed into areas that took them outside their original areas.

The Civil–Military Administration

After capturing Yambio, the SPLM/A had to ensure that it could keep the area from falling back to government forces, given that the neighbouring counties of Maridi and Mundri were still frontlines. To keep the area safe, groups of soldiers were posted all around Yambio and Nzara with outposts of between 35 and 70 soldiers on the roads to detect enemy movements. The military barracks were posted on the outskirts to minimise direct contact between civilians and the military. The evacuation of civil servants and the entire government administration before the arrival of the SPLM/A created a vacuum that needed to be filled.

> They [the SPLM/A] appointed military administrators and created 5 payams[14] in Yambio county—Gangura, Bangasu, Yambio town, Rangu, and Nadianguere—but we did not understand the titles of this new local government. ... They said

that at the boma[15] level there was a sub-chief and for the payam a chief. That's when they summoned all the chiefs and said that the army needed food.[16]

The objective at this stage was not to transform force into authority but rather to define force and reorder it so that civilians contributed to the war effort. It was about expansion, not consolidation, of rule. Although the movement aimed at restoring some sense of normalcy by empowering chiefs and restoring native administration functions, the mentality at the time still favoured the superiority of the military over the political/administrative leader. 'For those that grew up within the military the army was everything to them—knowledge, authority, future.'[17] This militaristic drive created the impression that the army was above politics, ideology, culture and tradition.

The CMA system had two main objectives: to stabilise and secure newly liberated areas, and to incorporate the population into the war effort through the chief's system. The system clearly wasn't underpinned by social and economic objectives, instead prioritising an extractive and conscriptive approach towards the population. 'The army, not the people, were at the centre of Garang's project' (Young 2012: 66–7) at this stage of the liberation. This militarised system was devised in such a way that commanders took the reins of administration, security and procurement of resources. Provision of services and rehabilitation of economic activities were not the CMA's main functions. This fell mainly under the auspices of the movement's relief wing, the Sudan Relief and Rehabilitation Association (SRRA), created in 1986 to act as a liaison between international NGOs and the SPLM/A. Soon after the UN's Operation Lifeline Sudan (OLS) began in 1989, it extended support to the SRRA. The SRRA had a 15-member secretariat and was headed by a secretary general, who was assisted by coordinators of different sectors: education, health, agriculture, stores and equipment, water drilling, veterinary, construction, accounts, projects formulation, religious affairs, public relations, field coordination and press. The secretariat was stationed inside the liberated areas in Kapoeta, which had been taken by the SPLM/A in January 1988. Within a year, Kapoeta had a functioning hospital with an operating room, laboratory and pharmacy, a library and renovated offices for the SRRA (Akol 2003).

At this stage, the movement was merely trying to replace the old political and administrative structures and did not aim to build a political base. Using the only organisational tools it had available, the movement structured the CMA system in line with the structures of the military. The SPLM/A's theatre of military operations was divided into axis, zonal and front commands, which were subsequently divided into independent area commands.[18] Zonal and area commands had the responsibility of appointing CMAs at the different levels of local administration while chiefs operated at the village levels. The CMA administrative authority was established using native and provincial structures in the zonal areas of military commands. The SPLM/A used the same local government divisions that had been in place in Sudan but changed their names to create a sense of a new administration (see Table 2.1). Using a skeletal governance structure, the CMA was simultaneously the civil administrator, the main adjudicator of legal cases, the head of the military in the area and the chief of resource organisation. Each CMA had the power to arbitrate and coordinate judicial matters by supervising chiefs' courts and having this system interact with SPLM/A-appointed magistrates. CMAs were also responsible for coordinating chiefs to provide the SPLM/A with recruits, food, porters and information. As the head of the county, the CMA would be under the authority of the regional commander but would be the ultimate authority of the district (payam) and rural councils (boma) that fell under his jurisdiction (see Figure 2.2).

Table 2.1: Old administrative system and SPLM/A system

Sudan Government	SPLM/A Government
Province/Area Council	County
District/Rural Council	Payam
Court Centre	Boma
Villages	Villages

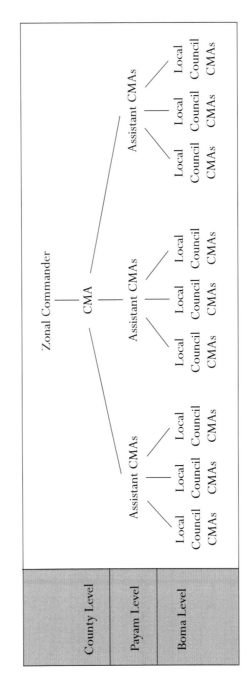

Figure 2.2: CMA system

The system was built on the foundation of allowing the chiefs' courts to continue functioning and as a result ensure justice, while families and civilians were given the responsibility of providing services to clinics and the wounded.[19] 'I was elected the first chairwoman of the county and had to encourage people to return to Yambio and begin forming associations to help the administration and the communities.'[20] Schools were re-established during the first years under the auspices of women's groups and churches. Government figures in 1989 indicated that, out of the 1,417 schools that existed in the South before the war, only 300 were operational.[21] The rehabilitation of the education system would be one of the greatest difficulties the movement would face. Testimonies from the SPLM/A leadership point to how the CMA system in Yambio was more organised than in other parts of the South, and committees for the delivery of services, although not a priority, were already emerging. Unlike many other areas, Yambio did not have a large presence of relief agencies during the first years of the CMA rule, which meant they were dependent on civilians for food and resources.

Militarisation of society

From 1990 to 1994, traditional authorities, civilians, civil servants, teachers and any member of the community had to undergo military training. This was for civil defence purposes—so that communities could defend themselves from enemy incursions or militia forces that ventured into the liberated areas—but it also allowed the SPLM/A to incorporate civilians into the movement. Chiefs were given military training and commissioned as officers. 'The first thing the SPLM/A did in 1990 was to take chiefs for forty-five days of military training which was difficult for the older chiefs. One chief from Nzara died during the training.'[22] A local party representative from Yambio described how 'Over 3,000 people from Yambio went for training in Moroto [an area in Eastern Equatoria near Nimule] and chiefs were taken to a separate training facility in Kidepo. Chiefs would learn the same skills as recruits: military, political and intelligence.'[23] The militarisation of social life would cause disruption at levels the SPLM/A didn't expect, and in the opinion of key leaders the militarisation of chiefs destroyed the structures of traditional authority. The paramount chief was given the rank of captain, while all executive chiefs became lieutenants. 'A chief who had the rank of lieutenant could not say anything to a SPLA Major. The new dispensation was upside down because chiefs were always revered,' and the most respected government title at the local level.[24] The objective of giving ranks to the chiefs was so that soldiers would respect them,[25] which pointed to the movement's inability to function and regulate social life outside of a militarised structure. The military training they underwent also affected the way chiefs related to their community, and they became more likely to favour their own family and clan than in the past (Deng et al. 2005).

Traditional authorities were expected to continue providing a system of local governance to their communities while functioning within the military structure. As chiefs, they had many roles. They were the gatekeepers or the go-between for the SPLM/A, reporting the problems and needs of the community to the movement and communicating SPLM/A orders to civilians. They organised food and tax collection, recruitment of soldiers and self-help projects. Chiefs had judicial and arbitration roles and were guardians of culture, traditions and customary laws (Deng et al. 2005: 12). While the SPLM/A interfered with and militarised the traditional authorities, it also depended on them to create pillars of social order. 'The social consciousness of the traditional society expressed in customary law, [was] so deeply ingrained that any developmental scheme, which disregard[ed] it could not find its way into the hearts of the people.'[26] The SPLM/A knew that it could not rule the liberated areas without the chiefs, given the fact that it lacked structured support from segments of the population, a political wing that could serve as a civil service, resources to provide services and any other ordering force that could replace the chiefs. Because of these shortcomings, the SPLM/A needed to govern through intermediaries. The movement tied its rule to authority figures who had prior legitimacy by inserting them into a larger organisational structure, a clear form of indirect rule.

However, unlike the organised British Lugardian scheme of indirect rule that rested on the three pillars of a Native Court,

Native Administration and Native Treasury (Mamdani 1996), the SPLM/A's rudimentary version of indirect rule rested on securing the immediate needs of ensuring order and obtaining food, rather than being an instrument to a system with a larger politico-administrative objective. The SPLM/A tried to restore the system of indirect rule that had existed in Sudan under the British, harnessing it so that it could be at the service of the SPLM/A. During British rule, the system of Indigenous Local Authority was adopted in the 1920s, which effectively gave traditional authorities executive and judicial powers. This system was based on ethnic and sectional boundaries and thrived in a context of homogeneity (Dak 1996) where communities were ruled within their traditional ethnic boundaries. This was a practice that had already re-emerged after independence, when the Sudanese Government revived the system of native administration in 1985 to serve 'as a practical vehicle of local administration' (Elhussein 1989).

Working within the confines of traditional rule gave the movement some relative peace with regards to any potential resistance emerging from the fact that it was perceived as being a Dinka movement. Traditional authorities were considered the backbone of the justice system in the liberated areas and generally in South Sudan. The first SPLM/A Chief Justice for Greater Equatoria described how 'the use of traditional authorities goes back to the beginning of the war, as in 1983–84 it was a time to organise and when the Penal and Disciplinary Code came out room was already given to the traditional authority in liberated areas'.[27] Yet, while the provision of justice was seen as a key pillar of legitimacy during rebel rule (Mampilly 2011), it did not initially earn the SPLM/A's full support and compliance from the population. The provision of justice and conflict-resolution mechanisms was divided between two types of laws: the SPLM disciplinary law of 1984 for the military, and customary law for disputes among civilians. Because of the nature of the war, justice was a vital sector that needed to be secured if order was to be maintained in the liberated areas. 'Trauma was in the head of the people and if civilians and the military committed crimes, they were brought to justice using A courts and B courts[28] and people settled.'[29] The military commander would in certain instances act like a court of appeal[30] if these courts were unable to make decisions that both parties accepted. Without tapping into this existing justice system and using it to maintain order, the SPLM/A would have struggled to secure rural peace. However, many military abuses by soldiers and SPLA officers went unregulated and unpunished by any form of SPLM/A structures.

In the early years, the effectiveness of the SPLM/A's civilian administration was premised on its ability to provide order and control local raids between different tribal groups in its liberated areas, with attempts at resolving issues of cattle rustling and community clashes going as far back as 1985[31] with firm and coordinated action by commanders and inter-tribal conferences (Johnson 1998: 66). Several magistrates who had been operating in the South under Khartoum's judicial administration joined the SPLM/A and continued to perform judicial duties in liberated areas. As per the 1984 SPLA penal laws, three military courts were established: the summary court martial, the district court martial and the general court martial, which would serve as the final appeal court (Kuol 1997). State laws at the time were not used in SPLM/A areas; rather, the legal code employed was that of customary law, as well as the SPLA penal code. Due to the lack of qualified judges in each battalion of the SPLA, the courts had to be mobile so they could move between liberated areas.

The SPLM/A was aware that if it interfered too deeply with the chiefs' system it could face resistance from groups like the Azande. 'When you divide a people, they can divide you,' warned a former civilian commissioner from Yambio.[32] 'Because we are a kingdom the chiefs are respected and if you want to succeed here you have to go through the chiefs.'[33] The chiefs' system in Zande areas was described as abiding by concrete rules of succession: 'Chiefs must come from the Avungara clans that are descendants of King Gbudwe and their rule is given to them by God. ... Not just anyone can be nominated chief.'[34] However, one case in Tombura may have served as an explanation behind certain allegations that the SPLM/A interfered and appointed chiefs. The movement decided to appoint a chief in 1990 for the Baranda people who, according to the Zande paramount chief, did not have a chief but used instead community leaders, as they lived in Zande territory.[35] A group of people not having a chief was an anomaly the SPLM/A had to address, and in cases where there was absence of an identifiable executive authority they were forced to discover or invent chiefs. As the main interlocutors with the civilian population, chiefs were created where they were needed. In this way, the paramount chief would answer to the highest SPLM/A authority; below him, the executive chief acted as an interlocutor at a lower level, and the headmen below him would act at the village level, coordinating respectively with their CMA counterparts.

Economic activities and relief

As the SPLM/A began to liberate and define its theatre of operations it also began to distinguish between different areas of the South according to levels of insecurity. Conflict areas were termed 'frontline emergency' while liberated areas were considered transitional and post-conflict areas. Each followed a classification of needs. Conflict areas were recipients of relief assistance, while transitional areas combined the use of self-reliance strategies with relief assistance, and post-conflict areas focused only on self-development. Yambio fell under the post-conflict category. Its economic potential in terms of agriculture, manufacturing and resources was never truly explored to the fullest, even though the government of Sudan managed to maintain the Nzara agro-industrial complex after independence in 1956. As with other regions of the South, the economy of the area was directed towards benefiting the North, through the exploitation of labour and resources. This sustained the SPLM/A's rhetoric of its struggle for liberation being a just war, and they used it as a mobilisation call in encouraging areas in the South to support the movement and otherwise be self-sufficient. The first few years of the SPLM/A's rule in Yambio were difficult, with the population facing challenges that ranged from food insecurity to lack of basic services, education, housing, clothing and tools for farming and basic sustenance. With the 1988 famine in Bahr El Ghazal capturing the attention of relief organisations—an estimated 250,000[36] southerners died from starvation—the region of Western Equatoria fell outside the parameters for receiving emergency relief. This left the SPLM/A and the chiefs to their own devices in terms of food security and service provision.

SPLA military farms were already operating in many areas in Equatoria, although the expectation was that civilians would contribute a part of their harvest to the military. Although there was no consensus on how this would work, it seemed that there was a rotation period of two months where soldiers would be between the rear and the frontline. Once they returned to their barracks, they would work three hours in their quarters and cultivate, either in collective or their own private farms (Herzog 1998: 29). Each battalion would establish a farm that grew sorghum or maize. 'During the rainy season there were limited military operations, so all units had to cultivate food for themselves ... In the SPLA Act and the Constitution it says that the military had to be used in development when there is no war.'[37] The reality, however, was that food was mostly secured by extracting it from civilians and chiefs. The SPLA would 'tax' civilians on the food delivered, or else violently appropriate food from communities.[38]

Until 1993, Yambio was completely isolated from much-needed relief assistance. Efforts were made to initiate economic activities and coordinate resources beyond the immediate need of sustaining the military effort and collecting food. The SPLM/A created an economic commission aimed at securing investment in the key areas of natural resources (namely gold in Kapoeta), livestock and fisheries (Deng 2013). Trade networks between liberated areas were also beginning to operate again as the SPLM/A secured more territory. Goods were moved from government-controlled Abyei through Yambio and on to Uganda in an intricate manner (Johnson 1994).[39] However, the CMA system faced serious challenges when in 1993 influxes of internally displaced people (IDPs) flowed into neighbouring areas of Mundri and Maridi after the Bor massacre (D'Silva and Sakinas 1999),[40] putting more pressure on already scarce resources. The wave of IDPs led international relief agencies to begin operating in Yambio in 1993, bringing with them the services required not only to assist the IDPs but also address the severe shortages faced by the local population.

The difficulty with assessing the CMA system was the lack of coherent explanations of the role of the CMA in the testimonies of several leading officers who became part of this administration. The system was experienced differently by segments of the population, with the leadership pointing to micromanagement and centralisation on the one hand, but on the other hand to the inconsistency of an unwritten and unregulated system. The CMA's 'word was therefore law, whether he was right or wrong, drunk or sane, corrupt or honest, patriotic or traitor' (Malok 2009: 182). There was a clear militarisation of society that led to numerous human rights abuses and a sense that the SPLM/A was an occupying force of Dinka soldiers in Yambio. The movement clearly lacked the necessary structures to govern the liberated areas, and they had failed to devise a clear objective of winning the hearts and minds of the people they were liberating. It was also during the CMA years that corruption emerged within the movement, with certain areas 'develop[ing] into a state of warlordism' (Kanyane et al. 2013: 109). 'Commissioners became powerful warlords that taxed the population ... instead of building institutions [they] were looking after themselves.'[41] The predation of some SPLM/A leaders and soldiers became systemic in some areas, a tendency that remained unchanged in peacetime. The military entrepreneurism of the movement during the war greatly informed the high levels of corruption, nepotism and the politically captured economy after 2005.

Although the CMA system had many shortcomings, it did create a structure upon which the CANS was built. The CMA system was the reason for the survival of the SPLM/A during its most challenged phase of 1991–94 (Johnson 1998). However, testimonies show that relationships between the movement and the masses were strained. 'We asked ourselves—why are people fleeing our areas? We are their liberators. So, we had debates about the difference of capturing a garrison town and liberating an area ... Liberation occurs afterwards because that happens in the minds of the people.'[42] Moreover, the traditional fabric of society had been disrupted in many ways. 'Original chiefs were laid off as they needed young people to sing the slogans of the movement. The administration in the bush helped to create ethnic conflict.'[43] However, the SPLM/A inadvertently corrected this mistake during the CANS period: it empowered the population by allowing communities space to experience the 'state' through its multiple forms rather than subjugating them to the authority of military commanders from other ethnic groups. Despite this, the SPLM/A never overcame the 'communitisation' of the nation to build a strong sense of a unified South.

The 1991 critical juncture and the impetus to transform

The SPLM/A's parallel state of New Sudan emerged in a context of national contestation when the movement was being challenged militarily, politically and symbolically. The impetus to transform the administrative system and build a political base was accelerated by the critical junctures experienced by the movement after 1991. Facing the prospects of a likely demise, the SPLM/A began to rethink its approach to governance and the politics of legitimacy. What propelled this shift was a multi-pronged shock that broke its military capacity, challenged its political legitimacy and reactivated ethnic fault lines dividing communities.

From May to August 1991, the SPLM/A would experience two sets of internal implosion: the loss of Ethiopia—its main patron, rear base and supplier of military and non-military support—and the splintering of the movement with the emergence of the SPLM-Nasir faction. The SPLM/A's dependence on Ethiopia from 1983 to 1991 went far beyond that of a patron–client relationship, with Ethiopian influence running far deeper than solely logistics. Its assistance included intensive military training of fighters, the instrumentalisation of refugee camps in Gambella and intrusive influence on the political direction of the movement. In May 1991, Menguistu Haile Mariam's government collapsed, leading to over 200,000 refugees leaving Ethiopia and migrating to Upper Nile. The SPLM/A had all its training facilities, communications systems, weapons arsenal, political schools and refugee camps in Ethiopia, and the fall of the Derg would destroy the infrastructure that had been a fundamental lifeline for the liberation struggle. 'The collapse of Menguistu was a serious setback. We were not prepared to relocate to any other country. We also believed we would liberate the south before the Derg would fall as we had sent 10,000 men to reinforce their side. We lost everything and our refugees had to leave.'[44] The SPLM/A then ordered all its bases and refugee camps to be relocated across the border. Some would move into Upper Nile and others to Kapoeta in Eastern Equatoria, creating a build-up of civilians in areas that would become divided by the factional split of the movement.

The year 1991 was meant to see the SPLM/A begin a process of reform, as evidenced by leadership testimonies claiming Garang had decided to begin working towards strengthening the political party in preparation for the possible defeat of the Derg. He realised that the movement would need to embark on internal restructuring and ideological recalibration to appeal to Western governments and donors. It needed a more liberal façade if it wanted to engage with the international community in order to maximise diplomatic support and the continuation of vital supplies from relief aid. A political school in Isoke, in Eastern Equatoria, was created in early 1991 to prepare the leadership and senior cadres for this ideological shift. The idea was 'to prepare cadres for social change and to install an ideology given that we had people of different backgrounds (students, army, former government officials) which all had different orientations'.[45] The school only operated for a few months.

On 28 August 1991, the second implosion occurred. Riek Machar Teny and Lam Akol, two members of the movement's high command, along with Gordon Koang Chol and other key military commanders declared on the airwaves of the BBC that they were staging a coup against Garang and unseating him as chairman. They did not succeed in overthrowing Garang, but the SPLM/A split with the Nasir faction operating from Upper Nile. The dissenting commanders alleged lack of democracy in the movement, human rights abuses, despotic leadership and the continuing need to liberate the South in a separatist armed struggle. They would issue the Nasir Declaration, signalling their break with the movement's policy of unity with Sudan (Akol 2003). Their appeal to key constituencies in the South made them a larger threat to the 'united' front against Khartoum than previous counter-insurgent ethnic militias that the SPLM/A had already contended with. The 1991 split meant the SPLM/A was now fighting a war on two fronts—with the government and with the Nasir faction—and as a result the movement lost most of the territory it had liberated since 1983. Most of Upper Nile, most of Bahr El Ghazal and Eastern Equatoria had fallen. Ironically, what had begun as a movement pushing for the liberalisation of the SPLM/A by removing Garang as its leader actually pushed Garang's faction towards key reforms that would liberalise the movement and lead it to adopt a new way of liberating the South.

A meeting of the Political Military High Command (PMHC), the movement's highest decision-making organ, in Torit was scheduled for September 1991, to discuss new ways to reorganise the movement. The timing of the SPLM-Nasir coup which splintered the movement was allegedly aimed at pre-empting this meeting (Malok 2009). The Torit resolutions were passed after 2 weeks of deliberations: one was aimed at reorganising a new administrative setup for the liberated areas of the New Sudan, and the other was for the movement to adopt the policy of self-determination (Malok 2009). At the leadership level, Garang dissolved the PMHC and substituted it with the General Field Staff Command Council (GFSCC), a larger forum composed of all SPLA commanders (70 at the time) with several specialised sub-committees entrusted with devising a plan to restructure the movement and create organs for socio-economic development, civil administration and foreign policy (Malok 2009). The SPLM/A's shift in strategy was the first time the movement concerned itself with creating a support base for the liberation struggle within the South.

The splintering of the movement invariably took on ethnic dimensions, creating deeper schisms in the social fabric of the South between the Dinka and the Nuer. In 1991, after the split, Machar's largely Nuer fighters, aided by the White army militias, attacked the town of Bor in Jonglei (Garang's home area) in what became one of the worst episodes of intra-ethnic atrocities. For 3 months, the White army surrounded and attacked villages mostly comprised of civilians, killing thousands in violent and grotesque ways (Martell 2018). The Bor massacre, as it became known, markedly became a leading grievance the Dinka harboured against their Nuer brothers. The SPLM/A retaliated brutally, with a counter-massacre in the Nuer town of Ayod, executing, burning and raping their way through the villages. In 1993, Ayod, Kongor and Waat would become the sites of a devastating famine. Cycles of revenge killings would continue, feeding narratives of collective victimisation and ethnic divisions that would re-emerge in the 2013 war.

In 1992, the Nasir faction was joined by several other armed groups to form the SPLM-United (renamed South Sudan Independence Movement/Army [SSIM] in 1994, a result of its own internal fragmentation). Other senior commanders like William Nyoun and Kerubino Kuanyin Bol (SPLA Chief of Staff) would also defect (Kanyane et al. 2013). Desertions would continue in the ranks of the SPLM/A, giving rise to movements such as the Patriotic Resistance Movement (PRM) and the Southern Sudan Freedom Fight (SSFF), organised by Equatorians Alfred Lado Gore and David Mulla respectively. By 1997, SSIM had signed an agreement with Khartoum calling for elections, self-determination and reconciliation, which resulted in the establishment of the Coordination Council of South Sudan (CCSS) as an interim government for South Sudan, becoming a parallel system to that of the SPLM/A's CANS. Despite this 'the SPLM/A's internal cohesion was stronger, not because of political and ideological awareness but rather because the contradictions between the South and the North were stronger than the internal contradictions' (Nyaba 1997: 68). Garang knew how to manage the internal contradictions of his movement and instrumentalise the radicalisation of the North after Bashir's NIF coup in 1989.

Despite this, the SPLM/A arguably never recovered the unity or military strength it had before the split. This catapulted Garang's movement into a greater sense of urgency to begin to create a 'state' and internal bases for support. Fighting an easily distinguishable enemy like Khartoum meant the movement could afford to delay the political aspect of generating popular support through a structured process of institution building, political education, indoctrination and production of social outcomes. However, fighting an enemy within the South, the SPLM-Nasir, that had that same capacity to generate legitimacy and capture the imagination of the population with a more democratic and secessionist rhetoric, was an entirely different threat. The SPLM-Nasir was also able to capitalise on the anti-Dinka sentiment targeted at the SPLM/A.

The SPLM/A held its first political and mass consultative meeting three years after this critical juncture moment. The First National Convention in Chukudum took place between 28 March and 11 April 1994, gathering community leaders, SPLM delegates, members of civil society and traditional authorities from all over the country. In many cases it took as long as 5 months of continuous marching for delegates from Southern Kordofan, northern Upper Nile and northern Bahr El Ghazal to reach Chukudum in Eastern Equatoria. Many delegates were killed by government offensives and aerial bombardments along the way. Chukudum became a reflective conference that allowed the movement to analyse, criticise and question the leadership on the path the movement had taken since 1983. The National Convention marked a stark shift in the strategic direction of the SPLM/A. Apart from the need to build a solid popular base and more permanent alliance with local communities across the South, the movement abandoned its broadly socialist ideology, embraced self-determination and defined itself as the guardian of southern Sudanese local customs, traditions and culture (Johnson 1998).

Civil authority for a New Sudan

Following the 1991 Torit Resolutions, a roadmap was created for the emergence of the CANS. However, the structure and the process of transformation were only formally initiated at the 1994 Chukudum National Convention. Chukudum had the principal objectives of creating structures for political, public and economic institutions; acquiring the mandate to negotiate on behalf of the people of the · South and other areas participating in the liberation struggle; and the separation of the three tiers of government (legislative, executive and judiciary) (Mai 2008). The CANS was meant to decentralise power and governance (although it never had the capacity to centralise) as well as promote political inclusion and economic development. Its strategy was genuinely informed by the need to address local grievances regarding the movement's past autocratic behaviour as well as engender loyalty from all ethnic groups (Mampilly 2011). The New Sudan state would emerge as the movement attempted to govern several areas of its five regions of Bahr El Ghazal, Equatoria,

Southern Blue Nile, Southern Kordofan and Upper Nile. By 1998, the New Sudan had twenty-nine counties spread throughout these five regions, with each county having an estimated population of between 100,000 and 250,000 civilians (Rohn et al. 1997). As a system of governance based on a party–state structure, this state project would encounter problems. For one thing, it would find it difficult to institute 'the necessary balance between peripheral pull and central control' (Nyang'oro 1989: 5–19). This mainly occurred because as an organisation it lacked political structures and strong mid-level collective leadership organs.

The SPLM/A's New Sudan would be structured with three branches of government. The executive would take the form of the National Executive Council (NEC), headed by Chairman Garang and comprised of twenty secretariats (ministries) dealing with different areas of governance. Ministers were appointed by the chairman, and the NEC was meant to sit every six months. The legislative branch would be based on liberation councils that were also a central political organ of the party. The judiciary branch was pillared on the principles of statutory and customary law, with the highest courts prioritising the New Sudan laws and the lowest courts deferring to those of the chiefs. Hierarchically, the chairman sat at the apex of this structure, followed by his deputy and a core group of military commanders, which included the five governors of the New Sudan regions. Below the governors came the county commissioners, followed by the payam and boma administrators. The 1998 SPLM Constitution further developed the role of the CANS as the authority regulating the relationship between the population and 'its government', in addition to that of the party/movement organs (Herzog 1998). Created as a party document and also as a guideline for the establishment of civil authority, the Constitution established the National Political and Executive Committee (NAPEC), which merged the roles of the executive and the SPLM political secretariat, bringing the ministries under NAPEC (Herzog 1998). This was an attempt to define political organs and have the party delineate all other aspects of the liberation, including the military. In Yambio, this centralising body didn't seem to operate or have a strong influence on how the CANS was implemented. The level of decentralisation was both a public management strategy and a political necessity, as well as an organisational imposition, given the inability to replicate structures of central power at the local levels.

As part of its process of creating a 'government' while simultaneously building the structures of the party, the movement had ambitious plans to introduce controlled elections. The objective was to create a state that would be regulated by the laws of New Sudan and the 1998 Constitution. However, in the absence of a functioning civil service and institutions outside of the military, the SPLM—as the political party—took over and dominated all tiers of government and civilian activities. Elections were held by some structures in Yambio but only at the local government level, leaving intact the composition of structures at the highest (regional and national) levels of power, which remained defined by military hierarchy. SPLM congresses at the county, payam and boma level were intended to be the supreme political body at the local level, with powers to elect and review the work of the liberation and executive councils (Rolandsen 2005). Governance expanded as the party was expanding, but it lacked the necessary level of cohesion and party structures. The SPLM/A understood that it would have to install a decentralised system of governance, given the same constraints that had led it to adopt indirect rule during the CMA years, but it was trying to establish a form of centralised control through the creation of party structures to guide this process of state formation at the local level. In this sense, the dominant party could be counted on 'to hold disintegrative tendencies in check' (Fainsod 1962)[46] in a system that was administratively decentralised.

The aim of the CANS was multidimensional. It was designed to translate an ideological concept into nationalist support, securing the hearts and minds of the people so that they too imagined the 'state' with the SPLM/A at its helm. It aimed to ensure a constant flow of recruits from civilian areas, and a continuous source of food, so that stable areas could support the fronts. It meant for Southerners to authorise it to negotiate for peace on their behalf, as a reaction to the Nasir faction negotiating with Khartoum. It was meant to guarantee the political support of the population so that the party would develop as a structure and build a stronger social base. It was organised in such a way that civilians were provided with services and NGO programmes coordinated for the advancement of the New Sudan. It was also meant to give the civil servants of the SPLM/A government the experience which would enable them to take over any administration during peacetime. Finally, it was a strategy for surviving the war, given that the conflict was going to be a long one. As a result, the movement was simultaneously attempting to build a political party, create a social base to secure legitimacy and build a parallel government to ensure hegemonic control and political longevity—all difficult and complex processes.

Shaken by the ease with which the Nasir faction gathered support, and the realisation that it was not the de facto liberator of the South, the SPLM/A attempted to transform itself and build its political base when it was at its weakest point. The element of explaining why the movement was fighting, and phrasing it in terms of protecting the rights of the people, popularised the liberation struggle. Interviews revealed a fundamental shift in how people saw the movement: 'In the beginning people did not understand the movement but in 1994 people's aspirations were respected.'[47] The Zande paramount chief reiterated that 'under the military there was no negotiation but after 1994 the administrative system changed and there were no orders, people started to negotiate again'.[48] The civilian population understood that the SPLM/A was fighting to liberate the country from Northern dominance. There was a need for the SPLM/A to begin delivering to the southern Sudanese a sense of what the liberation would achieve for them: a new political dispensation, a new governing culture, an opportunity to help shape the future and a sense of participating rather than merely being instruments for the war and the movement. The devolution of power to the local levels after 1994 transformed the perceptions and responses of southerners who began 'feeling that the Movement was their movement, and the struggle was their struggle' (Johnson 2003: 108).

In contrast to the unchecked authority of the CMA, the authorities of the new CANS system were given guidelines and mandates, as defined by the resolutions of the 1994 Convention. However, these proved to be too vague and lacking in implementation modalities to assist with the actual development of the different institutions.

During the first two years of the CANS, civilian structures faced many difficulties, namely lack of capacity, lack of funds and an absence of job descriptions that resulted in the duplication of roles and conflict between organs. Administrators each managed institutions in their own way, which led to corruption and inconsistency in governance. In addition, the military—accustomed to being the ultimate source of authority and having unrestricted power—now had to contend with cohabitating with other forms of authority. Several army officers and commanders found it difficult to relinquish the power and privilege they had been accustomed to for over a decade and resisted the transition from CMA rule to a separate civil administration. Another internal organ that resisted the CANS was the SRRA relief wing, which for years had been the civilian face of the movement. The CANS impacted the way the SRRA functioned, appropriating some of its power and responsibilities with several CANS secretariats taking the lead in key areas of service delivery.

Civilian and military structures had to be separated so that the political party became the main driver of the liberation struggle, the ultimate aim being to demilitarise society. Some SPLA officers, relieved of their military functions in favour of serving as CANS officials, felt that they were 'being rejected and abandoned' by the movement, that being part of the CANS was a demotion and punishment. The SPLM/A had learnt through its experience with the CMA system that there had to be less interference from the military in the everyday life of the liberated areas. The message now was that the liberation was for the people, and the movement was fighting a just cause supported by the civilian population. 'People began to feel that we were fighting for *them* and not that *they* were at the service of the army.'[49] Testimonies from the civilian population, community leaders and local administrators also supported this idea that there was now 'unity of mind',[50] and that 'when the CANS came people perceived it as things coming to normality'.[51]

Branches of government

The SPLM/A's ambition to create an entirely new state led it to begin developing the three branches of government in the liberated areas.

For some, this was an exercise in creating a veneer of democratic 'devolution', a façade to appease the international community (Mampilly 2011) that lacked the crucial exercise of empowering local government levels with the capacity to influence the central command. Several scholars agree that to a great extent the SPLM/A's New Sudan state was built on paper institutions rather than effective structures imbued with political and administrative legitimacy (Rolandsen 2005; Ohm 2014). This may be an oversimplified perspective of what the CANs achieved, certainly in Yambio. The New Sudan governance experiment was flawed, incomplete, sustaining too many contradictions and generally ineffective, but the shift from militarised governance to local civilian governance was still important. It built legitimacy, created a social support base and catalysed an internal SPLM/A reform process.

As per the New Sudan governance programme, the executive ran the civilian administration, the legislative became the basis for the building of party structures and the judiciary incorporated the chiefs into a formal structure of justice. The institutional arrangement of the New Sudan was based on five levels of governance: the national, the regional, and the the county, payam and boma levels. In each of these five levels of authority the three branches of the government were represented. It was a decentralised system that allowed the three lowest tiers of local government a degree of autonomy, while the regional and national levels ran in more centralised and hierarchical ways. The chairman appointed legislative and executive officials at the national and regional levels, but at the local levels he consulted with community leaders to determine who had the necessary popular acceptance, liberation credentials and record of efficiency. The governor, commissioners and payam administrators would at the same time be representatives of the executive, the legislative and the party, which further consolidated the creation of the SPLM/A party–state. Before the war, civil servants had been appointed to serve anywhere in the South, but after the movement began to develop its administration, it opted for the appointment of the 'sons and daughters' of the area to serve in the CANS civil service.[52] This meant that, in addition to the use of chiefs and other authorities, civilians and retired military officers were selected to govern their areas of origin.

Executive council and secretariats

The NEC was responsible for executing the policies and programmes of the SPLM/A, and the administration of the liberated areas. Comprised of several secretariats (ministries) and a decentralised arm of councils, the system was rendered ineffective by the leadership five years after its implementation. One of the many difficulties it faced was the fact that the executive had no permanent place of operations. Affairs were coordinated in a decentralised manner, without a central system of authority and coordination. The leadership would only get involved when problems emerged at the local level, as it believed that the party structures would be sufficient to mitigate any eventual problems of administration. This meant that continuity and supervision of the system were sporadic. In the first two years of the CANS, the NEC met only four or five times (Chol 1996), when, as the seat of the SPLM government, it should have been coordinating efforts and establishing protocols of governance in a more coherent and effective manner.

The NEC was represented at each level of governance through county executive executive councils (CEC), payam executive councils (PEC) and boma executive councils (BEC). Councils were elected and were constituency based, with women making up 25% of the council members. These bodies were meant to meet once a year and had the power to dissolve the legislative (the liberation councils) (Deng 2013). The different payams and interest groups throughout the county contributed input during CEC meetings. When they were in session, they facilitated an open dialogue with the civilian population and among different segments of society, the administration and the movement. They became grievance forums that allowed the movement to assess its performance. One problem that was continually brought up in these meetings was the abuse by soldiers, the administrators' lack of resources and the emergence of corruption, all topics that under a different system of governance could easily have been silenced and rules established to curb potential criticism.

Elections were also held at the local level with the participation of civilians, chiefs and the party. One report described how in 1998 a congress of Karika boma (Mundri county neighbouring Yambio) conducted a census of the population, deployed registration teams and informed the traditional authorities of the upcoming boma elections. Of a population of 8,794, roughly 4,500 participated in electing the chairman, the secretaries and members of the liberation council (Herzog 1998). The same report described how a Yambio county congress was held over a period of four days and discussions were led by the different payam representatives and syndicated organisation members, with reports delivered by the five congress committees (political, security, finance, administration and legal) (Herzog 1998: 18). There was a considerable effort to jointly find solutions to problems and ways to improve administration. Discussions were frank and open, with resolutions being proposed and passed to address issues as diverse as inefficiency of the county administration, inefficient tax collection and the misappropriation of funds.

Liberation councils

The National Liberation Council (NLC) was the legislative branch of government, but it also became the central committee of the party. This body was composed of 183 members at the national level from all areas of the South, with representation of different interest groups. The NLC was organised into 11 specialised committees to facilitate its mandate of legislating the laws of the New Sudan, approving NEC programmes and other executive decisions.[53] The NLC failed to meet for several years after its establishment due to the difficulty of reuniting all members in one place, given the vastness of the territory, the lack of transport and infrastructure facilities, and pockets of insecurity. Liberation councils were replicated at all levels of governance, including at the county, payam and boma levels. At the local level, the liberation councils also took on a political party function, playing 'the vital role of recruiting people of different constituencies using the chiefs and the CANS to join the SPLM/A'.[54] This was partly why they were elected by SPLM/A congresses (see Table 2.3). Chiefs were incorporated into the liberation councils so that the mission and vision of the movement could be taught at the grassroots level.[55] If any of the council members failed to comply with the Liberation Council Act, they were replaced by other members of the community.

Table 2.3: New Sudan government structure

	Legislative	Executive	Judiciary
SPLM System and Congresses	National Liberation Council	National Executive Council	(National) Court of Appeal
		Secretariats (Ministries)	
	Regional Liberation Councils	Regional Executive Councils	(Regional) Court High Courts
County Congress Elects ⟶	County Liberation Councils	County Executive Councils	County Courts
Payam Congress Elects ⟶	Payam Liberation Councils	Payam Executive Councils	Payam Courts
Boma Congress Elects ⟶	Boma Liberation Councils	Boma Executive Councils	Chief's Courts

Like the executive councils, their legislative counterparts also held elections. The boma liberation council (BLC) had 11 members, the payam liberation council (PLC) 31 members and the county liberation council (CLC) 51 members. These were constituency-based organs that were elected geographically in two distinct ways: through group/stakeholder-based representation and appointment-based representation. Civil society organisations (CSOs) were also given a certain percentage of seats to appoint members. This meant that, depending on the level of government, the councils would have elected officials by popular vote, officials elected by CSOs and members appointed by the leading authority—be it the chairman, the governor, the commissioner, the administrator or the head of organised forces (like the police).

Members of the executive councils would also become delegates to the liberation councils by virtue of office, making the debate less effective but also curtailing any potential checks and balances (Deng 2013). This was an attempt at integrating different groups of society into the SPLM/A state. It eliminated spontaneous interest articulation by establishing a limited number of functional groups under the tutelage of the state as central to the gradual process of authoritarianism (Nyang'oro 1989). This corporatist strategy would become more entrenched as the SPLM/A further blurred the party–state divide. It followed 'many regimes' inclinations to look for arrangements that ensure[d] their longevity' (Nyang'oro and Shaw 1998: 40). This became clearer with the movement's responses to local NGOs and civil society groups, explained later in this chapter. One main limitation of the liberation councils' experiment was its failure to create cadres to direct the new era of the liberation struggle. As a result, 'political enlightenment stayed only at the top and it didn't trickle down to the boma and payam levels. The SPLM never came down to remobilize people and change the mentality'.[56] However, these structures and their political commissars played a vital role in convincing the population of the need for a consolidated front, and in attempting to secure the legitimacy necessary to represent them. Chiefs, sub-chiefs and headmen were used to take the movement's mission and vision to the population, and they were incorporated into the liberation councils. Unlike the executive councils that stopped operating in the late 1990s, the liberation councils continued throughout the war and the peace negotiations.

Courts, chiefs and New Sudan laws

Following the Torit resolutions—which called for the establishment of the judiciary—a new penal code, a code of criminal procedure and a code of civil procedure were promulgated at the 1994 Convention, and the 1984 laws were repealed. The judiciary, based also on the 1998 Constitution, was given the responsibility of administering justice, overseeing the police, and acting in the role of custodian of the CANS. SPLM laws guided the traditional laws, although in the different courts system (chiefs' and New Sudan courts) both customary and statutory laws were enforced.[57] The SPLM/A made a concerted effort to bring the traditional chiefs' structures and customary laws into the formal system of the New Sudan. After the First Convention, the chiefs' position was formalised within the SPLM/A's administrative structure. The idea was to establish a legal system that would embrace the cultural identity enshrined in customary law while creating the conditions required to foster the rule of law and reduce ethnic tensions (Mennen 2010). However, the issue of building a governing system that sustained legal pluralism created problems. The harmonisation of legal proceedings was difficult in the liberated areas since different communities and ethnic groups had different ruling principles and systems of justice. In areas where there were IDPs of different ethnic groups cohabitating with local populations, there were difficulties in administering justice and mediating inter-community conflict due to jurisdictional issues. It was these gaps of customary jurisdiction where statutory courts would have to take the lead, although they did not always do so effectively. In most areas of the South, there was the problem of having parallel and unconnected systems of statutory and customary law. Attempts were made at making subject-matter jurisdiction, but this didn't succeed, and instead individual chiefs would adjudicate customary law as they saw fit (Mennen 2010). Testimonies from Yambio point to a functional coordination between the CANS courts and traditional courts, although some confusion arises when trying to explain how each operated differently. Again, the SPLM/A seemed to replicate a system that resembled a form of colonial legal pluralism whereby customary law was recognised if it abided by the basis of the state legal system (Tuori 2011).

The court structure in the liberated areas was comprised of different judicial institutions: at the top stood the court of appeal (headed by a chief justice), followed by high courts at the regional level.[58] County courts (statutory and customary) joined magistrates and chiefs, while payam courts were comprised of senior chiefs and boma courts were composed of three chiefs. The system of joining both sources of law and the two types of courts was meant to expedite justice and avoid backlog and over-bureaucratisation. County courts became the backbone of the legal system as they joined both statutory and customary law and shared jurisdictions on civilian matters. Five years after the creation of the New Sudan legal system, a conference was organised to evaluate its progress along with the difficulties of establishing the rule of law in the liberated areas. The result was a revision of twenty-five New Sudan laws and other reforms. The 1999 workshop on the Rehabilitation and Restructuring of Legal Institutions and Law Enforcement Agencies was aimed at reviewing several laws, creating an anti-corruption unit, addressing the problems faced by the judiciary and reorganising the courts system. One of the problems identified was the lack of clarity with regards to who presided over the courts at a local level. This issue was raised by the High Court Judge for the Equatoria Region, Deng Biong Mijak, who stated that while judges and magistrates sat at the Court of Appeal, the high courts, and the county courts, it was unclear what level of chiefs (whether the paramount chief, chiefs, sub-chiefs or headman) should preside over the payam and boma courts. This highlighted the difficulty the system faced in operationalising a modern judiciary with a pre-existing and well-established customary system. Both had to work together to establish law in the liberated areas and find lasting solutions to challenges of cohabitation. If issues were not resolved at the level of the chiefs' courts, then cases could be referred to the high court, in particular those involving murder, rape and stealing of government property. 'The High Court was military but there were also chiefs there that served as judges. I was a judge in Yambio for seven years and at the High Court we treated soldiers and civilians equally as citizens according to the law.'[59] According to other testimonies in Yambio, four chiefs—one from Maridi, one from Tombura and two from Yambio—were given legal training by Justice Deng Biong for a year to standardise the use of New Sudan laws.

There was an additional element that challenged the courts even further. Because of the IDP situation in Western Equatoria and the subsequent arrival of international NGOs to assist in relief and recovery efforts, cases in the early 1990s involved several aid workers who had committed social and moral crimes against the community. Kuol (2008) described how in 1995 an aid worker from Care International was accused of committing adultery with a Zande lady and received the sentence of paying 'Kasirbet' (house trespassing)[60] as compensation as well as a fine. Although NGOs were the lifeline of entire sectors of the liberated areas, the SPLM/A did not want to disturb community systems of justice and morality by allowing foreigners immunity. These fines foreigners had to pay for breaking local laws were also sources of revenue. With each case heard and its fines paid to the victims, fines were also paid to the courts. A structure of revenue sharing from the courts was set up that would be channelled to the war effort where the SPLM county authority would receive 30%, the army would receive 40% and the courts kept the remaining 30% (Kuol 2008).

Other bodies were created to provide greater guidance on recurring problems. In 1997, a land committee was established in Yambio where disputes over land and illegal seizure of property could be settled. Headed by a land officer, the committee attempted to mediate situations in which soldiers seized land from local civilian communities.[61] On average, five cases were heard per week. This body only functioned at the county level, while land disputes at the boma and payam levels remained the jurisdiction of the chiefs' courts. The focus of land disputes was particularly relevant in the Equatorian region, as agricultural communities interacted with pastoral groups that also needed to use their land. The issue of livelihoods and the clash between agriculturalist and pastoralist groups was one of the drivers of the antagonism between the Dinka and the Zande. The SPLM/A managed to create a working solution by having Dinka communities keep their cattle away from towns.

The national, regional and local levels of government faced several contradictions. The national level never truly existed for administrative and governance purposes but rather for military and strategic purposes. The county administration was the most effective level of government, as it exercised some degree of centralised execution while also understanding the different structures of the payam and boma below it. The county commissioner's office had its own departments of finance, information, agriculture, cooperatives and rural development, land, commerce, social welfare, youth, health, public works and police. Yambio had three commissioners during the CANS phase of governance, which showed a disposition for political rotation. Mary Biba was the third commissioner of Yambio, one of the first women to hold such a prominent role, and she stayed for six years (1999–2005). As commissioner of the county, she ran hospitals and healthcare centres, organised schools, dealt with NGOs and ensured that civil society groups were self-sufficient and able to produce goods to trade with Rumbek (another liberated area) and Uganda.[62] The SPLM/A was trying to appoint civilians to the roles of county commissioners, although once appointed they were given military ranks. The relationship between the CANS officials and the traditional authorities in this county and in its payams and bomas was considered one of the reasons why the SPLM/A's 'state' worked in Yambio.[63]

Still, the system encountered difficulties from the start. At the conference on Civil Society and Organisation of Civil Authority in April 1996, several of the structural and operational problems the CANS faced were discussed in the plenary (Chol 1996). The regional level of the New Sudan was conceptualised in a way that was contradictory to the objective of separating the military from the civilian aspect of the liberation struggle. Each of the five regions of the New Sudan was headed not by civilian but by military governors who would prioritise military affairs over all other aspects of governance. They were placed over the central level of the secretaries who acted as ministers of the New Sudan, instead of below them. The SPLM/A fused the different structures that were operated or supervised by the same members, only expecting the three branches to separate fully after the war (Herzog 1998). The governors, commissioners, payam and boma administrators would at the same time represent the executive, the legislative and the party, which only further consolidated the SPLM party–state as a single entity, replicating inefficiencies and extending structural deficiencies.

One of the many weaknesses of this approach was that it was unregulated and non-standardised, meaning the connection between local levels and central commands was weak. Local authorities were not structured according to rules defined by a larger SPLM/A political system but by local dynamics operating within the constraints of the SPLM/A institutions. Decentralised control, as opposed to a decentralised government system, was not an end for the movement but rather a means of ensuring sufficient control of large areas using minimal central leadership structures. Garang and his high command faced too many strategic obstacles to also be able to focus on day-to-day affairs of the civilian administration when they lacked the necessary structures of leadership. Orders were given at the central command level, but how they were implemented depended on the capacity, understanding and resources of the local administration. In the absence of a stable seat of government, during the first few years most of the secretariats operated from Yambio while the chairman moved with the military along the frontlines. When interviewees were asked about the system of receiving directives from the central government level (from the office of the chairman), their answers were not consistent. The absence of a clearly defined communications system for the CANS pointed to military commanders in the field receiving orders and then passing them on to the administrators.[64]

Service delivery and economic development

As the New Sudan government structures emerged, the SPLM/A needed to create alternative strategies for the delivery of services and economic development to accompany its 'state' project. The existing situation was that chiefs and relief agencies were used as service providers. The community was expected to provide the basis of its own education and healthcare, as well as provide their own food. Local NGOs were established for this purpose, with the assistance of international NGOs. This outsourcing of service provision and the minimal involvement of the SPLM/A was a lost opportunity for the movement to consolidate a social contract with the population. A key institutional aspect of legitimacy, handling the direct provision of services could have enabled the SPLM/A to build stronger bonds with society while developing administrative competence to deliver these services. However, the considerable presence of external organisations made the SPLM/A complacent.

By not directly providing welfare, the New Sudan state instead had to define what it was offering (freedom, empowerment and security) and the mechanisms it would use to shape the different encounters (councils, self-sufficiency groups, civil society). Its total dependence on foreign aid had another effect in that it undermined the social and political coherence of the South (Mampilly 2011), where international agencies dominated in every field except defence (Riehl 1994), which remained under the complete dominion of the SPLA. This did, however, allow for the emergence of civil society.

Popular participation: Civil society organisations

A driving concept of the New Sudan was the establishment of 'minimal government', which meant that the civil authorities would create an enabling environment in which civil society could develop (Herzog 1998). While 'minimal', the presence of the SPLM/A would be replicated at all levels, and the population was expected to participate in popular and syndicated organisations. The movement promoted the emergence of youth, women, farmers, workers and other groups that were given quotas of representation in the liberation councils. All the syndicated organisations came under the supervision of the Director for Popular Support in the SPLM's political secretariat. These organisations were party organs and encouraging people to work within the system rather than against it. 'With the CANS space was created for the participation of non-military personnel. It broadened the scope of the struggle, and the liberation struggle became bigger than the SPLM.'[65]

Testimonies of civil society members point to a belief that there was a space to operate in society regardless of partisan constraints and incursion of the SPLM/A. The New Sudan Council of Churches (NSCC), a coalition of pan-Christian churches—established in 1989 and headed by Catholic Bishop Paride Taban, and deputised by Protestant Bishop Nathaniel Garang Anyieth—had set the path for the emergence of civil institutions in the South. The idea had been to register the churches in South Sudan so that the NSCC could assist people in areas of faith and provision of services. In the late 1990s, the NSCC would take a leading role in several peace and reconciliation initiatives, in 'people-to-people' processes in Wunlit and Kejiko, among others. Working with churches allowed the SPLM/A to reach the population in different ways and strengthen their nationalist appeal, as well as bridge the divide between communities and ethnic groups.

Civil society was encouraged to develop its own organisations and take a leading role in the delivery of services. These were either syndicated organisations or initiatives supported by NGOs as independent organisations, including the New Sudan's Women's Associations, the Mundri Relief and Development Association (MRDA), the New Sudan Youth Association, the New Sudan Law Society, Sudan Medical Care (SMC), among others. Organisations also existed for traders and farmers, especially in areas like Yambio, Maridi, Mundri, Yei, Tombura, Rumbek and Tonj. One of the most effective farmers' organisations was the Yambio Farmers Association (YAFA). Established in 2000, YAFA had fifty-two groups of farmers that organised individual and family farms to produce enough surplus to trade between areas. The chairperson of YAFA explained: 'it was an order that the SPLM/A government gave to people to produce food … they called World Vision in 1995 to assist farmers to create a system so we could start using the Ugandan shilling to buy products we needed.'[66] The SPLM/A later created its own currency—the New Sudan pound—in Rumbek, but the experiment failed. The Ugandan shilling was used in Yambio, due to its proximity with the border, while the Sudanese pound was used in other liberated areas.

The Institute for the Promotion of Civil Society (IPCS) was another initiative that was coordinated by key SPLM/A leaders and civil society.[67] It began operating in Yei and Yambio in 1999. IPCS, a hybrid of local community initiatives and support from leading members of the SPLM/A, and other initiatives like it had as their main aim the strengthening of traditional authorities and the church (the main force behind development), as well as giving civic education to the military so as to forge better links with the population. The IPCS also aimed to teach people at the grassroots level about the roles of the liberation councils and the value of elections in their areas. However, their success was not always supported. 'The SPLA accused us of creating a parallel structure, but one was political [the liberation councils] and the other was for development. When you empower the community, you have accountability.'[68]

Women's groups also became very active from 1996 when programmes coordinated by World Vision and other organisations began skills training in Yambio. 'This idea of waiting for planes to drop food was not a system.'[69] The SPLM/A made it a point to reverse the exclusion of women from the public sphere that had been perpetuated under Khartoum's rule. There were as many as sixteen women's associations in Yambio.[70] These groups managed to break out of the traditional roles assigned to women in the old Sudan by spearheading income-generating activities like soap-making and tailoring. Later, women started attending adult training courses. 'With the Arabs they did not allow us to get skills. With the SPLM/A came changes and we had women's groups educating other women in home economics.'[71]

Civil society organisations had such an impact that international organisations highlighted their potential for spurring the development of grassroots organisations and democracy in the region (D'Silva and Sakinas 1999). Groups were created all over the Equatoria region, with many becoming important enterprises of change, such as the South Sudan Women Concerned Association, which had 5,000 women working on agricultural development projects in Kajokeji.[72] Testimonies pointed to the multiplying effect that some of these initiatives had and their impact in stabilising civil society behind the frontlines. The more cautious view of the genuine liberalisation of public space in the liberated areas highlighted the role of international non-governmental organisations (INGOs) being directly responsible for the emergence of local civil society groups rather than the local groups being part of an embryonic process. Had international organisations not taken the lead in supporting local NGOs, the public space of civil society in liberated areas would have remained smaller.

INGOs needed to strengthen their local counterparts, which led to the introduction of new institutions on the ground like the Sudanese Indigenous NGOs (SINGOs) (Rolandsen 2005). SINGOs became an important element in encouraging popular participation. Although they were financed by international NGOs, they largely operated on an independent level (Riehl 2001). In the early 1990s, hundreds of SINGOs were created in fields such as adult education, wildlife conservation and traditional medicine. As many as fifty SINGOS could have been operating in Western Equatoria alone (Riehl 2001). One of the difficulties mentioned with these civil society groups was the constant threat of *kasha* (forced recruitment into the SPLA), which would take away key members of the organisations and disrupt the process and expansion of the initiatives. An identity cards system was created to protect against *kasha* so that 'those that couldn't participate in combat, like teachers and farm workers, could do other jobs. The army needed justification of why men could not go to war'.[73]

Aid and service delivery

While this chapter will not attempt to portray the entire picture of international assistance in South Sudan during the war, or for that matter in Western Equatoria, it will briefly describe some of the activities that brought the NGOs into the New Sudan project. NGO presence and that of the United Nation (UN)'s Operation Lifeline Sudan (OLS) was a major driver in the delivery of basic services to the population during the war. The OLS—a tripartite agreement between the UN, the government in Khartoum and the SPLM/A—became the biggest ever UN-coordinated humanitarian operation at the time. Many areas had healthcare facilities, schools, boreholes and farming projects entirely funded and managed by international relief agencies and NGOs, under the supervision of the SRRA. Some have argued that OLS and NGO engagement with the SPLM/A had a direct impact on the formulation of political reforms in that it encouraged the creation of SINGOs to act as implementers, thereby forcing the SPLM/A to initiate local democratic and administrative reforms (Rolandsen 2005). Others, however, accused the UN and the international community of assisting the SPLM/A in sustaining its war efforts while also allowing it to take credit for service delivery that was entirely outsourced. Africa Rights argued that international aid operations in South Sudan extended the war by providing a constant flow of material resources that supported the SPLA's military activities and were also used for diplomatic and propaganda purposes.[74]

94

International NGOs' intervention in Sudan almost operated like a state within a state (Sharif and Tvedt 1994), in what has been termed the 'internationalisation of public welfare' (Duffield 1992).[75] Although the SPLM/A was a rebel movement, it was acting as a government in its areas, and this created a predicament for international organisations. The engagement was very new on both sides, with the international relief community not having 'yet considered what "normal" development activities could take place in a rebel held area and in an area called a war zone'.[76] But efforts to harmonise their work with the SPLM became important. Meetings between members of these NGOs, local commissioners, area commanders and SRRA members would occur regularly to coordinate activities and implement security procedures. This fell short of giving full international recognition to the SPLM as the governing authority of the South. However, the relationship between the SPLM/A and INGOs was tested and strained as the SPLM/A and SRRA attempted to officialise their role in governing South Sudan and bring international organisations under their control. In 2000, the movement issued an ultimatum to NGOs to sign a Memorandum of Understanding (MoU) or be forced to withdraw operations. The MoU established that, among other things, international organisations had to pay country fees to the SRRA for issuing work permits, ask for permission before interacting with local communities, and hand over control of the distribution of humanitarian assistance. Several organisations like World Vision refused to sign the MoU and evacuated. Their withdrawal from Western Equatoria resulted in the near collapse of the Primary Health Care programme (Riehl 2001).

Organisations like Catholic Relief Service (CRS), World Vision and UNICEF implemented a wide range of projects in Yambio, from income-generating activities (like the Tombura bicycle repairs cooperative) to food security projects (like the Fishpond rehabilitation project and enterprise development), among many others. USAID activities from 1993 to 1999 took innovative forms of development assistance, such as the rehabilitation of infrastructure and introduction of barter systems whereby basic items like soap and blankets were airlifted into Tombura or Yambio and exchanged for surplus grain produced locally by the community (D'Silva and

Sakinas 1999). The grain was sold by CARE (the implementing partner) to other NGOs to use for relief operations. While this Local Grain Purchase (LGP) programme was initially done by international organisations, the SRRA and the CANS began instituting the same system via cooperatives. At the boma level, primary cooperative societies were created that had a minimum of twenty-five farmers, while at the county level the cooperatives association was the entity managing all the lower levels. By late 1994, cooperatives and community development projects were underway, initiating the slow transformation of subsistence farming into market-orientated agriculture of agronomic crops, fruit trees and cash crops. The SPLM/A sought an agreement with neighbouring countries to allow for their respective currencies to serve as legal tender in the South for programmes of regional food monetisation. These LPG initiatives also allowed the international agencies to reduce the costs of humanitarian assistance.

As a result, the Secretariat for Agriculture, Forestry, Fishery and Animal Resources (SAFFAR) began the process of coordinating with international NGOs the growth of relief food inside the liberated areas. Rather than buying food internationally, aid organisations were able to buy locally from the cooperatives. This innovative idea used seeds and tools supplied by NGOs and led to related initiatives like the maintenance of feeder roads that could support trucks weighing seven tonnes, as well as the creation of rural stores to keep the produce (maize, sorghum, ground nuts, cassava, sweet potato), among other things. 'Market teams would go and buy in the rural areas for Care and World Vision and then the lorries would move to other areas in the South where there was food deficit ... we were maximising the humanitarian market.'[77] As many as 20 trucks per day could leave Tombura, and during the harvesting seasons (August and September) 6 Hercules C-130 flights could take off from the Nzara and Yambio airstrips bound for areas that needed relief.

This system of supplying food to the World Food Programme (WFP) and Food and Agriculture Organization (FAO) of the UN worked for ten years (1995–2005) and allowed for the creation of the County Development Revolving Fund (CDRF). 'Donors would provide the first funds of capital and operation costs and then we would use the money from the proceeds of the projects for other purposes.'[78] The revolving fund also functioned as a microcredit facility, enabling local communities to initiate businesses and small trade. Bigger businesses developed in areas like timber exploration and transport, but these were primarily controlled by SPLM/A commanders. In areas where there were cattle, SAFFAR devised ways to provide the necessary care for the 16 million heads of cattle. Tackling livestock diseases like anthrax and east coast fever meant it was necessary to coordinate veterinary services and vaccination campaigns from the boma to county levels, but also in IDP camps. Contrary to the agricultural inputs, that were free, the veterinary supplies were provided on a cost-sharing basis. Money would be collected by the county livestock officer and then reimbursed to the NGO that assisted with the provision of these services.[79] Because of these initiatives, the livestock population increased for the first time during the war, resulting in the frontlines being supplied more regularly with cattle.

Attempts were also made to address the capacity issue and lack of qualified personnel to administer projects. The Institute of Development, Environment and Agricultural Studies (IDEAS) was established in Yambio in 2000 with the aim of providing education and vocational training to civilians living in the liberated areas. It had as its motto 'The pursuit of knowledge through liberty and freedom,' with projects being led at a community level and allowing for work-based distance learning. IDEAS attempted to pioneer new ways of engaging the population with skills training in areas as diverse as farm management and local governance so that capacity was built internally. Another intensive course that IDEAS led at its campus in Yambio was the Civil Administration Training (CAT), where former Sudanese civil servants could put their skills and experience to use. However, once IDEAS's funding from UNICEF came to an end, the institute was no longer able to operate. Aware of the weakness of the CANS institutions, in 1997 the SPLM/A leadership requested that USAID design a programme to enhance its capacities for democratic governance and support economic rehabilitation (Deng 2013). This resulted in the creation of the Sudan Transitional Assistance Rehabilitation (STAR) programme to train civil administrators. The project had a national-level component for training the opposition coalition National Democratic Alliance (NDA), a county-level component for training local administrators and a community-level component for promoting economic recovery. Through these and many other projects, hundreds of administrators were trained. Yet, once external funding ended, the SPLM/A was unable to mobilise resources to continue such initiatives.

New Sudan education system

Education in the liberated areas produced a form of counter-hegemonic political discourse (Breidlid 2013) seen through the secularisation and adoption of a modernist education system by the SPLM/A. The curriculum was diametrically opposed to the one in Khartoum that Islamised education. The Sudanese education system was, in the SPLM/A's view, grounded in oppression and denied the region's rich heterogeneity of cultures, religions and belief systems. The SPLM/A highlighted in its Education Policy (2002) the need to counteract the 'assaults on the cultures and traditions of the indigenous peoples' that had marked the education system under colonial rule and under Khartoum.[80] Khartoum wanted to solidify the Sudanese nation–state under a political order based on Islamist values. By breaking with this policy of prioritising the knowledge of Islam above all others (Breidlid 2013), the SPLM/A sought to reverse the marginalising and homogenising tendency of the previous educational system. It initially used books and curricula from Uganda and Kenya before eventually developing a South Sudanese curriculum. Education was mainly provided by the churches, NGOs and the OLS, even though for the first decade of war interventions dealing with 'complex emergencies' were prioritised over more developmental ones like education (Deng 2003). OLS only began supporting community initiatives to rebuild the education system of the South in 1993. The SPLM/A would take another decade to produce its education policy of 2002. However, just like with other services, it faced many challenges, including lack of teachers, insufficient textbooks, recruitment of children to join the war effort, the need for children to work, food insecurity and the acute shortage of most necessities.

Education was meant to foster nation building, self-reliance, patriotism and the respect for other cultures and traditions. It was one of the founding tools the SPLM/A had set for building a new society. Its rhetoric of prioritising education seems to have been genuine, but the movement did not allocate resources to support international initiatives. As a result, communities carried the entire cost of maintaining the schools by contributing 100% of the fees (90% retained for the teachers and 5% for the school office, with the remaining 5% being paid to the assistant commissioner of the payams for his support staff) (Herzog 1998: 35). In the late 1990s, Yambio had 7 primary schools and 2 secondary schools with an estimated 12,000 students, of which 40% were girls. During this period, only 20% of teachers had received any form of training (Herzog 1998). With 97 operational facilities in Western Equatoria, the schools had only 928 teachers (Johnson 1994).[81] Schools existed in towns and payams but not in bomas, due to how isolated and far removed from each other they were.[82] Throughout the South, education was one of the biggest casualties of war. It was estimated that only 28% of the 1.4 million children in the South were enrolled in school in 2003, and less than 1% of those were girls (Breidlid 2013).

New Sudan health system

The New Sudan Health Policy was written in 1997. It was conceptualised to incorporate elements of the old healthcare system and the SPLM/A system, while harmonising traditional and modern medicine. The system was premised on the concept of primary healthcare (PHC), focusing on prevention, control of health problems, provision of adequate sanitation and water, family planning, immunisation and the treatment of common ailments. The PHC programme was run by community health workers that operated the healthcare units in the villages. However, it was the relief agencies and NGOs that were the lifeline of the healthcare system, despite the fact that the SPLM/A wanted the community to run this service. The SPLM policy stated 'that people owned their health care system as active participants and not just recipients ... as owners of the system'.[83]

Health facilities were overstretched, servicing an average of 17,000 civilians (including children) a month in Yambio alone.[84] Health services were managed at the different local levels through committees that fell under the County Health Authority (CHA) and National Health Authority (NHA) of the New Sudan. At the boma level, the chief would call the community meeting and elect 12 members into the health committee so that the health centre could be built. Each primary healthcare centre would have a consultation room, a treatment room and a pharmacy. This process was supervised by the payam and the CHAs, and directly assisted by NGOs that provided them with medication. The committees also identified who could become health workers and maternity healthcare providers. They would then proceed to training for a year in areas like Maridi, Rumbek or Kapoeta that had training centres.[85] While doctors were trained abroad, healthcare workers remained inside the liberated areas, with the Maridi Clinical Institute (2001) being the most advanced training institute.

The SPLM/A lacked the capacity and expertise to either compete with or attempt to design NGO interventions in the health sector. In fact, in 2000 the Catholic Church in Yambio threatened to withhold funds if the SRRA-run hospital was not taken over by the Catholic diocese of the county (Riehl 2001). As many as 100 NGOs worked with the CANS Health Department to ensure that there was appropriate medical care. 'Regional hospitals, like the one in Yei and Yambio, had surgery rooms—one male and one female—had over 200 beds, paediatric wards, dentistry, and ophthalmology'[86] and were run by international NGOs. Yet the system remained underdeveloped and unable to fully address all the health issues of the community.

Resources and taxes

With regards to taxation, the SPLM/A didn't manage to go beyond being a gatekeeper of the state. Gatekeeper states 'had trouble collecting taxes, except on import and export. ... What they could do was to sit astride the interface between a territory and the rest of the world collecting revenue and foreign aid, entry and exit visas' (Cooper 2002). At the county levels, the only sources of revenue came from taxing exports and imports, market fees, court fees, brewing fees and health fees at the payam and boma levels (Rohn et al. 1997). Once the Customs Department began functioning, taxes were being collected on imports (the Gibana tax)[87] and exports (i.e. of cash crops). Goods subjected to Gibana included agricultural products (like maize and cassava), cattle, fish and honey (Rohn et al. 1997). Imported goods were taxed at between 4% and 15%, depending on the item, with an additional tax for the county commissioner (Herzog 1998). Initially, the county authorities in Yambio tried to tax NGOs but had to exempt them after international organisations made an appeal to the SRRA office in Nairobi. However, NGO cars and motorbikes had to be registered with the police, who for a fee would allow them to function using New Sudan licence plates (Herzog 1998). The Yambio county congresses decided that soldiers participating in trading activities were also to be taxed, although enforcement of this policy would have been almost impossible, given that the soldiers themselves continued to collect taxes despite being prohibited from doing so by the movement.

A personnel tax (the Country Income Development tax) was also instituted by the Finance Secretariat, where locals working for NGOs would have between 3% and 10% of their salary sent directly to the civil authorities. Other revenues collected included road fees and travel permits (exit and entry visas) that were stamped by the SRRA but paid to the county authority. Although local authorities were requested to remit 70% of their revenue to the central level, revenues from exploration of natural resources or taxes from the civilian population were so low that they hardly managed to cover the running costs of the civil authorities. A 1997 study on three counties in the Equatoria region showed that their gross annual income in cash was between 1.5 and 4.5 million Sudanese pounds (the equivalent of US$4,000–9,000), with only a fraction of this available for the county administration (Rohn et al. 1997).

Following an economic conference in Yambio in 1999, a Natural Resources Technical Committee was created. The committee became operational in 2000, and teams were organised to begin a geological survey of the country, while other teams worked on surveying wildlife and forestry, trade and taxes operations. Working under this commission were the Secretariats for Finance, Transport and Mining, who attempted to coordinate how the exploration of natural resources (like teak and gold) could be efficiently managed to sell them in neighbouring countries. The commission prospected for gold in Eastern Equatoria and discovered many deposits of the mineral. 'By 1996 we had enough money to answer the immediate needs of the frontline, even medicine.'[88] 'We took forestry resources of Yambio to buy anti-aircraft guns,' described the head of the Natural Resources Technical Committee.[89] 'What forestry did was a miracle because it helped us with the ammunitions and transportation of fuel that allowed us to succeed in major military offensives like the taking of Raja to capture the oilfields.'[90] In the run-up to the capture of Yei and then the subsequent attempt to take Juba in 1997, several initiatives were organised to render teak profitable. In the later stages of the war, the exploration of timber became bureaucratised with the creation of the Timber Resources Evaluation Committee (TREC), which created a standard application form that authorised selective harvesting. This was to regulate the supply of teak and avoid deforestation.

Recentralisation of administrative decision-making

In 1999, there was a reversal of policy—termed by the SPLM/A a 'major shake-up'—within the New Sudan project that set back the decentralisation of decision-making. Garang decided to suspend the NLC sessions and reintroduce the SPLA High Command in the form of a Leadership Council consisting of fourteen senior commanders. The NEC was dissolved and parsed out into seven commissions that clustered several secretariats/ministries.[91] The leadership justified this on the basis that the administration of the liberated areas needed centralised and collective decision-making, as well as timely implementation of the SPLM/A's resolutions (Malok 2009). Governors were renamed SPLM/A Regional Secretaries while the secretaries (ministers) became SPLM/A Commissioners. All five SPLM/A Regional Secretaries became members of the Leadership Council, clearly an amalgamation of the powers of the executive falling under the control of the military. In Yambio, these central changes were seen as a return to militarisation. 'In July 1999 there was a return of the military and civilians could not give orders to the military.'[92] The fallback position for the SPLM/A when difficulties arose, and systems of administration stalled, was to revert to the military centralised structure rather than devise new mechanisms to alter the systems and empower institutions. This seems to have been temporary, as from 2000 onwards, with peace negotiations gaining momentum, the SPLM/A realised it needed secure structures to sustain the South during a transition period. Once a peace agreement was signed, the movement needed to have a strategy in place and build its capacity to define government institutions and a governance plan. As expressed by many leaders within the movement, the CANS was the most important factor that allowed the SPLM/A to take the reins of power from 2005 after the Comprehensive Peace Agreement (CPA), and in 2011 after independence. Although the CANS system had many shortcomings, it gave the movement some governing experience that prepared it for the transitional period and the creation of the Government of South Sudan (GOSS) and the Government of National Unity (GNU).

Conclusion

This chapter on Yambio has highlighted the localised, decentralised and loose form of the SPLM/A's parallel state. Grounded on social structures, it was pillared on the maintenance of rural peace, self-sufficiency, civilian participation and strengthening of traditional structures of authority. It sought to provide a relatively broad political programme that did not impose rigid ideological tenets on communities but instead secured their cooperation and consent by empowering them to act as agents of change. It instrumentalised forces of society, chiefs and aid agencies in working towards its political vision, thereby ceding power to these actors, rather than providing services and direct governance through its own political institutions. The different levels of government that functioned under the tutelage of the SPLM/A gained legitimacy in the way they were engrained in local dynamics. The SPLM/A understood that, had they not incorporated the civilian population into the struggle and creating a social contract with civilians and their leaders to reorganise society, they probably would have lost the war. There was a sense, as expressed in interviews, that the CANS gave the people of the South a government that was their own. Even if it was a 'bad government of our people it is always better than a good administration of foreigners'.[93]

The SPLM/A, however, failed to deliver a party and political structures that could link the local levels to the central command levels. Centralisation remained the policy of the militarily dominated movement that struggled to shed its behavioural DNA, while pushes for decentralisation were aimed at empowering communities and linking them to the political elites of the SPLM/A. This linkage never took root. Instead, the politics of survival led it to 'pre-empt the development of large concentrations of social control outside the state organisation' (Migdal 1988: 236), which led the SPLM/A to accommodate and balance different interests, thus weakening its political order. The most significant shift that occurred in the New Sudan was the change away from militarism and militocracy. Militarism was defined as the 'extensive control by the military over social life, coupled with the subservience of the whole society to the needs of the army,' while militocracy was the 'phenomenon of preponderance of the military over civil personnel' (Andreski 1971 [1954]: 185). The shifts experienced were in many respects informed by the 1991 critical juncture.

Before the 1991 critical juncture, the SPLM/A prioritised the unifying and hierarchical force of a military organisation and command structure. Ideological inconsistencies were replaced by pragmatic considerations, leaving the frictions between secessionism and unity unresolved. Proposed reforms were left sufficiently broad so as maintain respect for the diversity of the region's population, thus mobilising the peripheries and empowering the marginalised on political and economic grounds. The focus was on rapid military successes and gaining territory in what was expected to be a short war. The critical juncture forced the SPLM/A to address the structural weaknesses that had allowed it to reach a near breaking point in which it had lost almost all its territory, had no rear base or arsenal and was at risk of losing its social base. To survive the loss of Ethiopian support, the movement needed internal bases for support, logistics, provisions and operations. To survive the splintering and ethnic fragmentation of the liberation front, it needed to broaden its appeal to different communities by accommodating self-determination and ceding power at the local level. This made the SPLM/A turn its attention inwards to extend its internal support structures and mobilise communities for another cycle of prolonged war against Khartoum and the SPLM splinter groups. The changes it experienced had to be both pragmatic and deeply symbolic. As the political side of the liberation struggle became a priority, the movement was faced with the difficulty of not having trained cadres, skilled administrators and political commissars, which meant that their strategy was largely implemented autonomously at the local level. This resulted in a parallel state that attempted to corporatise society while maintaining the parameters of its gatekeeping presence in terms of development and service provision.

One of the SPLM/A's more strategic decisions was to outsource service delivery. In the same way that it used traditional authorities by reactivating native administrations during the CMA years, the movement also began to instrumentalise relief agencies. For over a decade of war, the SPLM/A had understood that the international community was going to operate in the South to assist with relief aid despite the diplomatic, logistical and security challenges faced. Externally, the movement had to take into consideration what the international community would accept as sufficiently state-like so that attributes of the SPLM/A project would count as recognisable state-building. If the movement was to negotiate in internationally sponsored talks on equal terms with Khartoum, it needed to project this kind of legitimacy. By building a parallel state, the SPLM/A also provided some measure of social and institutional predictability that allowed citizens of the New Sudan to begin to plan their futures, establishing a sense of normalcy during the war. Although services and economic development were financed and driven by external actors, the provision of security, justice and a political path that created symbolic capital gave the SPLM/A enough legitimacy and support to move its New Sudan project forward.

This governance experience arguably informed several of the reforms Garang set out to enact during the 2005–11 transition. After his inauguration as First Vice President of Sudan and President of the GOSS in June 2005, he began setting up structures for the first governing policies. Extensive interviews with his closest advisors and members of government reveal that, among other priorities, Garang wanted to launch the 'towns to villages' strategy in all 1,000 payams in the country, as well as create non-tribal caretaker governments at the local level. These were two among several other policies meant to address the dangerous dynamics that threatened to (and later did) unravel the hard-won political transition. As a rural development policy, taking the 'towns to the villages' would create 'rural cities', linked to the villages that surrounded them by feeder roads. The rural city was to begin as a resource centre at the payam level and would have the following facilities: 1) an administration complex for the executive, legislative, judiciary and chiefs' courts; 2) an education complex of schools and vocational training; 3) primary healthcare centres; 4) an agricultural complex with veterinary services; 5) an economic complex that would include microcredit facilities, solar power units and telecommunications; and 6) a cultural centre, as well as a police station (Deng 2013: 48). Garang's vision for development centred on transforming the country from the local level up, so that each 150-household village could be self-sufficient. A study was prepared in 2005 on how oil revenues could fund this initiative that encompassed the South.[94] This policy would allow for decentralisation of development, political power, financial budgeting and administrative priorities to be determined at the local level.

The second policy was meant to address the dangers of 'localisms'. Garang knew that tribalism and nepotism would haunt the new administration of the South, and that in some way communities would fall back into their smaller groups of solidarity, given the difficulty of forging a nationalist and integrating identity. He had learnt this through the complicated and delicate process of balancing tribal considerations among the top leadership of the movement. The pursuit of narrow interests and the resurgence of community and tribal imperatives would continue to haunt the process of transformation if leaders were initially selected from their communities to run their constituencies. Because of this, Garang came up with the idea of caretaker governors to provide the necessary link between the local and central levels. 'Garang didn't want the election of governors, he wanted rotation. As a traditional setting your community and family are the law, and he wanted to avoid this.'[95] The idea was to have a governor from a different tribe rule a state where he/she had no community affiliation or tribal representation so as to focus on the task of governing and avoid the pitfalls of nepotism and corruption.[96] The caretaker government was always referred to as the solution, 'to instil another spirit of cooperation and unity' (Schomerus and Allen 2010). Neither of these policies was ever implemented, mainly because Garang was killed, and with him died his vision.

Two years after achieving independence, the country would fall into a brutal war emanating from within the SPLM/A. Despite its efforts to correct the many pathologies within the state structure and the party, and despite managing conflicting interests among governing elites, the SPLM/A would not be able to contain the unravelling of the dynamics it had already experienced during the war. As a government, it ultimately failed to direct a path towards nationhood that unified the country. As a party, it failed to direct its commanders and strengthen structures of collective leadership. As a liberation movement, it lost its symbolic credentials that would rally diverse constituencies behind difficult reforms.

3

UNITA'S GOVERNANCE
JAMBA AND THE FREE LANDS REPUBLIC OF ANGOLA, 1979–91

'*War is a matter of Consciousness. It is not made to be destructive but to create a better world in a free land.*'

Jonas Savimbi[1]

'*Jamba was created to allow UNITA to combat the enemy in every way—with every task so that it wasn't just military but was about ideas, a confrontation of two state projects of two societies.*'

UNITA Colonel[2]

'*Ele tirou o fumo da aldeia e pôs a politica [He removed the smoke from the village and gave people politics].*'

UNITA Head Intelligence[3]

In the south-westernmost point of Angola, where the rivers Cuando and Cubango run along the borders of Namibia and Zambia, lay Jamba, a previously uninhabited sandy land that became UNITA's bastion of the revolution. Positioned at the 'Bico', the tip of Angola, Jamba comprised an area of approximately 12,000 square kilometres. 'As Terras do Fim do Mundo' (Lands at the End of the World), as the Portuguese referred to the area, it had the ideal terrain for the construction of rebel rear base, being supplied with important water sources, rivers and lagoons, and with enough bush cover to allow for military training and political activities. It was far from any airfield, which made it largely safe from being bombarded by government MIGs, yet its proximity to friendly neighbours meant UNITA could easily be supplied with capacity, resources and logistics.

Pushed to the limits of its ability to resist and fight government forces supplied by the Soviet Union and bolstered by Cuban troops, UNITA set up Jamba as the capital of its parallel state. Expelled from the cities in 1976 and plunged into the vast wilderness of rural Angola, UNITA retreated south where it was able to put its Maoist training into action. Most observers expected UNITA to disintegrate in 1976, yet it rose to become a resounding force for change (Marcum 1983).[4] It connected with the people, gave them politics and services and rebuilt its army. From a ragtag band of 1,500 soldiers, it would create a conventional force of over 60,000 troops in 1991. What was achieved in Jamba as an effective parallel state, mirroring the bureaucracy, standardisation, reciprocity and structure of a nascent government, became a story of competence, power and seduction.

From 1979 to 1991, Jamba became the embodiment of UNITA's capacity to govern a state within a state. Built as a training ground for its growing army of soldiers, commanders, cadres and civilians, Jamba served as a space for the movement to define a world order based on UNITA's redefinition of society and what it meant to be 'Angolan'. Over 12 years the movement would develop state-like organs for service delivery, along with a new society, maximising its control over people, territory and the imagined future. This was an intrusive and complex project that structured people, beliefs, norms, resources and strategies into a well-defined and centrally controlled rebel state. What made this possible was an alignment of leadership, the organisation and structure of the rebel movement, the iron discipline surrounding the tripartite structure (party, military, administration) and the embedded sense of a 'nationalist' purpose of liberating Angola which resulted from a structured strategy of education and acculturation. Traditional authorities and social systems were moulded to reflect UNITA's world order. The mass propaganda drives, including visits conducted for foreigners, created a myth-like idea of Jamba, but they had very real and long-lasting effects for those who experienced it. The purpose of Jamba was to rehearse governance and prepare cadres and leaders to govern a future state. It was a pragmatic exercise in expediency and survival but also highly symbolic as a projected political and social order for Angola.

This chapter traces UNITA's trajectory in devising a centralised governing strategy that allowed it not only to survive the war during the years under scrutiny, and to fight a stronger and better-resourced enemy, but also to build its popular support base. UNITA's wartime governance in Jamba expanded upon its previous structures of governance created during the 1966–74 war against the Portuguese. UNITA fought the Portuguese through guerrilla tactics and by neutralising their counterinsurgency strategies of population resettlements. With South African and United States support, UNITA would later fight the MPLA and the Soviet–Cuban alliance by producing a state alternative and staging a propaganda war aimed at delegitimising the MPLA post-independence state. Fighting the MPLA was as much a military matter as it was a question of wresting political legitimacy from an opposing vision for the nation and state. This change in strategy and organisational capacity was catalysed by a crippling military defeat for UNITA in 1976 that propelled the movement's response, 'the Long March', an attempt to rebuild itself. This turning point was the critical juncture that led to UNITA's decision to build a different kind of parallel state.

The creation of Jamba had several objectives. It was meant to support the movement in what was going to be a long war and provide an area large enough to begin building a semi-conventional army and train new recruits. It aimed to allow UNITA to develop its health and education programmes in order to populate the Free Lands with politically aware civilians and prepare a class of skilled workers. It functioned as the nerve centre for propaganda, political training and indoctrination, and it provided the leadership and the population living there moments of reflection and projection of a normal life so that they could have some relief from the tension of war. It also played

111

the important role of providing a stage for staff, cadres and structures to rehearse future governance. 'We needed to have a practice of governance and a way of managing people and inserting them into our structures so that we could get the pilot experience for the entire country.'[5] Jamba allowed UNITA the ability to project internally and externally the idea that it was running a parallel state as the ultimate expression of its 'sovereignty'. UNITA was attempting two things with this 'far-reaching project of engineering "a normal existence"' (Beck 2009: 349). First, it wanted to regulate and condition the behaviour of its combatants and followers by inserting them into an organisation that designed and controlled their entire existence so that politically aware, socially empowered and skilled members could reverse marginalisation. Second, this civilising project aimed to 'elevate' the southern populations and those from the 'bush' to the educational level of those in the cities as a way of correcting historical injustice. To this effect, civilian and political life in UNITA's military bases and its capital Jamba was staged 'to counter the threatening wilderness of the surrounding *mata* [bush]' (Beck 2009: 349) and all that it represented. For UNITA, the experience of Jamba revealed a deeper level of 'preparedness', a concept that dated back to the 1960s with the idea of creating a rural southern equalising force to empower the marginalised southern communities.

Physically located in an uninhabited and deserted area, Jamba was populated with civilians from all over Angola. This 'deterritorialisation' allowed UNITA the opportunity to embed the population and its fighters into a new socio-political reality. Jamba was never intended to become a second Luanda; it was always a provisional capital meant to provide UNITA with the necessary conditions and stability to stage its revolution and win the war. UNITA's state–society project was built on the creation of a new nationalist sentiment. Forging this new Angolan nationalism, based on opposition to foreign (Soviet Union and Cuban) occupation and perceived exclusionary MPLA practices, required redefining the concept of 'belonging'. Belonging and nationalism were in this way mutually reinforcing. 'When nationalists claim that national belonging is the overridingly important form of all belonging, they mean that there is no other form of belonging—to your family, work, or friends—which is secured if you do not have a nation to protect you' (Ignatieff 1994: 6). UNITA was meant to be that 'nation' in the liberated areas.

When the first peace agreement was signed in 1991, UNITA began moving its leaders and cadres to Luanda and the cities ahead of the first elections, which they expected to win. Jamba remained a symbolic base, but it had served its purpose. 'Nothing else was built in Jamba after early 1992—everything was built before because everything was geared to place technocrats and those with professions in other parts of the country.'[6] When the war restarted in 1992, and would rage for another decade, Savimbi positioned his headquarters in the Central Highlands, in the cities of Andulo and Bailundo. The governing experience there would be radically different, contested by the populace, politically driven by anger and without the underpinnings of national reform. Jamba was captured on 31 December 1999 by government forces that proceeded over time to systematically destroy most of the infrastructure and vestiges of the parallel state. Ahead of Operação Restauro's success in taking Jamba, UNITA began to destroy its most strategic assets, including the radio station. Leaders moved their families across the border in Zambia, but Jamba would be mostly taken as a functioning and equipped base.

Twelve years later, few vestiges would remain of the sprawling organisation and logistics of Jamba. The need to erase Jamba's history was an existential issue for the MPLA. In 2012, over 23,600 civilians still lived in the area, coexisting with a deployed battalion of the 51st Division of Angolan Armed Forces. Jamba was being governed by an administrator of the Licua Municipality, a former MPLA Women's League member who had been captured during the war and held prisoner by UNITA. Asked why she stayed behind in the symbolic capital of her enemy after 10 years of peace, her reply was 'because now I am the boss'.[7] Her fate too was inextricably tied to the experience of living in Jamba. Jamba today exists in the memories of the UNITA 'people', in the imagination of younger generations who seek to understand a history that has been erased by the victor's justice and historic revisionism, and as a small military outpost the government uses to 'punish troops'.[8]

This case study speaks directly to how the state was imagined—and how it was constructed, staged and experienced by its citizens—as an extension of the liberation struggle. It links the state and the imagined nation. The state was first and foremost an exercise in legitimation, more of an idea than a system (Abrahams 1988), in a continuous process of construction. The state-system and the state idea then became two distinct objects of analysis (Mitchell 1999).[9] For UNITA, the state-system and the state idea were indivisible, as one was an operational form of the other. To believe in UNITA's parallel state idea, the population, soldiers, and cadres had to experience it as a projection of a future political order. There was a need for the state to be 'constructed' in the minds of those leading the state formation process, so that they could visualise, and conceptualise, the structures they intended to form as vehicles for public goods. This state needed to exist 'in the hearts and minds of its people ... if they do not believe it is there, no logical exercise will bring it to life' (Strayer 1970).[10] However, in Jamba the state was also a matter of institutions, political culture and a UNITA-moulded society, true to its totalitarian form.

First bases and administrative units in military regions

During the first war of the 1960s and 1970s against the Portuguese, UNITA had already begun to develop structured guerrilla bases. From the onset, UNITA proposed to establish counter-administrations to allow it to propagate its political discourse and version of Angolan nationalism. During its first party congress in March 1966, UNITA defined its strategy to depend only on local capacity rather than wait for external assistance; to mobilise the peasants and guide them into a revolutionary party; to stage war as the only solution against Portuguese domination and apply an ideology that was valid in different circumstances; to form a democratic front and join the people in the interior of the country; and finally to prioritise the guerrilla fighter (Chiwale 2008: 97–9). This meant that UNITA had to operate deep within the Angolan territory and establish bases that would allow it to mobilise the population and expand operations. In following with its Maoist training, the principles of self-reliance, organisation and popular support were vital in the establishment of rural revolutionary bases.

The administration established in UNITA areas was premised on three key pillars: the respect for ethnic custom, a developed agricultural system and the organisation of community institutions. UNITA villages were populated either on a voluntary basis, with local chiefs choosing to bring their villagers behind UNITA lines; by force; or because the service delivery and societal assistance that the movement provided drew people in organically. In a move to reverse the gains of Portugal's counterinsurgency strategy of inserting populations into *aldeamentos* in order to isolate them, UNITA recruited villagers to resettle into their 'liberated villages'. In a similar manner, the Portuguese had hoped to win the war in Angola by denying the three liberation movements access to the non-combatant populations. In 1967, the colonial government's strategy began regrouping the population into strategic hamlets. These population resettlements took three different forms: the *aldeamentos* (strategic resettlements organised by the military in fighting areas), the *reordenamentos rural* (rural resettlement outside immediate fighting areas) and the *colonatos do soldados* (soldier's settlements where former servicemen were settled into strategic areas) (Bender 1972: 335). These settlement strategies extended the rule of the colonial power. 'While pre-war settlement attempts affected only several thousand Africans in Angola, these schemes affected more than one million Africans [20% of the population]' in the 1970s (Bender 1972: 337).

Understanding its military limitations when compared to its larger and better-organised FNLA and MPLA counterparts, UNITA relied primarily on political means to extend control over the population. 'The focus was on political mobilisation and gaining support from the population, as we had very few arms and military capabilities.'[11] Political commissars had the responsibility of mobilising support and ensuring that the war effort was supported with food, information and popular backing. UNITA instituted the policy that a soldier also had to act as a political mobiliser and establish contacts with chiefs. Each one of these policies would find expression in larger and more complex institutions as the post-independence war progressed and UNITA gained more terrain.

Bases were established within defined military regions to allow for the movement to increase its contacts with different communities and organise its guerrilla strategy. UNITA divided its operations into six military regions, *Regiões Militares* (RM)[12] or guerrilla zones commanded by a politico-military coordinator. Later in the war, the ultimate authority of the RM became the military commander who was the governor of the area and the senior representative of the party. Each region had its guerrilla force. As support grew with enhanced political mobilisation, bases were organised within the RMs. In May 1970, the Black Panther, Black Star and Black Fury military columns were created as part of a more defensive strategy, and with them greater detail on how administrative structures were to support the bases. Given that the movement depended on the population for its food, information and guidance in areas the guerrilla force had little knowledge about, UNITA subdivided its structures. The smallest was the cell, followed by the local committees, zones, sections, regions and finally the people's assemblies (Chiwale 2008). Each people's assembly was comprised of sixteen villages as a way of handing over political power to the different communities. Military personnel for their security and health facilities were supplied by UNITA, 'but all other services (schools, cooperatives, local political committees) were in the people's own hands'.[13] By the early 1970s the movement had already established 120 cooperatives and administered a large portion of eastern Angola.

Initially, bases followed a specific layout, and areas were divided along a main avenue. Structures were built like a *kimbo* (village) with a central *jazigo* (information post). Each camp would have a *njango*, a round, grass-roofed pavilion where village elders and guerrilla officers would meet. The main military camp also had schools, political indoctrination centres and served as a 'seat for a local parliament consisting of representatives ... of all the villages' (Alberts 1980: 252).[14] The administrative areas were clearly separated from the military structures, with areas for troops, logistics, administration and services. Surrounding the bases were ambush areas. Each base elected its own chairman and a village committee that dealt with problems and implemented the decisions of the branch. The branch was the next highest authority, composed of four villages, and was commissioned to train local militia and coordinate food supply. Civilians were armed with bows and arrows, as UNITA did not have enough firearms. Those who were not directly connected to the movement would remain in their villages with the People's Sentinels (the Republican force), whose mission was to protect the people and keep information contained.[15] The sentinels were trained for forty-five days and were envisaged as part of a public security force. 'In imminent zones [the frontline] they'd stay with the population or outside the base so there wouldn't be casualties of war.'[16] Seen as having strong patriotic fervour, the sentinels were there to protect and control the people, their belongings, provide information, assist with logistics and, when necessary, integrate fully into the guerrilla forces.[17] In return, the population was expected to provide loyalty, food and intelligence to the movement.

Traditional authorities

UNITA's dependence on traditional authorities stemmed from its need to have direct interlocutors with diverse communities and to outsource rule in villages to the chiefs. By incorporating the *sobas*, *sekulus* and *ocimbandas*[18] into their structures, UNITA was attempting to win the necessary legitimacy to govern the villages. This policy was directly contrasted with the MPLA's strategy of re-educating local leaders (Stuvoy 2002). Savimbi prioritised relations with the *sobas*, illustrating the movement's underlying belief that African traditions had to be respected and transferred into the new governing system that would replace the 'second colonial system' of the MPLA. Unlike the British, the Portuguese followed a 'systematic direct-rule policy where the paramount chiefs were not recognized, except for the Kongo king, and the *sobas* were reduced to village level executors of colonial policy' (Messiant 1998: 133).[19] This meant that Angolans, in the absence of traditional leaders able to present local claims or oppose colonialism, were dependent on Western institutions and on the elites formed by them.

UNITA tried to revive the powers of the *sobas* but inadvertently ruled the traditional authorities in a similar direct way, by placing them within a framework defined by the movement and the party, thus limiting their ability to contest UNITA's rule. However, traditional authorities did help shape the policies that governed these populations. They became the mouthpiece for the movement and the political coordinators of the civilian population (Heywood 1998). Moreover, *sobas* were used to resolve problems at the village level, operating the local village councils and coordinating all local administration matters under a UNITA framework. 'Every time something came up or changed during the struggle, we called upon the *sobas* to explain the situation to their people so that they could be enlightened.'[20]

UNITA later developed feedback mechanisms. *Sobas* would regularly meet with the leadership in Jamba and other bases, where they would also receive some material help for their families. A council, called the 'Parliamentarians', was set up for this purpose during the party's 6th Congress (August 1986). This advisory forum of elders and traditional authorities would meet annually in Jamba with Savimbi, who would take account of the problems in the liberated areas. If one commander was causing problems and this was exposed during these meetings, he would be demoted. This was confirmed in several interviews with senior and junior military officers.[21] Another testimony by a leading general mentioned the establishment of a consultative council in the Kwame Nkrumah base where elders were consulted and asked to provide ideas about the struggle, the people, health and other service areas that might have problems. 'They would bring proposals to Savimbi in meetings that happened every six months. ... These elders came from all RMs to meet in Jamba ... and ideas had to be brought from each of the different regions and those representing different ethnic groups. They were asked "how is the relationship between the troops and the people?" And if there was a problem an inquiry would be made' and action taken.[22]

Service delivery strategy

UNITA's dependence on the population, and its political programme of mass mobilisation, required a strategy for service delivery. Early on the movement understood the need to provide public goods and create the idea of a 'guerrilla republic' in spatial and political terms. While the movement had no rear base or 'capital' at this stage of the war, the idea of an alternate 'state' or Maoist parallel hierarchies of governance was already present. In 1971, 6 years after its emergence, UNITA was operating from bases in 5 (Moxico, Bie, Malange, Lunda, and Kuando Kubango) of Angola's then 12 provinces. The movement had already managed to extend both military and civilian sectors to these areas.[23] The 'liberated villages' brought together educational, health, agricultural and social service networks. Initially built by UNITA in the central highlands, these were successfully replicated in other parts of the country as the war progressed (Heywood 2000).

Early accounts of service delivery structures revealed they were guided by an emerging philosophy of guerrilla warfare but also of coordinated action to ensure civilian support. Journalist Franz Sitte reported on the existence of boarding schools in UNITA base camps and of kibbutz-like farms for developing agricultural activities. During one of Sitte's first visits in 1972, he described how he had to produce his UNITA pass and papers to the guard for stamping before he could enter the 'guerrilla republic'.[24] Sitte further described how the economy was carefully planned in each of the bases, where he visited with civilian working cooperatives to feed the army. Leon Dash, an American journalist who trekked across Angola with UNITA, reported how the movement had four hospitals and ten elementary schools in 1973.[25] 'In the forests children [we]re learning to write and do arithmetic, writing on wooden slates with charcoal or bits of mandioc instead of chalk ... Even at an early age they got some political indoctrination.'[26] Dash described how the rebels ran their own hospitals, schools, military training camps and collective farms.[27] In a commune-like society, UNITA organised civilians and provided 'education and medical services [that] had never been available to peasants here from the government', Savimbi told Dash. When independence came in 1975, over 90% of the Angolan population were illiterate.[28]

The report celebrating the sixth year of UNITA's struggle mentioned progress in the liberated areas and the movement's commitment to service delivery. A total of 12,000 children were in UNITA schools, and over 25,000 civilians had received medical care in UNITA health facilities.[29] These numbers were obviously exaggerated, given the limitations UNITA faced at the time, but they point to a strategy of providing a contrast to the 'enemy's' lack of development in the areas of education and healthcare. This issue spoke directly to the colonial distinctions that divided the Angolan population into the *assimilado* and *indigena* categories, with divergent levels of political and economic rights, where education and other services were used to deepen the class distinction. UNITA would use this same strategy against the MPLA during the second war, depicting it as an elitist urban movement dominated by *assimilados* and *mestiços*.

Seven years after launching its anti-colonial struggle, UNITA held its third congress, which was made up of 221 delegates, several UNITA representatives from Europe and leaders from all of UNITA's liberated areas in the Ovimbundu, Luimbi, Cuanhama and Chokwe regions. The congress reviewed the party statutes and elected a smaller, more efficient central committee (24 members) and politburo (10 members). It also reiterated its policy of uniting with the FNLA and MPLA and supporting attempts by several African governments in the formation of the Supreme Council for the Liberation of Angola. This unity would never materialise.

The 1975–76 critical juncture and the Long March

On 11 November 1975, UNITA and the FNLA declared Angola's independence from Huambo while the MPLA officially declared independence in Luanda as the post-independent government. The transitional arrangements of the Alvor Agreement that ended the Angolan war of independence and sought to establish a quadripartite government (made up of the three liberation movements and the Portuguese) to govern Angola until elections could be held in October had failed. This was meant to serve as a handover period to transition colonial Portuguese rule to Angolan independence. War was looming, with the FNLA and MPLA clashing continuously throughout 1975, but UNITA did not expect to be forced into a massive retreat by Cuban forces. However, 'on the 8th of February 1976, the Soviet and Cuban invasion chased UNITA out of the cities and each commander had to return to their areas in retreat'.[30] Numerous bombardments by Soviet-supplied MIGs and as many as 6,000 Cuban troops were involved in the fall of Huambo, which was faced with little resistance. On 10 February, Savimbi and several other leaders ordered the movement's followers to abandon the city and take to the bush (Bridgland 1987). The leadership understood strategically that the presence of foreign troops in Angola only a few months after the Portuguese army had withdrawn was a mobilisation tool. The military incursion produced such an effect, with soldiers targeting and killing 'anyone that was deemed as not being MPLA', that those who retreated from Luanda and then Huambo joined the war on UNITA's side, although not on any particular ideological basis or sympathy for UNITA.[31] A UNITA dissident explained that 'the MPLA made the mistake of killing people in the bush, it eliminated people to cause fear and they joined the guerrilla'.[32] UNITA was the target of five major military offensives from June 1976 to January 1977 (James 2011), which pushed it and key supporters deeper into the bush as they staged their Long March.

The movement's leadership and supporters began a retreat to the bush which would last fifteen years. Many would only return to the cities and the capital Luanda in 1991 with the Bicesse Peace Agreement and the 1992 elections. For the entirety of the second war, UNITA would operate outside the cities and dominate whole portions of the countryside. The retreat from Huambo in 1976 was a symbolically difficult one, as UNITA had lost its capital, and the movement needed to rethink how it would resurface and survive another long war. 'The only way to resist the Cuban invasion was to take this fight by stages: we advanced until reaching the stage of equilibrium and the stage of pressure.'[33] This meant that the movement would have to seek a safer, more isolated area to build its rear base.

On 22 March 1976, Savimbi began the Long March, a trek across the interior of the country with a group of supporters through the provinces of Huambo, Moxico and Kuando Kubango to the border with Namibia. The journey would last for seven months. 'The objective was to seek support and for the population to know of our existence so that we could spread our message. We talked to the people and organised them.'[34] 'We had the concept of a long war and needed to become hardened. Our time with the people was a time to educate, understand them and be useful so that they would hand over their children to the cause. We needed to sensitise them to produce and collect information.'[35] The Long March was described as one of the most important historical moments of the movement, engendering the 'realisation that people had to be empowered to save themselves'.[36]

The Long March became a moment of reflection for the leadership that allowed it to restructure the movement and reorganise itself. Savimbi was quoted as stating that the strategy had changed, and that 'from now onwards we will abandon conventional warfare for guerrilla warfare. … Now we will see who the true patriots are, because in the cities all are patriots but from today we will start walking. … Only the true revolutionaries will walk with us until the end' (Chiwale 2008: 221–2). An estimated 1,000 followers (over 800 guerrilla fighters and some 200 women and children) took part in the Long March, but only 79 survived the hardship of malnutrition, exhaustion and attacks from the MPLA (Bridgland 1987). UNITA was pushed back into using the bases that had been in operation during the first war as they retreated. From base to base, the columns of leaders, supporters and all those taking part in the Long March were under constant pursuit from the MPLA's army, the Forças Armadas Populares de Libertação de Angola (FAPLA) (MPLA's army) and from Cuban troops and airstrikes. During the march, the movement organised a party meeting in May 1976 near the Cuanza River (Chiwale 2008). During this meeting, the political bureau and central committee decided to 'reorganise the command of UNITA's army, Forças Armadas de Libertação de Angola (FALA) in order to clearly redefine the politico-military aims of our army of workers and peasants'.[37] It was during this meeting that Savimbi mentioned the need to produce a guiding manual for the guerrilla (*a Cartilha do Guerilheiro*) that would provide rules of conduct for the guerrillas and their interactions with the civilian populations.[38]

UNITA understood that the MPLA–Cuban–Soviet force was unable to win the war due to compounding factors it would later exploit. These included the vast territories that for over 500 years the Portuguese had never managed to completely control; the existence of rural populations and several ethnic groups that had no affiliation to the MPLA; an extended system of roads and railways where sabotage operations and ambushes were easily conducted; an economy destroyed by the liberation war; a civil service that was understaffed and inefficient; and high unemployment and lack of services in towns and villages. Most of all, UNITA's manifesto emphasised the 'bourgeois character of the Luanda clique unable to unite the exploited and oppressed masses; and the existence of UNITA as the vanguard of the poor and all the patriots opposed to the presence of foreign troops'.[39]

When those who survived the Long March arrived in Cuelei in August 1976, after walking for over 3,000 kilometres, the experience proved to be an enormous morale boost for the leadership. 'The march was the most profound experience of my life ... All of us who were on the march believed by the end of it that the war really could be won,' was the testimony given by Tito Chingunji (Bridgland 1987: 278). However, the Cuelei base, situated 150 kilometres from Huambo, proved to be inadequate, given its location in the central highlands, an area that was under constant threat of attacks. From there onwards, UNITA would move from military region to military region, from base to base, and would only settle permanently two years later in Jamba. In order to operationalise what the leadership had reflected upon during the march, the 4th Congress was convened in 1977.

The 4th Congress became the turning point for the restructuring of the party, as well as the defining moment in its strategies for combatting the MPLA. Over 1,600 delegates participated in the congress, held at a Catholic mission in Benda. The struggle, previously defined as one against Portuguese colonialism, was transformed into a 'struggle against Russian-Cuban' imperialism (Beck 2009). It was here that UNITA developed its 'Theory of Large Numbers', which would become a fundamental organising tool in mobilising Angolans. UNITA would rally the largest ethnic group—the Ovimbundu—as well as other smaller groups to form the governing majority in any future state. 'Many thought it was a tribalistic tendency to create Ovimbundu supremacy, but realistically only the Central Highlands could give us the men we needed to create a regular army capable of disarticulating the regime so we could move beyond the guerrilla strategy.'[40] But to achieve this UNITA needed to secure a safe rear base, one the MPLA and their foreign allies would never manage to attack. The movement would also need to operationalise the three branches of the movement—the party, the military and the administration—and create a feedback loop between them. It was at the 4th Congress that the political party structures evolved with the creation of the youth league *Juventude Revolucionária de Angola* (JURA), the women's league *Liga da Mulher Angolana* (LIMA) and trade unions (SINDACO).[41]

The UNITA society that developed became a ruralised and militarised experience, one in which 'strong political indoctrination, a blend of Maoist Stalinism and African populism ... was now directed against the "Luanda Creole dictatorship of the oppressed genuine Africans" ... As the war eliminated alternative choices, the evolution of opposition to the MPLA regime gave UNITA much of its political strength' (Messiant 1998).[42] The nationalism propagated by the MPLA was painted as one that stressed urban orientated rights and obligations, while UNITA rural nationalism was portrayed as being built on 'blood and soil' (Pereira 1994), yet neither of these two depictions was entirely representative. After fleeing south, a weakened UNITA began slowly receiving weapons from Zaire, Morocco, France and Saudi Arabia. As it began building Jamba in 1979, UNITA was also receiving support from South Africa, and by 1981 the movement had become strong enough to assume the offensive against the MPLA.[43] More importantly, it had built a strong political base and following.

Second liberation war

UNITA's second liberation war depended on building a conventional army and a political apparatus that would mirror the state in all its forms and institutions. Early on Savimbi understood that he would have to perpetuate another sense of Angolan nationalism. 'The history of nationalism everywhere seems to show that a conflict is much more intense when it expresses itself in terms of symbolic resources than in competition over mere material rewards' (Adam

1983).[44] As a result, political mobilisation and indoctrination took on a larger and more strategic role during this war, with UNITA making a huge effort to insert civilians into its political organisation and indoctrinate them to follow the political programme.

When areas were contested, or in the process of being liberated, commissars and party members would be sent to the villages to leave the message that UNITA was there to liberate and protect them. The idea was to transform the people into UNITA supporters, not to punish them. Another important element of their strategy was the need to instil fear of the MPLA and promote the perception that it was a threat, convincing communities that they needed UNITA as a defender (Pearce 2015). Once an area was liberated, chiefs would be used as the main interlocutors between the communities and UNITA leaders. If a general was from Moxico and the newly liberated area was in Moxico, he would be sent there to lead the party and its political strategy. While inserting UNITA elements among 'its' people was a strategy intended to bring immediate proximity between citizens and the movement, the ultimate ideological objective of this political education was to 'nationalise' the people and remove their 'ethnic elements'. In an interview with journalist Leon Dash in 1977, Savimbi explained the process of 'trying to get a man to switch from thinking of himself as a Cuanhama to thinking of himself first as an Angolan. It's very complicated'.[45] In a similar vein, the 'task of converting colonial subjects into national subjects— capable of responsible public conduct, loyal to the state and prepared to accept their responsibilities as the backbone of society' (Hansen and Stepputat 2005: 26) was a process UNITA took very seriously as it strove to produce a 'national people'.

In assessing the region, UNITA defined areas according to a control system: there were the government-held areas, the contested areas and the UNITA areas. 'The MPLA only controlled the provincial capitals, but the municipalities remained with us … we were in all the provinces although Huila didn't work well and Cunene and Namibe didn't have a large guerrilla presence. In 1985, we had reached the Lundas, Uige and Cabinda provinces,' explained a former commander of the Northern Front.[46] With the movement growing and the military's importance threatening to outweigh that of the political party, UNITA combined the political and the military in the role of the commander–cadre (*comandante quadro*). The military commanders' inferiority to the political commissar had proved problematic in battle conditions (Beck 2012). At a later stage, UNITA would train commanders to understand the basis of administration, political mobilisation and economic development so that this duality would never threaten operations.

UNITA's spatial organisation in the 1980s had four levels: 1) the republic, which was comprised of the liberated areas of Angola and functioned like a state with its capital in Jamba; 2) the compact guerrilla zones, which interlocked with the central state structures (in Jamba) and served as part of the first line of resettlement until people were allowed into the liberated areas; 3) the expansion zones where military operations were taking place; and 4) the line of clandestine cells that carried out infiltration and sabotage operations behind government lines. Each RM replicated the political and administrative structures that existed in Jamba, with representatives of the party and the different ministries. The military commanders of these RMs were expected to perform many duties, and because of this they had to undergo administrative training and political orientation classes. 'The objective was that when the war ended the military chiefs of yesterday would become the administrative chiefs of today ... we needed to manage a unit of 1500 troops and understand how to manage a municipality. The rest was a matter of amplification.'[47]

When expanding the bases in each of the military regions, the administrators would begin by conducting a census to gain an understanding of how many civilians lived in each area and subsequently coordinate with the military how to defend them. Each region had agricultural technicians who would teach the population to farm more effectively and yield bigger harvests. For such purposes, the bases created teaching areas and cooperatives. Everything that was captured was sent to the administrative centre to be divided among the civilians, the military and the administration. Health services were provided by mobile clinics at the village level. 'Later when MSF arrived in our areas they saw that we were already implementing important public health procedures like using dry pits as bathrooms ... our focus had been on preventive healthcare.'[48] Committees were created at different levels to coordinate the population from the region to the village. Each committee had a president who was elected by the population. The movement made sure that civilians chose their own leaders in order to maintain the necessary direct link with different communities. But to make sure that these leaders would become properly inserted into the revolution, they and their communities would be taught literacy, agriculture and the principles of the revolution.

UNITA's administration in other liberated areas was managed through local autonomous entities that were self-sufficient and ran independently of the rear base Jamba. In fact, Jamba was only the main supplier of assistance in military, political and logistical terms to the areas that were closest to the Kuando Kubango province. While food imports and other logistical supplies from South Africa were important lifelines for Jamba, areas without a direct supply link to Jamba had to depend on themselves for food and other supplies. 'There was a decree for self-sufficiency so that people would not depend on Jamba for food in the interior. Support came mostly in terms of medication from the rear base, but each military base had their own structure—hospitals, nurses, schools, food production.'[49] The idea behind this level of autonomy was tactical but also strategic. If one RM or one base within it fell, it was a self-contained incident that would not have wider implications for the organisation as a whole. The capturing of one area would not compromise the structures, information systems and functioning of the others. Each base ran as a structured entity within tight political confines, with its operational management defined in Jamba. The bases were all structured in similar ways and 'could be run by a sergeant that was almost illiterate because he would know where things had to be and operate ... everything followed a defined plan, layout and programme'. There was no room for error or interpretation.[50]

Tripartite structure: Party, administration and military

Although UNITA had emerged with separate political and military branches in the 1960s, it began to organisationally distinguish between the administrative, political/party and military roles of its leaders and members in the 1970s. These three areas were conceived as the three pillars of the movement's survival and expansion. Those that joined or were forced into UNITA had to be inserted into a socio-political framework that defined behaviour and redirected activities to suit the needs of the organisation. The military had as its leading motto for combatants 'weapon, hoe and pen', which broadly translated into the three branches of the organisation and the three areas that each UNITA member was being socialised into: rural development, fighting efficiency and education.

At the leadership level, the three areas had different commanding members: the Chief of General Staff for the army, the Head of Administration (acting like a prime minister) for civilian affairs and the Secretary General for the Party for political issues. Savimbi, as the High Commander, stood above this tripartite structure by tethering their authority to his vision and instructions, while also allowing a degree of decentralised control to trusted leaders who had shown loyalty and an ability to replicate his vision. The three structures were subordinate to the Political Bureau (the High Command) and the Central Committee (Toussie 1989). The administrative branch was comprised of several secretariats (ministries) that ran different areas and services for the civilian government in the Free Lands. Each branch and secretariat was organised vertically from the central authority in Jamba, with regional, zonal and smaller bases called 'positions' (Toussie 1989).

Military training

Before Jamba was created, military training was occurring in the Delta base near the Namibian border where the first unit of companies was organised. Although UNITA was already training forces in its existing bases in the interior of the country, it was only when they began establishing their bases in Kuando Kubango that semi-regular and regular forces began to receive training. FALA's first battalion, 'Samanjolo', was formed south of Bie and trained by Savimbi himself. While the rear base was being organised, training was being conducted in the Bico area by South African Defence Forces (SADF) trainers together with Angolan instructors. FALA organised into three types of military forces: regular, semi-regular and guerrilla columns (i.e. compact forces). The guerrilla forces were columns of thirty men, deployed rapidly and trained locally by instructors from Jamba. Semi-regular and regular forces received more complete and intensive training, which could range from a quick course of 90 days to 9 months. Troops were trained to resist hunger and thirst, and to survive long marches.

For this purpose, UNITA created the Military Instruction Directorate, which coordinated all the training given to the FALA. The directorate introduced instructors in combat forces to guarantee constant training. Their purpose was to observe the men in combat and correct them where they had failed or transfer them to form semi-regular battalions. Compact force units were used to destabilise the enemy and attack their supply and logistics lines. Semi-regular forces were used to engage directly with the enemy and secure territory. Until 1991, semi-regular forces were treated like regular forces, armed with some artillery, combat vehicles and vehicles mounted with anti-aerial and anti-tank mortars. UNITA also had between 15 and 20 commando platoons of Special Forces, each with 45 men. 'The specialised commandos were trained to destroy the enemy wherever he was and secure terrain. These forces trained for 6 to 9 months, and one man trained from these commandos had the training of 4 or 5 specialisations—infantry, working with mines, operating armaments like RPG-7, 60 and 82 Mortars ... they could do everything alone.'[51]

South African military instructors were training FALA semi-regular forces as early as 1979 at the Namibian border while Jamba was being built. As the area was being secured and training expanded to the entire RM66 (that included Jamba), several camps for military training were developed. Dotchi was where regular forces were trained, while compact forces would be trained in the *Batalhão de Instrução* neighbourhood of Jamba once the rear base was complete. The idea was never to concentrate many troops in one area. 'Dispersion was the maximum idea in Jamba so that we were not all together as aviation could strike and we needed time to manoeuvre into other areas.'[52] UNITA never allowed military instruction to occur in a political void; everything it did was deeply immersed in politics and indoctrination. After training by the South Africans was

129

concluded, 'our soldiers would go to another area and for a month we would take away the mentality that the South Africans had given them (that it was a fight against communism) and we changed it to a purely nationalistic mentality ... it was a political and philosophical change'.[53] Despite this, the SADF had a very strong influence on the design of the units. 'They had a say in who would command the troops trained by them.'[54] One commander described how 'the MPLA started using very complicated aviation—the MIGs—that had a severe psychological effect on us as they destroyed everything ... That's when we got the Stingers [from the United States] and when the first MIGs began dropping from the sky we knew the war could end soon, as their infantry would be defeated and we already controlled two-thirds of the territory'.[55] As the Americans began to take on a larger role in supporting UNITA after 1985, the movement appointed one of its officers to act as a 'handler' for the CIA representative stationed at their diplomatic mission within Jamba.

> Every day at 16:00 I would take a report to the Americans to indicate where the FAPLA were, all their movements, and they would in return give us satellite imagery. During the 1987–88 offensive, we had to report to them every time we used a Stinger missile, by recording the serial number of the weapon and the result achieved.[56]

Those interviewed echoed a strong confidence of the quality of training and the force's resulting ability to defeat a conventional army. 'UNITA was very creative in the military front—after training these forces it was very easy to send these men to train in Morocco, South Africa, Zaire and later the US, with General Charlie from the Pentagon training superior commanders and officers.'[57] Commanders were trained in Jamba, as there were better conditions for maintaining forces in such a vast area. After an officer completed his training, he was then sent back to teach his fellow officers, applying the cascade method of training at the fronts. UNITA placed instructors and commanders together in the same training courses, so that instructors could train future commanders. Their motto was '*Treinar fortemente para combater facilmente*'—Train vigorously to fight easily.

Jamba: A state of force aimed at structural efficiency

Political and spatial divisions of Jamba

Jamba, meaning 'elephant' in Umbundu, was the area chosen to build the capital of the Free Lands of Angola and UNITA's rear base (see Figure 3.1). Visitors brought in were kept under strict UNITA control. Local populations living in Jamba could only circulate in and out with special permits and documents, a tactic for preventing infiltration and escape of both enemies from the outside as well as citizens of Jamba. The area was chosen for its remoteness, as it was a considerable distance from Luanda and any airfield that the government could use as a base to destroy the movement's organisational capacity and military arsenal. The closest airport was Mavinga, but UNITA made sure that the FAPLA and their foreign allies never captured the town. The area for Jamba was also chosen because of its proximity to friendly neighbours Zambia and Namibia (then under control of apartheid South Africa) that could assist with constant supplies and where UNITA could build logistics bases.

A reconnaissance group, led by General Kanjimo, came to explore this remote, sandy area in mid-1978 where, the story went, they found the carcass of a dead elephant and decided to set up the movement's main rear base. The site needed to be large enough to support economic infrastructure, military training facilities and administrative structures. They started building the first military training facilities in 1978, with administrative structures only organised a year later, after the 12th Conference of the party.[58] After this conference, the three secretariats of political affairs, administration and portfolio of the masses would become the pillars of UNITA's governance strategy. As the structures were being built, the movement populated these previously uninhabited areas by sending word to family members in the central highlands of Huambo, Bie and Benguela to begin the long descent to the province of Kuando Kubango. Initially, Jamba was inhabited by a group of 600 supporters, elements of the leadership and their families.

Although Jamba operated in a centralised way and managed to deliver services, there was an element of mimicking the state that went beyond this functional aspect, manifesting itself is various

Figure 3.1: Map of Jamba

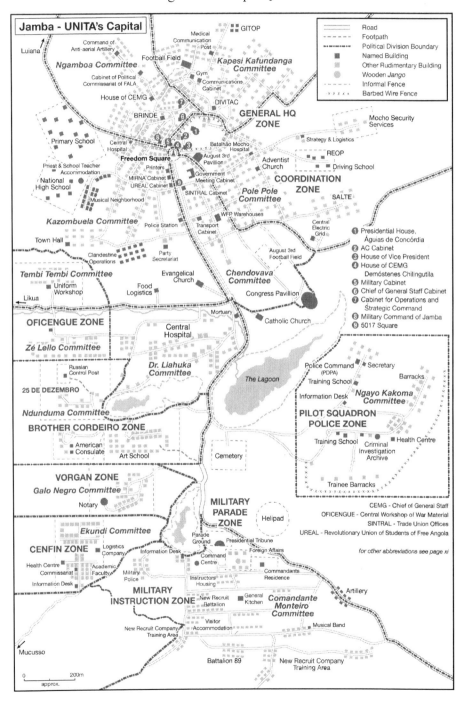

details that foreign visitors would mention when visiting Jamba. One was the traffic policeman who stood at a crossroads in Jamba (where the general headquarters and the road to the airport met), wearing white gloves and coordinating the almost non-existent traffic. Other such examples include the driving school, the military museum, the music conservatory and the public libraries. The element of imagining the state and inserting an element of urbanism in a rural rebel base was clearly in play here. This was part of UNITA's social engineering project that aimed at bridging the gap between the urban and 'civilised' elites and the rural and 'backward' populations that it governed. UNITA's symbols of 'civilisation and normality' in Jamba fed directly into the idea that a mythology of the ideal state 'empowers otherwise widely discrepant practices' when the 'myth is carefully cultivated inside the bureaucracy and … is constantly enacted through grand state spectacles, stamps, architectures, systems of etiquette' (Hansen and Stepputat 2001: 17). This also was in line with the understanding of the 'boundary-making effect of state practices' that required a constant imagining of the state through an 'invocation of the wilderness, lawlessness and savagery that not only lie outside its jurisdiction but also threaten it from within' (Das and Poole 2004: 7).

Layout and neighbourhoods

The first structure built in Jamba in August 1978 was the *Quartel General* (QG), the general headquarters. This area would develop into a large neighbourhood, cordoned off by tight security that would house the intelligence services, the party secretariat, the government ministries, strategic logistics operations, the houses of the leadership and presidential security services, the '*Mocho*'. QG would have civilian neighbourhoods that were serviced by primary schools, clinics and a high school. QG was also the site where the electricity grid was based, with electricity produced via large generators that were placed in the most strategic area of Jamba. Years later, QG would have a main square that would honour Savimbi's father, Loth Malheiro Savimbi, with a small train carriage positioned on an elevated cement platform displaying the number 5017, which was Loth's ID number when he worked on the Benguela railway.

Next to the square was the main library and the *Casa do Movimento* (Movement's House), which would become the seat of government where all the ministries operated. Near the 5017 Freedom Square were the trade unions, the Union of the Free Angolan Worker SINDACO and SINTRAL, and the Catholic and Protestant churches. Adjacent to QG was the *Coordenação* area where the main structures of the party were located, as well as the Politico-Military Commissariat.

In 1981, the second area to be developed was the *Batalhão de Instrução* (BI), the Military Instruction Zone, where recruits, whether voluntary or otherwise, would receive training, formed into battalions and units and then sent to two different military training fields near the Zambian border. As many as seven training fields were later developed, supported by mostly South African instructors. American instructors allegedly ran the Bumbu training field, and the camp in Missa was French run.[59] For every company of 150 men, there were 3 Angolan instructors and 1 South African. This level of organisation was what allowed UNITA to rapidly transform its guerrilla units into semi-regular and regular forces. As the war intensified, so did the conscription campaigns, as testified by several captured civilians living in Jamba as well as military instructors tasked with training new recruits.[60] BI would become a large neighbourhood that not only housed military structures and training facilities, but also had civilian neighbourhoods, a military band, instructors' living quarters and schools. This area housed the Foreign Ministry (the Secretariat for International Cooperation) and external relations offices for UNITA's diplomats and their foreign advisors. The secretariat was created in 1985–86 and was the body responsible for liaising with external partners, journalists and relief agencies. It held a crucial portfolio, as it expanded to have representation offices all over Africa, Europe and the United States. UNITA representatives from all the missions abroad would stay in the BI neighbourhood when they returned to their base in Jamba, and on many occasions they would come with diplomatic guests and foreign journalists to showcase the rebel capital.

Near BI was the *Parada Militar* (Military Parade zone), where large military processions would take place as a demonstration of UNITA's military might. Savimbi would discuss policy and strategy with his troops and hold several rallies as part of UNITA's constant effort to inspire its fighters and followers through carefully studied esoteric appeals.[61] All military equipment that was captured from government and Cuban forces would be paraded in this area, and every year on 13 May—the day UNITA was founded—large celebrations would be organised by the youth league JURA, the women's league LIMA and the children's league Alvorada.

The next structure to be built was the Central Hospital, which developed into a large health facility where the most severely wounded from the different fronts and military regions, as well as their commanders, would be treated. The Central Hospital serviced all the liberated areas. Close to the hospital was a neighbourhood where wounded soldiers and those maimed by mines who would receive rehabilitation therapy in the hospital facilities lived. The main hospital in Jamba was built years before the Health Secretariat was created. It was one of the pillars of Jamba's existence and an important lifeline to the struggle. It had 9 infirmaries—each with between 20 and 32 beds—and 6 surgery rooms, 3 for men and 3 for women. The hospital also had a trauma unit and an intensive care unit, maternity and paediatrics wards, a dentistry area and a physiotherapy ward for amputees and the wounded.[62] This facility had 'equipment for performing bacterial cultures, more advanced blood chemistries, serology ... and a unit for the determination of chemical weapons exposure' (Toussie 1989: 30). Throughout all the neighbourhoods, in Jamba there were clinics that assisted with smaller concerns like malaria and typhoid. Other more severe problems would be dealt with at the hospital.

Near the hospital was a lagoon which was where the first anti-aerial tower was located. The anti-aerial regimental command would later be stationed here and would be responsible for protecting Jamba from aerial bombardments. Over time, the rear base managed to erect eighteen anti-aerial towers that stood tens of metres above the tree line and had artillery pieces positioned above them to deter fighter jets. Although it is difficult to confirm, it seems that not a single plane was ever shot down by these artillery pieces, and they served more as a tactic of psychological warfare.

By the mid-1980s, all the structures were established and built in Jamba. The neighbourhood *Irmão Cordeiro* (Brother Cordeiro zone), named after a Catholic priest who had assisted Savimbi with his studies and hugely influenced him as a teenager, was where the US Embassy was positioned. 'The first US Embassy on Angolan soil was in Jamba not Luanda. The same happened with the French and the South Africans,' whose embassies were located in the 25th of December neighbourhood.[63] It was also the area next to where many of the cadre training activities occurred. UNITA maintained their allies in separate neighbourhoods as a control mechanism and to ensure that they never crossed paths unless such a meeting was planned in advance. The same occurred with the South Africans, whose embassy was near the Radio station VORGAN.

A system of bunkers (made up of buried fortified containers) in all neighbourhoods was created should the population and the leadership need to take cover from aerial attacks. More sophisticated bunkers were used in the QG by Savimbi and his commanders that served as war rooms to coordinate troops, weapons and supply movements. The leadership was instructed to have *copos* (cups) dug out for their individual use near their houses. Each *copo* would have a depth of 1 metre and was large enough to sustain one person, explained a former member of COPE and 4-star general.[64] All the other bases in the liberated areas also used this system. When government planes took off from Menongue (capital of Kuando Kubango), it would be detected by the radar system in Jamba and sirens would go off to warn the population to take cover in their bunkers or the *copos*.

Once Jamba was built, administrative divisions of local government were created to replace the village *soba* administration, focused on the municipality and neighbourhood approach. Because of its isolated location, UNITA did not need to compete with established traditional authorities in Jamba. Jamba's neighbourhoods were divided into municipalities and followed prescribed party structures of different political committees. All the neighbourhoods were equipped with primary and secondary schools, clinics to assist with minor health problems, areas for political mobilisation and feedback mechanisms that allowed the population to express grievances or inform on others that were causing problems.

The first UNITA parallel government only became fully operational in 1981, although it functioned with very rudimentary structures and lacked qualified staff to administer the functions in all the liberated areas. Numerous secretariats (ministries) were set up to develop the different governance areas. Each minister was responsible for their administrative units in Jamba and the military regions, and were held personally accountable by Savimbi for any shortcomings. These ministries delivered services to the populations in all areas under UNITA control, estimated to have numbered over 1 million in the late 1980s (Toussie 1989; Minter 1994). Jamba's population ranged from 25,000 to 100,000 in surrounding areas in Kuando Kubango. Overseeing these secretariats was a prime minister, a position occupied by Jeremias Chitunda until his death in Luanda in 1992.

At its operational peak, Jamba not only had functioning electricity and plumbing networks that provided neighbourhoods with running water and flushing toilets, but it was divided into functional areas that allowed industry, political activities, military training and cultural events to occur. By 1985, there was a specific department located in the presidency to coordinate the building of infrastructure for service provision: the *Repartição de Obras Publicas* (REOP). The water and electricity company—*Serviço de Agua e Electricidade* (SALTE)— was responsible for extending electric lines and the plumbing system from the boreholes to the population. SALTE had generator technicians who would face severe punishment if they allowed electricity to fail in Jamba, and the company was of such strategic importance that it was located in the QG neighbourhood. Jamba had a *Departamento de Direcção Geral de Pessoal*, the central registry and equivalent of a Home Affairs office, that dealt with issuing birth and marriage certificates. This department issued identity documents and driver's licences, which were later recognised by the government in Luanda. 'In 1991 during the peace process I exchanged my documents obtained in Jamba for the ones in Luanda and they were all recognised.'[65] Jamba's postal service, CITAL, had a system of postmen who ensured that mail was delivered and sent from the rear base to other UNITA military regions.

Relocation and population movements

Jamba needed a population to inhabit it. This led UNITA to begin a coordinated campaign of bringing people under its control and into the liberated areas. When word was sent out that people could find safety and services at the bases of Kuando Kubango, many came voluntarily from the traditional UNITA areas of the Central Highlands. UNITA leaders called for their families to start the weeks-long descent to Jamba, and many mobilised their extended families and communities. This type of mobilisation was like the recruitment strategy of calling on the pre-existing social ties of the Ovimbundu during the first war. Men and women volunteered to join the movement, following other family or community members, motivated by their kinship and ethno-linguistic ties to the organisation. However, attacks and Cuban offensives in the Central Highlands between 1976 and 1979 also contributed to an exodus of people fleeing south to safer areas. But as the civil war developed and the need to secure more followers and fighters emerged, UNITA developed a strategy of kidnapping people and bringing them under armed guard to the rear base and other liberated areas. Many of those captured were children who would be educated into UNITA's social order by being enrolled in the boarding schools in Jamba and then trained to join the armed forces. In these population sweeps, many MPLA supporters and FAPLA soldiers were captured, which meant that they would then find themselves in re-education centres and spending months in prisons. 'When people were captured, they'd first stay in the guerrilla support bases while they were being politically assimilated. Re-education was done at the military bases with the help of the party secretariat.'[66]

UNITA employed other methods of repopulation and building a large civilian base in its liberated areas, with *sobas* and village leaders choosing to bring their people under the movement. The allure of having access to services and other benefits outweighed the level of control and repression they were subjected to. Moving an entire population to an area under UNITA protection also minimised the risk of attacks had they remained in contested areas. *Sobas* were used to mobilise recruits for the army, with UNITA officials collecting the young men and women from the villages and taking them to the rear base for training. This forced recruitment of adolescents would become an important strategy for securing long-term combatants (Beck 2009).

Logistics

Around Jamba many logistics centres were operating, mostly because of their proximity to the border with Namibia. UNITA had over thirty smaller logistics centres in the liberated areas (James 2011) where trucks, ferries and porters would take supplies for civilians and the military throughout its territory.[67] The General Logistics Directorate was the organ responsible for collecting and distributing material. UNITA's most important logistical operations area was in Mucusse (Kakuxi), and it operated from 1978 until 1990. The Directorate ensured that the movement had all the supplies it required at the military and civilian level. At the logistics centres, items were organised into different centres (one for the collections of clothes, one for military support, among others). Everything had to be accounted for according to the following percentages determined by the leadership: 40% was tactical and 30% was strategic, and the remaining 30% was divided into 10% for reserve and 20% for commerce and trade with different communities. The strategic portion was apportioned to the fronts and the people in the rear; the tactical portion was considered working capital and was also divided between the military and the populations at the rear.[68] The reserve would not be distributed unless Savimbi gave the order.

Trade was regulated by the 'Kwatcha' stores that were run by the party. Although commerce was infrequent, UNITA maintained a mobile trading system where farmers could exchange surplus food for clothes, shoes, batteries, radios and other materials (Toussie 1989). Although some of these materials came as external assistance from South Africa and as a result of trade and purchases made by the movement, the largest source of supply was still the materials captured from the enemy. UNITA would use its guerrilla forces to target supply routes of the FAPLA with the aim of depriving troops of their materials and therefore weakening their position while simultaneously supplying FALA with new material.

Given the extension of its territory, UNITA had to devise ways of supporting the fronts without any initial or frequent aerial support. Transportation of goods from Jamba and its logistical bases on the Namibian border to the other liberated areas meant the movement would have to establish complex distribution systems. The Savimbi Trail, akin to the famous Ho Chi Minh trail during the Vietnam War, started in Mavinga near Jamba and went 130 kilometres up north towards the Moxico province. It functioned as the logistical supply lifeline to the armed forces and the administration (Bridgland 1986). The objective was to reach the Benguela railway, 800 kilometres into the interior of Angola, so that troops could be supported into consolidating positions. However, given the difficulty of the terrain and lack of infrastructure, most of the distribution had to occur using heavy trucks. Depending on the proximity and security of the fronts, columns of Samy and other cars would be organised to transport goods to different bases. UNITA's fleet of cars from South Africa—and the hundreds of captured vehicles of Polish, Soviet and Czech origin—were vital to the movement's capacity to keep the logistics flowing.

> Savimbi taught us that we should never send one car full of only one thing—so each Samy vehicle would take cans, maize, uniforms, weapons—so that if there was an attack all the other cargos could be integrated fully and we wouldn't lose our entire supply of uniforms all at once.[69]

Cars would reach the limit of the Kuando Kubango perimeter on the border with Bie province and the eastern belt of the Alto Zambesi (Cazombo), and from there the walking columns would take over. The cars would still reach the units operating near Mavinga, Lumbala N'guimbo and Menongue, but beyond those areas people would have to take the materials by foot to the different bases. Columns would take the cargo to their designated area and then pass on the materials to the receiving column that would continue along the trail. These were large columns, mostly comprised of villagers, that would spend weeks at a time walking for hundreds of kilometres. If they were walking to consolidated and liberated areas, then they would proceed in groups of 100;

if they were walking into zones where attacks were happening, columns would be much smaller in size.[70]

Economic programme: The Angolan road to national recovery

The experience of building and maintaining Jamba helped UNITA define the economic programme and development tenets that it would later use to campaign during the 1992 elections. In 1983, UNITA came out with a publication called 'The Angolan Road to National Recovery', published in Jamba, where it explained the principles of its reconstruction and economic programme. The development of human resources was a prerequisite for the second liberation, meaning UNITA had taken on the task of elevating the 'technical, professional, political and cultural level of the Angolan worker ... transforming workers through education, training and organisation'.[71] It believed that

> Education ... [was] key in raising the level of productivity and the standard of living; in unifying the country and bridging social, cultural and class differences; in raising the national consciousness ... Democratized education refers to the equality of opportunity for all school age children to attend schools at all levels, including university.[72]

In order to achieve this nationally, UNITA needed to achieve it in the liberated areas and more specifically to design its model and programme of services in Jamba.

The focus on rural development and 'the experiment of creating Jamba in an uninhabited area—that had sandy soil and little arable land, was characterized by extreme temperatures of desert like fluctuations, and was a bush area where wild animals roamed—proved that any area in Angola could be developed'.[73] UNITA advocated that in peacetime the state would need to embark on a rural development programme, given that 'most Angolans (up to 80%) were rural, illiterate, engaged largely in subsistence farming, with no services (no decent housing, no water supply, no electricity, no libraries, no recreational facilities, no hospitals, inadequate schools, no roads, no postal services, no telephone)'.[74] The movement wanted to reverse the trend of rural–urban migration and allow for the return of urbanised populations to rural areas, to what would be called 'socio-cultural gravitational centres'. This meant redefining the infrastructure and social landscape of the country to factor in the characteristics of the rural majority. The plan was ambitious, but it was never implemented, largely because war broke out again in 1992, but also because UNITA never took over the formal state. However, what the movement managed to achieve in the socio-economic area during the 1980s showed an adherence to this programme in the Free Lands.

Education system and leadership schools

The educational system was premised on giving basic education to all sectors of society—traditional authorities, soldiers, civilians and children—of the liberated areas. This led UNITA to devise a system of education that saw the establishment of schools in all the RMs, Jamba and the satellite bases, as well as the establishment of specialised schools for leadership and cadre training. From the beginning of the second war, literacy became mandatory in UNITA areas. The idea was to allow people to develop themselves: 'Man is the measure of everything that can be achieved on earth, and we have to enrich and cultivate him.'[75]

The National Secretariat for Education had three different directorates: for primary education, for the *Primeiro ciclo* (ages 6–9) and for the *Segundo and Terceiro ciclos* (until the age of 14).

> We didn't want to make reforms to the Portuguese schooling system because we thought it wasn't necessary to nationalise the schooling—it was preferable to know Portuguese as spoken by Camões and Gil Vicente[76]—and the manuals were conceived by people that had a lot of experience with the Portuguese schooling system. What we did was complement it with Universal History.[77]

Throughout the 1980s, the system developed into an arrangement of institutes and secondary schools run by priests, pastors, former Portuguese colonial teachers and Angolan teachers. In 1988, there were reportedly 975 primary schools and 22 secondary schools

(Minter 1994), an estimated 7,130 teachers and 225,000 students in the UNITA areas (James 2011). Although the schools followed the Portuguese curriculum, classes were also taught in several national languages. 'If people wanted to learn in Chokwe, Nganguela, Kimbundu and Kikongo, not only in Umbundu, they could … UNITA was not tribalistic because it brought everyone together from all over the country.'[78]

One of the first schools in the vicinity of Jamba was the Polyvalent Institute founded in 1979 and filled with teachers and pastors from the Dondi mission of Huambo.[79] Although some teachers and pastors came voluntarily, the majority were brought by force. Initially located in Bico, the Institute was relocated to Catapi, Luengue and then Chibujango as more free territory was secured. It taught hundreds of UNITA members and civilians along the way. The Institute gave classes in Portuguese and local languages, and from the fifth year onwards taught in English and French as well.

Until UNITA was able to begin training civilians and the wives of military personnel, teachers were initially recruited from the old missions and former public servants of the colonial days. A captured priest described:

> the pastors identified the curriculum that had to be taught in the schools—Portuguese, French, English, Latin, biology, universal history etc. … When I got to Jamba in 1982, I found many priests that had been captured except two that voluntarily went to Jamba—these were father Baptista Catombela [from Andulo] and father Damião [from Katchiungo]. Father Baptista knew Savimbi and was part of the transitional government helping with the education directorate on UNITA's side in the 1970s.[80]

School materials would mostly come from South Africa and Portugal, but at the Jamba Printing Press books and brochures on different subjects were being produced for local consumption. Jamba had connections with the Portuguese high school in the Congolese capital Kinshasa, and it received the school's programmes and curricula to assist with the design of its own schooling system.[81] In Jamba and other liberated areas, schools only taught until the 9th year (14 years old). The best students would be selected to study at the high schools in the Mavinga area and Boa Esperança in Licua, and would then study at the Portuguese school in Kinshasa. From there, they would proceed with a full scholarship to schools in Portugal, Senegal, France, Côte d'Ivoire or the United States, explained a student who had studied abroad in this scholarship programme.[82] 'If the student performed well they'd give him a certificate from Kinshasa, as students couldn't continue studying abroad with documents issued by UNITA.'[83] From 1988, the school in Kinshasa was no longer used as the vehicle to send students out, and the top tier of high school graduates would go directly to Portugal, the United States and France. This was assisted by the diplomatic effort of UNITA's diplomatic representations abroad.

The *Centro de Formação Integral da Juventude* (Centre for the Formation of the Youth) (CENFIN), created in May 1981, was a key institute in Jamba. 'CENFIN became a source of teachers and students—it was a nucleus to ensure continuity of UNITA's vision.'[84] It was a military academy divided into 6 companies (A through F), with each having between 300 and 400 students. It was initially constituted as a response to the influx of children and orphans that came from the interior. Thousands of students came to study at this male boarding school, either sent by their parents or brought by troops. Orphaned children captured in *recolhas* (civilian capturing rounds) would study at CENFIN and be schooled in the principles of military training. A CENFIN student described how 'to eat we had to march to the kitchen'.[85] Students were trained in multiple subjects that ranged from politics and the military to arts and culture, mechanics, tailoring and agriculture. 'Each company had a political and a paramilitary instructor ... and a mother figure [normally a LIMA lady] to give moral and social support.'[86] The LIMA 'mothers' would look after five children in each of the boarding houses until they turned 14. At the age of 15, the children would begin receiving basic paramilitary training and learn about guerrilla warfare and basic notions of defence.

UNITA prioritised leadership and cadre training during the second war. As early as 1975, Savimbi was already preparing staff to play a bigger role in the future of Angola by training them in Masside in Moxico province. However, it was only in 1983 that these leadership schools were extended to cadre training programmes. The main leadership school—the *Centro de Formação Comandante Kapese Kafundanga* (CEKK)—operated from 1981 to 1991 and was where military commanders and local administrators and commissars were trained. CEKK also prepared its students to become future administrators in a time of peace. Savimbi taught most courses at CEKK, although several members of the leadership who held doctorates and university degrees would also lecture. Over time, the curriculum developed into dealing with complex issues of political negotiation, party organisation and political mobilisation, social theory, public administration, law and philosophy.[87]

Training and industry

Part of UNITA's plan to change Angola and rebuild it after the war entailed equipping a generation of Angolans with the technical know-how for reconstruction and economic development. Investment in human capital was one area the movement went to great lengths to develop. Civilians were selected to receive training at the industrial school of Nova Aurora, created in 1986 and located forty kilometres outside of Jamba. Angolan colonial teachers and technical experts would give training in as diverse areas as mechanics, electrician training, carpentry and plumbing, among others. Nova Aurora was conceived to lead the self-sufficiency drive of the liberated areas, and it had a sawmill that employed over 300 workers who prepared hardwood for export in Namibia.[88]

Other areas of expertise were taught at the Technical School for Agriculture and Livestock (ETAPE), created in 1985 and located in the 3rd of August area near Jamba. At ETAPE, trainees would learn about different farming techniques, irrigation mechanisms and mechanical farming, with courses lasting 2 years. The school managed to train over 2,250 medium and basic agricultural experts (*técnicos*) who were later deployed to all the liberated areas to guarantee food self-sufficiency. The Antonio Capalala School near Rivungu was created in 1983 to train nurses and health professionals. Students were awarded nursing certificates after eighteen months of training and six months of practical work, with courses taught by Angolans but also South Africans.[89] Capalala later developed a laboratory-training programme and followed the curriculum of the World Health Organization for 'public health laboratories in the Developing World' (Toussie 1989: 33). Over time, UNITA would create eight health worker training schools in the liberated areas that provided two-year courses for medics and other health technicians. 'The medics would receive instruction in elements of anatomy, pathology, pharmacology, first aid, and public health' (Toussie 1989: 33). Other professional training institutes were developed to prepare a UNITA civil service. A secretariat school run by Ana Junjuvili trained women for 12 months to work as personal assistants and secretaries in the UNITA administration, teaching them Portuguese, maths, French, stenography and dactylography. Several of its teachers carried diplomas from schools in Paris and Abidjan (Muekalia 2015).

The Central Workshop of War Material (OFICENGUE) in Jamba was the industrial complex where weapons captured from the enemy would be restored and recuperated. The workshop began operating in 1978, although it only had two vices and 164 men to assist with making the necessary transformations of the armament to repair weapons. 'Before I went to the bush, I had been a metalworker in the CFB railway and that's why I was sent to work in this workshop. We made adaptations of vehicles so we could mount weapons. We repaired all sorts of weapons—carabines, AK-47s and even T-32 and T-55 tanks.'[90] It developed into a war material workshop where artillery cannons F76mm, BM21 and BM14, as well as other weapons, could be repaired. 'A chief mechanic at one workshop devised a new kind of a rocket launcher from parts taken from helicopter firing pods' (Burke 1984: 21). Between 1984 and 1989, the workshop had over 600 people working there from 7 am to midnight. During military offences, the workshop would operate 24 hours a day.

OFICENGUE was divided into 1) the section for weapons, 2) the workshop that made handles for weapons out of wood, as well as prostheses which were sent to the hospital, 3) the electric section in charge of the large generators, which also repaired weapons that had electric components, 4) the metal/ironworks section, 5) the carpentry section that made furniture and 6) the crafts section that made presents for international visitors or for when Savimbi would go on state visits. 'We sent several wood carved gifts to the White House when Savimbi visited President Reagan'.[91] The transformations that many of these war materials underwent meant that people living in Jamba were able to have functioning tools and materials from the industrial complex serve as household items. Next to the OFICENGUE was the General Factory of Fatigues where 500 machines, each of them assigned two tailors who would switch between 12 hour shifts, would produce military uniforms 24/7 to send to the fronts. A vital part of UNITA's order was that its soldiers always be presented in professional gear and proper uniforms. 'All regular troops [wore] leather boots and locally made uniforms consisting of khaki olive-greens, or dark blue depending on the unit' (Burke 1984: 21).

Agriculture

UNITA's economic programme focused on rural development and community farming. In 1975, the movement was already locating the technical staff at a national level in the liberated areas so that they could start developing demonstration camps to assist communities in enhancing their crop production. 'Because we hardly had any staff and had one technician per 100 farmers, we decided to organise seminars to talk about cultivating, combating plagues and also home economics so that people understood they could support the family and sell the surplus.'[92] The system around Jamba was organised in a more centralised manner with UNITA farms and other joint ventures with local villages (Stuvoy 2002), supervised from Jamba by the Agricultural Secretariat. The secretariat further provided maintenance of the large farms, selected the agricultural sites for resettlement of displaced populations and allocated land (Toussie 1989). UNITA would supply these relocated people with a plot of land, seeds, tools and food until the first harvest, so that they could farm the land and later contribute to the food stalls (Toussie 1989). Throughout the liberated areas but especially in Kuando Kubango, UNITA introduced several crops to areas that hadn't grown them before.

The Agricultural Secretariat had regional units throughout the liberated areas that would follow different programmes. In areas close to the frontlines, the population was expected to contribute food. Bridgland described how in 1981 resistance collectives, one of the joint-venture initiatives between UNITA and the population, operated by bringing chiefs under UNITA areas and having villagers work a day a week in these collectives and in exchange being allowed to work their private plots using the collective's tractors. The movement claimed to have had nine of these collective farms at the time, yielding considerable harvests. In 1981, one of these resistance collectives was reported to have harvested 150 tonnes of maize from fifty-four hectares of land (Bridgland 1986), and the harvest projected for 1982 exceeded 350 tonnes from an expanded area of 100 hectares. Large grain storage facilities were kept away from the fronts, located in Mavinga, Lomba and Kueyo and with a total storage capacity of 5,000 tonnes (Toussie 1989).

Production centres were opened in different locations around Jamba, and in Benda, Capacala, Xilemba, Xicosi and Lomba, supported by tractors and irrigation systems that allowed for the farming of beans, corn, soya, sweet potato and horticulture.[93] It was unclear if these production centres were initially just providing food for the armed forces or if they were also tending to civilians' needs. It seemed, however, that Jamba mostly sourced its food items from Namibia and South Africa, and some testimonies pointed to agricultural activities only beginning in the outskirts of Jamba in 1988 with the impending withdrawal of support from Pretoria.[94] Agricultural centres were reported to have existed around Kuando Kubango in 1984, but they operated more like demonstration areas than large farming enterprises. Food distribution in Jamba was done every two weeks through neighbourhood committees that were responsible for the equitable distribution of food to each household. Each committee was comprised of 150 people, and they would calculate the amounts necessary for distribution. Everyone would receive 1 kilogramme of maize flour and rice, which corresponded to 4 days' worth of food.

In 1983, the Ministry of Agriculture under Engineer Salupeto Pena began investing in training experts and in diversifying production areas. 'He instilled a more scientific method of work in the existing staff and also ensured that they understood the nature of the soil in UNITA territory by personally surveying all the liberated areas.'[95] The ministry did a reconnaissance of the land, soil and climates, dividing them into categories: 1) clay-like soil near rivers and lagoons, which was used for vegetables and cereals, 2) high ground where corn, massango and massambala (more resistant forms of maize) was grown and 3) other types of soils. As a result, the liberated areas were divided into 30 different agricultural zones where different crops, techniques and systems of agriculture were introduced. In the 1990s, UNITA was operating 53 collective farms, totalling 25,000 hectares, and producing maize, vegetables and other foodstuffs (James 2011).

The Ministry sent the agricultural experts trained at ETAPE to all the liberated areas. The experts had different levels and ranged from the medium expert (equivalent to the former regents, with 15 years of experience), the base expert, individual promoters of agriculture and rural mobilisers. Once trained, they would be distributed in the politico-administrative coordination centres that existed in the south, centre, north, east and west of the country— with expansion into Cabinda. They created demonstration sites in each village and experimentation camps in each sector. 'They'd teach the techniques of cultivation and agriculture and introduced scientific knowledge regarding the choice of land, the type of plants that each land could support, the harvests etc.'[96] These agricultural experts would recruit the community leaders and empower them to become the mobilisers and promoters of these initiatives in order to win the population over to the new ideas and methods.[97]

> The *sobas* were the opinion leaders of the communities and were also trained at ETAPE so that there was effective coordination of agricultural activities. ... The key to our success was political mobilisation—the idea that we could count only on our own people, and people mobilised everything for the troops. We operated under an iron-like discipline.[98]

One of UNITA's biggest failings in the second war was its inability or unwillingness to use money. While trade was conducted in other liberated areas, this was not the case in Jamba, and the UNITA leaders spent almost two decades not knowing what monetary policy was. 'I didn't know what money was and what it meant—this was what we lacked in our state.'[99] This was the foundation of a utopian system where there was no commerce (although there was a barter system), no currency, salaries were not paid and citizens would 'contribute according to their capacities and receive according to their needs' (Roque et al. 1988: 430).[100] Only a few members of UNITA's leadership dealt with money, in particular those who were in the diplomatic sphere and those dealing with logistics.[101] Internal sources of revenue were strictly controlled.

Resource extraction

Resource extraction and UNITA's war economy were dominated by the Ministry of Natural Resources (MIRNA). This ministry developed and expanded into the third war (1992–2002) as UNITA faced the withdrawal of major sources of external support. Even when UNITA was receiving significant external support, it still devised an alternative economic system, which was the basis from which the movement's war economy in the 1990s emerged (Stuvoy 2002). By 1979, the movement was using multiple supply routes to export internally generated sources of revenue: ivory, gold, rhino horn and animal skins (Stuvoy 2002). From the beginning, MIRNA operated with a hierarchical structure that was not dissimilar to that of other ministries. Its minister was responsible for coordinating with and reporting to command structure (COPE), while the vice minister coordinated activities at the field level in different areas of resource exploration. Below him, the director general gave tactical instructions to the MIRNA delegates and articulated the work of all the delegates in the different fields of resource extraction. Delegates were based at the RM level and specialised in prospecting for gold, diamonds, ivory, animal skins, timber and so on. These men were trained in France, South Africa and Côte d'Ivoire. Given the number of resources available throughout the liberated areas, every front and its respective commander had to respect the areas determined for resource exploration and ensure that enough troops were deployed to protect them.

At the 5th Congress in 1982, the first diamonds were identified in Kuando Kubango near the Chimbunjango River close to Mavinga.

They were of poor quality, so their trade wasn't able to sustain the war, but it was sufficient to sustain diplomatic efforts.[102] By 1983, UNITA reportedly had foreign diamond merchants flying into Jamba (Bridgland 1986), although it was unclear how the movement first began to export diamonds. UNITA was thought to have used its access to South Africa to reach international diamond markets, but it also could have relied on its Zairean supply routes (Cilliers and Dietrich 2000; Bridgland 1986). These were the initial stages of the movement's diamond empire, which would develop exponentially during the 1990s.[103] UNITA claimed that by 1986 it had exported US$386 million in diamonds from mines they had attacked and from within the liberated areas.[104] The increase in the movement's diamond revenues in the 1990s was concurrent with the capturing of mines from government areas and the expansion of MIRNA into the Lunda Norte and Lunda Sul, Kwanza Sul and Bie provinces. It was only in 1992 that UNITA began to trade in diamonds on a mass scale and the diamond trade took on an industrial capacity (Cilliers and Dietrich 2000).[105] UNITA's war economy in the third war would go on to change significantly (and is not covered here).

Healthcare system

Delivery of healthcare services was functional in UNITA areas even though the movement spent many years without any external help in this sector. An assessment by the US State Department in 1989 noted that the UNITA healthcare system was 'the most complex and widespread civilian administration' (Toussie 1989: 29). Civilian health units existed in the liberated areas but were also run in the contested areas. UNITA began its healthcare programme in the early 1970s before independence with Eduardo Sakuanda, a trained nurse from the missions, conducting rudimentary surgeries and amputations. 'By 1976 we included the delivery of health in our political campaigns,' explained the former Health Minister.[106] The movement first began to structure the health services for the military, coordinated by ex-Portuguese military officers who helped train people. Then, faced with having to provide for large numbers of civilians, UNITA began to devise strategies to deliver civilian health services. The system separated the military and civilian health

151

areas, each of which had its own staff, although the infrastructure was shared.

Médecins Sans Frontières (MSF) began to help the movement in 1983, providing a doctor and a team of nurses and supplying the health staff in the Capacala Hospital with some medication. 'Luanda called them the white coated mercenaries.'[107] MSF trained medical staff, assisted those wounded in battle and assisted in all health development areas. Anabela Muekalia, assigned as a translator to the MSF team, described in 1984 how a permanent support group led by Captain Amos Chissende accompanied the medical team of one doctor, a lab technician, a nurse and a midwife. This support group consisted of ten soldiers, a cook with three helpers and a radio team. In later years, the Red Cross, International Medical Corps and Médecins du Monde would assist UNITA, but the needs of the liberated areas far exceeded the assistance given. There were not enough doctors. UNITA only had a few trained doctors, and most of the healthcare services—including lifesaving surgeries—were done either by nurses or by *clinicos* (medical assistants). It was these assistant doctors that led the hospitals and the clinics throughout UNITA areas.[108]

The Health Secretariat was set up in 1988 in Jamba and was run by Dr Ruben Sikato, one of UNITA's only doctors. Dr Carlos Morgado was the medic in charge of military healthcare and was Savimbi's personal physician. All the doctors had received their medical degrees from Portugal, but the equipment and medication that they used was bought in South Africa. 'Timber was sold and exported to Namibia as one of the ways we devised to start buying medication.'[109] The Health Secretariat became the main depository for medication and was responsible for distributing supplies and managing personnel at the national level, even though the different RMs had semi-autonomous healthcare systems. The ministry estimated that it provided health services to over 500,000 people in the liberated areas. All medical treatment and medication were free of charge, given that money was not used in the liberated territory of Angola. Neonatal and pregnancy assistance was provided for all women. UNITA aimed to provide inpatient delivery services to all pregnant women who would 'stay in hospital from 7 to 30 days before delivery and up to 7 days following delivery for uncomplicated pregnancies' (Toussie 1989: 35). In 1988, a training centre was set up around Mavinga, while an ontological health code was also being devised. All health professionals of the fronts and zones were called to Kuando Kubango province to become familiarised with the methodology used and the hierarchy installed under the national Health Secretariat. Training was then expanded at each military region. 'Physicians, nurses, clinicians, midwives, and supervisory technicians received formal training in UNITA's (8 training) schools and abroad' (Toussie 1989: 33).

While Jamba had a central hospital, other hospitals and clinics existed throughout the liberated areas. The number of medical staff was difficult to ascertain fully, but rough estimates are that military health services could have had 3,000 nurses and civilian health services 3,800 nurses (Minter 1994). UNITA reported in 1989 that it had 8,608 health workers, of which 55% were within civilian jurisdiction (Toussie 1989). Three different types of medical units operated throughout the liberated territories: central hospitals, with a capacity of 200 beds and equipped to conduct surgeries; regional hospitals, each with a capacity for 150 patients and equipped for small procedures; and over 500 clinics that assisted in neonatal care and basic health services (Roque et al. 1988). In 1983, UNITA claimed to run 5 central hospitals and 22 regional hospitals, and to be treating over 67,000 people every 6 months (Barata-Feyo 1985). By 1989, the movement ran 8 central hospitals, 28 regional hospitals and 35 local hospitals (Toussie 1989). Because of the large presence of anti-personnel mines, there was a large number of amputees in the region. UNITA ran a prosthesis factory in Jamba where amputees used locally sourced materials (wood and rubber) to make prostheses. The factory in Biongue, several kilometres from Jamba, was assisted by a Belgium NGO, and would become the main site where prostheses were made.[110] The Biongue base had over 3,500 civilians and catered for 1,800 amputees, who were rehabilitated physically but were also trained in other work areas to which they then contributed at the rear base (Roque et al. 1988).

A politically structured and controlled environment

A key element of UNITA's social order was its ability to control the discourse, history and worldview of its followers.[111] The movement achieved this through extensive programmes of acculturation and education, through the control of information and through the 'normalisation' of daily life. UNITA valued instances where soldiers and civilians could experience moments of recreation and normalcy to envisage how life would be during peacetime. This was part of the movement's strategy to win the hearts and minds of the population. UNITA's national radio station VORGAN played a fundamental role in this, while other mechanisms provided necessary measures for countering any creeping doubts or potential dissent among the population. UNITA's intelligence services and communications systems were some of its strongest organisational aspects.

The Information Secretariat and VORGAN Radio

UNITA's propaganda strategy became more clearly defined in 1977, during the 4th Congress. 'In the mountains in Huambo we produced pamphlets that even arrived in Luanda ... We produced a periodical called *Grito da Liberdade* [Freedom Cry] that reached the urban centres.'[112] The propaganda division developed into a large organisation with different sections for spoken, written, audiovisual and psychological operations propaganda. It later used the printing press in Jamba to produce the necessary material. 'I was a commissar, and my specialty was in military propaganda in psychological operations (I trained with the Brazilians) to produce propaganda material through the printers in Jamba and also through VORGAN in the *Patria Livre* programme.'[113]

UNITA's Information Secretariat was responsible for managing information within and outside Angola. The *Voz da Resistência do Galo Negro* (Voice of the Resistance of the Black Cockerel), VORGAN, was UNITA's radio station, a powerful propaganda tool that allowed the movement to communicate to all the provinces of Angola. It began operating from Namibia and first aired on 4 January 1979. Its programmes reported on battlefield losses with the intention of breaking the spirit of the enemy, but they were also used to explain

UNITA's cause. In 1988, VORGAN began operating with the assistance of technology and equipment from the CIA, and would completely revolutionise the movement's ability to communicate with Angolans outside of the liberated areas. It had two large transmitters, each with three antenna towers, and was powered by two generators.[114] VORGAN functioned in all the liberated areas, with 280 radio stations located throughout the country and cared for by over 1,400 radio technicians. The technology was so strategically sensitive that security in the VORGAN compound in Jamba was very tight, and access was restricted to only a few technicians: 'no one else, not even those that worked directly in Savimbi's office, could access the transmitters area'.[115] 'In 1999, when UNITA began to abandon Jamba ahead of the military offensive that would retake it, among the structures that were destroyed with explosives were the VORGAN transmitters.'[116]

The radio station was thought to have operated using three frequencies assigned by the Voice of America: from 6:00 am to noon (9.700 kHz frequency), from noon to 19:00 (11.830 kHz) and from 19:00 onwards (7.100 kHz) (Albuquerque 2002). It was inaugurated on 8 May 1988 in its newly refurbished cement installations in Jamba and broadcast 24 hours a day with different news, cultural and political programmes. One programme that explained the revolution was 'Galo Negro—the Awakening of a New Dawn for Angola'. All programmes passed through the Information Secretariat to check for content. Others were broadcasted in Portuguese and all the national languages. There was a centre within the VORGAN compound that received international news from all the major news agencies in Europe, the United States and Africa, and transmitted it throughout Angola. At the VORGAN installations was the Kwatcha UNITA Press (KUPA) that would launch a monthly international bulletin in three foreign languages (Roque et al. 1988). KUPA would send dispatches all over the world to UNITA diplomatic missions on a daily basis. Kwatcha (meaning 'wake up' in Umbundu) News then began producing an official bimonthly newsletter of the Free Angola Information Service, which operated from Washington.

Communication system and intelligence

Initially, UNITA's communication system was very rudimentary, using couriers to carry messages between the commands in 1976/77. After a few years, the first radios were captured, but UNITA was still unable to function without the courier messenger system. In 1978, 'UNITA forces, equipped with handheld Racal radios, used coded messages to remain in daily contact with all their units and bases over a 900-set two-way radio network' (Burke 1984: 21). UNITA was able to build a stable base of communications run by General Andrade, who worked to streamline communications for Savimbi and his commanders, and to intercept the enemy's communications. In 1979/80, the Directorate for Administration of Transmissions was already functioning and had a transmissions centre that was subdivided into: 1) cryptography, a department known as 'The Kitchen' where messages were coded and decoded; and 2) an explorations and radio area that did reception and transmission of messages. The transmissions centre had an Office of Studies and Analysis that dealt with the production of coding systems.

The communication structure was divided into different regions and organised through networks that covered different liberated areas. 'Each network covered four RMs, and each of these regions also had their own sectors. Each sector controlled an area and different codes were devised for each of the regions—so we could maintain security in information, and if this was captured the rest of the country would not be exposed and fragile.'[117] The main idea behind the system was to centralise information in the office of the President and the Party, so that he was aware of everything that occurred in the liberated areas. Daily messages were sent with different levels of urgency. 'Information had to come in two or three times a day. Reports were laid out by priorities and Savimbi read absolutely everything and would respond by recording orders and giving orientations to the country and abroad. These recordings would then go to communications and be transcribed into a written document.'[118] By 1990, UNITA had over 1,000 operators working in the five different sectors of communications, in what had become a complex system of communications and interception for different areas and intelligence fields.

The communications structure and system for UNITA was divided into five large areas: the Directorate General (DG) located in Jamba, the High Commanders communications, the Office of Interceptions (GITOP), the intelligence service (BRINDE) and Special Operations. Initially, the DG structure of communications was developed in two areas in Jamba and later in four different military regions in the centre of the country (RM 50/35/19/71) to support the military units. The motto of communications was 'Speed and Secrecy'—efficiency in coding and secrecy as to who had access to the information.

Working in interception was the *Gabinete de Intercepção Tecnico e Operacional* (Office of Operational and Technical Interception) (GITOP). 'With GITOP we managed to intercept communications in Russian, French, Spanish and English to know the strategy of the enemy.'[119] GITOP had three large areas: 1) wiretap/listening, where radio workshops would disable the broadcast system so that the radios only had receivers; 2) decoding, where messages at the wiretap section would be decoded and clarified; and 3) study and analysis of enemy systems of communication. At the communications centre in Jamba, there was also a training facility for DG and GITOP operators, who would then proceed to specialise in either wiretaps, decoding, finding patterns or analysis. Operators were also sent with the different military units.

The third area of communication was BRINDE (see below), which had its own structrure and staff, and dealt with communication for the intelligence and security services. This large structure controlled thousands of people, as each liberated area had its own BRINDE representation in the military regions. The fourth area was Special Operations, which operated in Rundu from 1984–89. The Cuito Cuanavale offensives of 1987/88 had special communications centres that worked with the South Africans to support the troops on the ground and collect information. This information was then passed to the SADF, and airplanes were sent to destroy certain targets.

The fifth area for communications was that of the High Commander. For several years, there had been a separate centre for transmissions that dealt only with messages for Savimbi's office, but it took on a more structured form in 1989/90 when it became the Division for the Transmissions of the High Commanders (*Divisão de Transmissões do Alto Commandante*) (DIVITAC). DIVITAC had two areas of internal communication: first, when the president spoke to the politico-administrative structures and as commander for the military; and second, for external communication, whose operations were turned towards diplomacy and UNITA representatives worldwide. After 1992, during the third war, the communication system operated in a more limited way. While GITOP was moved to Bailundo in 1993/94, DIVITAC was taken out of Angola and operated from Côte d'Ivoire.

Control mechanisms, re-education and justice

UNITA didn't develop a complex justice system with courts to ensure peace in liberated territories. Rather, it depended on commissions to intervene and deal with problems as they emerged. Society in Jamba and the surrounding areas was so controlled that there wasn't much room for intercommunal conflict or any other social disorder to occur and threaten stability. When such episodes did occur, they were dealt with very harshly to ensure that people would remember the repercussions of acting against the system. 'If there were disputes, the leadership would be consulted and they would be resolved via political dialogue and consensus. The party was the organ to resolve problems.'[120] The Ministry of Justice was only created in 1991 at the 7th Congress, ahead of the peace agreement, with the formal separation of civilian and military justice systems. There were different legal codes for civilian justice and military justice. Civilian justice worked through commissions and a justice delegate who would intervene 'when there were problems ... He would invite the *sobas* and their counsellors to discuss the problem and the sentence ... but the last word was held by the military commander of the RM for both civilians and military matters'.[121] 'People knew the laws as the party explained them to everyone and norms could not be transgressed,' explained a former political commissar in the propaganda directorate.[122] The police would become involved in criminal cases that fell outside the reach of these mediation mechanisms.

158

If people were found to have committed a crime or broken the rules governing Jamba, they would be sent to re-education camps in the Nova Aurora area. Punishment in Jamba also included jail time, or summary execution, but in other liberated areas prisoners would be punished by forced labour working on agriculture and transportation of materials. *Esquadra Piloto* (The Pilot Police Zone) was the area in Jamba where the police stations and criminal investigation divisions were located. Some prisoners were the responsibility of the Interior Secretariat while others were of the security service. The underground prison cells were also located in this area to accommodate for political prisoners and MPLA troops that were captured.

The *Brigada National de Defesa do Estado* (Brigade for the National Defence) (BRINDE) was created in 1980 to serve as UNITA's internal police and intelligence service. Until 1974, such services fell under the *Serviço de Segurança Geral* (SSG), which operated at the guerrilla level and controlled infiltration areas. BRINDE eventually came to coordinate hundreds of operatives under several branches of security.[123] The department was subdivided into information areas dealing with 1) foreigners, 2) prisoners of war, 3) the president and leadership security and 4) infiltration and counter-intelligence. All these department areas had branches throughout the country in all RMs.

> In Jamba many wanted to escape with Nzau Puna in 1991,[124] and we needed to know who wanted to escape to prevent leaks and denunciations. We had an independent network of security to inform on others ... whoever revealed having doubts while abroad in the diplomatic mission would be sent here into the interior.[125]

All activities were directed at ensuring that there was cohesion and loyalty among the population, and that there was no infiltration from the enemy. At the more local level, neighbourhood committees were used as mechanisms for control and information collection. They had a chief, a sub-chief and a secretary for each neighbourhood, and they used the *Control Book* to register any anomalies that might arise within the daily activities of the community. Whatever was registered was then sent to BRINDE.

To effectively manage information and intelligence gathering in the liberated areas, the head of BRINDE coordinated his activities with the head of the Military Intelligence Service (SIM) and the office of the Chief of Staff of the army. SIM was created in 1978 and initially ran out of the Muandonga base before being transferred to Jamba. The head of SIM, General Peregrino Chindondo Wambu, was trained in South Africa, Morocco and West Germany. At its operational peak, SIM had over 2,500 staff that detected enemy operations, produced intelligence reports and gave vital information to operational commanders. The organisation operated from 1978 until 1992 but took on a different form after the third war began.

One legacy that severely damaged UNITA's external image during the 1990s was its incident of witch-burning in 1983 in Jamba, where over 20 women and their children were accused of being witches and burnt alive. In the run-up to their summary trial, there had been episodes of wounded soldiers in the hospitals being smeared with faeces and having their medication stopped. In an environment where infiltration was avoided at all costs, and where the movement could not afford fear and doubt to take root in the imagination of the population, a trial was organised to punish those who were inducing this fear and disrupting the harmonious and strictly regulated system exercised in Jamba. The hearing was oral, and in the presence of the civilian population several women were called out from the crowd and thrown into an open fire, together with their children. This incident was orchestrated to instil fear in the population and reassert control. It was about curbing the presence of any kind of enemy, even an imagined one, at the rear base. According to some sources, Washington was well aware of UNITA's bloody past, including its witch-burning episodes.[126] The CIA was present in Jamba as a permanent feature throughout the mid- to late 1980s, so it is impossible they would not have known.

UNITA was also known for its internal purges of high-level cadres and commanders. Famous generals were accused of treason and sentenced to death on Savimbi's orders. Many of these killings occurred in Jamba. If commanders or UNITA diplomats were thought to be misdirecting the cause or diverging from their mandates, they would be summoned to the rear base and the party would deal with them accordingly; this could mean a military rank demotion, prison time or death. Waldemar Chindondo, former Chief of Staff, was one such commander, as was Vakulukuta. Both were killed in 1984. Their bodies were buried in unmarked graves outside of Jamba's official cemetery to pre-empt any future dissent. The assassinations of Tito Chingunji and Wilson Dos Santos, and their families, in 1991 was another episode that seriously hurt the movement's external image and caused a wave of defections from high-ranking officers, including the former Secretary General of the party, Nzau Puna (at the time Interior Minister), and co-founder Tony da Costa Fernandes. According to many inside UNITA, these killings were related to disputes over women. 'It was rumoured that Tito had been having an affair with Savimbi's wife and that he had to be accountable for this. The same had happened to Waldemar Chindondo, who was killed so Savimbi could keep his wife.'[127] Others explained that Savimbi might have felt challenged by Tito's proximity with key US decision-makers in Washington. There are few certainties regarding these deaths and the defection of Puna and Fernandes. Many senior leaders abroad or at the military front were always slightly afraid to be called back to Jamba, not knowing if they would leave alive. Executions of several leaders would continue throughout the third war (1992–2002) with levels of extreme paranoia and ritualistic killings widespread among the movement.[128]

'Guerrilla Democracy': Feedback mechanisms

Forums for community engagement and feedback were held regularly throughout the liberated areas. The main forum used was the Warrior's Flame meeting (*Chama do Guerilheiro*) whereby civilians, UNITA leaders and the military would meet once or twice a week to discuss community issues. These meetings were presided over by the leader of the community, and the objective was to allow for the voicing of tensions and frustrations. These meetings were a regular occurrence in Jamba and in all the RMs. They would begin with a recreational activity: 'we'd have a dance of some sort; they could be traditional dances like Kassumbe'.[129] After that, the political and military issues would be brought to the floor, and people could express themselves freely. These sessions had the objective of correcting wrongs and readjusting the pace and progress of the liberation.

The military also had a feedback mechanism where the lowest ranks were allowed to voice their opinions. The Soldiers' Committee (*Comité do Soldado*) were gatherings of 50 soldiers from the regular forces, of 20 soldiers from the semi-regular forces, and of 7 from the guerrilla forces. They were opportunities for identifying problems so that military discipline could prevail, and they were used as a participation instrument to encourage a meeting of minds between the soldiers. 'If soldiers agreed they didn't want a certain commander, Savimbi would have him removed after receiving feedback from these meetings.'[130] The President's office would be informed of any misconduct or dissatisfaction reported during these meetings, in accordance with the main policy that commanders had to set an example so that soldiers could follow and be held accountable. There were strict rules defined by the disciplinary code and the punishment would suit the severity of the issue. 'If one soldier was found to have taken the wife of another, he would be subject to 50 whips. ... If it was an officer who had done this he would be demoted.'[131] Debate was encouraged, and these committees were described as UNITA's experience with democracy in the bush. 'A 4-star general could face questions from his soldiers at these sessions. ... They were political structures that had the effect of being a counter-power.'[132]

Cultural events and the performance element

The *Pavilhão VI Congresso* (VI Congress Pavilion) in Jamba was built in 1986 and was one of the areas where people would come and enjoy cultural evenings. The social activities in Jamba were aimed at creating a sense of normalcy like what was experienced during peacetime, where football matches were attended and traditional dances organised, to ameliorate the constant pressure of living in a war environment. The 3rd of August Stadium, named after Savimbi's date of birth, was another area where cultural and sporting activities were organised so combatants could decompress during their rest and recuperation period. The stadium had a football field and basketball courts where tournaments were organised. It also had a playground for children. 'When we left the frontlines, we would come and rest, we would read, play ping pong, and football tournaments with the two teams—the Red Stars and the Black Stars.'[133] One of the main objectives of having such recreational and sports activities, which included the opening of a martial arts centre, in the bases was to create a projection of normal life. 'It allowed us to diminish the shadow of war and to believe that we would live beyond this.'[134]

Creating 'normality' (Beck 2012) was part of a larger strategy of consolidating UNITA's world order. For normality to be effective, it had to be part of a set of new symbols and devices; part of a process of 'inventing tradition'; a 'process of formalisation and ritualisation' when 'a rapid transformation of society weakens or destroys the social patterns for which the "old" traditions had been designed' (Hobsbawm and Ranger 1983: 4–5). The populating of Jamba with 'deterritorialised' and uprooted communities facilitated this. The spatial and political definitions of Jamba confirmed the idea that 'the identity of a place emerges by the intersections of its specific involvement in a system of hierarchically organised spaces with its cultural construction as a community or locality' (Gupta and Ferguson 1997: 36).

Cultural events also played an important performance role for foreigners who visited Jamba. Journalists and foreign diplomats who reported such occasions helped solidify the idea of Jamba being a theatre of governance and projected a particular image abroad. After visiting in 1983, Portuguese and French journalists described how the main stadium was decorated with giant handpainted murals of the faces of UNITA's leaders and posters with the party slogans. The stadium with giant posters depicting how UNITA saw the war. 'Soviet-made jets bombing villages, bearded Cuban soldiers bayoneting terrified women and children, and triumphant guerrillas overrunning government positions.'[135] 'At the centre of the stadium were three FALA platoons with their AKs. ... Around the stadium were three thousand civilians and when Savimbi arrived they erupted into dances and singing' (Barata-Feyo 1985: 23). Savimbi then gave a long speech, and at the end there was a display of all the activities that UNITA coordinated: a truck exhibiting what was done in agriculture, with farmers feigning working on a pyramid of earth; tailors using their sewing machines; mechanics repairing items; fisherman displaying their catch on fishing boats placed on top of the trucks; teachers and their students; and nurses taking soldiers' blood pressure.

Conclusion

This chapter on Jamba has highlighted the totalitarian and utopian nature of UNITA's parallel state. Unlike the SPLM/A, that relied on strong social structures to build the basis of its state, UNITA integrated and acculturated every social force in the liberated areas. The parallel state was the motor behind society's transformation, the power behind economic development and the political direction the county was intended to take. UNITA's governance in the first war focused more on autonomous commands and smaller-scale villagisation strategies, coupled with the use of traditional authorities and structured political work. It progressed into centrally managed structures that focused on regulating behaviour, instilling operating procedures and embedding the principles of disciplined work, education and combat. Jamba was meant to demonstrate UNITA's capacity to govern. The institutional features that the Republic of the Free Lands took on were similar to those of totalitarian regimes, with a monistic centre of power, an official and enforceable ideology, and the mass mobilisation of the citizenry by the single party (Linz 2000). All this was done with the aim of legitimising UNITA as the only political alternative for governing Angola.

UNITA's organisational capacity was premised on its political programme. Organisation was aimed at securing logistics, educating followers and fighters, and maintaining services, but also coordinating the entire Republic of the Free Lands. Each secretariat and security organ had a defined structure that followed a hierarchical chain of command and answered to the central command body COPE. Every aspect of the military as well as civilians' lives was controlled and regulated so as to be indoctrinated with political legitimacy at every juncture—at the fronts, at the rear base, within the community and at social events. Without the political and party organisation, and the training programmes that came with this social engineering project, UNITA would not have been able to govern the Free Lands in the same structured way. The military presence alone could not have achieved what the movement managed in the areas of health, agriculture and education. Savimbi and his commander–leaders saw the two first wars (against the Portuguese and then the MPLA–foreign alliance) as first and foremost theatres for political combat, supported by military operations, and because of this developed the party and administrative structures required to defeat the enemy on all fronts.

Before the 1975–76 critical juncture, UNITA had prioritised its political organisation to rally constituencies that were not represented by the other two liberation movements. It had placed its leadership inside the country as a legitimising force and rooted itself at the village level, with political cells providing basic services to the population. The ease with which it was militarily defeated and expelled from Huambo led the movement to build up its military capacity so that it would mirror a conventional army. To survive the war, UNITA would need to develop its political rhetoric in a way that would damage the liberation credentials of the MPLA as the country's first independent government, and it would need to train, equip and build its army. In the 1980s, UNITA deepened its controversial and politically costly alliance with apartheid South Africa. As Savimbi explained, 'if a man is drowning in a river and someone holds out his hand to rescue him, that man is not going to check who that hand belongs to first'.[136] In this way, UNITA managed to receive the logistical support and training it needed from Pretoria to transform its guerrilla forces into an army capable of withstanding attacks from Cuban and Soviet-supported government troops. UNITA also repositioned its political ideology in a way that appealed to both internal and external audiences. Despite being a disciple of Maoism, Savimbi understood that he had to position UNITA as a beacon for containment of communism in the region if he was to attract the support required. The parallel state was in this way a key legitimising and logistical instrument for the movement's national constituents and international allies.

After the Bicesse Peace Agreement was signed in 1991, Savimbi gave orders for all his ministers and thousands of cadres to begin their move to the cities and start the political campaign for the September 1992 elections. Although Jamba continued to operate, the capital would be run instead by a governor, his deputy and several mayors. 'The governor looked after everything, including water, energy and commerce. ... Jamba opened its first markets as General Chitombi started to liberalise trade by injecting dollars so people could trade with Zambia and Namibia.'[137] The governor was also responsible for politics, administration and security, but each of these areas had their respective vice-governors. The population that stayed behind was able to continue receiving services and develop other activities like trading and small businesses, but the general feeling among citizens was that they had been abandoned. In the run-up to the peace agreement, Savimbi had already begun implementing his strategy of educating his most trusted commanders in politics, economics and other disciplines that would prepare them for their transformation into civilian leaders. Ministries were created to fully shadow the exiting government in Luanda, and senior cadres were listed to become members of parliament. Lower-level technocrats and civilians trained in key areas needed for the reconstruction of the country were also sent to the cities. Thousands of civilians left the bases of Kuando Kubango, returning to the Central Highlands after almost two decades away. UNITA's leadership was convinced that they would become the ultimate rulers of Angola, elected in free and democratic polls, with the legitimising presence of the UN and the Troika (US, Portugal and Russia). This meant that after 1991 no other structures were built in Jamba, and most of the leaders had left the capital of the Free Lands with the intention to never return. Their destination was now the cities. They had to begin preparing for an urban life, leading communities that had not received the level of 'political education' that would result in their unwavering support for UNITA, while setting up structures for future governance and the running of the political party throughout the country.

The collapse of the electoral process in 1992 and the subsequent Halloween Massacre of UNITA leaders and supporters brought an abrupt end to all the political work undertaken by UNITA and Savimbi in preparation for peacetime politics. A church report claims that over 20,000 people were massacred in Luanda over the course of three days.[138]

> I believe we lost between 100,000 and 300,000 people in Luanda and the other provinces where the government staged their *limpeza* [cleanse]. Everyone that was from the South was killed. The worst killings were in Luanda, followed by Huambo where we couldn't really sustain a defence because our logistics had stayed in Kuando Kubango. Lubango, Benguela and Uige also saw heavy fighting and killings. It was all organised in the same way with the use of police, PIR, *fitinhas* and the civil defence.[139]

The three-day massacre depleted UNITA of some of its most valuable cadres and leaders, after the creation of a single army and the DDR process had already taken away several of UNITA's most qualified commanders and officers. It also changed the political calculus of the movement with regard to the next stages of war. When the 1992 war began, UNITA relocated all its most strategic assets, like the VORGAN radio and the intelligence services, to the key bases of Bailundu and Andulo in the Central Highlands. The movement would struggle to enact the same level of political control in diverse, urban and politically hostile populations, so it adopted very different operating procedures. It focused instead on military success, and by August 1993 UNITA controlled 70% of Angola. The following years oscillated between peace talks and fighting, with varying degrees of military escalation and intensity. The structured and hierarchical organisation that had served UNITA in transforming its military capacity and running a parallel state in the previous decade allowed it to develop a sophisticated resource extraction industry. In 1996, Andulo became the centre for the commercialisation of diamonds, with UNITA controlling as much as 70% of Angola's diamond production and generating an estimated US$3.7 billion.[140] The last four years of war from 1998 until 2002 would deeply traumatise the country, leaving millions politically and physically displaced.

Although for the last 10 years of the war (1992–2002) UNITA focused more on military operations and less on building a parallel Angolan reality, the political project that Savimbi and his commanders had led during the second war had a far-reaching impact on Angola's

167

social fabric. UNITA's project was so intrusive towards the people who had experienced it that the integration of many individuals and communities into the Angolan 2002 post-war reality was difficult. For many, they felt estranged from the society they were now part of and did not feel represented by the state they lived under. 'They were stuck between the UNITA society that no longer existed and the life they were living under a political party and state that they believed reject[ed] them' (Beck 2009: 352). 'The men and women that had spent their lives with UNITA appeared like aliens in today's Angolan society' (Beck 2012: 118). If Angolans had begun the second liberation war with some differences between them in terms of region, race and class, they certainly had them deeply ingrained in their political and historical memory after the war. This was a direct result of the political propaganda and indoctrination programmes that both UNITA and the MPLA had used to win over the 'soul' of the nation.

4

COMPARATIVE STRATEGIES, DILEMMAS
AND RESPONSES

*'There is a soul to an army as well as the individual man, and
no General can accomplish the full work of his army unless he
commands the souls of his men as well as their bodies and legs.'*
US General Willian Sherman[1]

*'Men make their own history, but they do not make it as they please;
they do not make it under self-selected circumstances, but under
circumstances existing already, given and transmitted from the past.'*
Karl Marx

Insurgent states lie in the flux of many dynamics. They reflect the
challenges, convictions, resources and support insurgent movements
can harness, as well as the levels of legitimacy they attain. The
previous chapters on Yambio and Jamba briefly described the main
strategies and sources of legitimacy for both movements, hinging
heavily for the SPLM/A on justice and the space for civil society,
and for UNITA on service delivery and the credible projection of an
Angolan alternative state and political order. Both the SPLM/A and
UNITA managed to remake a national collective at the sub-national
level, persuading this collective that it was its legitimate provider of

169

political goods. Both political projects were meant to legitimately represent the marginalised and disenfranchised against a state that was exclusionary, predatory and culturally assimilative. Both UNITA and the SPLM/A needed legitimacy at the macro and micro levels as they broadened their wars territorially and introduced governance as a feature to project legitimacy externally while harnessing 'the right to rule' internally. The language of stateness and the actions they took to provide protection and representation to and of 'their' people were symbolically important and linked to specific outcomes. Legitimacy also related to 'a psychological property of authority, institution, or social arrangement that leads those connected to it to believe that it is appropriate, proper and just' (Tyler 2006: 375).[2] It was an ordering process of wielding power without violence, 'generated with reference to local norms, identities and realities which resonate with target populations' (Worrall 2019: 47).[3] In the case of the New Sudan and the Free Lands of Angola, legitimisation strategies were dependent on and constrained by the tools the SPLM/A and UNITA had at their disposal and how they chose to wield them. UNITA's tight organisation and capacity to deliver sustained levels of service and aid to its populations gave the movement legitimacy and moral authority. The transactional aspect alone of distributional outcomes was, however, insufficient to sustain support. UNITA also provided its constituents with recognition and linked their social identity to an imagined future where they had agency. The SPLM/A's strategic use of the traditional courts systems and emphasis on maintaining rural peace gave it legitimacy, which only grew when it recovered the popular aspirations of the South across many communities for self-determination. It managed to symbolically attach the fulfilment of these aspirations with the success of the rebellion it led. The decentralised aspect of SPLM/A governance also enabled civil society organisations to flourish in support of the liberation, igniting some unique collaborations with external aid agencies, such as the revolving fund.

Both movements ultimately created the necessary reciprocal relationships with non-combatants that they needed in order to continue waging war. Force and coercion were transformed into authority, creating this layer of legitimacy, as the population oscillated between active and passive compliance, obedience and varying levels of submission to and support for their rule. Scharpf (1998) made the interesting distinction between input legitimacy—which implied that the governed played a role in the process of rulemaking—and output legitimacy, which required that the governors provide collective goods to improve the quality of life of the population. In the dimension of input legitimacy, collectively binding decisions originated from authentic expressions of the constituency that were self-determined rather than imposed by 'exogenous will'. In the output legitimacy dimension, the government employed its powers to serve the common interest of the constituency by addressing problems that individually its members could not solve. By default of the 'local' form of the SPLM/A parallel state, input legitimacy characterised the New Sudan project. In allowing civilians, local leaders, traditional authorities and civil society to govern with relatively minimal oversight, the SPLM/A enabled its constituency to take part in rulemaking in Yambio. While UNITA defined and manifested a problem that needed to be solved, it instrumentalised the need for representation and redress of a population that otherwise had no power. For them, UNITA provided the ouput legitimacy that reflected geographic, ethnic and cultural distinctions in need of integration, agency and political participation.

This chapter will assess the aspects of rebel agency—leadership, ideology and organisation—that gave form to the parallel state. It will use the rebel-system as a framework for the comparison. The approach to the civilian aspect was covered in the empirical chapters on Yambio and Jamba. This chapter will provide the historical, temporal and circumstancial context for the governance of Yambio and Jamba.

Leadership

The leadership of John Garang de Mabior and Jonas Malheiro Savimbi was the element that most defined whether the movements would succeed or fail in governing their wartime rebel-states. Leaders bear the ultimate responsibility for the outcomes of their movements, as they make the vital strategic decisions affecting complex relationships and institutions. For insurgencies that aim to produce a different society, state and sense of nation, leaders need to inspire high levels of devotion to the cause, ideally articulating the vision, defining the organisation, providing training and accountability mechanisms to secure discipline, allegiance and group cohesiveness. A leader's ability to retain political control, combining both power and authority, determined his capacity to shape the actions and dynamics of other leaders, combatants and members. A leader's grasp on political control also determined how and why followers and fighters chose to obey them. The SPLM/A and UNITA were two highly personalised insurgencies, absolutely dominated by their two charismatic but authoritarian leaders. The strength of command they wielded was in many ways a contributing factor to their movements' failure at forging new pathways of war and peace. The ideologies and political messages they reworked, rehashed and self-tailored became important binding mechanisms for fighters, civilians and cadres as they founded parallel states and societies. The decision to establish different types of governing strategies and institutions reflected their biases, prejudices and personal experiences. They aimed to attain a higher level of political representation and correct the failings of the past while avoiding the trappings of existing social and political divisions. To achieve their reform, they needed to bring together a critical mass of supporters and leaders of different constituencies, by aggregating similar needs and interests while reconciling divergent ones to create a normative system that was broadly accepted. These two leaders stood out for their unmeasured ambition to achieve something visible of revolutionary and reformist proportions; for their drive and tenacity to find solutions at all junctures; for their confidence in carrying out important unpopular decisions; and for their realistic perspectives of what was required and what was possible so that their actions would be aligned with shifting opportunities. These were all crucial for allowing UNITA and the SPLM/A to wage decades of war and create their parallel states.

It was their reformist visions and ideological conceptualisations of self-styled political projects that brought about two movements that were ideologically incoherent and yet rallied considerable constituent support and pleased diverse external patrons. Cold

War patrons for both movements, each on opposing sides of the ideological spectrum, greatly influenced the directions of their wars but for neither were determining ideological hinderances that blocked other reformist elements of sub-nationalism, Africanism and tradition. Both UNITA and the SPLM/A led two liberation campaigns for reformed countries based on reimagined nations and states, yet they rallied sub-national groups—the broader South in both cases. They portrayed their nationalism as a unifying call for change but invariably took on regional and ethnic dimensions. UNITA's ideological definition began in the anti-colonial wars and matured during the post-independence conflict as a continuation of the struggle against foreign interference and the denial of Angola's traditional culture. The initial depiction of the SPLM/A as a vanguard movement for a 'united Sudan under a socialist system' was primarily a reflection of the influence of the Ethiopian Derg. It was perceived by a few from within the intellectual strata of the movement as being post-ideological rather than providing political orientation for different stages of the liberation. The SPLM/A's vision of a New Sudan shifted over time, just like UNITA's perspective of a free and democratic Angola, both with the impetus of breaking down the shackles of imperialism and marginalisation. Both movements aimed to change the power structures in their countries, dismantling what they perceived as being discriminatory, elitist and unrepresentative political orders that specifically marginalised in the people of the South.

While UNITA's ideology survived the death of its founding leader when Savimbi was killed in 2002, the SPLM/A would drift into a political and ideological vacuum after Garang's death in 2005. The New Sudan vision would die with Garang, revealing the lack of structured political work and ideological strength that had gone into creating a pathway for peacetime. UNITA's vision for a free and democratic Angola would suffer deep contradictions during the last decade of war (1992–2002), an extension of the contradictions created by its totalitarian nature, but the movement would experience a revival during the second decade of peace, particularly after 2012, when depicting the MPLA as serving elitist and foreign interests conditioning the lives and livelihoods of the people would once again resonate politically across segments of Angola.

Savimbi and Garang led two complex rebellions and survived several internal and external threats. Factionalism, dissent, asymmetrical warfare, loss of external patrons, diplomatic pressure, among others, were challenges that required tailored responses and strategies in order for both leaders to survive at an organisational and capacity level. They understood that to wage a successful rebellion they needed a unified command where rival groups or communities would agree to subordinate their own interests to align with the overall interests of the movement. For the SPLM/A, this meant adopting a military structure; for UNITA, it meant a political party structure. Given the centralised structure of both Garang's and Savimbi's leadership, decisions of military importance, political strategy, the day-to-day administration of war, governing the liberated areas and managing resources fell on them. The capacity of each to determine the political vision of his movement and alter it when necessary to gather international support, while simultaneously projecting a war of visions and societies, was also key. Both Garang and Savimbi wanted to be recognised as 'sovereign presidents' (Johnson 2008) who, unlike warlords and other rebel leaders that aimed merely to seize power, wanted to be seen as the legitimate representatives of their people who they defended. They both sustained the necessary esoteric appeals by interpreting existing grievances, enhancing them and popularising them in ways that their constituents would embrace as their own and seek remedy for.

UNITA and the SPLM/A's leadership pursued a combination of transformational and transactional control. Transformational leaders appealed to followers through a transcendental mission and 'mutual elevation that convert[ed] followers into leaders and leaders into moral agents', while transactional leaders approached followers with 'an eye for exchanging one thing for another' (Burns 1978).[4] As transformational leaders, both Garang and Savimbi provided an inspiring vision aimed at reducing narrow self-interest and factionalism; as transactional leaders, they regulated behaviour in 'which ambition countered ambitions, and factions countered factions' (Burns 1978) so that emphasis was on the creation of new political orders. Savimbi and Garang's leadership traits, while essentially different, shared several common characteristics. They formulated the movement's vision and manipulated the population's grievances while enhancing sub-national cleavages to further political mobilisation and create a new nationalist platform. They sustained alliances that were often contradictory to their own rhetoric and incorporated political principles to reflect the plurality of internal and external audiences. Both tailored organisational responses to address key shortcomings during the war through military and political skill and strategy. They provided inspiration and operational direction by engendering devotion to the cause and promoting collective interests that superseded all others by articulating an ideological vision (Freeman 2014). Both leaders balanced the imperatives of operational, strategic and inspirational leadership, at times chaotically and violently, while aiming to wield complete centralised control over the destiny of their people and armies. Neither ever lost the political control of the liberation, despite dissent and fragmentation.

Characteristics of the founding leaders

The leadership of both Garang and Savimbi was made more complex by the wars they fought, the social cleavages they experienced and the difficulties within their own movements. Garang was a highly intelligent and charismatic man, a natural leader who was humble yet unrelenting in his determination to dismantle the regime in Khartoum.[5] He was 'a man who had always known how to juggle a stone and an egg without losing sight of either' (Waihenya 2006: 69). Garang was one of the few Sudanese politicians who was able to rally significant support for a unified country (LeRiche and Arnold 2012). His strategic alliances with northern opposition parties, and his understanding of power dynamics in Khartoum, made him a considerable threat to the Sudanese government. However, his critics described him as indecisive, authoritarian and incapable of dealing effectively with his enemies.[6] Garang also failed to instil discipline within the movement to curtail the many war crimes committed against civilians. Garang's leadership was key in bringing about several military and diplomatic victories for the movement. His death in 2005 and subsequent developments in the SPLM/A show that he had a unique way of balancing difficult decisions and power struggles. Under a new leader, the SPLM/A would, by default of the peace agreement, succeed in achieving independence in 2011 but would collapse internally, resulting in a war of genocidal proportions in 2016.[7]

Savimbi was also a man of exceptional intelligence, whose public speaking ability inspired many to follow him unconditionally.[8] 'It did not matter what [Savimbi] said just as long as he spoke—telling them what to do, how to do it and how long it would take. They would follow.'[9] His commanders admired his self-discipline, organisational capacity and relentlessness. He was described as 'that rare coincidence of history, a throwback to the great tribal leaders of Africa—Tchaka Zulu, Msiri, and Jomo Kenyatta'.[10] He prided himself on his African roots and knowledge of traditional culture, and he spoke several Angolan languages. Those who accompanied his movement through many stages of political and nationalistic development point to how Savimbi truly believed in transforming Angola. This image rapidly changed in the 1990s, partly due to testimonies of defected UNITA leaders who confirmed MPLA propaganda with descriptions of Savimbi's violence, but largely due to his own mismanagement of dissent and the crimes committed. 'Savimbi did not die in 2002, he died in 1992 when the electoral process failed. From then onwards he stopped believing and no longer had a political programme.'[11] The war Savimbi staged from 1992 through 2002 was purely destructive, revealing his sense of betrayal and resulting intense paranoia.[12] Under a new leader in 2002, UNITA would work hard to sanitise its image and slowly rebuild confidence with key constituencies, but it would fail for two decades to provide the necessary accountability to MPLA misrule.

Experience from previous movements and peace agreements

Both Savimbi and Garang were products of the political moments they emerged from and were themselves informed by the histories of insurrection of those who came before them. The historical context within which they emerged was crucial. A period of crisis or turbulence was generally more open to leaders who proposed radical change (Roberts and Bradley 1988).[13] Both leaders recognised the deficiencies of the status quo and 'effectively articulate[d] for followers ... how the future vision [would] remove deficiencies and fulfil the hopes of followers' (Conger and Kanungo 2012: 9). They provided 'orderly interpretations and explanations for all perceived social, economic and political "realities"' (O'Neill 1990: 75).

Both Garang's and Savimbi's personal histories were naturally intertwined with the history of their country, perpetuating a sense of grievance and injustice that required a collective response. Both established their liberation movements in a context of existing movements that were in principle fighting a version of the same cause. Upon graduating from the United States in 1971, where he had received a PhD in Development Economics, Garang returned to Sudan and joined the Anyanya I movement for a short period, with the peace agreement being signed a year later. For Garang, Anyanya I had played an important role in the resistance against Arab domination, but it had failed to impose change on how Khartoum dealt with the South. Because of the political wrangling and bickering of the southern political elites and the way they had lost control of leading the South due to weakness in negotiating and a lack of strategic thinking, the SPLM/A came to disregard any initial internal calls for democratisation, collective decision-making and political discussions in favour of a disciplined and structured military command. The 1983 Manifesto highlighted the shortcomings of Anyanya I, accusing it of implementing 'fake governments, complete with its Western-type cabinet' comprised of a bourgeoisified southern bureaucratic elite. The perceived inefficiency in its leadership sustained by the dual command of the political party and the Anyanya military arm that were headed by different people led Garang to amalgamate power to avoid contradictions. He became the commander-in-chief and chairman of the movement.

Savimbi was also impacted by disillusionment with how the anti-colonial struggle was being waged by existing movements, and he criticised the MPLA and FNLA for basing their leadership in Congo Brazzaville and Kinshasa. He believed the leadership of any liberation struggle had to be on the frontlines, and because of this UNITA led its liberation from inside the country. Although Savimbi's initial sympathies had lied with the 'progressive' MPLA, he nevertheless joined Holden Roberto's União das Populações de Angola (UPA) (later renamed FNLA) in 1961 and became the secretary general of the movement and later its foreign minister in the government in exile. Savimbi would become disillusioned with UPA's approach to the liberation struggle, despite it claiming to have very similar ideological stances to UNITA. Its capitalist, pro-Western stance contrasted sharply with the MPLA's Marxist orientation, even though the latter would only become explicit after independence in the mid-1970s. Savimbi openly disagreed with Roberto's 'tribalistic leadership' at a meeting of the Organisation of African Unity in 1964, where he accused Roberto of incompetence and corruption. He also criticised the MPLA for failing to be more inclusive. The Ovimbundu, Savimbi's own ethnic group and the largest in Angola, did not have a political force to represent their aspirations (James 2011). As a result he would build alliances that would bring the Ovimbundu, Chokwe and other smaller ethnic groups under one movement. Both Garang and Savimbi took inspiration from the shortcomings of the previous movements to craft new and improved strategies, but they also defined the universe of their liberations differently from the previous movements: Garang's constituents would include all the Sudanese, not just southerners; Savimbi's constituents would include the 'totality' of Angolans, not just the southerners of the central highlands. These aims did not fully materialise.

The experience of failed peace agreements would also impact these leaders. The failure of the Addis Ababa agreement and Khartoum's continuous violations would impact Garang's conduct of the war and negotiations. In January 1972, Garang wrote to Anyanya I leader Joseph Lagu suggesting the necessary conditions and strategy for the talks with Khartoum, including the sustaining of two armies and two administrations and highlighting the failure of constitutional guarantees against the 'barbarities of Arab nationalism and chauvinism'.[14] The failure of the peace agreement was blamed on President Nimeiri's abrogation of key provisions, the imposition of Sharia law, the mismanaged integration of forces and the dividing of the South into three regions. But blame was also assigned to the politicians of the South, whose divisionary and factionalist manoeuvres became self-defeating, which Garang had somewhat foreseen and later criticised.

Unlike Garang, who didn't play a formal role in negotiating the Addis Ababa Peace Agreement, Savimbi was very committed to securing the political outcome of the 1975 Alvor Agreement. He believed in the possibility that the agreement would secure UNITA's political role in independent Angola. Although all three movements began implementation in early 1975, the accords did not prevent the FNLA and later the MPLA from making military moves to take power. Fighting would continue, and the MPLA's request for additional support would lead to mass inflows of Soviet aid and hardware, as well as Cuban troop reinforcements that, by 1976, numbered between 10,000 and 14,000 (Marcum 1978). In a publication issued by UNITA's observer mission to the UN in February 1976,[15] the movement identified the difficulties faced by the 1975 transitional government as: 1) the lack of a national army and police to maintain public order, 2) the administrative inexperience of the members of government and the impact of partisan politics and 3) the fact that Portugal was clearly favouring one side—the MPLA.

Both Garang and Savimbi would use these lessons to inform their negotiating positions in future peace agreements. That was why the 2005 CPA saw two standing armies and two separate administrations during the transition in Sudan. For UNITA, the lack of an integrated security apparatus in 1975 was corrected by the creation of the Angolan Armed Forces (FAA) as a result of the 1991 Bicesse Peace Agreement. UNITA also worked to counter the unpreparedness of their cadres when it came to holding administrative positions in government. The previous wars, the movements fighting them and the resulting peace agreements would inform in very direct ways the manner and structure of UNITA and the SPLM/A.

Founding the movement and structuring the leadership

The ways in which Garang and Savimbi came to head their two movements was very different. UNITA was founded in March 1966, in the Chokwe village of Muangai in Angola, through a consultative process that began in Zambia among different Angolan elites. At its inception, UNITA elected a Central Committee and adopted a constitution. The SPLM/A was founded in July 1983 in the Gambella region of Ethiopia, operating with provisional structures which would later be replaced by a military high command. While Savimbi was behind the idea of UNITA and rallied support inside and outside Angola with key constituencies and leaders, Garang secured his position following a leadership dispute moderated by the Ethiopians. As early as 1975, Ethiopia's military government, the Derg, began to politically organise refugees in Gambella and Addis Ababa in what became known as 'Project 07' of the Defence Ministry, which assisted in the formation of the SPLM/A (Yihun 2013). Menguistu's regime was fundamental to the SPLM/A's initial formation and survival in that it armed the movement directly, providing it with rear bases and training camps and curbing dissent. While Garang had maintained contact with the different groups opposing the Addis Ababa agreement in the 1970s, there were other more senior contenders from the Anyanya II movement who were positioning themselves for the chairman role. Garang's task was to organise and structure a movement that would join several existing groups mobilising for war.[16] It took months of leadership negotiations in Ethiopia before the SPLM/A was formed.

UNITA began as a small group of which Savimbi was the undisputed leader, while Garang had to contend with a divided leadership that would challenge his authority throughout the war and cause deep rifts in the attempt to create a united front. Garang fought several movements and militias, leading to continuous negotiation and incorporation of existing rebel groups. Garang more so than Savimbi would have to contend with the fact that the 'organisation was not built from a clean slate; instead, it reflected the terrain of collective action available to leaders' (Staniland 2014: 78), many of whom had previous experience in the wars of the 1960s, in government and parliament, and as founders of Anyanya I and II. Savimbi would face different constraints, as the two other Angolan liberation movements were already spearheading the anti-colonial struggle. He had to balance different interests while also developing a political agenda that differed from that of the FNLA and the MPLA. It was a difficult proposition, given his predecessors in the MPLA and FNLA already had backing from several African countries, military experience which he would have to contest and contrasting political messages around which he would have to reposition his new movement.

In structuring the command of their movements, both leaders had to compromise with key commanders, many of whom would later be sidelined and purged. In August 1983, Garang was elected chairman and commander-in-chief of the SPLM/A at Itang Camp, where he structured a Provisional Executive Committee (PEC). The PEC was comprised of several committees which dealt separately with the military, administration, justice, finance, political and foreign affairs. It was meant to lead the revolutionary movement in mobilising the population and determining the politico-military strategy for the war. However, the PEC ran into several difficulties with internal power struggles in 1985, effectively ending its role, despite the fact that it served a more multifaceted function and could have taken the lead in developing the party and administrative structures during the 1980s. Instead, the leadership became structured around military seniority.

The Political–Military High Command (PMHC) that replaced the PEC was comprised of the five SPLM/A founding members: Kerubino Kuanyin Bol, appointed deputy chairman and deputy commander-in-chief; William Nyoun Bany as the chief of general staff (CoS); Salva Kiir Mayardit as deputy CoS for security and military operations; and Arok Thon Arok as deputy CoS for administration and logistics (Arop 2006). The only two politicians of the PEC, Joseph Oduho (who had chaired the Political and Foreign Affairs Committee) and Martin Majier (who had chaired the Legal and Administration Committee), were no longer part of the leadership when the PMHC was formed (both had been imprisoned from 1985 until 1992), making it a command structure comprised only of soldiers. The difficulty of managing the different issues of seniority, political ambitions and contrasting interests would lead the movement to continually define itself in terms of military hierarchy and the seniority of its founding members, even after independence in 2011. This was reflected in the way the first governing strategy of the CMA was conceived and managed. As seen in Chapter 2 on Yambio, even the chiefs were given military ranks and incorporated into the command structures. Only after 1991, when the need emerged, were more collective decision-making processes secured by political imperatives to structure relationships in the liberated areas.

181

Savimbi's quest to begin a third front of the liberation in Angola would lead him to unite several organisations represented in Zambia in the early 1960s. The new nationalist unit would draw upon three constituencies: the defectors from the FNLA whose group, led by José Kalundungo, became part of the 'Amangolans';[17] an Ovimbundu Congo-based association; a student union, União Nacional de Estudantes Angolanos (UNEA), led by Jorge Valentim; and several leaders based in Zambia from Chokwe, Lwena and Luchazu groups that were organised as self-help organisations (James 2011). As the group of activists entered Angola in 1968, UNITA became the only liberation movement whose leadership operated within Angola. UNITA claimed its distinctiveness also on the basis that it sought to represent ethnic groups that did not find direct expression in either the FNLA (whose leaders and followers came from northern Bakongo provinces) or the MPLA (which was composed of urban elites, *mestiços*, *assimilados* and Kimbundu-speaking constituencies). UNITA claimed to represent the total union of Angolans and in particular the Ovimbundu masses of the central highlands, the Chokwe, the Ovambo, the Ganguela and other groups from south-eastern Angola. Savimbi's difficulty was in mobilising diverse groups into a coherent organisation, rather than a leadership dispute that led him to structure the commands the way Garang was forced to. Essentially, Savimbi faced a constituency issue and Garang a command issue, both of which were tied to the difficulty of overcoming problems due to disparate causes and interests.

Both UNITA and the SPLM/A divided their leaders to cover different military areas and manage other portfolios. Priority was given to placing trusted senior commanders at the different fronts and military regions, after which other roles and responsibilities would be distributed to develop the initial structures of command. UNITA's co-founders[18] were selected to run these areas following the hierarchy of 1) the military FALA that would have a supreme commander, a chief of staff, regional chiefs of staff, district commands, military councils and village forces; 2) a congress, a 12-member political bureau and a 25-member central committee with councils all the way from the party level to the village level as of 1969; and 3) the administrative structures defined at national, provincial, district, council and village levels (Chiwale 2008). In 1987, the leadership was restructured into a strategic organ that dealt with the politics of the revolution, the *Commando Operacional Estratégico* (COPE); a political commission that approved strategies; and a commission that implemented deliberations. COPE was the main strategic and operational command structure that brought together the military, the party and administration. Members of COPE included all the senior leaders of these branches, including intelligence agencies, who were there 'to help complete and advise Jonas Savimbi'.[19] There were also two separate COPE structures in the North and in the South of Angola that the office of the chief of staff followed closely.

Garang would also increase the numbers of the initial founders and enlarge the high command structures, both as a necessity, because the war was expanding to different areas, but also to further develop the representation of different communities. In early 1986, 10 additional senior officers were appointed to the PMHC as alternate members.[20] They were vital to the organisation at the operational level but were not decisive for strategic decision-making, and they had no veto power. The enlargement of the PMHC was meant to enable it to function as a council and parliament that would draft the movement's laws, decide on deployments of military commanders and operations, and deal with humanitarian organisations (Mach Guarak 2011). Each of its members would lead operations and administer the liberated areas under their purview. Yet the enlarged PMHC did not have the same coordinating capacity that COPE had for UNITA. It continued to embody the same structural challenges of amalgamation and lack of differentiation, seeing as the PMHC was the political party, the administration command, the military and the judiciary, with little understanding of separation of powers.

The SPLM/A's command structures blended 'autocratic control with an anarchic reactionary system premised on continual negotiation between Garang and the movement's upper echelons' (LeRiche and Arnold 2012: 41). The central command structures did not operate as forums to meet and discuss operations, monitor success and redirect strategies. Garang, as a result, retained the centralising authority, despite the challenges of controlling a vast territory while lacking proper communication systems, even when the 'importance of local cultures and tribal units conspire[d] against his ability to micro-manage' (Young 2003: 426). Garang also needed to retain control, allegiance and direction of the commanders on the ground. This was done at the local level through the cohesion of units under different commanders and at the national level through Garang rather than the PMHC. The ad hoc nature of the PMHC, an organisation that seldom met and was aimed at military rather than political decisions, meant that these mechanisms were hardly a blueprint for governance structures in the liberated areas. The forms taken by these structures in Yambio were influenced by interactions of governance with chiefs, civilian engagement and local political structures (e.g. liberation councils) rather than being consistently defined and reproducible institutions throughout all the SPLM/A liberated areas. In contrast, the structures in Jamba were created with the aim of being replicated at all levels of the liberated areas, as they were based on standards of operation, with defined hierarchies and reporting systems. The centrality of leadership structures and their ability to command all other areas of operation were reflected in the administrative capacity and design of the institutions of the parallel state. In Yambio, the central command had a tenuous influence on administration; in Jamba and other liberated areas, it was the ultimate authority.

Ethnicity and balancing interests

In stratified countries like Angola and Sudan, where communities lived relatively isolated existences and had few intersections for building an inclusive nationalist sentiment, the management of ethnicity and regionalism was crucial for the development of UNITA and the SPLM/A. Both movements managed these cleavages enough to ensure military cohesion and success, but not sufficiently to create strong political platforms for containing ethnic and community shocks by rival commanders, nor to build consensus across regions during peacetime politics. Both movements had to contend with several delicate balances. Criticism emerged that these movements, despite their nationalist appeal, were dominated predominantly by the ethnic group of their leaders. The SPLM/A was accused of being a Dinka-dominated organisation; UNITA was seen as a predominantly Ovimbundu organisation. Both Garang and Savimbi understood that they needed to empower commanders and political leaders from different regions and ethnic groups in order to secure the support of their constituencies and fighters. They also knew that retaining control of civilian populations in liberated areas meant they would have to provide for the inclusion and empowerment of local leaders. Yet, both Garang and Savimbi would continue to be criticised for their overdependence on recruits and commanders from their respective ethnic and regional strongholds.

Although the leadership disputes Garang faced in Ethiopia were based not on ethnic divisions among the Nuer and the Dinka but on the ideological issue of unity or secession (Johnson 2003), the first year of the SPLM/A was spent trying to neutralise the threat posed by two Nuer leadership contenders Akuot Atem and Samuel Gai Tut of Anyanya II (Johnson and Prunier 1993). When Atem and Gai Tut were killed in 1984, their rebellion was taken over by William Abdallah Cuol, who led an entirely Nuer force (Johnson 2003). The Dinka–Nuer fault line worsened after the 1991 split, as the two factions encouraged Nuer and Dinka civilians to attack each other (Johnson 2003). 'Initially, the [Dinka] refugees from Upper Nile and Bhar El Ghazal considered themselves to be the proud owners of the SPLM/A. The few of us from Equatoria who identified with the movement were considered mere "supporters" or "sympathizers"' (Wondu 2011: 144). Many Equatorians were initially sceptical about the objectives of the movement, seeing it as a tribal organisation aimed at restoring Nilotic domination. Several communities and groups took up arms against it over land and boundary disputes, while others—including the Murle of Pibor and the Mundari of Terekeka—were armed and instrumentalised as anti-Dinka militias by successive regimes in Khartoum (Johnson and Prunier 1993). While Sudan enhanced ethnic fault lines, the Angolan government chose to weaken UNITA with other political and military tools rather than ethnically fragmenting its constituent base. The war strategies of the enemy would therefore impact how different interests were balanced at the leadership level and within the organisations. Both Savimbi and Garang had to provide responses to the counter-insurgency strategies of the enemy forces.

The accentuation of these localised and ethnic counter-responses to the SPLM/A would pose a multitude of challenges during the 22 years of war. Initially, Garang was able to strategically bring in several other groups. Elements of Anyanya II—like the Upper Nile units, commanded by Captain Oyay Deng Ajak and Captain John Kulang Pot—joined the SPLM/A in October 1983. Anyanya II groups operating in Bahr El Ghazal and other young recruits from Eastern Equatoria also joined at that time (Malok 2009). The SPLM/A continuously absorbed forces from different militia groups and armed movements, which contributed to the difficulties of maintaining a unified command and structured movement. One of its key strategic decisions was to incorporate the different zonal commanders, from the Nuba Mountains (Yusuf Kuwa), the Blue Nile (Malik Agar), Darfur (Daud Bollad) and Western Bahr El Ghazal (Daniel Aweit), to expand its operations and give the movement a truly national character (Johnson 1998). By the late 1980s, the SPLM/A had secured a base in Eastern Equatoria, which meant that it 'could move beyond the Nilotic heartland. ... It also demonstrated that they could move, albeit tentatively, beyond the North-South border, and expand the war' (Johnson and Prunier 1993: 135). In fact, it was the fighters from the Nuba mountains and Abyei who were instrumental in liberating Yambio.[21] To counter the perceptions that the SPLM/A was a Dinka army, Garang placed Brigadier Samuel Abu John, a Zande, in the leading position of governor of the greater Equatorian region, which was reassuring to the people in Yambio. Despite this and efforts at the local administrative and military level to empower local commanders, the movement would still carry the Dinka label. After the 1991 split, the leadership council of the SPLM/A was comprised of seven Dinka members and six members from other communities. The issue was not the overrepresentation of one group but the fact that the SPLM/A did little to fully embrace other groups (Young 2003). Yet, at the local level, the SPLM/A allowed the 'sons and daughters' of their areas to take the political and administrative control of the liberated areas, which allowed the movement to accumulate significant nationalist political capital.

Savimbi also understood the difficulty of uniting disparate groups and initially opted to allow representation of different communities in the leadership. When this proved to be ineffective, he centred his commanders, political and administrative leaders around him in a tightly controlled and defined structure that coordinated all their operations. He used these structures to extend control to the local levels by empowering local leaders and appointing military commanders from the area to ensure effective coordination. Savimbi was concerned with erasing the localisms of communities as he forged a nation, much like Garang was; but unlike Garang, who failed due to weak political structures, Savimbi managed to subvert local interests to advance his political objectives. This was a strategy of layering command structures in such a way that they were all absorbed into a defined political world order.

Although the support base of UNITA had an ethno-linguistic regional nature (southern and eastern Angola), it projected itself as a nationalist movement. Yet it would struggle to get mass support from the constituencies rallied by the FNLA and the MPLA. As a direct response to the perceived Bakongo tribalism of the FNLA, UNITA initially decided to appoint three vice-presidents from different ethnic groups. The idea at the time was to achieve ethnic balance and have the Chokwe, who made up most of the movement's supporters in 1966, play a key role. 'The first [vice-president] was Smart Chata who was a Chokwe, the second was Salomon Njolomba, a Chivale from Bazombo, the third was Moises Muliata, a Banda from the Lundas; these leaders were given these roles also because they had already formed "proto-political organisations".'[22] 'In 1969, at the II Party Congress, UNITA ended this vice-president situation because only Chata wanted to fight in the interior ... we couldn't have figureheads that did nothing.'[23] The party had begun to divide itself into ethnic factions between 1966 and 1968, in particular while Savimbi was under arrest in Cairo for nine months. Upon his return in mid-1968, Savimbi found the movement divided into groups of combatants led by Samuel Chiwale, Paulino Moises and Samuel Kafundanga Chingunji (Weigert 2011). He would face the difficulty of having to reorganise his movement and assert his authority after having his leadership challenged.

At the II Congress in 1969, Savimbi appointed a Cabindan, Miguel N'zau Puna, as the secretary general and as the main political commissar of the forces, a move meant to demonstrate the national rather than regional character of UNITA (Marcum 1978). Throughout the movement's history, UNITA would have at its helm non-Ovimbundu leaders such as leading commander Antonio Vukulukuta (Quanhama), Ernesto Mulato (Bakongo) who served as Secretary for Administrative Coordination, Antonio Dembo (Mbundu) who served as vice-president from 1992 until 2002, among others. Despite this, the Ovimbundu nationalism that emerged during the anti-colonial struggle was different from that of the Mbundu (MPLA) and Bakongo (FNLA) populations because of the sense of cohesive identity and group solidarity that had been aided by the historic role of Protestant missionaries in the country (Heywood 2000). In the 1980s, this nationalism was laced with Ovimbundu political ideology that skilfully incorporated traditional beliefs (Heywood 1998). During the anti-colonial war, UNITA recruited from communities in the East and South, but as it moved into new areas in the 1980s it began recruiting from northern regions. Yet the Theory of Large Numbers—developed in 1977 to rally the Ovimbundu for war, like the SPLM/A had rallied the Dinka populations initially to secure large numbers of fighters—would later be used by critics to present UNITA as an ethno-regionalist and tribalist movement. Throughout their wars, both movements would recruit and mobilise across their countries, transforming their armies into multi-ethnic forces, although they would never truly shed their sub-national character.

Defections and purges

Disunity in rebel movements could lead to their defeat. It could undercut political and military organisational structures, deepen factionalism and affect combat support and the ability to plan, orchestrate and integrate military operations; but it could also lead to the diversion of material and personnel, and undermine external support (O'Neill 1990). Avoiding this and mitigating the effects of disunity were priorities for the leadership. On many occasions they were pre-emptive in their response, but in others the leadership had to contend with the fallout of division and subsequent purges. Both Garang and Savimbi were known to purge their commanders depending on their perception of threat, factionalism and the emergence of additional centres of power. By 1990, Garang had imprisoned several of his top commanders, including founding members Martin Majier, Joseph Oduhu, Arok Thon Arok, Kerubino Bol and others. However, Garang had a restrained approach that Savimbi would not develop. Savimbi was able to exert a level of control over UNITA's social order that was not possible on the SPLM/A's political and social terrain. The response to dealing with any issues in the SPLM/A was to create a committee, formed of representatives from different ethnic groups, to address people's concerns (LeRiche and Arnold 2012: 41). This revealed Garang's realistic understanding of the fragmented and diverse social terrain he faced and how loyalties were not so easily secured through nationalist appeals and centralising commands. The more nefarious aspects of the purges of the SPLM/A are yet to be fully divulged. While the Derg and Ethiopia's security services facilitated the control of dissent within the SPLM/A and alerted Garang to coup attempts during the first decade, several other commanders took key roles in countering dissent and ordering the killings of their fellow comrades.

Savimbi's brutal purges would eliminate not only the commanders but members of their families. One of the first incidents that shocked the leadership of UNITA was the allegation that a group of officers was planning a coup against Savimbi in 1981. Several senior commanders—including Chief of Staff Waldemar Chindondo, Commander Samuel Chiwale and then Foreign Secretary Ornelas Sangumba—were accused of plotting this coup, though this was never proven. Chindondo and Sangumba would be summarily killed, their bodies never returned to their families. Chiwale would survive but experienced a serious rank demotion. In 1991, the defections of Nzau Puna and Tony da Costa Fernandes would create irreparable damage to Savimbi, as they would make revelations about his role in the killing of Tito Chingunji and Wilson do Santos, as well as the witch-burning episode. In the war of the 1990s, many other senior commanders would be killed. Those who escaped—General Sachipengo Nunda (later appointed by the MPLA as Chief of Staff of the Angolan Armed Forces) and General Jacinto Bandua (appointed

Head of Psychological Warfare for the Angolan army), among others—would surrender to the MPLA.

While it is difficult to fully grasp what exactly happened and how these purges were justified, the commanders who stayed beside Garang and Savimbi would have had at one stage or other members of their families, communities and close friends killed, yet they would remain with the movements. The reasons to remain had to be much stronger than the fallout of defecting or abandoning the liberation struggle. Either way, both leaders and their closest commanders would have to invariably deal with the difficulties of managing divisive rifts without allowing their actions to escalate into purges that would weaken the cause, the morale and the structures of the movements. The vacuum created by the removal of key commanders also required the commander-in-chief to reposition other senior leaders and adapt structures so that command and control was assured.

While the role of these founding leaders was pivotal to their movements' trajectories, they did not do it alone. Beside Garang and Savimbi were military commanders, civilian leaders, intellectuals and politicians who made up the leadership backbone necessary to wage war on multiple fronts. They were instrumental in supporting their presidents when it came to devising strategy, giving legitimacy to the cause among diverse constituencies and advancing the design of the organisation. Without them, Garang and Savimbi would have struggled to sustain complex military operations; rally external support; manage intelligence organs, clandestine cells, logistics and communications; and diffuse internal dissent and factionalism. Their stories will need to be told one day and their contributions recognised.

Comparing these two leaders provides a clearer understanding of the lessons they applied from previous movements and peace processes, and how these factored into changes in organisation, leadership structures and negotiating positions. Garang understood that diversity of political objectives (some groups wanted secession while others sought autonomy and reform in the Sudanese context) and ethnicity would generate greater difficulties for creating a unified front. He opted for military efficiency and placed all the potentially fractious commanders, intellectuals and politicians within a hierarchical chain of command. This became the ultimate equalising strategy. Unable to command civilians and chiefs in a fully incorporated military hierarchy, he chose to devolve power to the 'sons and daughters' of each liberated area. Savimbi understood that, despite the Ovimbundu constituency not having its own political force, he would need to unite them and bring in other groups to build his third avenue for liberation. Although the political objectives that UNITA defended were essentially the same as those of the MPLA and FNLA until 1975 (to achieve independence), Savimbi understood that he needed to build his cause around political, not military, achievements. He experimented with placing leaders of different ethnic groups as vice-presidents but this led to fragmentation rather than unity. This led Savimbi to embrace cohesion around structures and political coordinating principles creating an executive stranglehold to eliminate contestation. The structures Savimbi built to support his leadership enhanced his autocratic control, more so than those of Garang, who obtained only a portion of the same hegemonic power despite being accused of running the SPLM/A 'out of his briefcase'.[24]

Ideology and political programmes

Understanding ideology, political programmes and war strategies allows for a clearer perspective of what these movements wanted to liberate, how they proposed to do it, which internal fault lines they needed to address and who they wanted to mobilise. While ideology was a system of ideals and the ideas spawned by those ideals, a political programme was a summary of the political party or movement's aims and principles, as well as a statement of proposed action. Ideologies provided a set of goals on how society and the liberation struggle should be organised, and the methods chosen to achieve this objective. War strategies had a military focus on how armed forces were employed to secure political and economic objectives by applying force. All three therefore had reinforcing elements. Assessing whether movements were capable of applying such ideals in their governing strategies of the liberated areas revealed important shortcomings and contradictions, mainly around the movements' capacity, the strength of their convictions, how they resonated with different constituencies, and their mobilising strategies.

The symbolism of anti-colonial liberation movements throughout Africa was framed within the paradigm of 'representing the oppressed, those wanting freedom and independence', as embodying the nation. In this way, they had a 'common theology' which stated that, regardless of its sins, the liberation movement was righteous and not only represented the masses but actually were the masses, and therefore could never be wrong (Johnson 2003).[25] This framing was employed mostly during the anti-colonial struggle, not so much by post-independence rebel movements, and highlighted the difficulty faced by second liberation movements in devising alternative strategies and political programmes to justify the continuation of war. This required a deeper unpacking of the conditions of national decay in new calls for revolution that emerged outside the colonial setting into one of continued marginalisation, failed governance, corruption and disillusionment with existing political arrangements and elites. Both UNITA and the SPLM/A framed their struggles as a fight against discrimination and the imperialist stances of elitist, exclusionary and unrepresentative governments. Yet their ideologies and political programmes were filled with complexity and contradiction that fed mobilisation and recruitment but stifled political growth and the drive to create a unified nationalist platforms.

Reform rebels had to determine in greater detail why their cause was just by mobilising, enhancing or creating grievances. This would form the basis of their new nationalism, linking ideology to different levels of local solidarity (Collins 2013).[26] By mobilising sub-national grievances, they attempted to carve out a 'people' that they represented and were responsible for liberating, yet they also needed to appeal to the national level while neutralising the contradictions between their rhetoric about the 'oppressed' and other communities they wanted to represent. Their parallel states were built in peripheral and rural areas, tapping into sub-national dynamics and relying on existing forms of local authority. They did this while trying to avoid the trappings of localisms to project a national agenda. UNITA and the SPLM/A aimed to correct the perceived failings of previous nation- and state-building endeavours, in the name of those excluded from these projects. The movements attributed these groups recognition and sought to empower them, while trying to erase the visible and invisible social and physical boundaries within their nation–states. A new nationalism had to be created for the justification of the second liberation, but also a new concept of the state had to emerge. It would do so through the projection of a deep clash of societies, state projects and visions.

Diverse ideational tools were used to organise collective action and sustain mobilisation. This meant tailoring messages for internal audiences (diverse communities, leaders and local allies) and external audiences (diaspora, patrons, regional hegemons) at different times. External patron support proved to be fleeting and driven by self-interest, and over two decades of war the SPLM/A received support from countries as diverse as Libya, Ethiopia, Eritrea, Uganda, Kenya, the United States, Norway and Cuba. UNITA too had many contradictory benefactors such as China, South Africa, the United States, Saudi Arabia, Morocco, Zaire, Senegal, Côte d'Ivoire and several European governments. Its alliance with apartheid South Africa was strategic but damaging, foreclosing the possibility of support from many other African nations and liberation movements. The eclectic array of patrons led both movements to balance flexible political positions with the unflinching resolve of their reform agendas. They had to guarantee that their political stances wouldn't alienate patrons but also wouldn't compromise their nationalist visions either. The populations that UNITA and the SPLM/A attempted to rally were also not homogenous groups, sustaining differences in ethnicity, socio-economic conditions, religion, race, levels of education, geography and experience of oppression, which provided different challenges and opportunities to the movements. Ethnic and religious antagonisms alone were insufficient conditions to spark rebellion unless they were accompanied by other conditions that favoured insurgency: marginalisation and poverty, political instability and contested spaces (Fearon and Laitin 2003). Rebel leaders had to understand the social fabric they were mobilising, and integrating ideologies with locally relevant political issues and social understanding furthered the mobilisation of different constituencies and social groups. The SPLM/A was able to redirect existing mass anger in the 1980s but unable to reorder such anger so that it would not turn against the movement in the form of different militia groups, thus failing to build a unifying political project across localisms and sub-national ethnic identities. To define a constituency to mobilise, UNITA had to enhance anger and frustration and define this as a sub-national issue with national implications, but it failed to project an integrative form of nationalism. The choices made during these initial stages found organisational expression to address the challenges of cohesion, integration, mobilisation and survival.

The ideologies crafted by UNITA and the SPLM/A out of historical grievances and utopian visions brought together many political ideals, pragmatisms and inconsistencies. They were self-styled ideologies that morphed over time to reflect local conditions and geopolitical shifts. From a unionist, secular and vaguely Marxist stance, the SPLM/A shifted to a Western-leaning ideology of self-determination and state reform. The vision for a New Sudan allowed the SPLM/A to define the aims of the war and who the enemy was, which became its strongest mobilisation tool, even if most southerners had secessionist ambitions. However, while the SPLM/A's ideology defined what the solution was, it failed to provide a strategy to achieve it. UNITA's Afro-traditionalist, socialist ideology combined a particular type of nationalism with a centrist, Western-leaning stance while heavily applying important tenets of Maoism. Its combination of contradictory political ideas, however, never suffered a significant shift during the civil war, even as it moved on from the anti-colonial war, which meant that the strategy defined—and the public policies defended—were deeply ingrained within the thinking of the leadership and supporters. Unlike the ease with which the SPLM/A redirected existing frustration and anger with Khartoum's failings, UNITA had to build on the sense of disenfranchisement and nationalist anti-colonial sentiment to justify a post-independence war against the MPLA and the Soviet–Cuban interventionist force. Yet UNITA's hybrid ideology gave it a level of permanence that the SPLM/A's ideology never achieved.

UNITA's ideology balanced several contradictions and inconsistencies. A general close to Savimbi explained that the internal realities of Angola that could only be economically and socially addressed with left-wing policies while externally right-wing policies were what secured UNITA much needed support. 'This led Savimbi to defend two policies and have two faces.'[27] Savimbi explained that 'from Mao and the Communists I learned how to fight and win a guerrilla war. I also learned how not to run an economy or a nation'.[28] This hybrid approach was explained coherently in several elite interviews. 'UNITA wanted to come up with its own revolution and not just be seen as a leftist revolutionary movement. That's why we studied the French and American revolutions, the Vietnam War and the political ideas of great strategists.'[29] UNITA wanted to define its ideology as fundamentally Angolan. 'In Africanism we defended the capacity to keep our values. ... The MPLA had the politics of acculturation and destruction ... they wanted to destroy everything that was Angolan, as it was the only way to perpetuate their regime.'[30]

UNITA's objectives during the second war were first the withdrawal of the Cubans, second to change the ideological principles of the MPLA—which was communist and acted contrary to Angolan society—and third to reverse the practices of marginalisation and exclusion.[31] UNITA's programme for Angola was explained by the four words on its coat of arms: socialism, negritude, democracy and non-alignment. Under socialism, UNITA would establish a collective production system and the planned development of the country. The concept of negritude meant that UNITA believed the 'cultural African identity of all the peoples of Angola is a pillar to the concept of national unity'.[32] Under democracy, UNITA used free elections to give Angolans the 'opportunity to give their views on those political economic and social problems that affect their lives' and form a government led by the majority.[33] As for non-alignment, UNITA's foreign policy ensured its independence of action in that cooperation with countries was based 'on reciprocal interest, mutual respect and non-interference in internal affairs'. In this way, the movement reflected the ideology of external alliances, the national character of society that they envisioned and also the piecemeal approach of combining different ideological tools to structure and justify the liberation.

The SPLM/A referred to itself as a socialist revolutionary movement in 1983 but proved to have a loose adherence to its ideological roots. The movement did not develop the vertical party hierarchy that linked mass popular horizontal organisations and a strong political party, as was normally associated with Marxist liberation movements. The imposition of socialism by the Ethiopians would also bring into question the commitment of the top leadership, as none of SPLM/A's five initial founders were known for their communist credentials (Arop 2006). Intellectuals in the movement pointed to the fact that these top commanders had little understanding of communism or socialist doctrine and applied the principles in a repressive manner. As a result, the SPLM/A was described as lacking ideological or political consistency. A leading commander explained that 'the brand of our socialism—which was a mixture of what was happening in Tanzania, Kenya, Ghana and Zambia—would reveal its nature as the pace of the struggle progressed. We did not want to commit dogmatically, so everyone was fighting. We had so much anger that we were fighting without an ideology'.[34] This idea that the SPLM/A essentially operated with its main unifying force the opposition to the North has been linked to the over-militarisation of the movement (Young 2003). Its 1983 manifesto was criticised for lacking the political direction that most liberation movements' founding documents developed. Its greatest weakness was 'the gap between establishing the validity of its cause and the realistic political strategy for realising its goals'.[35] Yet the lack of dogmatic rigidity or defined revolutionary principles brought together pastoralists, workers, peasants, students and intellectuals, allowing SPLM/A to become a 'melting pot for all these ethnic differences ... giving them a political and national context and form for the first time' (Nyaba 1997: 27). After the fall of the Derg, the SPLM/A shed its Marxist–socialist mantle, a pragmatic shift aimed at securing Western support.

The lack of ideological unity within the SPLM/A leadership also contributed to this hybrid nature that, unlike that of UNITA, was not only a matter of expediency with regard to alliances, but also a consequence of weak ideological and political structures. In 1985, the PMHC was said to have divided into groups of socialists, communists and capitalists, that 'instead of looking at themselves as revolutionaries, Bonga and Bilpham politicians looked at themselves through the lens of former political affiliations' (Mach Guarak 2011: 308). After the 1991 critical juncture and the emergence of the 1998 SPLM Constitution, the New Sudan took on a different form. The reform programme could be applied in five national settings to accommodate different forms of self-sufficiency, viewing the New Sudan as: 1) a unified country under a secular and democratic government; 2) a confederation; 3) a united secular African state; 4) a united Islamic Arab Sudan; and 5) two separate countries. These five models were meant to keep northern opposition parties, southerners and external allies engaged. In both cases, the critical junctures of 1976 and 1991 led UNITA and the SPLM/A to provide greater clarity on the reforms they proposed and the political contours of the countries they wanted. Despite their different definitions and degrees of consistency, both movements established their political programmes on reformist ambitions that defined the enemy and their constituent bases as opposing forces. Their hybrid nature was a consequence of having to accommodate different interests and needs while representing a vision that tried to unite such diversity.

Nationalist ambitions

The nationalist cause was for UNITA and the SPLM/A a matter of projecting a political endeavour to correct the failings of the first liberation and empower the disenfranchised people they claimed to represent. It also aimed at projecting a new national identity. The issue of nationalist, ethnic and sub-nationalist mobilisation would find expression in different moments of the movement's strategies. It was nationalism based on existentialist differences of instrumentalised sub-national grievances, yet called for unity of the nation. The difficulty with this kind of nationalism was the 'epistemological illusion that you c[ould] be understood, only among people like yourself' (Ignatieff 1994).[36] Both movements failed to build a nationalist platform uniting different communities that would have an enduring legacy. The nationalism that UNITA and the SPLM/A intended to create would never escape the paradox of its intended universality versus its local manifestations,

197

or its political power versus its philosophical incoherence (Anderson 1991). The way both movements conducted their political programmes ultimately led them to build an artificial construct of the society they were trying to represent. They had to craft a relatively unexperienced 'commonness' of oppression and project a future of aligned and reconciled interests, needs and values. They were trying to do two things in this way: to construct their alternative vision of the state and the nation by providing a platform that could unite disparate and diverse groups, and to forge the necessary nationalist unity that would help contain factionalism and dissent.

The SPLM/A's main challenge was creating a united front from a political setting that was characterised by tribes (Young 2003). It was because of this level of fragmentation that Garang was also against defining the war as solely a 'southern problem' rather than as a Sudanese problem. The movement needed to go beyond localisms, and war had to be taken to the north.

> The oppressor has divided the Sudanese people into northerners and southerners; westerners and easterners, Halfawin and the so-called Awlad El Balad who have hitherto wielded power in Khartoum; while in the South people have been politicized along tribal lines resulting in such ridiculous slogans as 'Dinka unity', 'Great Equatoria'. 'Bari speakers', 'Luo unity' and so forth. The oppressor has also divided us into Muslims and Christians, and into Arabs and Africans.[37]

Garang proposed that a new nationalism emerge, which he termed 'Sudanism', to stand in opposition to all the sub-nationalisms and political groupings. It was meant to unite all religions, ethnic groups, regions and cultures of the country and thus create a new Sudanese national identity. Yet Garang's insistence on fighting for a unified Sudan did not reflect the goals and aspirations of the many southerners who wanted secession (Akol 2003). Few structures within the movement reflected this cross-regional and supra-ethnic nationalism that balanced the power of Dinka leaders with those of other communities. The only institution that had a national character were the armed forces of the SPLM/A, as the administrative and political structures were developed mostly at a local level and empowered local leaders rather than being guided by national leaders and nationally defined political objectives. More importantly, the SPLM/A's unity position became a missed opportunity to create a binding nationalism from the mass spirit of resistance among southerners who supported the movement by virtue of their animosity towards the North. The lack of a defined southern nationalism capable of diluting insular tribal loyalties, and the failure at nation-building via political education due to the movement's lack of political structures, enhanced divisions in the South and localised the movement's administration experiment. While UNITA created popular support around its ideals and rhetoric, the SPLM/A's lack of political depth in its New Sudan vision fragmented a political setting that could have possibly been united.

The centrality of structures in UNITA and the ethnic diversity of the leadership gave a national character to the different branches of the movement, although the Ovimbundu were still the majority ethnic group. UNITA's constitution stated that 'without identity, cultural pride and proper civilisation ... the country runs the risk of disappearing'.[38] During the second war, UNITA rallied nationalist sentiment on the basis that the MPLA was not a black Angolan political party, but was a minority government, kept in power by non-African nations (Cuba and the Soviet Union), dominated by *assimilados* and *mestiços* who were complicit in the subjugation of black Angolans.[39] From the perspective of 'UNITA's black nationalism, the Soviets and Cubans represent[ed] an extension of white rule' (Marcum 1983). Ironically, the MPLA also pointed to the presence of foreign advisors and South African troops in UNITA areas to disqualify them. This informed the way legitimacy was contested on both sides. Despite UNITA's efforts to redefine Angolan identity, there was a 'powerful stream of Ovimbundu nationalism' underlying its Angolan nationalism (Heywood 1998: 148).

The nationalist ideals defined by UNITA and the SPLM/A were deeply linked to the confrontation of societies and clashes of visions that essentially were built along these sub-national concerns and needs. Although clearly aware of the need to build ethnically heterogenous movements to secure national identity, UNITA and the

SPLM/A failed to politically overcome the paradox that 'successful mobilisation requires, not the abolition of ethnic sentiments ... but rather the politicisation of ethnicity for nationalist purposes' (Chabal 2002: 200–1). The ultimate test for both would be whether they could win over supporters and leaders from the enemy camp. Both failed at this, as UNITA's political identity was not accommodating of other perspectives and never managed to make significant inroads into the MPLA's support base. It wasn't just a matter of ethnicity, it also entailed class distinctions, racial identities and different approaches to culture and tradition. The SPLM/A also failed at convincing the northern Sudanese (despite some support from the North and its strategic membership in the National Democratic Alliance) of its ability to represent all the facets (including Arabism and Islam) of Sudan's identity.

Confrontation of societies and visions

Both UNITA and the SPLM/A built their liberation rhetoric and programme around the belief that the enemy they were fighting held a vision and a state project that not only contradicted the very fabric of society (as they saw it) but was also a direct threat to the values held by the people these movements claimed to represent. It was a war of visions in Sudan and a clash of societies in Angola. To achieve the legitimacy of representing these groups, the SPLM/A and UNITA had to project divisions and frame their fights as existential, but also create the governing structures in the liberated areas to demonstrate their own version of 'stateness'. The motivation for creating parallel states in this regard partly emanated from this political positioning. The contours of the state project in Yambio and Jamba had to be understood within this context.

Conceptions of the state and their alternative visions for reform mattered. They mattered because they provided a blueprint to structure governance and arguably the design of institutions. They were the experienced element of the reform programme for their supporters and constituencies. For UNITA, the creation of a critical mass of civil servants, political leaders, engineers, doctors, administrators and so on aimed to advance the social order proposed by the movement. It was meant to provide the opportunity for an entire segment of the population to become a force capable of countering the assimilated elites of the MPLA and the 'imperialist' project it sustained through its collaboration with the Soviets and Cubans. For the SPLM/A, it mattered because building alternative state structures in direct opposition to Khartoum's state was part of the resistance. This led the movement to change names of administrative units, to organise consultative forums, to allow women to partake in economic and political life. It was about devolving power to the masses. To maintain symbolic and political capital, and to help overcome the many governance shortcomings, both movements enhanced their previous positioning to build a society that was loyal to the state.

For UNITA, this meant projecting

> a confrontation of two societies ... while Luanda had 500 years of contact with civilisation, Huambo [central Highlands] only completed 100 years [of its founding as a city by the Portuguese]. Here we had two different classes and two different societies ... When the Portuguese came and went to the coast they used blacks—chiefs, *chipaios* [slave traders] and *assimilados*—to fight the indigenous people of the interior. A conflict was created between the native in defence of the interests of the colonialists and those in defence of their own areas. People started seeing the black man that came with the white man as their enemy. This was the perception that was being created, that in the North and coast they are 'superior' to the South and the interior—those that came from the bush. Only with the passing of time did this battle unravel and the interior produced people to go and study in Portugal.[40]

This explanation used the Ovimbundu as an example of the disenfranchisement experienced by other people, and was framed as a matter of correcting historical injustices.

The war of visions in Sudan was over competing versions of the state and the nation. The SPLM/A and the Khartoum government were on opposite poles when it came to the secularisation of the state and the political characteristics of the system that supported it. 'The crisis of national identity in the Sudan emanate[d] from the fact that the politically dominant and economically privileged northern Sudanese Arabs ... den[ied] the African element in them' (Deng 1995: 484). For Garang, 'the central problem of the Sudan was that the post 1956 Sudanese state was essentially an artificial state, based on a political system and institutional framework of ethnic and religious chauvinism, and after 1989 on Islamic Fundamentalism. It was a state that excluded the vast majority of its citizens'.[41] The system that Khartoum operated could not be reformed, it had to be brought down so that 'in the ruins of the old we build a new Sudan'.[42] In this way, Sudan was 'still looking for its soul, for its true identity' (Khalid 1989: 127). Khartoum was imposing a syndrome of dependency in the South, as expressed by a colonel in Yambio, who explained that even to make bricks you had to get permission from Khartoum, which was another way of dominating people. The SPLM/A would counter this with programmes to allow people to become more self-sufficient and self-reliant. Yet like UNITA it also failed to accommodate the values of communities that did not experience this marginalisation. Other groups and movements fighting against the government in Khartoum, like in Darfur and elsewhere, were not ready to deny their own Arab and Islamic identities. This highlighted the difficulties that reform movements faced in attempting to represent many constituencies and align different interests into a political programme, yet never fully overcoming the unintentional narrowing of their proposed identities. Many in Sudan and Angola who were against the NCP and MPLA nevertheless felt unrepresented by the identities built by the SPLM/A and UNITA. As a result, the mobilising of different societies called for by UNITA and the SPLM/A did not result in the platform for inclusive empowerment the movements had hoped for. Rather, it created divisions in the social fabric of their countries because of the mutually exclusive formulations of the state and society they used, which were unifying for the purposes of war but destructive for the purposes of peace.

Organisation

The unpredictability of war, the disruption it effected on social structures and the difficulty of mobilising fighters and civilians to sustain a cause in the face of hardship and bloodshed demanded exceptional motivational and organisational skills from the movements' leadership. Political and military structures facilitated the absorption of the shockwaves of unpredictability; they also allowed for social systems to find new expressions, while creating the incentives and survival strategies for those engaged in the conflict to stay the course. Rebel movements needed to accomplish many tasks to make up for the fact that they were disadvantaged in the face of a stronger, better resourced and mobilised enemy. They had to control their organisation, recruit fighters, determine tasks and responsibilities, prevent defections, organise military operations, fundraise, establish communications and logistics systems that eluded government surveillance and ensure structures existed to survive multiple and consecutive threats. Organisation was one of the biggest factors that enabled rebels to compensate for the material superiority of adversaries (O'Neill et al. 1980). Organisations had to account for many dilemmas and the choices they made to ensure survival and optimisation of efforts. Opportunities were opened and closed by organisational structure (Staniland 2014). The two most difficult organisational challenges related to collective action and principal-agent problems (Jones 2017). Launching an insurgency required the mobilisation of fighters and supporters who had to overcome the accompanying risks. Different incentives (material and nonmaterial) helped ease this collective action problem, but this meant the movement needed to establish organisational structures and processes to retain support from the population and orientate their motivations for doing so. Lichbach (1995) proposed four solutions to the rebel's collective action dilemma: market, contract, community and hierarchy. Material incentives alone would not result in collective action without being 'supplemented by civil society (community), a constitution (Contract), or state (hierarchy)'. The principal-agent problem required other strategies to retain fighters once they had been mobilised, which included incentives and penalties for defecting but also required recurring engagement, indoctrination, monitoring and reporting systems. As insurgencies grew, they factored in several constraints of decentralising control, contract enforcement with supporters and the need for longevity not just immediate successes.

Organisationally UNITA and the SPLM/A couldn't have been more different. One was highly centralised with effective command structures at all levels, governed by a strong political wing and defined ideology. The other was decentralised by default, although headed by a controlling leader; lacked effective command structures linking different organs across the organisation; was not governed by a strong political wing; and fought in a relative ideological vacuum. Both movements developed the initial tools and structures they had prioritised at inception. They added structures following critical junctures but didn't alter their fundamental driving force and ethos: the SPLM/A remained militarised, and UNITA was guided by the political wing. They both understood that to compensate for material and other shortcomings they had to build a triad of self-reinforcing organs that would widen the scope of participants and entrench their vision at the local levels.

The first purpose of organisation was to ensure cohesion and centralise structure of command and control so as to provide political direction and discipline while managing incentives to secure allegiance. For UNITA, this meant simultaneously developing the three branches (party, administration, military), culminating in a centralised command headed by Savimbi. All branches were subordinated to the political transcendental cause of national justice and path correction. For the SPLM/A, the command structure absorbed all different areas under Garang with mid-level decentralisation at the military level and lower-level decentralisation for administration, with all subservient to the military hierarchy. Attempts by the SPLM/A to develop its three branches never changed this dynamic.

Given that direct military confrontation with a stronger army could result in a crippling defeat, movements needed other strategies to neutralise the support enjoyed by the state and strengthen their defensive capabilities. The development of administrative organs allowed groups to out-administer state authorities in their areas of local operation. The provision of services to different communities compensated for material and other shortcomings relative to stronger opponents. Groups that provided social welfare benefited in three ways: their provision of public goods highlighted the state's failure to fulfil its social contract; they offered populations alternative institutions in which to place their loyalty; and, once loyalty was secured, the population contributed to providing a steady stream of resources to help battle the regime (Grynkewish 2008).

In the Yambio chapter, the CMA system revealed how the SPLM/A militarised society as a governing strategy; it used the tools available to socialise its supporters into a military hierarchy above politics, ethnicity and regional divides. But it also revealed how the military was society's most important multi-ethnic institution and the main vehicle in promoting nationalism. It was through the military that civilians and their chiefs were given ranks and were able to take part in managing the SPLM/A-liberated areas, even when this created more animosity against the movement than it generated a following. During the CANS era, the SPLM/A allowed local power dynamics to determine citizenship of the New Sudan even as the political organs were trying to build a national platform of unifying symbols. Despite this, the military would throughout the war continue to define the leadership, identity and vision of the movement. UNITA, on the other hand, had a political view of organisation, and citizenship was achieved through training and political education so that communities not only understood and experienced UNITA's version of statehood, but they internalised its narrative of what it meant to be Angolan. This was a far more complex, intrusive and structured approach that also implied militarisation but was premised above all on socio-political engineering and control. 'UNITA leadership set out to design and control the entire life world' (Beck 2009: 349) of their supporters, fighters and populations. The SPLM/A did not have this objective, partly because the South Sudanese world order was so vehemently opposed to northern hegemony that the rallying call for mobilisation was already set out. The SPLM/A also lacked the political tools necessary to re-engineer society and identity. The fragmentation of the South also forced the movement to defer to the localisms and traditional authorities, imposing military hierarchy and discipline to appease differences, neutralise dissent and override tribal affiliations.

Both movements had to define structural differentiation based on hierarchy of power, functional differentiation based on division of labour (O'Neill 1990; Staniland 2014), and had to devise ways to coordinate these and other structures within a framework of rules and regulations. This was relevant to civilian governance insofar as the tools used to sustain structures, and to secure recruits' and leaders' allegiance, were the same tools used to build parallel states, reflecting the level of centralised and decentralised control, as well as the levels of persuasion and coercion. As a result, 'because political and military leaders had different preferences, policy outcomes were shaped by the institutional framework within which these groups interact[ed]' (DeVore 2012: 60). These frameworks were determined by core organising principles. For UNITA, it was democratic centralism. For the SPLM/A, it was a form of military-focus strategy with a corporatist component that relied on the conditions of believing that popular support was sufficient to keep the movement going and it therefore did not require extensive political organising efforts (O'Neill 1990).

The SPLM/A 'was not organised as a liberation movement, merging with the people and carrying out social reform. It was organised as a hierarchical army, broadly on the model of its opponent'.[43] The SPLM/A's decentralised approach was less a strategy and more a result of the need to outsource governance to chiefs, civilian leaders and aid organisations. It functioned also at the level of military operations and autonomy of commands during the CMA and CANS eras. The SPLM/A was 'able to harness local grievances by offering to liberate and preserve local custom and livelihood against the very real threat of religious, political and economic reorganisation from Khartoum, not by imposing a uniform "revolutionary" administration based on principles drawn from other liberation movements' (Johnson 1998).[44] While this may have been the case, the SPLM/A's lack of uniform administration and effective political organs was also its weakest element as a parallel government.

UNITA placed the political party as the coordinating structure of the movement. It also had a very clear distinction between the party and the movement. 'The movement represented everyone—from thieves to religious leaders—but the party was more selective and operated in circumstances that went far beyond the armed conflict.'[45] The revolution was to benefit all, but only those truly committed to UNITA's vision were members of the party. UNITA's political party created an administrative arm for civilian rule that wielded centralised control over all aspects of civilian life. The movement adopted a position of political dominance where its fighters, leaders and civilians had to be embedded in its ideological conception. The local population had to alter their perceptions to truly join the liberation struggle; civilians who were not persuaded by UNITA's vision had to nevertheless operate in politically controlled spaces.

Organisational capacity was also dependent on the stability of structures and their ability to provide continuation in leadership consultation and issuance of directives. A key difference between the two movements was the itinerant nature of the SPLM/A's headquarters, their mobility, lack of definition and lack of roots in one area which would have allowed for development of structures, training, consultation, leadership coordination and course correction. In this regard, having had its rear base in Ethiopia deeply impacted the SPLM/A. The movement failed to develop a central capital for political and administrative control, and different SPLM/A commanders explained that the headquarters were in different areas and played different roles. For some, Torit and then New Site was the political capital, while Rumbek was the administrative capital and Yei was where the military command was based. This changed at different times throughout the war. The movement had several headquarters for operational purposes: 'the tactical HQ was in Kidepo between Torit and Kapoeta, Yei was the administrative HQ after Yambio, while John Garang and his main officers (chief of military intelligence, communications, operations etc.) were the mobile HQ'.[46] A senior SPLA commander explained that the mobility of the movement's capitals and headquarters was intentional because wherever Garang was stationed was where the headquarter was for that day. Each commander had his headquarter, with about five in all the military regions, revealing a level of autonomy that would have created differences in the way the liberated areas were governed.[47] While having a mobile headquarter seemed innovative and a potentially effective way of overcoming centre-periphery dynamics, it failed. It failed not because of its conception, which reflected the decentralised military and administrative structures of the SPLM/A's parallel state, but because it lacked a unifying political arm for levelling out the inconsistencies and contradictions that weakened the war effort and that linked the local level to the central command.

UNITA took the opposite approach, with one UNITA ideologue explaining that 'we couldn't operate a transformation in a transitory situation', referring to the difficulties of the post-1992 war when the movement had moved from different bases in the central highlands despite having had Bailundu and Andulo as their headquarters.[48] For UNITA, having Jamba as the main rear base and capital became one of its key factors for success at the organisational level. This also allowed UNITA to effectively coordinate violent and nonviolent activity and create the basis for the new society they aimed to build. The movement's inability to reproduce this system after the 1992 war revealed how it was an inflexible system, and arguably unable to be applied to larger urban centres.

Political party structures

After their critical junctures (1976 for UNITA and 1991 for SPLM/A), both movements began to better coordinate the dual structure of the party and the military, even though the SPLM/A was developing the party structures along the way. Coordinating the dual structures also implied they worked as separate organs. UNITA would hold regular congresses and conferences, building a strong political foundation with these policy-making forums vital in defining and refining their strategy over the years. Congresses were held every four years where Savimbi and other leaders were re-elected. Conferences and central committee meetings were a yearly event, while the political bureau met every 3 months. The movement adopted as its three methods of work the principles of democratic centralism, collective leadership and criticism and self-criticism, which required the separation of political and military structures. The movement did this between the 1969 and 1973 congresses, with the nomination of a secretary general for the party and a separate chief of staff for the army. For UNITA, annual party conferences were big events that aimed at restructuring the movement, reviewed internal regulations and reformulated strategies. The XII conference of June 1979 was attended by 1,062 delegates from all the party structures, including the people's assemblies, local committees, mass organisations and missions abroad.[49] Compared to the SPLM/A, these elective conferences were as logistically challenging as the 1994 Chukudum convention which the SPLM/A was only able to replicate a decade later. Even then, it only held one such consultation during wartime, as opposed to UNITA that held several.

At the top of UNITA's hierarchy was the cabinet of the President and the commander-in-chief, which was a military as well as a politico-administrative cabinet. This was followed by the chief of general staff's office, the strategic organ COPE, the party secretariat and general administration. By 1985, UNITA had brought the leadership of the party and the armed forces under the Executive Committee, which had 12 permanent members (ranging from front commanders to the secretary general of the party) and 5 additional members. It was followed by the National Committee, which included Savimbi, the members of the Executive Committee and an additional 33 members. The National Committee was elected at every party congress and was charged with executing the movement's policy, which was then implemented by the party's secretariat. Although the party took a prominent role, Savimbi like Garang still centralised decision-making power in a smaller group and a more restrictive organ. The main difference was that every few years under UNITA's party system the party would elect and re-elect key leaders, holding different portfolios, and the compositions of different organs.

The SPLM/A would only develop the dual structure of separating the political (SPLM) from the military (SPLA) after the 1994 convention. The structural and organisational results of the Chukudum convention would in principle alter the movement significantly. In practice, the separation functioned better at the lower levels than at the senior leadership levels. The SPLM/A did not have distinct command structures for administration and political structures, although it did have the SRRA humanitarian wing that was arguably considered an initial administrative structure in the 1980s. What the SPLM/A did was fuse the party with local government and administrative structures, as both were developing simultaneously. The General Field and Staff Command Council (GFSCC), formed in February 1992 and composed of a group of 61 military leaders, was the interim government structure until the convention was held. This meant more collective decision-making, an element that was missing during the PMHC era. Some SPLM/A leaders pointed to the fact that, while Chukudum established a government-like organisation, it failed to change the way the movement was run and decisions made. Others stated that Chukudum created a culture of conferencing that allowed for a process of sharing ideas, brainstorming and establishing collective responsibility for the liberation process. It also allowed those who didn't carry guns to become freedom fighters (Wondu 2011). The congress and other large policy conferences held by the SPLM/A in the 1990s were not dissimilar to how UNITA conducted its leadership consultations. However, over the course of 30 years, the SPLM/A only held 3 conventions (in 1994, 2008 and 2016), while UNITA held 13 congresses, 4 extraordinary congresses and numerous central/national committee meetings.

Meetings of the different political party organs were sporadic for the SPLM/A. Upon its formation in 1994, the National Liberation Council (NLC) was unable to meet regularly, and as the central committee it remained ineffective. The disorganisation of the SPLM/A's structures led to a partial reversal of collective decision-making in 1999/2000 that saw the creation of the Leadership Council, which reinstituted a similar structure to the PMHC. The Leadership Council was an amalgamation of the executive and the party, and it effectively took over the functions of the NLC and the NEC (Deng 2003). It was transformed into the Political Bureau following the 2004 SPLM Strategic Framework for War to Peace Transition but would only be formally created in May 2008, 3 years after the SPLM had begun functioning as a government. Essentially, the SPLM/A would only develop political party structures 20 years after its founding, with links between the political and military areas of the SPLM/A remaining tenuous even after the 1994 reforms.

The ultimate test for the political structures of both movements would come after the deaths of their founding leaders. When Savimbi died in 2002, UNITA managed to transition into peacetime politics and fully disarm (partly due to its military defeat but also to the belief that the party could rebuild itself and compete in the democratic process). Savimbi held one last party meeting in late 2001 in the bush to prepare his leaders and cadres for UNITA's transformation into a political party. He gave them a set of steps and policies they needed to implement, knowing that he was not going to survive the last assault on UNITA.[50] When Garang died, the SPLM/A morphed into a more personalised and less institutionalised structure. Any traces of collective leadership disappeared, and political consistency with the vision of a New Sudan was discarded in favour of political expediency ahead of the 2011 independence referendum. Despite having attained the goal of reaching power, the SPLM/A would splinter into several factions in 2013.

Three other areas differentiated UNITA's strong ideological grounding in its liberated areas from those of the SPLM/A. The political groundwork of educating cadres, building an army of political commissars, structuring effective propaganda and communications systems, and expanding political structures through syndicated organisations revealed the structured organisation of one movement and the neglect by the other. UNITA had a vast enterprise of propaganda, education and political commissars at the service of its war effort. The VORGAN radio, the Kwatch press and the thousands of communiques sent, both abroad and to the interior of Angola, since the 1960s created a powerful structure that fed the movement's social engineering project. A vast network of communication and intelligence directorates guaranteed that information was secured and updated. UNITA's leadership was fully aware of what happened on the military, political and civilian fronts. The movement established leadership schools and far-reaching education programmes to ensure indoctrination and allegiance.

In contrast, the SPLM/A had less extensive and elaborate systems of communications and propaganda, lacked a strong ideology directorate that trained and empowered political commissars and lacked syndicated organisations for the first decade of its liberation. Political education occurred initially in Ethiopia, as a wholesale import of the curriculum of Ethiopian political schools that taught 'Marxist philosophy and hard dialectics to peasants and secondary school dropouts' (Nyaba 1997: 54). The SPLM/A was criticised for failing to invest time, resources and effort into creating the body of political commissars and cadres needed to build political structures and socialise the masses. This lack of political mobilisation 'led to institutionalized militarism, warlordism, relegation of conscious political discipline and social harmony to brute force, military authoritarianism and absolutism' (Nyaba 1997: 55). Key SPLM/A leaders recognised this deficiency. 'The building of capacity was thought of later. We should have done this concurrently. Some did get courses in Cuba and in Addis, but there was no clear plan to send fighters to schools. The Institute of Revolutionary War in Gambella and Bonga only worked until 1991 and was for officers and intellectuals.'[51] The Department of Ideology, under the command of Amon Mon Wantok and Alfred Lado Gore, played an important role in the 1980s, helping train political commissars in Itang and Bonga in Ethiopia. However, this department became an institution that also served to eliminate or exile those perceived as 'enemies of the revolution' (Malok 2009).

One of the few propaganda tools the SPLM/A had was Radio SPLA. The radio first aired on 12 October 1984, and for eight years it proved to be instrumental to the war and disseminating the SPLM/A's mission. Policies and changes within the movement were announced on the radio, with programmes aired in English, Arabic, Zande, Dinka, Nuer, Shilluk, Nuba, Bari and Juba-Arabic. Programmes would include news from the battlefield, an analysis of the political situation in Sudan, the vision and mission of the SPLM/A, calls for material and human mobilisation for the war, among others. When the movement retreated from Ethiopia in 1991, they brought a mobile transmitter and broadcaster and tried to re-establish the radio from Torit, but this too came to an end when Torit was captured in 1992. Attempts were made to re-establish Radio SPLA inside other areas, but this failed due to the instability after the Nasir split. Instead, the movement turned to print media to disseminate information inside and outside the country through editions of *SPLA Update* monthly and others. However, the publication was limited as a mobilisation tool.

Propaganda and communications contributed to organisational complexity by assisting in coordination, internal specialisation and indoctrination required to maintain allegiance. Its purpose was to unite support for common goals, distinguish enemy groups and separate spheres of legitimacy. For those it united, it was meant to convince followers and future supporters of the righteousness of the course of action taken. Conversely, it built layers of demoralisation and division for those it treated as enemies, and it used them as targets for anger. The use of psychological warfare, of which propaganda was an integral part, could vary in intensity, capacity and diversity, but it was key to manipulating people's attitudes towards their wars. The choice of medium depended on the audience being targeted (recruits, different communities, state sponsors, diaspora, government forces or allies). It also depended on the technological capability, communications infrastructure, resources and ability to coordinate different operations.

Had the SPLM/A been able to implement far-ranging indoctrination strategies and broad propaganda tools to socialise fighters and politically mobilise civilians, it could have more easily united the many disparate groups that inhabited its political and military universe. Cohesion at leadership levels suffered throughout its liberation campaigns, for many different reasons including personal animosities, ethnic rivalries, ideological differences and transactional interests. This made it even more urgent to bring in a unifying political operation. Instead, the military provided a structure, hierarchy and language of violence and reward that all could understand regardless of ideological, communal or regional schisms. But this structure was based on the frivolity of power in a setting of war that would not translate to the political magnetism needed to govern civilians and build a nation. In contrast, from its foundation in the 1960s, UNITA understood the need to socialise the masses into its revolution but also knew the value of producing propaganda aimed both at the interior of the country and externally, to counter the exiled politics of the other two movements. During

213

the second war, these propaganda tools would become more sophisticated, imprinting ideas, narratives, versions of events and justifications on those fighting, those observing and those opposing. UNITA's success in this regard kept at bay many of the potentially fractious rifts that could have led to the movement's unravelling due to the totalitarian nature of Savimbi's leadership. But it wasn't just propaganda that kept elites together, it was the deep-structured political work that led many to blindly follow the path set out by UNITA's socio-economic vision for the country and the political reform it promised.

Military organisation

Writing on civil–military relations, Huntington highlighted that 'the military institutions of any society are shaped by two forces: a functional imperative stemming from threats to the society's security and a social imperative arising from the social forces, ideologies, and institutions dominant within society' (1957: 2). In this manner, the military was equally a factor of politics, of society and of the different institutions that brought people together. Both UNITA and the SPLM/A developed semi-conventional armies that fought against government forces with the same intensity as two standing armies. Militarily, both movements produced very effective command structures that allowed for operational autonomy and the competent exercise of centralising control. The scale of military operations of these movements required them to coordinate multiple operations and run effective communications systems and complex logistical lines, as well as maintain a supply of weapons and adequate distribution of resources.

What contributed to the level of military success for both was the structured and systematic training by elements of two large armies—Ethiopia for the SPLM/A and South Africa for UNITA—in the safety of a rear base that was not threatened by enemy forces, coupled with mass recruitment campaigns which rapidly built the movements' capacity to move beyond guerrilla attacks. Yet this development occurred for UNITA after its critical juncture, while for the SPLM/A it occurred before the critical juncture. This meant that the way the armies were built either incorporated the parallel state as a pillar of military survival (UNITA) or did not factor in civilian support as being intrinsic to military survival (SPLM/A). While UNITA shifted its military strategy after the critical juncture to enhance its capacity to combat government forces, the SPLM/A maintained its strategy of having an amassed army after the critical juncture in order to replicate previous successes. This revealed that the leadership's entrenched interests and operating procedures were harder to reform after critical junctures when they were already cemented in organisational structures, even if leadership did go on to adopt new strategies. The inability to correct this would cause great difficulties for the SPLM/A even as the liberated areas were being locally managed, with problems emerging between civilians and abuses by the army. The military therefore did not accompany the political and administrative changes. Rather, an amalgamation of forces would further the lack of structural and political definition given the expedience of militia alliances that remained largely outside the SPLA.

The level of reform the SPLM/A army was open to after the 1991 juncture was limited by its previous military victories and the need to regain military control after defections and mass losses. The formula before 1991 had been successful in military terms, and this hampered the extent to which military commanders and officers were willing to give into civilian and political control. This reform–resistance was cemented at the leadership level. These commanders were placed above the executive ministers, positions, as explained in the Yambio chapter, weakening the political command of the army. For UNITA, the extent of political training and development that existed before the critical juncture allowed the movement to build a mass army in a politically controlled way, which reversed the balance of power as reflected in the SPLM/A case. In UNITA's case, the army was at the service of the wider political project; it was one instrument in a coordinated three-pronged socio-political and economic strategy. This empowered the administrative branches, enabling them to coexist with authority next to the military branches. The party stood above both, as political commissars were at the fronts engaging the FALA and continuously imbuing them with UNITA's political ideology.

Having a parallel state and shadow government required the projection of military power as a form of state power. The movements had to project power throughout different areas of the country as a way of undermining their enemies' authority and intimidating their troops, while simultaneously attracting support by virtue of military victories. The rebel army was also the first structure to make significant inroads into different areas of Angola and Sudan where the movements were not dominant, especially in areas that were not naturally sympathetic to liberation, as was the case of Equatoria for the SPLM/A and northern provinces for UNITA. In analysing the parallel state, it becomes clear that the military was a tool for mobilisation, for representation of different constituencies and for cementing the advances of the liberation struggle on the ground. The military was also a source of antagonism, and the violence it perpetrated against civilians often generated rejection of rebel rule. The strategies used to continue fighting in a sustained way, even as the amount and accessibility of resources differed, was for UNITA and the SPLM/A a matter of aligning military fronts and divisions outside and alongside administrative units and logistics channels. When these didn't always align, governance strategies shifted and adapted to less centralised and more localised forms, as was the case with Yambio but not Jamba.

Militarily, the SPLM/A followed a conventional army structure to accommodate the mass recruitment and number of fighters it had to organise. At its peak, the army could have numbered over 400,000, in following with the Soviet tradition of massed armies,[52] although other estimates point to 100,000 (de Waal 2015). The smallest unit of the SPLM/A was the platoon of 12 men, and its largest unit was comprised of between 10,000 and 12,000 men. Each of the divisions of the SPLA were then subdivided into reinforced brigades. The movement divided military operations into different categories of Axis Command, Zonal Command and Front Command.[53] The five Axis Commands were commanded by the five permanent members of the PMHC, while the four Zonal Commands (that were for independent military areas) were commanded by alternate members of the PMHC.[54] By September 1989, Garang created three fronts: the Bright Star Campaign (BSC), headed by Garang; the New Funj

Campaign (NFC), headed by Willian Nyuon; and the Kon Anok Campaign (KAC), headed by Salva Kiir. As mentioned earlier, the pursuit of rapid military successes in the 1980s subverted several important reforms that the SPLM/A should have undergone to counterbalance the social stratification and presence of different militias they confronted. Garang chose to balance interests and incorporate groups into a massive military machine rather turn them into a coherent national force. It would take the SPLM/A almost four years before it could begin staging large military offences after the 1991 critical juncture. Slowly it managed to rebuild its capacity and began the process of absorbing different factions into its ranks. In 1995, William Nyuon's group was reintegrated with the Lafon Declaration; this was followed by Kerubino's group in 1998, Peter Gadet's group in 1998, the SSDF Fangak group under Taban Deng Gai in 2001 and then the reunification with Riek's group and the SPLM-United under Lam Akol in 2002. The SPLM/A's strategy of integrating different groups with diverging political views never changed after the critical juncture. In 2005, the South could have had as many as 50,000 troops associated with 60 other armed militias.[55] This would be reflected as a major difficulty in the CPA and post-independence years.

The disintegration of the SPLA along factional lines in 2013 was part of the problem of the movement not having instituted a basis for a disciplined army that would undergo defence transformation and submit to civilian rule. Another issue that would haunt the SPLM/A leadership in 2013 was the ethnic composition of the army and in particular the senior command. Although the movement had recruited from all five regions of the New Sudan, it remained under the control of the Dinka and some Nuer commanders. 'The only standing army was predominantly Dinka; other nationalities were always recruited at the campaign level to liberate certain areas. They were overwhelming during the capture of Yei, Torit etc. But in the end the other ethnicities were sent home and only the Dinka and the Nuer remained.'[56] This testimony described what occurred during several campaigns in the 1980s and 1990s, although these divisions were reflected in the composition of many battalions after independence. At the time of independence in 2011 the SPLA could

217

have had as many as 25 militia groups in its ranks bringing it's total force to 200,000, with differing loyalties. In addition, after 2011 the Nuba and Blue Bile units of the SPLA returned to their areas and took on their own liberation against Khartoum as the SPLM-North. In heterogeneous settings like Angola and Sudan, the ethnic composition of the army's command and fighters became important, and the balances struck would either consolidate previous gains or unravel them.

UNITA's armed forces, the FALA, were created and organised around the slogan of revolution and reconstruction. By 1974, UNITA claimed to have 4,000 trained guerrillas, although this was an overestimation (Marcum 1978). Over the course of 1976–86, UNITA became a fighting force that directly contested and fought against the better-armed FAPLA. In 1981, the first brigades (12th, 21st, 53rd, 34th and 45th) were formed and began operating as independent units. UNITA was present in all the provinces by 1984, making massive inroads into non-Ovimbundu areas (James 2011). By 1990, FALA claimed to have 20,000 regular troops, 18,000 semi-regulars, 20,000 compact guerrillas and 35,000 dispersed guerrillas, although numbers could have ranged anywhere between 28,000 to 90,000 (ibid.). The level of expansion and innovation the movement enjoyed during these years was due to the training and stability of the rear base, and the need to engage the MPLA forces on all levels, as the latter were supported by the superior armies of Russia and Cuba. UNITA's areas of military operations were structured around 5 strategic fronts and 22 RMs, with each being subdivided into military sectors and military detachments. Military detachments under each RM worked closer to the cities and operated like clandestine cells. Zones were created according to the geographic terrain. Strategic fronts established in 1983 were: 1) Esperança Negra in the Lundas, commanded by General Nunda; 2) Estamos a Voltar in the Central Highlands, led by General Chendovava; 3) the RM25 Front of Cazombo and the East, led by General Chilingutila; 4) A Frustração do Povo, north of Huambo until Malange; and 5) the Southern Front. These were established immediately after Savimbi finalised the first year of CEKK strategy training for commanders. Each front grouped together five RMs. 'Savimbi did not manage the autonomy of these sectors. It was the chief of staff of the front that was responsible for running the military and politico-administrative affairs.'[57] UNITA had several rotations of chiefs of staff of the army. From 1966 to 2002, UNITA had nine chiefs of staff of the FALA.[58] Despite its military focus, the SPLM/A had fewer chiefs of staff in its rotation.[59] Both movements were able to decentralise their military commands to allow for operational autonomy in each of the different fronts and military regions. This was a major contributor to its military effectiveness and the extension of administration of territory.

The differences in terrain, technology and weaponry used by the opposing armies, and the military strategies of the enemy—the use of proxy militias by the Sudanese army, and the sophisticated weaponry aided by Soviet advisors and Cuban troops by the Angolan army—impacted their organisations. Ultimately, both UNITA and the SPLM/A created military organisations that in many aspects mirrored the characteristics of the enemies they were fighting. Strategically, they only needed to be as organised and effective as the government forces they were fighting against, or at least organised and effective enough to neutralise their advances. In Angola, a large part of the war was characterised by large campaigns with sustained battles. In contrast, Sudan's counterinsurgency strategy was done on the cheap, using ethnic militias to support and conduct operations. These liberation forces were created differently. Unlike UNITA, which began as a guerrilla force, the SPLM/A began with two battalions of army defectors and several armed groups. Garang reflected in 1996, 'We did not start as a movement in the classical way of Latin American liberation movements ... we started as a mob. We have been in a series of reforms, reforming a mob.'[60] The organisational challenges of coordinating this mob were different to those of building a rebel army from guerrilla units to brigade-sized forces, as was the case for UNITA.

Military success was always underpinned by effective logistics. Logistics were the sinew of war from the beginning to the end. They were the backbone of organisations and determined their capacity for staging complex, simultaneous and decisive operations against the enemy. Yet, logistics for insurgencies could make a little go a long way, while for government and counterinsurgent forces a whole lot was never enough (Vlasak 2007). Several elements made up this logistical infrastructure: supply networks and bases, local and external support dimensions, logistic cadre development, transportation, concealment and deception, technological application and explosives, rural and urban aspects, printing and disseminating directives, money-raising approaches and phased support for guerrilla movement growth (Turbiville 2005). Movements had to be able to coordinate logistics to allow for armament, ammunition, gasoline, food, troops and other materials to move between fronts and liberated areas, but they also had to differentiate support to operations of special units and small cells, all the way to battalions and brigades. The coordination of supplies across numerous jurisdictions, neighbouring countries and further afield also entailed other organisational elements such as external representatives and lobby efforts, military and political contacts and a financial structure to ensure the transfer of funds. A key part of logistics related to the communications systems used for military operations, logistics, communication between bases and specialised areas of leadership communications, intelligence processing, coding and counterinformation. The support provided by the military logistics systems of the South African defence forces to UNITA, and the Ethiopian Derg to the SPLM/A, had the greatest impact on the movements' ability to survive the first decade of their wars. The SPLM/A had used the Gambella region of Ethiopia as a fundamental part of its logistics system until 1991, where even refugee camps had become logistical support centres (Nyaba 1997). The rapid military successes of the SPLM/A in the 1980s and its capacity to regroup in the mid-1990s revealed a movement that had very strong logistics systems. These instrumentalised international aid, regional support and armament from diverse sources. Transitioning from guerrilla to conventional warfare required serious investment in logistics infrastructure and associated capabilities for UNITA in the late 1970s. During the 1980s, Savimbi's trail allowed the movement to use human couriers to move supplies through enemy areas. UNITA's rear base inside Angola, near a friendly country, allowed it to be resupplied without much constraint through Namibian territory. The high stakes of its war and the mass injection of resources, in particular after the repeal of the Clark amendment by the US Congress in 1985, allowed UNITA to vastly expand its bases to support the transfer of weapons and other supplies. As UNITA grew and began waging a conventional war in the 1990s, while also governing urban areas, its logistical capacity progressed and extended to its diamond extraction enterprise.

Conclusion

The founders of two of Africa's most resilient insurgencies were complex leaders. Savimbi and Garang were talented politicians who manipulated regional and national emotions, electrified their supporters and terrified their opponents. UNITA and the SPLM/A were both the creations and vehicles of their founders, who believed in their duty and right to govern as presidents of their people. In varying degrees, Savimbi and Garang felt they had a patriotic mission in which they played a messianic role to liberate their people from oppression and 'savagery'. Arguably, only two strong, strategic and centralising leaders could have forged a new nationalism aimed at uniting disparate groups, mobilising the population for a reformist war that not everyone fully understood (unity instead of secession for the SPLM/A, and an anti-imperialist war post-independence for UNITA) and appeasing accusations, ideological contradictions from internal audiences and external patrons. Strategy, ideology and alliance building were 'a commerce conducted in as many currencies as there are interested parties' (Luttwak 1987: 220), a phenomenon both leaders grasped well as they navigated the level of internationalisation of their wars within Cold War politics. Yet they were considerably different in how they organised for war. While both demanded loyalty and commitment to the cause, Savimbi focused on ensuring that his commanders engaged in collaborative work that legitimised the political order they operated. Garang balanced ethnic and regional fault lines by engaging his commanders with a compelling purpose which united disparate groups. They both learnt from the mistakes of the insurgencies before them, the dissolution of previous peace agreements and the capacity of their societies to sustain protracted wars.

The strength of both leaders' political message increased as they overcame crushing defeats, UNITA in 1976 and the SPLM/A in 1991. These critical junctures threatened to dismantle both organisations, render their ideologies irrelevant, and disarticulate their command structures and armed forces. Both leaders chose different solutions and pathways to survive. Both reformed their leadership and second-tier command structures to ensure control over the liberation; they decentralised control over specific areas by striking different balances.

At a leadership level, Garang had to show strength in 1991 to avoid the movement's collapse and motivate troops to keep fighting after huge losses. He understood that the centralising and authoritarian tendencies had to be corrected if the movement was to avoid fracturing further, and he began creating forums for greater consultation, like the 1994 national convention of the party. While there was a level of displacement in leadership structures to allow for more collective decision-making, many structural factors impeded their functioning: the lack of a central command base, the de-concentration of governance across unlinked liberated areas, ill-defined and weak political structures. At UNITA's leadership level, the 1976 critical juncture forced Savimbi and his officers to retreat and build the movement's military capacity while formulating different political and administrative strategies. The key to this was the creation of the rear base in Jamba where leadership could train and direct the war effort. Leaders from different ethnic groups were nominated to lead the three branches of the movement, but this was based on political and military expediency, allegiance and skill rather than the need to balance ethnic interests. This aimed at ensuring a level of efficiency and control that would sustain national rather than local objectives. The leadership schools and training programmes allowed UNITA to create a class of cadres and commissars that became key to operating the governing systems in the liberated areas. The SPLM/A lacked this political groundwork, which exposed it more to the detrimental effects of tribal divisions. Political disputes among its leaders risked becoming tribal conflicts, which they did in 1991. Tapering over this dynamic through military hierarchy and an ill-defined ideology was a strategy for war, not for governance or peace. UNITA, unlike the SPLM/A, was training its people to govern, preparing for peace as it grew militarily. This element alone would partly explain why UNITA survived as an organisation in peacetime and its leadership remained united after its defeat, while the SPLM/A imploded and factionalised after victory.

The hybrid and self-styled ideologies of the SPLM/A and UNITA brought in the strengths and weaknesses of ethno-nationalist (Clapham 1998; Sambanis 2001) and revolutionary (Kalyvas and Balcells 2010) ideologies. Movements that mobilised through ethno-nationalist ideologies tapped into existing and socially defined issues. Revolutionary ideologies faced a more difficult mobilisation path of having to justify the change in political order, which had both an element of unpredictability and a projected belief in the capacity to rule differently. Defending a second liberation as a just and necessary cause projected the two movements' political programmes as existential struggles aimed at protecting the marginalised and disenfranchised from an exclusivist, elitist and discriminatory state. For both UNITA and the SPLM/A, the clashes of societies and wars of visions had to rally support from different constituencies, aiming at mass recruitment of fighters but also of civilian support. Civilians were crucial because they would provide the justification for having a new society and new political order. Above all, it was the promise of strength to the marginalised communities they rallied that became the most successful political tool.

Post-1991, the SPLM/A was able to rally key constituencies under a loosely framed ideological and political project—the re-conceived New Sudan vision—that allowed for greater buy-in from local communities and incorporated broader possibilities for self-determination. This aligned the movement's aims with the southerners' visceral desire for independence. Post-1976, UNITA adopted a new political programme; it reformulated its objectives and moved to capitalise on the presence of foreign troops to launch a nationalist war. It strategically replaced the Portuguese imperialists with the MPLA 'neo-imperialists' as the enemy. The post-critical juncture strategies defined by both movements would factor the parallel state as a key pillar of military, logistical, political and symbolic survival.

The organisational divergence between the SPLM/A and UNITA revealed two different approaches to governance. The SPLM/A's weak political organisation led it to decentralise governance to the grassroots level and the chiefs. Its militarised ethos allowed for the permeation of a culture of militarisation and the mythologising of virtues of the fighter, which distorted the balance of civilian and military interests and needs, and at whom the liberation was aimed. UNITA's strong political structures meant Jamba was under very tight political and administrative control, where all aspects of life were coordinated. The necessity of creating an equalising southern force factored deeply in UNITA's move to have politics dictate all other aspects of its campaign, including the military and society. UNITA had in this regard a more rigid and dogmatic approach than the SPLM/A, which made it more vulnerable to change. The SPLM/A was less effective in replicating structures and providing standardised governance. This did not mean that the SPLM/A lacked organisation; rather, the opposite was true. The movement managed to rally tens of thousands of combatants and organise their operations in a highly diverse social and military terrain, securing territory that faced such numerous challenges as lack of infrastructure, isolation and lack of resources. This comparison showed that organisation could take different forms as long as either the political or military wing was robust enough to provide unified leadership structures and the ideational, administrative, territorial and relational capital to rally and sustain collective action.

Post-critical juncture, both movements defined a three-pronged approach to their liberation campaigns that combined the party with administration and the military. Organisational development had to 'accompany the escalation of violence' (O'Neill 1990: 94) but also had to provide responses to the defeats experienced. The SPLM/A organised around military structures until the complexity of the war enhanced political and social fragmentation within the southern resistance, necessitating stronger and more inclusive strategies to incorporate civilians and chiefs into the political structures. The military had to recalibrate its conduct and war ethos. Fighters would become administrators, working parallel to civilian leaders and traditional authorities, without any political training. Yet, the

SPLM/A never fully achieved its separation of civilian/political and military authority due to its weak political tools used to alter the behavioural DNA of the military. This implied building political structures to rally communities and govern them using untested and ungrounded political tools. This drove the movement to outsource governance to existing local structures and instrumentalise aid agencies as service providers. At the organisational level, UNITA formulated a complex multi-tiered organisation that coordinated all the facets of war and governance, while socially engineering an army of fighters, cadres and a social base of civilian support. It continued organising around political structures but focused on building the necessary military capacity to move beyond the guerrilla warfare stage. All structures were imbued with politics and the justification for the war. The party became the nation for the citizens of the Free Lands of Angola. The three branches of the movement—military, party and administration—became coordinated and structured in ways that allowed for the reproduction of institutions in all the liberated areas.

The legacy of these structures and the experiences of civilians in the liberated areas of the SPLM/A and UNITA were clear in the testimonies provided during the research. With all their failings and their successes, these parallel states and their corresponding orders managed to provide not only the necessary military, logistical and political but also the social lifelines required to recover from crippling defeats in 1991 and 1976.

5

RISE AND FALL
SUBSEQUENT CRITICAL JUNCTURES

'Look at its past, and you can tell its present; look at its past and present, and you can tell its future.'

Mao Tse-Tung

Understanding change, crucial choices, the transitions they catapult and the legacies they leave behind are key to identifying the resilience and composition of insurgency leadership, organisation and ideology. Both UNITA and the SPLM/A experienced crippling setbacks in multiple areas during critical junctures. Those faced by both movements experienced the three components of 1) 'a period in which elites find themselves obliged to make significant choices and take action in response to the crisis', 2) 'the choices and strategies embarked upon, which [shaped] the new arrangements, [were] understood as themselves constrained by past choices' and 3) the 'choices made and actions taken in this period [shaped] the nature of the state and state-society relations for some relatively significant time to come' (Villalon and Huxtable 1998: 7). These shocks led to structural shifts that allowed for a different approach to war and governance. The impact of the critical junctures led these movements (that had pre-existing governing strategies) to

227

establish the idea and function of the state as an integral pillar of their survival strategy.

The histories of these two parallel states and the agentic shifts that led to wartime state building guide an understanding of what the SPLM/A and UNITA are facing in the present. Just as the SPLM/A and UNITA emerged as a response to and partly from past struggles for liberation and peace, the future of South Sudan and Angola will carry elements of their past. UNITA's military defeat in 2002 and the SPLM/A's taking of office in 2005 did not erase the effects that the experiences of wartime governance had on the population, state–society relations or how perceptions of justice and freedom were formed, expectations (mis)managed and different identities reconciled. The residual effects of the experience of living under UNITA and the SPLM/A were evident in the interviews with many leaders, civilians and lower-level cadres who reflected about the time they were stakeholders in the future of their country. Even if these recollections were merely symbolic and sustained by a distorted recollection of history, they reveal how the political orders of Angola and South Sudan are still divided along several of the same fault lines with differing degrees of state disengagement, real or perceived marginalisation, social division and lack of national unifying symbols.

Although at opposing poles of victors' revisionism (SPLM/A) and a fight of the defeated against historical denial (UNITA), history has become a political tool that too often ignores the lessons provided of unreconciled societies, disputed political legitimacy and imperfect state- and nation-building exercises. Both countries are facing a mismanaged transition from war to peace, despite one war culminating in a military victory and the other in a negotiated settlement. Angola and South Sudan are once again experiencing forms of contestation. South Sudan is engulfed in a conflict that is swelling to genocidal proportions, where the response on all sides is the collective punishment of communities. The history of the liberation and the SPLM/A no longer holds a unifying capacity, as the leadership in Juba remains unable and unwilling to reactivate the structures of the party to decentralise power and decision-making and reverse the usurpation of power by Dinka elites. As a failed state, South Sudan has few if any institutions that can rebuild confidence in the state and begin repairing the damage caused to the country's social and political fabric. While Angola is still at peace, the exclusionary politics pursued by MPLA elites have continued unabated since 2002. Entire segments of the population survive outside formal structures and do not recognise the legitimacy of the government. The discrimination against and marginalisation of several constituencies, used by UNITA to advance its own political agenda during the war, are still realities in Angola. The contestation of societies and war of visions remain symbolic and relational realities.

Just as UNITA and the SPLM/A chose to take different paths in 1991 and 1976 out of a set of different choices, the subsequent critical junctures posed choices for the two movements that would reverse many developments and result in different rebel-systems. The parallel states were a product of the alignment of several conditions and characteristics after the 1976 and 1991 crises. Their dismantling was also a result of significant shifts. Two subsequent sets of critical junctures, from the result of an evolutionary process of several key events, would alter the ways UNITA and the SPLM/A had functioned earlier (see the timelines in Appendices 1 and 2). In many ways, the first post-reform critical junctures of 1992 for UNITA and 2005 for the SPLM/A provided the 'antecedent conditions' and the legacies establishing the 'mechanisms of production and reproduction' (Collier and Collier 2002: 30) for the second set of post-reform critical junctures. For the SPLM/A, it was 1) the death of John Garang in 2005, and 2) the outbreak of civil war in 2013 that resulted in fundamental and perhaps irreversible shifts. For UNITA, it was 1) the collapse of the Bicesse Peace Agreement and the resumption of war in 1992, and 2) the death of Jonas Savimbi and the Luena Accords in 2002 that altered the way it had previously operated. In all four internal elements, these movements would suffer tremendous shifts. This chapter links UNITA's and the SPLM/A's leadership traits, ideological contradictions, organisational strengths and shortcomings, and relationship with civilians to the paths of war and peace that led both movements into irreversible military and political losses. It provides a short timeline and analysis of events through the decades that followed the dismantling of the wartime parallel states up to events in 2022.

The wars in Angola and Sudan took opposite forms of resolution. Having already experienced two failed peace agreements, Angola's war would end in the military defeat of UNITA. Conversely, the SPLM/A would implement all its default positions of independence and political hegemony in a negotiated settlement. The explanations for whether a conflict ends in defeat and victory are neither linear nor simple. However, an overriding decisive factor was the role played by the international community in sanctioning and weakening UNITA and in bolstering the SPLM/A. Yet decisive shifts also occurred within the movements that led them down fundamentally different paths.

In the 1990s, UNITA altered its governing strategy to become a much more militarised project, governing new areas and several cities, facing international isolation and building a huge diamond-extracting enterprise to fund the war. UNITA began fighting a war to punish the government, and the political transformative agenda was abandoned. In the Central Highlands, the movement's symbolic capital, UNITA would face contestation and struggle to define a 'people' to liberate. Organisationally, structures were built and developed for the war machine and diamond-extraction sector, and the power of the political consultative organs was reduced. The Free Lands Republic was dismantled in many ways during the post-1992 war. Political education and skills training were not structured, and coordination of the administrative units was ineffective in the landscape of governing several cities and under constant threat of losing territory and aerial bombardments. The evolution of the leadership and its political ideology, as well as organisational changes of the 1990s, would lead to the military defeat of the movement and the death of Savimbi, rendering UNITA unable to challenge the MPLA's hegemony for 20 years. The 'equalising southern force' would never reach power, and the marginalisation felt would become more pronounced in the post-war years as reconstruction efforts were designed to exclude key segments of the population and empower the Luanda elites.

The SPLM/A, on the other hand, was operating under a successful peace agreement, supported by international guarantors, when Garang was killed in 2005. The Troika (United States, United Kingdom and Norway) were deeply committed to supporting the implementation of the Comprehensive Peace Agreement (CPA). Reforms initiated by Garang that reflected the governing lessons of the CANS were discarded under the leadership of Salva Kiir, yet the country continued to function, largely thanks to the UN peacekeeping mission present ahead of the 2011 independence referendum. The parallel state had been dismantled due to the CPA agreement and the intrusive state and nation-building agendas of international partners; the elements that had made the parallel state operate at the local level stagnated and were not built upon. The SPLM/A's failure to function as a party directing government policy became visible as it lost the ability to diffuse leadership disputes. It also lost the ability to project a vision for the independent state. Militarisation of power at the leadership levels in Juba as well as the local levels, coupled with corruption and nepotism, would lead to the ethnicisation of politics and fragmentation of the party, military and society. This evolution, beginning in 2005, culminated in the December 2013 crisis when the SPLM/A splintered into three factions and a new era of war started.

UNITA's 1992 and 2002 critical junctures

UNITA's downfall began in 1991, after several miscalculations and the first failed elections that resulted in the legitimisation of the MPLA-led government, pushing UNITA into a spoiler role. In 1992, when UNITA underwent its first set of critical junctures that would result in its defeat, no one could have predicted that a movement known for its resilience and political acuity would be militarily crushed. A decade of war would only end when the second critical juncture occurred, the killing of Savimbi in the province of Moxico on 22 February 2002. From then on, UNITA would struggle for 20 years as an unarmed political party to provide any real opposition to the MPLA, who effectively consolidated its power and shut down all avenues for independent thought, action and organisation that could threaten its hegemony.

231

Within UNITA, there was a clear understanding that the critical juncture of 1992 changed the course of its liberation, perhaps more so than the death of its founder in 2002. Debates within UNITA's leadership reflected on the mistakes the movement made after 1992. Key generals lamented the choice of war rather than the alternative political fight with the mediation and assistance of the international community. Others highlighted the few options they had available immediately after the 1992 Halloween Massacre, which decimated UNITA's leadership and was interpreted as an effort to permanently shut down the possibility of any Ovimbundu taking power in Luanda. Some UNITA leaders even questioned whether the signing of the 1991 Bicesse Peace Agreement was a mistake. Savimbi himself spoke of this (Muekalia 2010). Numerous military victories in the run-up to the peace agreement in the 1980s left UNITA in a position to keep pushing ahead militarily until it could capitalise on the end of the Cold War and their symbolic and material consequences for the MPLA. Although the 1987–88 Cuito Cuanavale war—then the biggest international engagement in Africa since the Second World War, with Cuban, Soviet and South African forces involved—ended in a military impasse, the objective of removing UNITA from its strongholds failed. It also showed that UNITA could not be defeated militarily, despite the government forces' superior military capacity in terms of air power and sheer number of ground troops.

The critical juncture of 1992 began with two decisive moments that catalysed a series of events. The first was the 1991 defection of two senior Cabindan leaders, Miguel N'Zau Puna (then UNITA's interior minister) and Tony da Costa Fernandes (then foreign minister), who fled Jamba afraid that they would take the blame for several killings. The second was the killing, months earlier, of Pedro 'Tito' Chingunji and his brother-in-law Wilson Dos Santos that shocked the world—in particular Western supporters of UNITA— and greatly contributed to turning the tide of support away from the movement.[1] It became a source of great embarrassment for the Bush administration and US congressmen who had greatly buoyed Savimbi. Chingunji, a charismatic and respected diplomat, had been UNITA's representative in the United States, while Dos Santos was the movement's representative in Portugal. Both leaders and their families, totalling thirteen people, were executed in Jamba. They were later accused of plotting a coup against Savimbi with CIA help, although there was no evidence of this. When Puna and Fernandes defected, they exposed the truth behind the purge, as well as a series of horrific episodes that further damaged UNITA's image, in particular the witch-burning episode described in the Jamba chapter. They made clear the dangers the people of Angola would face if they elected Savimbi in September 1992 (Valentim 2011). The defection of these politburo members initiated a period of fragmentation that would plague UNITA right until the end.

Savimbi expected to be the first elected President of Angola. President Reagan's support for the rebel leader, which culminated in several White House visits for Savimbi, positioned him as the solution to Angola's push for reform and liberalisation. The purges revealed UNITA's darker side and its totalitarian aspect, which had been dismissed by the overriding interests of the superpower rivalry. In the 1990s, Bill Clinton didn't feel the need to support a movement that sustained several undemocratic traits, despite the MPLA being just as centralised and authoritarian as UNITA.

> Savimbi's image never recovered from Tito's death and the burning of the witches episodes. Washington thought—'that if he did that do his friends what would he do to others', and they made an agreement with the MPLA to stop him. That's why, after everything that happened in October 1992 and the killings of UNITA leaders, there was no international condemnation. And Tito's death was not Savimbi's fault—nor did the order come from him. It was the security people that misinterpreted and had the two families killed.[2]

The fact was that many had been killed on Savimbi's orders over the years, making it difficult for Washington to continue viewing Savimbi as a beacon of hope and democracy for Angola. No one will ever truly know (or admit) who gave the order to kill Chingunji and Dos Santos, but the episode haunted UNITA for decades. Before the 1992 elections, 'it was very clear to Savimbi that the US had redirected their interest in Angola—it was now economic interests above the fight against communism. The Americans shifted their weapons from one shoulder to the next'.[3] The US had abandoned UNITA due to superseding economic interests triggered by the shocking revelations of UNITA's internal purges.

Despite these transformative events, the 1991 Bicesse Peace Agreement brought about a pathway for peace and reform in Angola. It was celebrated internationally as a model for post-Cold War peacemaking. This period of hope was short-lived when the 'generally free and fair' elections (the expression used by UN Special Representative for Angola Margaret Anstee) of 1992 were tainted by bloodshed in Luanda and a return to arms by both parties. Despite professing a will to negotiate, UNITA and the government continued to purchase large quantities of arms while engaging in sporadic but intense fighting. The reasons for the failing of the Bicesse Peace Agreement are complex and multifaceted, with blame divided among all parties—including the UN and international observers. Observers in Angola pointed to UNITA's leadership miscalculations on how they operated and campaigned in Luanda prior to the 1992 polls. Savimbi's rhetoric was at times aggressive and intimidating; he appeared armed and wearing military fatigues, which alienated the urban elites and voters. With electrifying demagoguery, he rallied great support but also scared many off, creating the popular expression, 'The MPLA steals, but UNITA kills.' Moreover, MPLA propaganda of a violent, rural and barbaric movement had taken root in the memories of many in the 1980s and was not easily dislodged. Unlike Garang's experience in Khartoum, when he visited the capital after the CPA and was greeted by millions of supporters, Savimbi was entering a hostile environment in Luanda that stood firmly against UNITA's political project. The MPLA had branded itself as an urban, modern, multiracial movement, exposing multinational nationalism. Luanda was its territorial, symbolic and representational capital. In the background fuelling the electoral debate and campaign trail were the divisive issues of regionalism, class, ethnicity and race. Neither the MPLA nor UNITA were able to fully sway voters on either side. UNITA's strident us-or-them campaign, a reflection of its indoctrination strategies, alienated many voters who were ready for change but whose 'support had to be won through a campaign of inclusion' (Heywood 2000). In contrast, Dos Santos, ran a sophisticated campaign designed by a Brazilian public relations firm that focused on painting the picture of a civilian leader who could take the country into the future. Savimbi was still defending himself against the accusations made by defected leaders Puna and Fernandes, which cemented his image of a perpetrator of human rights abuses and violence.

On 29 and 30 September 1992, Angolans voted in their first elections. With hindsight, holding elections while both parties had not yet fully demilitarised and the joint army was incomplete was a mistake. The UN and the troika made many errors along the way but none more so than Savimbi and Dos Santos, who prepared for war and zero-sum victories even as they implemented the clauses of the Bicesse Peace Agreement. Evidence was mounting of electoral fraud—the opposition pointed to numerous irregularities, revealing that the elections were heavily tilted in favour of the MPLA—but neither the UN nor the troika ever fully investigated these claims, despite concerns raised by international observers and journalists. On 16 October, it was announced that the MPLA had won the parliamentary polls. The results of the presidential race revealed that neither leader had passed the 50% threshold—Dos Santos had 49.57% and Savimbi 40.07% of the vote—which meant a second round was required. Less than two weeks later the Halloween massacre in Luanda would occur, decapitating UNITA's leadership and pushing the country back into war. In a premeditated move, having distributed weapons to civilians in the capital and repurposed key military units as Rapid Response Police, the MPLA oversaw the killing of UNITA members, supporters and leaders. The killings that began on 31 October severely and permanently wounded UNITA. Savimbi had already left the capital for Huambo after being warned of an assassination plot by a senior MPLA general that knew this would set back the country, but several of his senior leaders remained behind. They were captured, tortured and killed. Among the UNITA members killed in Luanda were the movement's vice president Jeremias Chitunda, the secretary general Adolosi Mango Alicerces and top negotiator Elias Salupeto Pena, a member of the joint political military commission and Savimbi's nephew. Killings of UNITA members, supporters and anyone deemed to be 'from the

South' were merciless, fuelled by fear and dehumanisation. Over 2,000 people were arrested, including several members of UNITA's political commission. The MPLA staged this clampdown on UNITA, claiming that the rebels had attempted a coup. The reality was that UNITA had thirty-five platoons of armed men in Luanda, totalling 420 troops. It would never have attempted a coup with so few men in the context of a highly fortified capital and a burgeoning securitised state. UNITA had been politically outmanoeuvred.

UNITA was also abandoned by the UN. The electoral manipulation that occurred in 1992 was pinned on the rudimentary stuffing of ballots, the replacement of ballot boxes and the use of ghost polling stations, but also with the use of a computer programme—a language and data management system called DBase III—that allowed for the manipulation of data. 'DBIII recording systems were used in voting areas that had a standard algorithmic increase in MPLA areas of 10% automatically and UNITA a 15% decrease automatically. MPLA duplicated outcomes—there were fifteen polling stations with the same numbers.'[4] The government also used mobile polling stations to reach different communities in the country, yet these were neither monitored by observers nor did they have opposition delegates on board.[5] Reports by several members of the Comissão Nacional Eleitoral (CNE) (National Electoral Commission) 'raised considerable doubt whether Angola's election was actually free and fair'.[6] Observers from the German component of the UN mission claimed in their report that several polling stations had closed at noon on 30 September 'when they had attained the statistical target of 1,000 ballots cast. The voters still waiting to vote, often hundreds, were sent away'.[7] UNITA prepared a document for the UN Security Council's Ad Hoc Commission, sent to Angola in October, whereby it detailed and analysed a systemic pattern of election fraud. This document showed how there were discrepancies in the CNE's computer records that provided identical results across different provinces, using the example of the MPLA receiving 11,668 votes in Kwanza Norte, Lunda Norte and Bie, while UNITA received 7,757 votes in each of those same provinces. The party also requested a full investigation into the operation of the ghost polling stations, as well as the disappearance of 66 ballot boxes. UNITA demanded to know the security of the two million additional ballots, printed by the De La Rue company in London that the MPLA had hired to transport ballot boxes when the UN was mandated to transport them.[8] In fact, De La Rue had printed over 7.2 million ballots for 4.8 million voters.[9]

The opposition's claim of electoral manipulation was never fully investigated by third parties. While the ad hoc delegation of the UN Security Council, presided over by the Cape Verdean ambassador, was sent to Luanda to discuss the matter they took no action. 'The UNSC delegation told me that the UN had spent too much money already and it could not afford to repeat the process so the claims of irregularity would not result in any action.'[10] On 17 October, the UN Special Envoy for Angola, Margaret Anstee, ratified the electoral results, declaring them 'generally free and fair' and foreclosing any possibility for the opposition to find political redress. Others were not as convinced. Former US Assistant Secretary of State Chester Crocker claimed that observers had no way to evaluate the elections (Simpkins 1996). The UN had 400 election observers for 6,000 polling stations. A confidential UN report dated 9 October 1992 concluded that there had been irregularities which could have affected the overall result of the election, whereby 'the volume of votes lost or gained by each candidate could, taken nationally, be significant as to distort the final results'.[11] UN Undersecretary for Peacekeeping Kofi Annan confirmed the existence and validity of this confidential document during a 20 December interview with South African paper *The Star*, but otherwise the UN took no action.[12] Anstee was reported as having spent sleepless nights before declaring the results free and fair, all the while knowing that the UN had detected irregularities. Journalist Jill Jolliffe, a harsh critic of UNITA, claimed that Anstee called 'Boutrous-Ghali after receiving the final report to request instructions having been told she should ratify the results of the elections at all costs, since a budget did not exist for the holding of new elections and Angola had fallen on the list of UN priorities'.[13]

A shift also occurred in Washington, although the United States' role in supporting and derailing the peace process has received little attention in the historical analysis of Angola in the 1990s. 'As Bicesse was being signed, Washington told the parties that after the signature it would recognise the MPLA. It went back on its word maybe because there was a change of administration from Bush to Clinton. This created huge problems.'[14] This was somewhat unexpected, given the direct support the United States gave to UNITA in the run-up to elections, with Congress approving a transfer of US$35 million to the movement. This support would undergo a radical shift in policy under the Clinton administration in 1993, which not only recognised the MPLA government as the legitimate representative of Angola, forestalling the possibility of using any leverage the United States still had to influence UNITA, but also closed off permanently the possibility of a second round of presidential elections and a unity government. Months before the official recognition, an MPLA representative had been present at Clinton's inauguration.[15] President Clinton's recognition of the MPLA government opened the door for US investment in Angola in March 1993. In August 1993, the *Wall Street Journal* reported that Clinton's National Security Advisor Tony Lake was instrumental in lifting the ban on provision of lethal supplies to Luanda, which was a violation of the Bicesse Peace Agreement under the 'triple zero' clause.[16] In September 1995, the United States pledged US$190 million to support reconstruction at a donors' conference in Brussels. By 1996, the United States was purchasing two-thirds of Angola's exports, which accounted for US$2.6 billion. US private investment in the nation was expected to exceed US$4 billion in 1997, with Chevron planning to invest a yearly US$700 million in exploration and development of Angola's oil sector. Economic interest had clearly overridden democratic and peace imperatives.

The MPLA won the diplomatic war by casting itself as the legitimate representative of Angola, causing UNITA to become a pariah isolated from international interlocutors. The MPLA won the propaganda war by rewriting the events in Luanda as UNITA rejecting the election results and taking the country back to war. Ultimately, neither group was prepared to accept defeat at the ballot box. After suffering heavy initial military loses, with UNITA occupying 70–80% of Angola in 1993, the MPLA was able to reconstitute its army and recapture territory. This was the beginning of a decade of war. This war had different characteristics at different parts of its timeline: the fighting of 1992–94 became known as the war of the cities, after the brutal sieges of the state capitals of Huambo and Kuito in 1993. The years 1994–99, where peace held somewhat during the implementation of the Lusaka Protocol, were marked by levels of great asymmetry between resources and military capacity of both parties. They were also atypical in that UNITA was part of the 1997 government of national unity in Luanda but was fighting it in the countryside. The last three years, 1999–2002, were essentially a counterinsurgency war. UNITA was reduced to guerrilla tactics again, with the government implementing a devastating scorched-earth policy in the rural areas.

UNITA would struggle on many fronts to govern the cities of its ethnic heartland in the Central Highlands. Undergoing constant bombardment and shelling from government forces, the movement was unable to implement the same political conditioning and education it had in smaller, more contained areas of the liberated zones and bases. It was also unable to secure the supply of goods to urban areas, or replicate the supply chains of government-held municipalities, and it struggled to win over constituents after the brutality with which they had conquered the cities.

> The administration experience of the cities had been harder for UNITA, harder than in Jamba because: 1) we didn't have external support, 2) the territory was much bigger as we controlled 75% of the territory—Zaire, Uige, Kwanza Norte, Huambo, Kuando Kubango and Huambo etc., 3) the sanctions were very conditioning for us. I wouldn't say that UNITA managed to govern Huambo. What UNITA did was to build an administrative structure to guarantee basic services. The Kuando Dam worked, the schools and hospitals worked and there was order.[17]

The movement struggled to adapt the culture of power it had wielded in Jamba to the cities that were more diversified and less controllable.

Yet, some elements did work. 'In Huambo we paid salaries to the administration—teachers, etc. We would send fleets of cars to Namibia and the DRC to buy salt, oil and clothes—this is how we lived for two years.'[18] Neither UNITA nor the SPLM/A during their strongest administrative phases during the war had ever truly experienced ruling large urban areas. Savimbi stated in 1988 that it was not in UNITA's interest to defend or *abastecer* (refuel and feed) provincial capitals or cities, but rather to control the surrounding territory to make these cities 'prisoners' (Roque et al. 1988: 42). This had been a strategy of disruption and sabotage against MPLA-held urban centres. In the 1990s, as UNITA governed several cities, it faced hostile populations that had been politicised by the MPLA and become accustomed to the territorial control of the government.

> The attitude of people in the cities was not the same, or the demography—more people, more problems, and more difficulties, and we didn't have time to educate people, mobilise, persuade and engage in deep dialogue. What remained more with the people in Huambo was our inexperience in administration—but don't judge us without context because things cannot be seen in parcels. There was inexperience, need and war and there was nothing that could be done. Expectations were a different story.[19]

For many in Huambo and Kuito who had experienced UNITA's rule in 1993 and 1994, this period was associated with deprivation, violence and fear, decimating the support UNITA had built up in the areas in the 1980s (Pearce 2015).

Experience in the rural areas of the Central Highlands, though not uniform, was different. There were continuities in the form of governance experience with those of the 1980s (Pearce 2015). However, as government forces reconquered territory from UNITA, the movement lost its ability to control its people in these areas and in the process lost the trust of those who had once accepted UNITA's authority (Pearce 2015). As UNITA faced difficulties, it began losing its core areas of local support (through the loss of territory), which pushed it into areas where support was less widespread, leading the movement to tax and pillage populations. People moved in and out of UNITA and government-controlled areas not because of partisan loyalty, or because they inherently believed in the political project of either, but because of their need for security and food. The warring parties saw this differently, and 'an act of migration became an act of defection' (Pearce 2015: 155).

UNITA was sanctioned numerous times by the UN during this period. The first set of sanctions, imposing an arms embargo, was adopted unanimously by the United Nations Security Council (UNSC) in September 1993. The embargo required all weapons and military hardware coming into Angola be sent to points designated by the government (James 2011). The second set of sanctions were applied four years later in October 1997, prohibiting UNITA members from travelling abroad and ordering the closure of all overseas UNITA offices. The third set of sanctions was placed a year later in July 1998, freezing UNITA's bank accounts and banning its diamond exports.

Touting international sanctions, both the MPLA and UNITA circumvented the arms embargo using revenues from oil and diamonds. Both would produce sophisticated and intricate mechanisms to feed their war strategies. UNITA's main source of revenue, used to procure arms and sustain its political structure, came from its trade in alluvial diamonds which began after securing the Cuango Valley that held the most valuable stones. Already in the late 1980s, UNITA's mining capacity had reached US$14 million worth of exports (Cilliers and Dietrich 2000).[20] For UNITA, diamonds were a matter of survival. They transformed the movement's war economy by expanding its resource base so it was able to depend on its own capacity of generating revenue following the loss of support from South Africa and the United States, as well as its increasing isolation from the international community. US support to UNITA during Reagan's administration could have amounted to US$40–60 million a year at its peak (Minter 1994). This would pale in comparison to the estimated amount of revenue UNITA was receiving in the 1990s from diamonds, thought to have been as high as US$3.7 billion between 1992 and 1998.[21] The movement built a sprawling diamond enterprise as it conquered the diamond fields in the East and South. From 1992, UNITA focused on increasing its operation to industrial-like production, which allowed it to create conventional forces and use different armament. 'In 1995/6, we conquered a lot of territory but the correlation of forces of the MPLA was superior—they had aviation, cavalry and artillery, so UNITA focused on 1) long-range artillery, 2) tanks that were superior to those of the MPLA and 3) anti-aerial arms.'[22] The sale of diamonds enabled the movement to stock its arsenal. By the mid-1990s, UNITA had established the Cuango Mining Corporation, a joint venture with David Zollman from the Belgium trading firm Glasol and George Forrest, who held major interests in diamonds in Zaire (Hodges 2004). This was one of several international partnerships that allowed UNITA to run the world's largest illegal diamond operation.

Time and resources were invested in setting up a sophisticated and efficient operation, that included training divers and evaluators, servicing airstrips, administering auctions and establishing wide networks of buyers and traders. MIRNA had to rapidly develop capacity. UNITA sent MIRNA employees abroad to learn how to evaluate the different stones so that it could create control mechanisms and an evaluation commission. MIRNA would deploy delegates to all resource-extraction areas to account for the stones collected and ensure that these were sent to the general cabinet of the ministry. Once the diamonds were counted, COPE would be informed of their amount and value so that UNITA's strategists knew what had to be commercialised. Diamonds between 15 and 24 carats were sent to be commercialised, while anything bigger was sent directly to Savimbi to be held in the Treasury. From 1993 to 1999, Luzamba would become UNITA's diamond capital, although auctions and operations would occur in diverse areas. The movement's Vice President Dembo was responsible for diamond output and sales, and he coordinated mining throughout different provinces. At its peak, UNITA's diamond operations were thought to have had a work force of 100,000 miners (Hodges 2004).

In 1996, Andulo became the centre of the commercialisation of diamonds, and 'people came in airplanes from all over the world'.[23] As the diamond trade expanded, UNITA introduced the US dollar in the Lundas areas where people were allowed to open stores and trade with the DRC. Taxes were collected by the then administrator of the Lundas, Menezes Sahepo, who also worked for MIRNA. UNITA created governors for independent zones in the diamond-rich Lundas provinces, and the administrative organ was entirely directed towards guaranteeing exploration and constant supply of revenue. Everyone profited from the rebel exploration of diamonds, including De Beers, whose hypocritical stance against blood diamonds tried to hide the fact that it had profited from diamonds sold by UNITA. A Human Rights Watch report in 1994 claimed that De Beers had admitted to spending US$500 million a day in purchasing legal and illegal diamonds in 1992 in open market transactions.[24] The majority of UNITA's commercialisation routes passed through the DRC, and it had taken to buying offices in Mbuji-Mayi, in East Kasai province, and Kinshasa. When Luanda succeeded in aiding Laurent Kabila's rebellion that toppled the government of Mobutu Sese Seko in 1997, UNITA redirected export routes through Zambia. Efforts to understand how UNITA was able to move across international borders and participate in the global diamond trade despite sanctions revealed the role played by key allies the DRC, Burkina Faso, Zambia and, to a lesser extent, Rwanda, South Africa, Namibia and Côte d'Ivoire.[25] Details of UNITA's diamond operations and trade could fill an entire book, so could not possibly be fully explained here. Nevertheless, the organisational capacity that the movement had developed in the 1980s was a driving force of this operation, coupled with the efforts of its external relations offices and leaders.

During the implementation of the 1994 Lusaka Protocol, negotiations occurred to allow UNITA to retain mineral rights in exchange for the withdrawal of its military from diamond areas. In December 1997, UNITA withdrew from the Cuango valley with the expectation that the government would award its companies the rights of exploration. This never happened, especially after the country went back to war in 1998. Even as the movement lost military capacity, diamond mines and territory, it still managed to secure US$100 million from diamond sales in 2000.[26] While diamonds funded most of UNITA's logistical and civilian needs, the movement never discarded the need to produce its own food. In the 1990s, UNITA was operating fifty-three collective farms, totalling 25,000 hectares, and producing maize, vegetables and other foodstuffs (James 2011). Neighbouring countries remained vital as transit points, service providers and suppliers of essential commodities like fuel, generators, batteries and medical supplies.

UNITA's collective leadership structures operated throughout the last few years of the war, by far the most devastating, even as it lost territory. Political consultations, policy deliberations and strategies defined within party structures led the response to peace negotiations and strategic recalibrations after military defeats. The eighth party congress occurred in Bailundu, in February 1995, and 1,200 delegates attended from all 18 provinces (James 2011). The congress approved peace plans for Angola and called for the disarmament of civilian militias in Luanda, as well as the withdrawal of foreign mercenaries. An extraordinary Congress was called in August 1996 to discuss the offer made to Savimbi to become Dos Santos' second Vice-President which was debated and rejected by an overwhelming majority of delegates. In October 1999 UNITA would hold its ninth congress after the fall of Andulo and Bailundo. This would be the last congress the movement would conduct with Savimbi as its president. The following party congress occurred in June 2003 in Luanda, electing Isaias Samakuva as its new leader. In the late 1990s, UNITA's political structures remained the commanding organs of the movement and the military. It had established four political commissions, subordinated to the General Political Commission, that dealt with different areas. The first political commission was charged with political affairs, foreign relations and information, headed by UNITA's vice president Antonio Dembo and the foreign secretary Alcides Sakala. The second concentrated on executing strategies for administering UNITA areas, coordinated by the secretary general of the party, General Lukamba Gato. The third was mandated with administering justice and coordinating the security services, chaired by Celestino Kapapelo. The fourth commission was charged with coordinating all military affairs, headed by the chief of staff general Geraldo Abreu Kamorteiro. These four bodies were coordinated by the central body, chaired by Savimbi.[27] Militarily, UNITA retained the office of general staff even as it lost its semi-conventional capacity for war. Until the end, key generals would retain the functioning of their units, which included telecommunications, logistics and political coordination. By mid-2001, UNITA had divided the country into three theatres of operation, each led by a military commander with a chief of operations and a political commissioner.[28]

However, its political cohesion would suffer. In the aftermath of the 1992 elections, and the bloodbath that followed suit, UNITA was left with severe internal contradictions, particularly as some elements supported the Lusaka Protocol and others didn't. At the 1995 party congress, the Huambo factions and the Bie-Benguela factions became defined, although the underlying tensions between these two camps spanned the history of the movement. More significant were the divisions between the UNITA leaders in Luanda, who sought political compromise and wished to deescalate militarily, and those based with Savimbi at his Bailundu and Andulo bases in the Central Highlands, who had more aggressive agendas. The Luanda UNITA believed that complying with the DDR process would give it the political space to rebuild its organisation, while the Bailundo UNITA wanted to delay demilitarisation for as long as possible so as to use military gains to extract greater concessions.[29] In 1997, when the Government of National Unity (GURN) was formed as a result of the Lusaka peace agreement, the divisions became entrenched as 70 UNITA deputies took their seats in parliament, 4 took their posts as ministers and 7 as vice-ministers. UNITA's Luanda city elite would find themselves distanced from the grassroots level of the movement—a tendency the movement struggled to reverse after its 2002 defeat, when it became a political party in the capital. As the last years of civil war started in 1998, a group of leaders broke with UNITA, calling themselves *UNITA-renovada* (renovated UNITA) under the leadership of Eugenio Manuvakola and Jorge Valentim. *UNITA-renovada* was, to an extent, a fabrication of the MPLA, who had been working hard to persuade UNITA parliamentarians to distance themselves from Savimbi. This faction never posed a serious political threat. From there onwards, the government closed diplomatic channels and dialogue with Savimbi, opting instead to deal with *UNITA-renovada*. For Dos Santos, Savimbi's refusal in 1997 to take the largely symbolic and powerless position of vice president of the country foreclosed any role he could have at the centre of Angolan politics.

Just as Jamba was falling in 1999 to government forces, so were the bases of Bailundo and Andulo. These bases were strategic and symbolic, and the retreat signified the third and final time UNITA attempted to govern in its ethnic heartland. In the run-up to its

245

withdrawal from these bases, UNITA was hit by a series of defections and betrayals that 'played as critical a role as airpower and artillery in forcing UNITA to abandon its bases' (Weigert 2011: 149). Several senior officers would defect after Savimbi begun punishing and killing commanders for disobedience in the aftermath of military losses. These senior officers—General Jacinto Bandua, Col. Alcides Lucas Kangunga, Col. Joao Antonio Gil and others—took with them crucial information about UNITA's military infrastructure and gave the government details on logistics, communications, arms purchases and intelligence (Weigert 2011). UNITA political prisoners and military officers would be detained in Andulo, and many were killed for their mistakes, doubts and insubordination.

> On 24 October 1999, I was taken by the UNITA commandos that I had trained to be killed. I escaped and ran 600 metres while they shot at me. I surrendered to the nearest FAA troops, and they didn't believe that a general had escaped and thought it was a trap. I was put on a plane to Luanda where I called my mother crying in despair and disbelief. If it hadn't been all the killings at that time, the war wouldn't have ended in 2002. All of this weakened UNITA—it was not the strength of the government but the decadence that developed in UNITA.[30]

Savimbi's growing paranoia and loss of control, as testified by people who lived or visited Andulo, led to widespread purges and other mistakes that were a primary cause for the movement's downfall. Unconfirmed accusations point to several executions of key commanders, including that of General Bock, whose inability to follow orders led to the loss of crucial positions in Bie, weakening the defence of Andulo and leading to its eventual capture by government troops.[31]

The retreat from Andulo and Bailundo signified UNITA's loss of territory and a permanent location for operations. From then on, the movement would no longer be able to administer areas inhabited by civilians or create a stable political centre. Although the movement was thought to still have 500,000 people who depended on it, their interactions with civilians were predatory and instrumental.[32] Falling back on their guerrilla training, the movement decentralised command and control, giving regional commanders more autonomy over military operations. Retreating from Andulo were thousands of civilians organised into groups of 1,500, heading for the Moxico province and later crossing into Zambia. A member of female battalion 89 explained:

> That's when the difficult march began. We divided ourselves in groups some went to Kwanza Sul others north and others east— after this march we left to Zambia as it wasn't yet the moment to surrender and we'd fall into the hands of the army. Instructions were given by the leadership for the elders to go to Zambia and the troops would protect them. After that people were divided into groups of 100 or 200 as we retreated.[33]

Nangweshi was the main Zambian refugee camp that housed the UNITA elders, women and children, and relatives of the leadership, created in 1999 to shelter the refugees from Jamba after it fell. [34]

Months of trekking across the eastern provinces of Angola in smaller guerrilla groups allowed the leadership to evade government forces. In April 2001, UNITA held its 16th Annual Ordinary Conference in Moxico, where Savimbi spoke for five hours in what became a deep reflection of the mistakes made and the shortcomings of the movement.

> The conference from 13th to 16th April near the Cunguene river was organised by General Numa who was from this region. We reflected on our mistakes and prepared the party to return to the cities. We discussed a peace plan and negotiations with the church so that they would mediate. Savimbi named Samakuva and Jardo Muekalia as the reformers.[35]

Savimbi instructed UNITA's external mission to contact Ambassador Ibrahim Gambari at the UN to serve as a bridge for dialogue. Numerous appeals for negotiations went unheeded, as the MPLA had an operation to hunt, track down and eliminate Savimbi well underway. This was the last time many of UNITA's leaders would meet with Savimbi as UNITA's leader.

In October 2001, the FAA launched their counterinsurgency sweep that would surround Savimbi. With the help of Israeli advisors and equipment, Savimbi's satellite calls were intercepted, which helped to better position the whereabouts of his column. UNITA leaders and the core group of soldiers that travelled with these columns in Moxico province were increasingly weaker, malnourished and lacking medicine. In December, Dos Santos reiterated that Savimbi had three choices: surrender, capture or death (Weigert 2011). In early February 2002, FAA forces managed to capture or kill several key generals and political leaders, even though Savimbi had broken down columns of fighters to avoid detection and capture.

On 22 February, the FAA managed to break through the small protection rings around Savimbi, who was left without any form of communication. Surrounded by fewer than 20 members of his column, Savimbi was encircled by FAA forces and shot six times, in the head, torso, arms and legs. As his body lay on the ground, he was shot at close range several more times. A few hours later, a helicopter arrived and took away his body to be displayed with national and international audiences. The pictures taken were reminiscent of images of Che Guevara's corpse, lying open-eyed and bare-chested on a stretcher somewhere in Villegande, Bolivia, where he was killed in 1967. Savimbi's body was initially shown with his olive fatigues, his eyes half-open and his trousers sliding down, a gunshot wound on his neck visible, as he lay on the ground. This anticlimactic end of a warrior, admired and feared by many, signalled the end of the war. The leadership of UNITA fell to Antonio Dembo, the vice president, who because of a prolonged illness would also succumb to wounds in March 2002. Conspiracy theories soon emerged that Dembo had been killed because UNITA could not be led by a man of Mbundu (greatly associated with the MPLA support base) rather than Ovimbundu descent. This was the second critical juncture that would end UNITA's military liberation and force it to fully transform into a civilian-led political party.

With the death of its leader, UNITA created a management commission headed by General Paulo Lukamba Gato and 13 members (generals and civilian leaders) tasked with uniting the party until a national congress could be held to elect a new president. This interim organ was replaced by a standing political committee that operated like a reconstituted political commission. Its work ended in

June 2003, when the party held its ninth party congress in Viana on the outskirts of Luanda, with about 1,500 delegates attending from all eighteen provinces (James 2011). The presidency of the party was contested by Gato, Dinho Chingunji and Isaias Samakuva. Samakuva, with a less militaristic image than Gato and his mostly political and diplomatic contribution to the struggle, won overwhelmingly. Ernesto Mulato was given the vice presidency and Mario Miguel Vatuva the role of secretary general. The congress rewrote the party statutes and discussed strategies to expand its political platform across the country. The task to begin building party structures in all eighteen provinces was monumental.

After Savimbi's death the government proceeded to deal directly with the military commanders, negotiating the terms of the ceasefire, rather than bringing in UNITA's political leadership in Luanda and elsewhere. For the MPLA, peace was a matter of demilitarising the country, ensuring its own monopoly on violence and dismantling UNITA's capacity for war. Nowhere did the need for political compromise, the economic development of rural areas, decentralised government or steps toward reconciliation of communities properly factor into the government's calculations for peace. The Luena MoU, signed in April 2002, determined the parameters of peace on the MPLA's terms. Although benefiting from a general amnesty for crimes committed and integrating 5,000 more troops into the FAA, UNITA was in no condition to negotiate a more balanced agreement. The great majority of its leadership in the bush were emaciated, sick and broken by years of guerrilla warfare and the attrition of the government. It was important for the government to dismantle UNITA's structures in rural areas by resettling UNITA-affiliated populations into areas administered by the state, which was contingent on becoming identified as an MPLA member (Pearce 2015).

The demobilisation of UNITA soldiers and officers became an exercise in humiliation. The DDR process was badly mismanaged, leading to the deaths of thousands of ex-combatants and their families in quartering areas (Roque 2021a). The process was entirely managed by the Angolan government, with the FAA responsible for logistics and later resettlement. The quartering areas were forcibly closed, a political decision that went against military advice, and ex-combatants and their dependents were spread out around the country. It was a very clear policy to dismantle and disburse UNITA core supporters so that the movement would not have areas where their political identity, narrative and historical legacy thrived. Even so, UNITA had left such a deep organisational legacy that UNITA village structures were said to be replicated in IDP camps as well as refugee camps in neighbouring countries after the end of the war. Despite years of brutality, displacement, hunger and the loss of community members, UNITA supporters at their core never managed to shed the alienation they felt as a result of the MPLA's political project. They had lost the war, and with it went the possibility of experiencing the project of a reformed nation and society as espoused by UNITA. Yet the political legacy and the mythico-history (Malkki 1995) that remained were impenetrable. This spoke directly to the strength of the movement's ideology but also to years of propaganda and acculturation.

President Samakuva would lead UNITA from 2004 to 2019, through three elections and several small crises that could have led to bloodshed in Luanda. Encounters with the unfairness of a securitised and corrupt governing system over the years put UNITA in a position to either openly contest or strategically retreat to avoid confrontation with the police and other security units. As a result, they never used their large capacity for mobilisation of street protests, even when the brazen theft of the 2017 polls that elected President João Lourenço inspired the population to seek more vocal reactions. UNITA would, during the three post-war polls, seek remedy in the courts, which reaped no results aside from there now being a historical record of fraudulent practices. In 2008, UNITA's seats in parliament went from 70 to 16 (the movement had won only 10.3% of the vote), but in 2012 they increased to 32 members (representing 18.6% of the vote) and then to 51 members in 2017 (26.7% of the vote). Yet their impact on the direction of national politics was nominal. The MPLA would hold a two-thirds majority of the 220-member parliament following all the polls. The ruling party put its hegemonic power to considerable use, fully directing the political order of Angola and appropriating its economy towards the benefit of an exclusionary development programme. Samakuva managed to rebuild UNITA and restore its base support in the rural areas while also widening its appeal in Luanda. The people's disillusion and oversaturation with MPLA rule aided this, and by 2012 UNITA was in a position to win the provincial vote of Luanda, given its wide support in the overcrowded and underdeveloped *bairros* and *musseques* of the capital.

As an opposition party, UNITA would grow its base in the Central Highlands as well as, unexpectedly, in the provinces of Luanda and Cabinda, which had no significant historical links to the movement's liberation campaign throughout all its years of armed struggle from 1966 to 2002. UNITA's progression in peacetime politics and the way it grew as a political force defied assumptions that the structures and aptitudes of former military movements were ill-suited to peacetime political engagement (Pearce 2020). This trajectory also defied the neo-patrimonial thinking that, without access to resources, political parties would become marginalised from power and unable to cultivate a base (Pearce 2020). UNITA's resource base was, as expected, greatly reduced in peacetime. As a party it received some money from the government, from its members and donations, but it could not possibly compete with the MPLA at times like national elections, where its funds were dwarfed by the MPLA's resources. For example, in the 2008 elections, UNITA was given US$17 million for its campaign while the MPLA had over US$300 million at its disposal (Roque 2008). During the 2012 elections, each opposition party was given state funding on a proportional basis, which meant that UNITA would receive US$10 million annually.[36] UNITA's growth as a party in peacetime was also aided by the fact that entire segments of the population felt marginalised by the MPLA's modernist development project of reconstruction. Added to this was the lack of access to services and employment opportunities that opposition members and supporters faced. Without MPLA membership, their access to the state was minimal, especially given the fact that MPLA specialist committees dominated entire sectors and industries. Despite, or because of, these difficulties UNITA retained a strong political identity that resonated with its base but also began appealing to a cross section of society in the cities, especially the urban youth who became increasingly disenchanted with the government. The appeal to these youths—who had little to no recollection of wartime identities, generational loyalties or the appeal of cultural and African authenticity (Heywood 1998)—was the language of social and economic justice UNITA wielded.

While the need to distance the peacetime UNITA from the wartime UNITA meant staying silent in some instances, other difficult legacies could only be discussed privately. The party began to reconnect with its ideological roots a decade into the post-war political setting. In December 2011, at UNITA's eleventh congress, the principles of Muangai (the place where UNITA was founded in 1966) were reaffirmed. Almost fifty years later, calls for equality and democracy, the need to develop the countryside to benefit the cities and safeguarding the interests of the Angolan people above foreign interests still resonated ideologically with the reality in Angola. In January 2013, a senior leader of UNITA explained that the civil war confrontation between two societies and two states was still alive today.

> There was no care to talk about the technical discourse of equality and culture. Here we live the creole culture—where the culture of our country is being modernised, which has resulted in permanent elites and cliques. We feel used and despised. Today we feel that the *Bailundo* will never reach power—that they should only sweep the streets and *capim* [tall grass]. In the national assembly one parliamentarian even still referred to us as '*os sulanos*' [the southerners]. Because of this, latent tensions return and are inflamed this way. The Bakongo have the same feeling.[37]

Later that same year, Samakuva would openly revive an old discourse that the MPLA served the interests of foreigners and its own elite, breeding discrimination and subjugating Angolans. His opening speech at a political commission meeting stated that after thirty-eight years of independence Angola was undergoing a period of asphyxiation and absolutism like in 1973 (before independence), in which the MPLA 'discriminates against the "langa" [the bakongo] and humiliates the "sulanos" while dividing the money among its own and not allowing people from other parties to prosper economically or legitimately attain political power'.[38]

Organisationally, UNITA would begin to tap into its structures of service provision that had given them state-like legitimacy with civilians during the war. Pearce (2020) identified three examples of this in the Central Highlands. He describes how after 2008 UNITA began to establish projects relating to education, cadre training and famine relief, setting up a school in an abandoned building in Bailundo and running a cadre-training programme teaching the party's history, organisation and mobilisation. Pearce also mentions an initiative where UNITA led a convoy of food to drought-affected areas in the southern province of Cunene after collecting 10 tonnes of food from supporters. Numerous testimonies also referred to the use of UNITA doctors and nurses, tapping into networks of solidarity, when members could not get adequate medical care in state hospitals.[39]

UNITA's membership would swell from 900,000 in 2002 to over 3 million in 2019.[40] In November 2019, the party elected a new leader—Adalberto da Costa Junior, a dynamic politician who eloquently spoke truth to power in parliamentary debates. Da Costa Junior was heavily committed to seeing UNITA take over from the MPLA in the August 2022 elections. His ascension in UNITA, however, was not an easy one. An internal battle for the presidency of the party—between Samakuva and Da Costa Junior's camps—revealed the party's many fault lines along regionalism and race. It became a very ugly affair with the potential of splitting the main opposition party. At stake was the loss of an old unspoken tradition of having UNITA led by a Bie-born leader (both Savimbi and Samakuva were from the province of Bie) of African, not Afro-Portuguese descent (which UNITA claimed was a feature of the MPLA elites). Da Costa Junior was born in Huambo and was of mixed race. He embodied everything that the MPLA had deemed UNITA wasn't; he was urban, multiracial, sophisticated and he appealed to a multinational audience across ethnicities. When he won the presidency of the party, Da Costa Junior faced the arduous job of reconciling the camps to avoid defections and a politically divided UNITA.

Da Costa Junior placed as his deputies Arlete Leona Chimbimba, and Simão Albino Dembo, the nephew of previous vice president

Antonio Dembo. The former youth leader Alvaro Daniel was secretary general, signalling the rise of the youngest generation of UNITA leaders, none of whom were the old politico-military heavyweights of the past. This, however, scared the government, aware of the difficulties it faced with rising levels of poverty in the cities, a looming famine in the South, high unemployment and growing dissatisfaction among the youth. Strategically, Da Costa Junior reached out to Abel Chivukuvuku, who had defected from UNITA in 2012 to form his own party, the CASA-CE, which rapidly became the second-largest opposition party. Chivukuvuku had long and important ties to UNITA spanning back to the war and peace processes of the 1990s. Considered a political heavyweight and charismatic, Chivukuvuku (as leader of the newly formed PRA-JA platform) would align himself with Da Costa Junior and another party, *Bloco Democrático*, led by MPLA dissident and intellectual Filomeno Vieira Lopes. Together, these three leaders and their supporters formed a broad-based opposition platform to contest the 2022 elections. The *Frente Patriotica Unida* (Patriot United Front) (FPU) joined intellectuals, youth, civil society and politicians from different regions of Angola, hoping to bring about the end of the MPLA's time in office. The government responded with an unrelenting and sustained attack on Da Costa Junior. 'I don't understand why they fear him so much, I've told them [MPLA leadership] that no one knew who Adalberto was during the war, he was not a senior general in UNITA. But yet he makes them so nervous.'[41]

In October 2021, the Constitutional Court, acting as an electoral court, cancelled the election of Da Costa Junior as UNITA's leader on the basis that he could not qualify due to holding dual nationality. Da Costa Junior handed in his Portuguese passport months before the UNITA congress. UNITA regrouped, fundraised and, in December 2021, held another congress to re-elect Da Costa Junior. There followed months of harassment, political intrigue and scandals fabricated by the intelligence services, coupled with the freezing of UNITA accounts and other measures meant to dissuade members from retaining him as their leader. This was the first time courts became overt political instruments in manoeuvring MPLA interests. The highest court in the land was at the time headed by

Laurinda Cardoso, a member of the MPLA's politburo, and included Fátima Pereira da Silva, wife of Manuel 'Manico' Pereira da Silva, the president of the MPLA-controlled National Electoral Commission. An Angobarometer poll in January 2022 revealed that UNITA would win the elections with 60% of the vote; the MPLA would only secure 28.4%.[42] An Afrobarometer study revealed in April 2022 that UNITA would win the vote in Luanda, with the national result being split between the MPLA with 29% of the vote, UNITA receiving 22%, while 46% remained undecided.[43] The MPLA-dominated parliament, unhappy with these results, passed a law regulating organisations conducting polls. Among the hurdles it created against civil society measuring the political pulse of the population was the requirement that organisations must have starting capital of 45 million kwanzas (approximately US$110,000) and that polls must be analysed by the executive before being published. Three decades after the traumatic 1992 polls, UNITA was well placed to take the government, reflecting a general yearning for political renewal.

In August 2022, Angolans gave UNITA, as part of the FPU coalition, an electoral but unrecognised victory. A parallel count held by the opposition proved the 24 August elections to be fraudulent, but more importantly it revealed that a majority of voters rejected the idea of another 5 years of João Lourenço's presidency. They voted for change. Because of this, all institutions were instrumentalised to uphold irregularities and entrench securitised power. Among the remarkable elements of this election was the opposition's defeat of the ruling party in the capital Luanda, that represented a third of the electorate. Urbanites, the educated youth and even MPLA supporters voted for UNITA. The MPLA lost the vote of the rank and file of the military and elements of the police, as revealed by results in the polling stations near barracks. The electoral fraud was perpetuated by changing results and interfering with the ability of opposition delegates to keep record of the result sheets from the polling stations. There was also the matter of interfering with the voters' registration by keeping 2.7 million deceased voters on the lists. Having a large number of 'ghost' voters gave the MPLA a buffer to play with numbers and justify different results in specific provinces. Contracting the Spanish company INDRA, which was accused of

255

facilitating electoral fraud, in the logistics and technology systems was another contributing factor to the obfuscation of the electoral process. The state media also played a key role by allocating 90% of its coverage to the government and the MPLA. A week before the election, the CNE made two key changes that were clearly counter to the electoral law. On 16 August, the administrative body decreed that the result sheets used would not include a total number of voters in each of the polling stations, allowing for the possibility of numbers being altered after voting. The CNE then determined the national tally centre would be restricted to 5 electoral commissioners and a 'technical group', limiting access to all other 11 commissioners and denying them, the press and civil society the fundamental right to witness how results were being processed.

UNITA appealed to the constitutional court, calling for a recount and a comparison of electoral sheets in its possession with those used for the official result. Angola's constitutional court decision on 8 September revealed it was a partisan instrument, perpetuating injustices and invalidating the sovereign power of the people. Forsaking the constitution, they broke their own laws. A conclave of 10 justices failed to fulfil its most fundamental role, which is the respect for public probity. Official results awarded the ruling MPLA 51% of the vote and UNITA 43.9%. The opposition FPU conducted its own parallel count with 94% of the result sheets from the 13,200 polling stations which revealed a difference of over 533,000 votes, placing UNITA ahead with 49.5% and the MPLA with 48.2%. The court dismissed the case and refused to demand that the electoral commission show its result sheets and how it tallied the final result. A dissenting judge called for transparency, denounced the reasoning of her colleagues and ended by quoting Plato that justice should never produce injustice.

João Lourenço inaugurated his government on 15 September with the capital Luanda under siege. Military, police and presidential guard units were deployed to secure key arteries and strategic government and economic infrastructure, and were placed within populated neighbourhoods. Columns of armoured police vehicles and military Russian-made Kamaz trucks with artillery pieces lined the streets of key suburbs. Populated areas that voted for the opposition—including Rocha Pinto, Samba, Zango, Viana and Cazenga—became heavily militarised, bringing back memories to the older generations of the war and political massacres of 1977 and 1992. Military tanks lined the streets in an unprecedented show of force. Not even during the worst years of the war did Luanda have the entire security apparatus on display in an act of public intimidation. Lists of opposition leaders meant for elimination were circulating on social media. Several had received death threats, and activists across the country were rounded up and arrested. UNITA's old guard, mainly the generals, cautioned Da Costa Junior and the youth against protesting en masse in Luanda. 'We knew that those that survived in 1992 would be killed now, that they would decapitate UNITA once and for all, and we needed to be here to fight in elections to become the next government.'[44]

From a defeated, ideologically adrift and reputationally bruised movement, UNITA had managed over 20 years of peacetime to rebuild its base and position itself to politically defeat the MPLA through elections. This was a testament of the strength of the party structures and the legacy of collective leadership that had been retained since the 1970s. The party reframed its ideology as one of representing the marginalised masses and defending the unity of Angola above foreign interests and dictatorial tendencies, and this message resonated with diverse constituencies. UNITA's organisation and structures became an asset to mobilise funds, people and help where needed. Unlike the wartime years, where its leadership eclipsed many other political strengths, the post-2002 UNITA began a discreet and gradual rebuilding of the party without the 'big man' exuberance of Savimbi. Even when it wasn't capable of politically dethroning the MPLA, UNITA understood the need to play a long-term game.

South Sudan's 2005 and 2013 critical junctures

The signs of the SPLM/A's implosion had been clear for many years—certainly after 2005, when the movement changed leadership and embarked on a militarised, kleptocratic state-building path that overrode the fundamental reforms of political transformation,

257

national unity and sustainable development. The 2005–11 transition, initiated under the CPA, attempted to undertake several structural reforms without reforming the SPLM/A itself as a political party shedding its liberation legacy of militarism, nepotism and assimilation. Despite this, the hope and optimism that unified southerners behind the SPLM/A in 2011 created the impression that the country could rebuild and prosper. In 2011, a referendum in Sudan split Africa's largest country in two without clearly defining a border or how oil and infrastructures were to be shared, exacerbating many other micro-conflicts and setting the stage for future war. Six decades of war to liberate the South from northern domination resulted in the physical separation of the two regions but brought little else to the people of South Sudan, who remained impoverished, lacking services and divided. The SPLM/A was not solely responsible for this, but it played a key role in mismanaging a very difficult transition from war to peace, and as an independent state. Two critical junctures led the party down a path of decadence and factionalism resulting from the death of John Garang in 2005 and a violent leadership dispute in 2013.

Several factors explain why the SPLM ultimately failed to transform itself in peacetime. First, there was the structural challenge of operating with a revolutionary legacy that centralised authority and command, which negated the concept of separation of powers and of being mandated to serve. Operating with a revolutionary tradition of hierarchical command and a legacy of a militarism, the leadership had difficulty in adapting to other types of behaviour that did not adhere to a rigid pyramid of power and unbending loyalty, with divergent opinions perceived as dissident and undisciplined (Roque 2014). Second, there were operational aspects of distinguishing between the state and the party, and in the governance sequencing of who should lead who. Policy was crafted at the government level as opposed to the party level, with the driving force of balancing the interests and representation of the various communities. Peacetime mobilisation did not follow a party line. Instead, it saw the integration and political accommodation of potential spoilers and militia groups into an overinflated megastructure that threatened the future definition, vision and ideology of the SPLM (Roque 2014).

The third factor was tied to the party's lack of institutionalisation. The structures existed, but the party organs met only sporadically, and some individuals and key interests eclipsed the ability of these structures to operate independently. Finally, the party was still grappling with divisions among the elites and the vision of the SPLM. Under the leadership of Salva Kiir and his 'big tent' approach that incorporated many other armed groups into the SPLA, this factor worsened and de-characterised what were the last remaining elements of a core group of SPLM/A historical loyalists. The Garang loyalists were slowly sidelined under Kiir, while former dissidents and problematic leaders outside the SPLM/A were brought into the inner circles of power. A southern intellectual explained it perfectly: 'If we fail to make democracy within the party, we cannot make democracy within the nation. We cannot take defeat. It would be interpreted as mutiny—to rebel against the state. All we have are leaders and not the party or the grassroots.'[45]

Many of the structural constraints identified as barriers to the SPLM/A's transformation could have arguably been overcome under the leadership of Garang. His death in 2005 was a turning point for the SPLM/A and the South. His centralising grip on the movement had kept in check many of the fragmenting tendencies of ethnic competition and tempered the sentiment of Dinka supremacy. He was, however, already facing internal divisions to his rule. The 2004 leadership meeting in Rumbek became a pseudo-trial of Garang's leadership of the SPLM (Pinaud 2021). Salva Kiir led the charge, and with him stood a broader group from Bahr El Ghazal and a few non-Dinka leaders. Kiir clashed with Garang over claims that the movement was being mismanaged, that Garang ruled the SPLM as his personal fiefdom and that there were no processes of inclusive decision-making and internal reflection. As a result, 'Salva went to Yei with his troops and began mobilising Garang's enemies like Paulino Matiep and his militias to prepare for war, because Garang was preparing to replace Salva with Nhial Deng at the meeting.'[46] Ironically, it was Riek Machar who helped diffuse the situation. 'Salva presented Riek with fifty-two reasons and complaints, and Riek showed him the list he prepared in 1991—they were almost identical. He told Salva that it is better to unite to achieve peace and he also said, "you don't want to be the leader of a faction—I have had that experience",' recalled a former SPLM minister. The 'SPLM strategic framework for war to peace transition' policy document emerged because of the 2004 leadership crisis and recognised that before the democratic transformation of Sudan could occur, they first had to bring about the transformation of the SPLM itself. This 2004 document called for the reorganisation of SPLM structures: transforming the NLC into a Central Committee tasked with revising the party documents; holding a National Convention to elect rather than nominate the SPLM chairperson and members of the NLC, who would then elect the political bureau, deputy chairpersons, and other office holders; and the formulation of a post-conflict recovery and reconstruction strategy. It was this 2004 document that Rebecca Nyandeng, Garang's widow, quoted in her intervention at the 6 December 2013 press conference where several SPLM leaders publicly criticised President Kiir's chairmanship, blaming him for the poor governing record, lack of collective leadership and paralysis of the General Secretariat. This meeting in December 2013 set the stage for what Kiir would interpret as an attempted coup, sparking an intractable war.

Despite the internal reflections of 2004, the movement headed into the 2005 transition with a conflicted understanding of what the path forward would be. Some within the SPLM/A contended that Garang's focus was on reforming the centre in Khartoum to secure change for the South, whereas Kiir was uniquely interested in achieving independence for the South in 2011. Garang had defined several policies addressing the many social and economic fault lines identified during wartime governance that had the potential to politically unravel the South if left unaddressed. The SPLM/A's experience in governing and misgoverning their liberated areas for three decades provided them with a deep understanding of the fissures and challenges at the local and regional levels that governing the new state of South Sudan would entail. These included factionalism and segmentation within the party, tribalism and nepotism, and a resurgence of Kokora[47] due to development inequalities of different states. They also included insecurity and loss of legitimacy of law enforcement agencies and the difficulty of sustaining a nationalist project that would keep all communities united, as well as of creating a social contract between the government and its constituents in the context of sustained external delivery of services and development. 'We were building a country that had contradictions and needed to create a new model of higher values that everyone could subscribe to. A constitution was not enough, as laws do not make a society. Policies needed to be foundational, so they help us interact as a people and not facilitate us to reject ourselves.'[48] The words of this SPLM elder from Equatoria, who accurately predicted the devastating intra-elite conflict, carried a strong message that Garang had already identified. Transformative change had to occur simultaneously within the structures of the movement—and more importantly within the leadership—and within society. Garang began preparing for a transformation that would occur simultaneously within the SPLM as a party, within the SPLA as the military and within the CANS as the new administration. The first policy directives in 2005, as the Government of South Sudan (GOSS)—the autonomous entity of the Government of National Unity based in Khartoum—was being inaugurated, therefore, dealt with the establishment of caretaker governments, a professionalised civil service, the reform of the party and the delivery of services through villagisation.

The policy of creating caretaker governments aimed at curtailing the dynamics of nepotism and violent kleptocracy that had crept into the local fiefdoms of state governments. 'Nepotism is like a garden—you see characteristics of the owner and the individual. Today a government office or institution is not national, it is the preserve of a tribe. The thinking is: after all who paid dowry for this seat?'[49] Garang knew that tribalism and nepotism would haunt the new administration of the South, and that in some way communities would fall back into their smaller groups of solidarity given the difficulty of forging a nationalist identity that could bring together all the different communities of the South. He had learnt from the complicated and delicate balance of interests and ethnic considerations among the top leadership of the SPLM and SPLA that kept the movement under a tightly controlled hierarchy of the military. The few times the movement tried to address diverging interests and opinions, or internal calls for reform, had resulted in political crisis that would invariably take on factional and ethnic dimensions (as seen in 1991, 2004, 2008 and 2013). The pursuit of narrow interests and the resurgence of community and tribal imperatives would haunt the process of transformation if leaders were initially selected from their communities to run their constituencies. In light of this, as well as the lessons taken from the disputes and tribal conflicts in the liberated areas, the SPLM chairman came up with the idea of caretaker governors that would be the ultimate state authority and provide the necessary link between the local and central levels.

After the CPA, the South, in accordance with the normalisation of the northern structures, divided its regions into 10 states where each state would have a governor. The fact that the South inherited 10 states was problematic for the SPLM because the movement was used to governing based on three greater regions. The emphasis on decentralisation by the SPLM leadership aimed at addressing Sudan's legacy of marginalisation. As per the policy, the caretaker governor of the state would not originate from the area, thus avoiding the pitfalls of corruption and conflicts of interest. The idea was to have a governor from a different tribe rule a state where he/she had no community affiliation or tribal representation so that there would be a focus on the task of governing. Garang therefore nominated Riek Machar (from Upper Nile) to be the governor of Western Equatoria; Wanni Igga (from Central Equatoria) as governor of Upper Nile; Daniel Awet (from Lakes state) to be the governor of Eastern Equatoria; Lam Akol (from Upper Nile) to be the governor of Western Bahr El Ghazal; Kuol Manyang (from Jonglei) to be the governor of Northern Bahr El Ghazal; Deng Alor (from Abyei) to be the governor of Jongeli state; Pagan Amum (from Upper Nile) to be the governor of Lakes state; and so forth. Privately among members of parliament and the government, the debate resurfaced in 2012 as to bringing back a programme that would ease tensions between tribes. The caretaker government was always referred to as the solution, 'to instil another spirit of cooperation and unity'.[50]

The second policy, dealing with the creation of a civil service, would be premised on using what already existed. For decades the South had been governed by different entities—the Khartoum government and SPLM/A—which resulted in several inconsistencies that needed to be resolved before it could have a functioning GOSS. In 1994 federalism was introduced by Khartoum, but this had no impact on the liberated areas functioning under CANS. The South Sudan Coordination Council (SSCC) served as the public service in areas of the South controlled by Khartoum during the war. The relationship with the states was very tenuous, as the governors dealt directly with the central government in Khartoum. The SSCC also faced serious communication and access difficulties, as garrison towns had entire areas surrounding them under SPLM/A control. However, the employees of the CCSS system were professional civil servants and were capable of providing the necessary assistance to the new administration during the CPA transitional years. The CCSS civil servants had the know-how, training and organisational capacity that the CANS operatives lacked, while the CANS administrators understood the basis upon which the SPLM would build a new state.

Under Garang's policy, the transformation of the CANS would begin with the incorporation of civil servants from the CCSS. A committee was formed comprising Samuel AbuJohn, Nhial Deng Nhial, Lual Deng and others, who were given the mandate to assist in this process of integration and transformation. The CPA did not consider the issue of the civil service in great detail, nor did it include implementation modalities, which resulted in an overinflated and inconsistent public service. Garang's policy was meant to devise guidelines and benchmarks of implementation. The CCSS public service would therefore take the lead. However, after Garang's death, priority was given to the CANS cadres, followed by the diaspora members who had supported the movement, and only then to those who had worked in garrison towns, even if the latter had a greater level of professionalism. The argument at the time was that those who had fought the war needed to be given a seat in government, regardless of qualifications, as a reward for their loyalty.

Garang's third policy dealt with the party–state transformation. The building of the SPLM's party structures and the necessary forums for consultation and debate at the local levels did not follow the lessons posed by the liberation councils during the war. As legislative bodies of the CANS, the liberation councils also became party organs that allowed for the population, chiefs, civil servants and civil society members to engage in debate and address the affairs of the community at the local level, while also bringing all those groups under the political banner of the SPLM. Garang knew that there was a weak link between the SPLM leadership and the grassroots, that the party had weak institutions and discipline.[51] The need to transform and strengthen the party and its institutions was a result of the assimilation of the party into the state. However, this did not translate into better communication with civilians or enhanced state–society relations. Instead, policy was dictated by the presidency's policy priorities and decisions. The post-2005 government, and in particular the presidency, ruled without consulting or engaging with the SPLM, creating deep divisions within the party and allowing local-level calculations of power to be negotiated politically with the presidency. Attempts to prematurely separate the state from the party, when neither were institutionally capable of taking on the roles they were assigned, created opportunities for conflicting dynamics and interests to emerge. By 2012, key NLC members claimed that the party needed to 'get back its chairman' so that the SPLM could start determining the policies of the reconstruction and the state moving forward.[52]

Garang's final policy, 'Taking the towns to the villages', dealt with the issue of rural development and building rural towns through service provision and economic infrastructure so that communities could become self-sufficient and less dependent on the main cities. Garang's vision for development centred on transforming the country from a rural-development perspective, aiming for each 150-household village to be self-sufficient. He was so intent on this that he was willing to budget part of the oil revenues to fund this South-wide initiative.[53]

At Garang's request, a study was prepared in 2005 by David Deng Athorbei to understand what the costs would be to fully implement this policy, like the *ujamaa* of Tanzania. According to some high-ranking SPLM/A members, a census was considered to determine how to allocate the oil revenues according to population size rather than county size so that this development path could be effective. Implementation of this approach, together with lessons learnt from CANS partnerships with international NGOs, could have resulted in a very different socio-economic landscape in the post-conflict reconstruction period. Had the SPLM been able to play a more active role in providing services rather than outsourcing them to external actors, the process of embedding a state within the population would have given it the basis for a stronger social contract. It would also have developed administrative competence within government. According to testimonies from his advisors, Garang intended to address this legitimacy gap that had emerged during the war due to the presence of the UN and other relief organisations.

Garang's death in July 2005 threatened to draw the country into war. A thirst for vengeance and retribution had driven several military officers into a state of readiness. 'Units had mobilised to march on Kampala and Khartoum, as we suspected that Museveni and Bashir were complicit in our chairman's death.'[54] To this day, no one knows if and why Garang was killed. Madam Rebecca Nyandeng was credited with having appeased these sentiments as the leadership retreated in New Site to determine the path forward: 'After the death of Dr John, there was a near split between Garangists and Salva's group. Salva was surrounded by a group that had tenuous ties to the SPLM/A's liberation history. These included Dominic Dim, Justin Yac, Bona Malwal, Telar Deng and Aleu Aleu.'[55] Under the chairmanship of Salva Kiir, the SPLM/A would take a different direction. Garang's vision was abandoned in 2005, as the new political dispensation was unable or unwilling to implement this vision, as the country was fully in the throes of integrating external solutions and state-building models. Institutions established were suited to the running of a federal political system. The North operated under the values of Sharia law and the South under a secular system. Both sides maintained their respective armies and created a third integrated force, the Joint Integrated Units. Omar Al-Bashir remained the president of Sudan, deputised by Garang as first vice president, and Ali Osman Taha as second vice president. When Salva Kiir took over as first vice president of Sudan, leader of the GOSS and chairman of the SPLM/A, he embarked on a different path. His focus was on the South, not on implementing the New Sudan vision. The end point was the referendum and achieving independence. The impression created by the GOSS and the international backers of the SPLM/A was that independence was more important than democracy (de Waal 2014).

Two dynamics under Kiir's leadership were particularly problematic: corruption and militarised assimilation. Although these were legacies of the war, from 2005 onwards corruption evolved in South Sudan from mismanagement at the highest levels of power to a more generalised practice that characterised entire state institutions. Locally across the different regions, many grievances were pinned to economic terms of marginalisation, disenfranchisement and expropriation of resources. At the national level, elites fought over the means of extraction, production and economic power to advance narrow military and political interests. All this was achieved through mechanisms that perpetuated corruption, nepotism and patronage. The situation was worse in the oil-producing states of Unity and Upper Nile because of the 2% of oil revenues given to state authorities, and there were accusations that revenue from oil was being directly used to mobilise, train and arm militias.[56] The revenue these oil-producing states received became commonly referred to as 'the missing two per cent'.[57]

The second dynamic referred to the aftereffects of Kiir's 'big tent' process of assimilating and integrating different armed groups and militias. At the time, the UN[58] and many diplomats praised these actions as conciliatory and strategic, a solution that kept the South from erupting into more violence stoked by Khartoum as well as unaddressed local grievances over land, cattle and other resources. The détente achieved by Kiir and the peace established by the absorption of other armed groups was an important stabilisation strategy at the time, but it would have difficult consequences in the following years. The integration of Paulino Matiep's militia, the South Sudan Defense Forces (SSDF), as part of the 2006 Juba Declaration was a large component of Kiir's 'big tent' process. This move was problematic on several fronts, notwithstanding the fact that during the war the SSDF had been an effective ally of Khartoum. The SSDF invoked people's hatred of Garang, the SPLM/A and the Dinka, to justify their alliance to the government.[59] Because the SSDF was comprised of several militias and tribal self-defence groups (operating in Upper Nile and the Equatoria regions), it was an unavoidable step to pacify the South. The predominantly Nuer SSDF could have been comparable in size to the SPLA, which increased ethnic prejudices and transfigured the SPLA's ethnic composition (Pinaud 2021).

These militiamen never formally recognised themselves as SPLA, nor did they shed their more localised and narrower agendas. Despite sustained efforts by donors and international agencies to professionalise and train the SPLA as part of the DDR and security sector reform process, the South Sudanese army remained predatory and lacking in discipline, and when unpaid it would resort to looting and violence against civilians. Many historical grievances and narratives of unreconciled ethnic massacres were also part of the undercurrent of factors that accelerated several of these inter-communal conflicts. Tensions in the South were also fuelled by poorly disciplined security forces and the creation of private militias. Between 2008 and 2009, cattle raiding, fighting between clans and boundary disputes over grazing lands killed 2,500 people and displaced over 350,000.[60] In 2009, the SPLA army consumed over 40% of the GOSS budget, a number that would increase in the post-independence years. The South's defence budget had increased from US$586 million in 2006 to over US$1 billion in 2011 (de Waal 2015). The real number of SPLA soldiers was unknown, although the African Union placed the number at 200,000 in 2014.[61] The importance of the army remained above that of the nation.

As South Sudan became a securitised state, other forces were being strengthened and armed as an enlarged security apparatus moved towards securing the political project and power of key politicians. The National Intelligence and Security Services (NISS) became a powerful institution that would terrorise perceived dissenters, civil society members and journalists. Directed by the Office of the Presidency, it became a political police unit which aided in the increase of state repression and securitisation. Several militias, like the Dinka Mathiang Anyoor recruited in Bahr El Ghazal, were created as a counter-power to political and military elites and to uphold the political hegemony of key leaders. Post-2011, Salva Kiir strengthened his presidential guard, the Tiger Battalion, as tensions within the SPLM rose. Like him, many other generals-turned-politicians also built their own personal armies.

Together the two dynamics of corruption and militarisation, against the backdrop of weak political institutions and a diluted ideology and political programme, led to the creation of a kleptocracy in the form of a militarised, corrupt, neo-patrimonial system of governance (de Waal 2014). The levels of patronage and accumulation of wealth by political and military elites increased as the GOSS gained access to oil revenues. The integration of armed groups in 2006 increased the government's neo-patrimonial tendencies, giving future rebellions the idea that their integration would result in positions of power and access to resources which would facilitate clientelist networks along tribal lines.[62]

Two moments during the CPA years (2005–11) revealed the many weak points of the SPLM as a political party and its default instinct to subvert democratic and consensus-based rules: the second national convention in 2008 and the first general elections in 2010. The SPLM held its second convention in Juba in May 2008, fourteen years after its first convention in Chukudum. There were high expectations, with members believing that the transformation agenda as well as the policies on deployment of cadres and other governing policies would be discussed. There was some reorganisation of the party's organs and a revitalisation of the roles of the youth and women's leagues, but otherwise important discussions were avoided and collective leadership structures remained organisationally inept. The leadership of the party was not prepared to manage all the congresses' elections, resulting in senior cadres losing their seats. The convention was paralysed for a week while the leadership decided who would be number two in the party, an issue that threatened to divide the SPLM into regional and ethnic power centres (Yoh 2010).[63] While there was initially a consensus to have only one deputy, the status quo was maintained with three deputy chairmen—Machar, Wani Igga and Malik Agar (later replaced by Daniel Awet). This marred subsequent political initiatives to reform the party, and difficult discussions ended up being postponed or avoided. The three camps of the president, Machar and Pagan Amum (the secretary general and Garang loyalist)—that later factionalised in 2013—were already defined in 2008. This was a factor very few chose to remember and address in the following years.

It seemed like nothing was ever simple in Sudan. The April 2010 elections, regarded as some of the most complex polls in the world, used a mix of electoral systems: the president was elected by a two-round system, a simple majority voted in governors and state and national legislative assemblies were elected by plurality (60% representing geographic constituencies and 40% on the basis of proportional representation at state and party list level). The polls saw over 15 million registered Sudanese electing the President of the Republic, the President of South Sudan, 25 governors, representatives for the National Assembly, the South Sudan Legislative Assembly and state assemblies. The logistical enormity of the task added to the difficulties of guaranteeing full and unhindered participation. Voters in the North were casting 8 ballots while voters in the South cast 12, with a choice of 72 political parties and 16,000 candidates. The SPLM was unable to arbitrate the contestation of 340 members within its own party running against the candidates approved by the political bureau in the electoral race. This was a clear sign of the party's internal fragmentation. Of these 340 SPLM candidates who decided to contest independently, 6 ran for governor position in Jonglei, Central Equatoria, Eastern Equatoria, Northern Bahr El Ghazal, Upper Nile and Unity state. The mismanagement of this process within the SPLM, with reports that the political bureau would disown these officials, enhanced existing schisms within the party. If primaries and other internal elections had taken place within the SPLM, the issue of independent candidates could have been avoided. Several candidates who ran as independents later staged rebellions in Jonglei, Unity and Upper Niles states, namely those led by David Yau Yau, George Athor, Johnson Oliny, Gatluak Gai and others.

The exercise revealed that the movement had no structures or appetite for internal democracy, which further enhanced the imperative of maintaining a delicate ethnic, interest group and regional balance above the pursuit of a political vision (Roque 2012). One of the reasons the members of the top ruling organs of the party continued to be nominated rather than elected was to maintain this delicate balance that provisionally kept the party from fracturing. 'If key figures were voted out this would be interpreted as a tribal matter and the result would be serious conflict.'[64] This was the argument used to excuse the lack of internal democratisation and accountability, but it was also a realistic assessment of difficult dynamics that would lead to the implosion of the SPLM in 2013.

The process of liberation in South Sudan had not ended with the achievement of independence, as per the SPLM/A's assessment, but rather was an ongoing process that involved continuous negotiation and sharing of power. In some parts of the country the population began to feel that they had been politically demobilised, with little or no influence on policy nor any stake in the political system. The SPLM found itself with the mandate to rule the South using a structure created by a power-sharing agreement, with institutions that remained ineffective and lacking capacity, struggling to define its own centre of power that resonated with the party and the population (Roque 2012). Partly, because of this, the party was unable to transform the state and instead collapsed into the state.

The conditions for statehood in South Sudan ahead of the July 2011 independence were highly debatable. The massive investment by the international community and the UN in building institutions, creating conditions for economic development and ensuring the implementation of the CPA had by 2010 revealed a state-building exercise that was more a legitimation of external interventions than it was locally embedded and politically functional. Despite this, the end goal remained independence even if all the signs screamed of a country ill-prepared to govern itself. Unsurprisingly, the January 2011 referendum resulted in 98% of the 3.8 million voters choosing to separate from Sudan. The months that followed saw great hope and jubilation among the population as a sense of historical justice and catharsis swept through the South and the SPLM. With the liberation complete, the hard task of governing would test the shaky foundations of political leaders', state structures' and different communities' capacity to find a common trajectory. The future had arrived, and no one knew what to do with it.

The first post-secession cabinet, as announced in August 2011, was composed of 29 national ministries and 27 deputy ministers, the president, and the vice president. The distribution of posts was carefully considered so as to allow for representation of other ethnic groups and curtail the appearance of Dinka domination. This was achieved by transitioning key ministries that were previously held by the Dinka to other groups: the Ministries of Defence went to General John King Nyuon (Nuer), Finance and Economics to Kosti Manibe Ngai (Equatorian), Interior to General Alison Manani Magaya (Equatorian), National Intelligence and Security to General Oyay Deng Ajak (Shilluk) and Justice to John Luke Jok (Nuer). In terms of regional representation, the new cabinet had 10 ministers and 10 deputies from the greater Bahr El Ghazal, 9 ministers and 11 deputies from greater Upper Nile and 10 ministers and 6 deputies from greater Equatoria.

However, this new cabinet was a cause for heated debate in Juba and throughout the diaspora, in particular among civil society that at one end claimed it was a broad-based government (as four ministers and five deputies were non-SPLM members), while at the other end accusing the president of not only promoting Dinka Rek domination of the Warrap elites but also subverting the influence of Dinka Bor. Critics also pointed to the fact that some of the new cabinet ministers had been aligned to the NCP, as was the case with Alison Magaya (who joined the SPLM in June 2011) and Agnes Lukudu (who was previously deputy chairman of the NCP in the South). Elements within the SPLM criticised the nomination of General Magaya, questioning the logic of placing the internal security of the new country in the hands of an 'enemy'.[65] In their opinion, the SPLM was subsuming the opposition rather than engaging with it and contesting its policies. Other interpretations saw the president as surrounding himself with elites from his state and bringing former adversaries into the circle of power around him, whereby only he could manage the dynamics and become the ultimate arbitrator.

Efforts by some members of the NLC and the politburo to reform the SPLM in 2012 would begin setting the stage for the crisis that later erupted. In February 2012, the politburo of the SPLM announced that the party was resolved on further re-structuring itself and developing new strategic goals, to reflect the political separation with the SPLM-North and the structural changes of the post-independence political setting. An NLC meeting took place from 26–29 March, the first since 2008, aiming to transform the structure and vision after independence, while endorsing a future national programme. The NLC was preceded by a political bureau meeting on 24 March that had ended with unreconciled and unsettled positions. The NLC meeting was described as disappointing, where only the views of key leaders and ministers were heard and issues were 'bulldozed' over to maintain the status quo.[66] At this NLC meeting, Secretary General Pagan Amum proposed a road map for reform, yet the border war between Juba and Khartoum that had erupted took precedence. Some contended that the 2012 Heglig oil dispute, which had triggered the conflict, was the perfect excuse to avoid the difficult discussions during this NLC meeting that was to set the stage for the Third National Convention, ahead of the first post-independence elections in 2015. By engaging in a border war, the president recalibrated the need for national cohesion and patriotism in the face of external aggression, but this was a short-lived solution, and the issues within the party would resurface. In late 2012, a group of SPLM political bureau members toured the country, allegedly to thank the population for their support during the liberation years and the referendum. Instead of being welcomed at the local level, the SPLM was widely condemned for having lost its vision and failed at delivering services and good governance.[67] In March 2013, Riek Machar and Pagan Amum allegedly confronted Kiir, blaming him for the party's failure and making their intentions to run for the chairman's position known.

In July 2013, Kiir dismissed the entire cabinet, replacing it with new political allies who lacked party credentials. In November 2013, he dismissed all the party structures and officials, except elements of the secretariat, on the grounds that they had outlived their mandates. In a last bid to call for party reform and restore order within the party, a reformist group of SPLM leaders supported by Machar and including Amum called a press conference on 6 December to highlight the many problems and fault lines within the SPLM. Their objective was to call a politburo meeting to determine the agenda for the NLC meeting. The assessment made by these leaders was an accurate portrayal of the difficulties faced by the SPLM. In their press statement, they stated:

The SPLM is NOT a ruling party. In practice decisions are essentially made by one person, and in most cases directed by regional and ethnic lobbies and close business associates surrounding the SPLM Chairman. The efforts to transform the SPLM from a liberation movement into a mass based political party have totally been frustrated by the Chairman. General Salva ignored the grassroots views and demands garnered between July and August 2012 for the SPLM re-organisation. ... There is no formal communication between the party organs at the national level and those in the States, County, Payam and Boma levels.

These SPLM leaders also claimed that Kiir had

instructed the State Governors to appoint their preferred delegates to the SPLM 3rd National Convention scheduled for February 2014. The intention is to side-line and prevent SPLM historical leaders and cadres categorised as 'potential competitors' from participation in the Convention. This is very dangerous move and is likely to plunge the party and the country into the abyss.

The structural pathologies that haunted the SPLM as a movement before and after its 1994 transformation were clearly highlighted by these statements. Despite the diagnosis being correct, it was too little too late to correct the course the country was taking. President Kiir bypassed the politburo and convened the NLC meeting on 14 December. This was a clear violation of the party's constitution and likely stemmed from the fact that the president had lost his ability to persuade the political bureau to act in his favour, with 14 out of 19 its members supporting Machar's call for reform.[68] From Kiir's perspective, this was tantamount to an internal coup attempt. All these events became a fatal runway to the second major critical juncture of the 2013 civil war.

On 16 December 2013, Kiir appeared before national television dressed in military fatigues and announced he had averted a coup attempt in Juba, which he claimed had been staged by Riek Machar, Garang's widow Rebecca Nyandeng and several key SPLM leaders.

Fighting had erupted the day before within SPLA barracks and rapidly spread in Juba. In the capital, Nuer, civilians were selectively and intentionally massacred by forces allied to the government. While Machar escaped Juba, the group of SPLM reformers were arrested in their homes as killings continued. Among those arrested were Pagan Amum, Oyay Deng Ajaak, Kosti Manibe, Majak D'Agoot and John Luk, who would become known as the SPLM-Former Detainees group. Rapidly the war took on ethnic dimensions, with dividing lines being drawn between the Dinka and the Nuer. Revenge killings of Dinka by Nuer would spiral in Akobo and Bor. Riek would form the SPLM-In Opposition (SPLM-IO) faction, drawing his fighters from defecting units of the SPLA and some armed civilians in Nuer areas. The first unit from the SPLA to join the SPLM-IO was Peter Gadet's 8th Division in Jonglei, followed by several SPLA units comprised of re-incorporated anti-SPLA militias (Johnson 2014). Equatorians and other smaller ethnic groups stood on the sidelines of this war, something that would change in 2016.

When the civil war broke out in 2013 and the success story of South Sudan collapsed, the SPLM/A had been in power for eight years, heavily supported by the international community and its neighbours. Over US$4 billion of international aid had been invested in the country, and an endless amount of training, advising, restructuring and political support given in establishing the newly formed state. Yet few efforts focused on reforming the political ethos of the governing elites. The SPLM was unchallenged in every way, which brought about a complacency reminiscent of the first decade of war. Little was done to restructure the collective leadership or to shift the focus from the militarisation of politics (many governors found it acceptable to have private militias). The party became divided into three main fronts: President Kiir's faction (the SPLM-In Government), Machar's SPLM-In Opposition faction and the reformers' SPLM-Former Detainees faction. Alone, none of these factions had the necessary traction or capacity to lead a reform process and govern the country. This intra-SPLM war would displace over three million civilians, killing an unknown number of non-armed and armed southern Sudanese. It would reverse all the reform efforts, exponentially expand the reach and action of the security apparatus and effectively enhance local and ethnic divisions. For the first three years until the signing of the 2016 peace agreements, US$1.5 billion was spent yearly in humanitarian aid, an amount that would increase following the declaration of famine (de Simone 2018).

In 2016, South Sudan found itself in a situation of anomaly on several fronts: it had two ongoing political processes as represented by the Arusha SPLM Reunification Agreement and the Intergovernmental Authority on Development (IGAD)-led Agreement for the Resolution of the Conflict in South Sudan (ARCISS). While Arusha focused on the internal reform of the SPLM as a party with a joint single agenda, ARCISS focused on three SPLM parties and as such could be implemented without SPLM reunification. The shortcomings of the IGAD-led process resulted in an elite compact between two of the largest ethnic groups. Adding to existing difficulties were the factionalism and divisions within the government and SPLM-IO with differing agendas, both of which were used to sabotage the agreements. Their agendas were dominated by fear of losing positions and access to power, which translated into financial stability. The SPLM continued to be considered the only vehicle to power, with competition for power and leadership dictating long-term strategies for attaining the presidency. Claims of widespread human rights violations, crimes against humanity and war crimes resonated in several reports, including President Obasanjo's AU Commission of Inquiry report and the numerous findings of the UN panel of experts, resulting in the future establishment of a Hybrid Court (HCSS) as per ARCISS.

The implementation of both ARCISS and the Arusha agreements stalled, although Arusha was more successful in bringing the parties together. Ahead of the final signing of ARCISS, President Kiir produced a list of reservations his government had regarding the agreement. Some intellectuals jokingly stated years later that Kiir had fully implemented the reservations and not the peace accord. Several presidential decrees were also passed that hijacked important national conversations on future governance arrangements. The decree of October 2015 creating twenty-eight states (out of the 10 states) was the most controversial. While supported by a large constituency—in particular the Dinka—as a popular response to calls for decentralisation, the move was opposed by other communities. The redrawing of state, county and payam boundaries became a political issue aimed at enhancing ethnic proportions of power rather than respecting community boundaries and securing peaceful relations at the local level. The creation of more states also distorted representation proportions in parliament, in the SPLM's political bureau, in the NLC and among delegates for the National Convention. The twenty-eight states impacted the economic viability of the state, placing administrative structures under more pressure and further revealing the inadequacy of the civil service. Ethnic lobby groups were becoming increasingly stronger among different constituencies and key elements of the leadership. The Dinka Jieng Council of Elders (JCE) was thought to be behind many presidential directives, openly stating that South Sudan should be ruled by a Dinka. The narrowing of the democratic space increased as security agencies took over power in Juba. The press and civil society faced sustained threats and intimidation. A Transitional Unity Government, as mandated by the ARCISS transition, was inaugurated in April 2016 after many delays and tensions in the implementation of political and security arrangements.

In June 2016, a series of deadly clashes between government troops and SPLM-IO forces in Juba led to a full-blown assault by the SPLA on SPLM-IO cantonment areas in Jebel and the residence of the first vice president, Riek Machar. Tensions in the capital between Machar's presidential guards and SPLA members around the presidential compound J1 had produced a powder keg, with any confrontation likely to set off an explosion. The result of the June clashes was over 300 deaths, the displacement of 40,000 people, attacks on civilians and UN protection of civilians' sites, the killing of two peacekeepers, mass looting and the rape and assassination of NGO staff. Versions of events and trigger points differed, with each party accusing the other of political and military wrongdoing. The most likely explanation was that a combination of intentional actions with the aim of derailing ARCISS resulted in many unintended or unforeseen consequences. Machar fled Juba on 9 July. The deployment of MI-24 attack helicopters and ground forces gave credence to claims that there was a massive manhunt for him. SPLA units spent weeks in hot pursuit of the vice president and his entourage in Central and Western Equatoria. Equatorian militias and rebel groups helped defend Machar, understanding that they themselves would not be spared by government forces, helping him enter the DRC where he was extracted to safety by the UN mission several weeks later (Roque and Miamingi 2017).

Days after Machar's departure from Juba, Kiir appointed Taban Deng, an SPLM-IO minister in the transitional government, to replace Machar as first vice president. The SPLM-IO effectively splintered, one of several schisms that the opposition would suffer. The international community and regional allies would scramble to find a solution to this crisis as the war deepened. By not dealing adequately with some existing conflict triggers, the peace agreement ARCISS exacerbated them. As a power-sharing arrangement, it resulted in ethnically exclusionary political alignments that isolated more diverse and non-partisan communities. This led to the militarisation of ethnicity as different communities that fell outside the power-sharing agreement came to realise that in order to play a political role in peace they had to be armed (Roque and Miamingi 2017). This view was compounded by the perception that ARCISS shared power between the Dinka and Nuer and allowed them to control rewards to members of other communities, thus filtering those communities' concerns through the interests of the two dominant groups.

Localised conflicts increased in 2016, enmeshing localised issues with national grievances and power grabs. Armed groups proliferated outside the ARCISS framework, continuing to fight the central government or their neighbouring communities. Depressingly, it was clear that there were few if no nationalist symbols, political agendas or social forums to bring communities together. The liberation struggle's symbolic capital had been exhausted among the political elite and the grassroots constituents. Alliances were based on the convergence of interests in some areas and on identity in others. By 2017, South Sudan was engulfed in a mutually reinforcing war system. This war was more decentralised. Several drivers of conflict—some new and others accentuated by the conflict—emerged, namely badly managed decentralisation, corruption, marginalisation, ethnic rivalries and exclusionary politics, as well as unaddressed local grievances that fed militias and insurgencies countrywide (Roque and Miamingi 2017). With a daily production of 135,000 barrels of oil in mid-2018, the government managed to increase its annual budget to US$166 million (up from US$103 million the previous year). The majority of these funds were used to sustain the war effort and patronage networks. An investigation by Global Witness revealed how the state-owned Nile Petroleum Corporation (NILEPET) became the president's choice vehicle to funnel millions in revenues to the National Security Bureau led by General Akol Koor (also on the board of NILEPET) and different ethnic militias. The economic drivers of the conflict became more visible yet were left unaddressed by any of the diplomatic interventions within the region.

In 2018, the Revitalised-ARCISS agreement was signed, setting out additional reforms and rebooting the transitional period. Five years later, these reforms were largely unimplemented, a national unity government was only partially formed and the parties held opposing views to almost every issue. Unsurprisingly, the implementation of the security arrangements and the transitional justice mechanisms were the most difficult. At the time, the government and SPLA believed in a military victory despite the serious rift after Paul Malong, powerful army chief, was removed from his position and put under house arrest in May 2017. This divided the government's military front but also the Bahr El Ghazal Dinka unity. The rift entrenched these divisions within Warrap Dinka communities, more particularly as numerous defections to Malong's recently formed South Sudan United Front (SSUF) movement held significant symbolic and political weight. The former governor of Warrap and co-founder of JCE, Lewis Anei Madut, put his support behind the SSUF. Telar Ring Deng, once a close advisor to President Kiir, became the secretary for external relations for the SSUF. While several opposition groups had been fighting each other, the SPLM-IO actively encouraged Malong's military objectives, given that it had opened a front that the SPLM-IO had been unable to open itself in the Bahr El Ghazal region. In August 2019, two groups joined forces with the SSUF—namely Thomas Cirillo's South Sudan National Democratic Alliance (SSNDA) and Pagan Amum's Real Sudan People's Liberation Movement (R-SPLM)—and became the United South Sudanese Opposition Movements (SSOMA) umbrella.

In February 2020, a government of national unity was inaugurated. President Salva Kiir formally reappointed Riek Machar as First Vice President of South Sudan, James Wani Igga as second vice president, Taban Deng Gai as third vice president and Rebecca Nyandeng (John Garang's widow) as fourth vice president. Government officials, however, continued to dismantle the opposition, courting the defection of senior leaders, further fragmenting an already fragile alliance and enhancing sub-national fault lines as communities further rejected each other. In August 2021, Machar's military chief Simon Gatwec attempted an internal coup with the help of Johnson Olony and later Henry Odwar. Olony split with Gatwec, and months later Kiir would sign bilateral agreements of force integration with both. By early 2022, over 10 senior commanders had defected from the SPLM-IO and the SSUF.

In August 2022, over 21,000 new troops were placed into the new unified army as per the R-ARCISS agreement. The new force, totalled at 83,000 personnel, was to be divided between VIP protection services, the police, national security services, prison, wildlife and civil defence forces. The government and SPLM-IO had agreed to split senior positions, but with commanders defecting from the opposition and joining the South Sudan People's Defence Forces President Kirr asked for 60% of the positions.[69] The strategies remained the same of co-optation, division and elimination. Over fifty years, the SPLM/A had learnt little. The transitional period, dated to end on 22 February 2023, was extended for two more years, creating fears that during this period more would be done to undermine the fragile peace and undercut the power-sharing arrangements that existed between the parties, with the hardest provisions of the agreement yet to be implemented. A constitution had to be written, the security apparatus had to be reconstituted and elections would end the transitional period. By January 2024, the great majority of South Sudanese needed humanitarian assistance (over 9 million out of a population of 12 million), with 2.3 million living as refugees in neighbouring countries and 2 million displaced internally. The international community and the SPLM/A are heading for another critical juncture as a winner-takes-all election approaches in December 2024. Neither the parties, the guarantors, the UN or the different communities are anywhere near prepared to hold elections. The only solution would be to institute a system that would devolve power to the states and regions, rotationally at the centre and highly decentralised at the provincial levels, which seems like an impossibility given the machinations of elites.

The level of collapse and failure of the SPLM/A as a political project, movement and leading organisation after the critical junctures of 2005 and 2013 cannot be understated. The crisis the country faced was catalysed by the bad governance of the movement, the failure of its leadership, the lack of political structures and the ill-defined ideology that failed to rally and unite the nation.

Conclusion

The paths of war and peace embarked upon by the SPLM/A and UNITA could have been avoided, although they were heavily underpinned by organisational, political and leadership constraints. Strategic miscalculations factored into their demise as much as effective leadership decisions had led to their adaptability and survival in the previous decades. Just like leadership, ideology and political programmes had been the main drivers of the movements' ability to survive the critical junctures of 1976 and 1991, and they remained the key contributing factors to the way both responded to the subsequent critical junctures leading to defeat (UNITA) and internal war (SPLM/A). When the visions of their founding leaders died, the SPLM/A and UNITA changed. In post-independence politics, the SPLM/A lost its political direction, lacked a nationalist vision and factionalised. Political structures were further destroyed, and policy was conducted according to personal preferences, with military power determining individuals' political positions in government. Neither Isaias Samakuva (who had been President of UNITA since 2002) nor Salva Kiir Mayardit (who took over the SPLM/A in 2005 as chairman) were as capable of steering the party's political vision in the same way to avoid factionalism and determine effective mobilising strategies for peacetime politics. In the SPLM/A's case, its leadership traded in rents, opportunities and resources to secure loyalty and mobilisation. In UNITA's case, leadership without power and resources traded on the mistakes of their political foes.

These leadership failings and constraints came from the movements' founding presidents too. After 1992, Savimbi gradually lost internal and external support. His paranoia and purges, as well as the escalation in military operations, would lead to greater atrocities being committed against the civilian population. UNITA would face international isolation, crippling sanctions and constant defections of military leaders. Savimbi lost political control of the liberation in 1992 and failed to repackage the political message in a way that justified another decade of war. Samakuva was left with the difficult task of shedding the movement's brutal and militarised image, which he managed in the post-war years. Yet under Samakuva, the party split (in 2012, with the creation of CASA-CE under the leadership of UNITA leader Abel Chivukuvuku) and has only in the last few years managed to rally and reorganise its support base. In a decade, the party had grown its membership to 3.1 million, a result of the political strength and party structures that UNITA had built during the 1980s. However, as the main opposition party in Angola, it continued to be outmanoeuvred by the MPLA and ultimately failed to better capitalise on the regime's governing failures.

Once Kiir took over the SPLM/A, he abandoned the polices that Garang had defined for peacetime state-building: to launch the 'towns to villages' policy of non-ethnic caretaker governments, the development of a professional civil service, the downsizing and streamlining of the SPLA into a national army and the instituting of party reforms within the SPLM. Kiir sought instead to manage governance challenges through the 'big tent' approach of integrating militias and disaffected politicians, which further diluted the SPLM's political definition. Garang had adopted this strategy during the war, but Kiir failed to understand that such a strategy during peacetime would militarise politics. During the first 6 years of Kiir's tenure, the country implemented the CPA peace agreement and there was a clear governance agenda defined by the international community. After independence in 2011, the country lacked a vision for a post-independent nation. The party structures remained underdeveloped, and the SPLM/A was unable to direct government.

Ideologically, both UNITA and the SPLM/A in the subsequent critical junctures failed to realign the political identities that they had devised during the war with new political programmes in peacetime. Even during the war, merely having an anti-identity (rejecting the identity imposed by the state) was not enough for these two movements. They had proposed alternatives as a direct response to a sense of exclusion felt by Angolans in the interior and South and southerners in Sudan. In perpetuating a sense of being under continued imperialism and revisited colonialism from Khartoum and Luanda, both UNITA and the SPLM/A became the vehicles to emancipate the populations they considered to be experiencing this marginalisation. Neither movement managed to reinvent this wartime rhetoric to continue mobilising constituent support with peacetime programmes that would separate them from other political actors and reinforce the legitimacy they had sought. UNITA began depicting itself as the opposing force to the MPLA by default of the government's failings. However, UNITA failed for almost fifteen years to produce a political identity of exclusion for its supporters (uniting other communities that remained represented by other parties, the PRS [Partido de Renovação Social] and the FNLA) when all the ingredients were present: the MPLA's nepotism, corruption, elite enrichment, partisan state institutions and so on. UNITA instead tried to make inroads into MPLA strongholds like Luanda, which it managed by virtue of the MPLA's governing failures rather than UNITA's own political programme for reform.

At the organisational level, both movements saw obvious alterations during peacetime. The very weaknesses and strengths revealed during the war at the organisational level were replicated in peacetime, despite the need for the movements to alter their form and their objectives. In the 1990s, UNITA prioritised securing territory and military victories, abandoning many of its strategies for politically governing the populations, which left many UNITA communities feeling abandoned.[70] It built an extensive diamond extraction enterprise and distribution network that maintained services in the liberated areas, but these were ultimately turned towards military operations and the leadership's survival. MIRNA, the ministry governing resources, would become the most strategic of the administrative branches. The organisation had become even more coercive, but it lacked the political justification to secure support and mobilisation. The fact that UNITA was swiftly losing territory in the mid-1990s meant that it was unable to continue running leadership schools, skills training, and healthcare programmes in the same way.

As an opposition party, UNITA abandoned most of its structures that enabled it to function as a shadow state, although it maintained its shadow cabinet. Although it disbanded many wartime institutions after 2002 as it fully demobilised and disarmed, UNITA would reactivate a few after a decade of peacetime politics. The BRINDE was said to have been redeployed to provide intelligence to keep the leadership safe from constant security threats by the government, and cadre training schools began functioning in Huambo province to continue building political structures and cadres. For fifteen years, UNITA struggled to reorganise itself, despite having a strong political party base, which revealed a division within the leadership between those who remained in urban areas versus the rural constituencies. Although it began to empower youth leaders, it also continued to rotate the same leaders and cadres. This was partly a result of the deeply destructive final years of the war that layered different forms of disengagement at the leadership level—constraining its ability for renewal and reinvention—and within its support base by failing to win over supporters of other parties.

The SPLM/A, on the other hand, remained a highly militarised organisation where party seniority reflected the military hierarchy of the wartime Politico Military High Command. Internal leadership disputes emerged and took on ethnic dimensions as the party failed to accommodate divergent interests and build the political structures necessary to curb the tendency for power grabs from elites. The SPLM/A would opt to retain its amassed army and integrate several militias instead of streamlining the SPLA in preparation for northern aggression ahead of the 2011 referendum. Party organs would become redundant, as the government was directing policy through

Kiir and a group of non-SPLM leaders, creating divisions within the party. Decentralisation efforts during the transitional years and after independence failed to link local leaders to the central government and further isolated the local level, allowing ethnic fiefdoms to emerge under the domains of key commanders/governors. The SPLM/A would continue to expect international agencies to provide services to its population, to run and fund almost exclusively the education and health ministries,[71] and would struggle to manage its oil revenues. These organisational shifts, catapulted by changes at the levels of leadership and ideology/political programme, resulted in the reduction of both movements' support bases and the narrowing of their socio-political areas of operation.

During interviews, civilians, chiefs and community leaders compared the experiences of war with the experiences of peacetime state-building, and they judged the mistakes committed post-war much more harshly. Memory and nostalgia played an important role, but they also indicated the level of impact sustained by societies and communities when experiencing orders that created certain expectations that never materialised. In South Sudan, the SPLM/A was judged with the same level of intensity as that experienced in Angola during MPLA rule, despite the movement being the same organisation running the wartime and peacetime reform programmes. In Angola, the people emerging from UNITA areas were in many cases estranged by the functioning of the MPLA government. Because of their experience under UNITA's social order, certain groups of cadres criticised the lack of services post-war and the inability to apply the skills training and education they had received under UNITA. They were denied a role in peacetime reconstruction, as all sectors were dominated by MPLA specialist committees that determined who was eligible for employment and who could benefit from the peace dividend. For the South Sudanese, the CANS, despite their shortcomings and inefficiencies, created an expectation of greater proximity between the governors and the governed that never came to fruition due to the power plays between Juba and the peripheries. Services were provided by NGOs and funded by international donors, effectively disowning the state in the eyes of many communities.

Both UNITA and the SPLM/A lost gravitas in the eyes of the people they claimed to represent, lost legitimacy as representatives of the excluded and failed to fully unite different constituencies. The closest the peacetime SPLM came to achieving the level of unity and mass support it had enjoyed during the 1990s was during the 2011 referendum and the 6 months that followed until independence was formalised. Since the 2013 war, the ethnicisation of the party and political groups has increased. President Kiir was openly accused of promoting Dinka hegemony and instigating ethnic massacres against the Nuer, the Equatorian groups, the Fertit, Murle, Shilluk and other communities. UNITA's relations with civilians were badly affected by the 1992–2002 war, when the movement committed mass human rights violations against the population. Rebuilding trust and support in peacetime would become a huge challenge. UNITA would only regain political strength after the 2012 elections by mobilising in key strongholds, venturing into other areas and appealing to the youth by placing young leaders in key positions. Old mistakes, entrenched power dynamics, governing failures and ineffective reform solutions would haunt UNITA and the SPLM/A as they navigated more challenging years. Subsequent critical junctures reduced their legitimacy, erased liberation credentials and the justness of their cause, and threatened to invalidate a historical journey that held existential meaning for millions.

CONCLUSION

'Here we have people trained as mechanics, teachers, carpenters, nurses, tailors etc., and if there is work in the city we are not allowed to access it. There is discrimination. The government stipulated that all the Africans are inseparable and that there are no party differences, because now there is only one party. A person that comes with UNITA does not have rights; but the elements of the government and the military all have rights. We have nothing to eat and nowhere to go. Rights exist only in the books on national reconciliation because in reality people are being physically and psychologically punished. We live in a condition of punishment. We are now only visitors.'

UNITA Village Leader, Moxico province (captured when Savimbi was killed), 2004

'I remember the level of organisation here [in Jamba] and if they had managed to transport this level of organisation to the entire country we would have a better Angola today. Those who were educated in Jamba are the best ones today. It was a different world here. Even today we stay here until life changes. We still have people in Zambia and Botswana because they do not trust that the government will change. They are waiting for UNITA to come to power.'

UNITA elder and logistics captain, Jamba, 2012

'Instead of people converging to write a constitution we were writing a constitution for a political party. There is a need to distinguish a forum for a party and the state. The political programme of

287

the SPLM failed—it did not socialise the masses and reduce the impact of tribalism. We are a weaker state because of this. We should have built nationalism. Looks like we are mercenaries. Because mercenaries come to implement some functions. The real owners of South Sudan are still to come.'

SPLM/A cadre, Juba, 2012

'We liberated and now you build a nation. We cannot do two things. The leader of the SPLM was Dr John [Garang] and he laid a strong foundation. Leader of separation is President Salva and founder of the new nation. Now we need to decide what will be in the next 30 years—what type of governance, economic growth, society we want to build. We need a Dinka leader for the next few years—Museveni also acknowledged this—as we cannot give the presidency to a minority, not while the country is illiterate, uneducated and unprepared.'

Senior military SPLM/A leader, Juba, 2012

Reformist wars balanced many binaries: two opposing states, clashing conceptions of the nation, two opposing societal formulations, parallel economic structures and programmes, and two forms of sovereignty. In each side of these equations the political order was organised around the prospect of violence and existentialist destruction, but also of rebirth and restoration. These wars and the rebels fighting them highlighted the crisis of the nation–state in Angola and Sudan where the conceptions of a stable territory, containable population, conformity and homogeneity, and identifiable sovereignty were challenged on many fronts. During specific periods of both wars, social order, legitimacy, authority and a form of responsive governance coexisted with the many forms of destruction. As a result, the *state* and *nation* were fluid, temporal and shifting entities. The parallel state, like the state it aimed to destroy, became a crucial part of the functioning set of boundaries, hierarchies and socio-economic and political motivations that sustained heterogeneous communities within the nation–state. The resulting identities and nationalism left deep divisions in peacetime Angola and South Sudan. The opening quotes of this chapter bear witness to the exclusion of the defeated (UNITA) and of the victors

(SPLM/A). Two movements, living very distinct moments in their political lifetimes, embodied the deep pathologies and fault lines of the social fabric and political orders they navigated post-conflict. For UNITA, this would become an asset, for the SPLM/A a liability. UNITA ultimately repositioned itself as representing the excluded, while the SPLM/A would reveal itself to be owning the nation not representing its people.

This study of the SPLM/A and UNITA has highlighted how the wartime parallel state was a fundamental resistance tool to the contested central state. Its symbols and structures embedded the concept of the state in the minds and lived experiences of its constituents. It mediated the idea of a liberated, normalised and reformed state that could function during wartime and that enhanced the power of the local/peripheral levels as catalysts for state-making, not on the margins or borderlands of war but at the very heart of the conflict. The understanding that 'war makes states' (Tilly 1984),[1] and that war was not synonymous with chaos when 'clearly, order [wa]s necessary for managing violence as much as the threat of violence [wa]s crucial in cementing order' (Kalyvas et al. 2008: 1), was an experience that cut across divergent contexts and conflicts. Although, today, externally driven models of state-building, global changes in warfare, the privatisation of coercion and capital and other features of current wars may raise questions over whether these continue to make states (Leander 2004),[2] the experience of parallel states globally shows that the interactions between violence, ideology and the organisational survival of 'corrective' liberations can produce states. However, the making of the state in the case of UNITA and the SPLM/A moved beyond the Tillian fiscal–military paradigm of coercion, extraction, distribution and production, and included the development of organisations and interactions that were aimed at socialisation, regulation and normalisation (Pincus and Robinson 2013). They sought to introduce certainty, predictability and procedure into an environment that was otherwise characterised by mass violence, destruction and disintegration.

The parallel state also shed light on the temporal utility of the state, serving multiple purposes at different times, under the guise of diverse political principles and social objectives. It considered the mobility and fluidity of institutions and interests, bringing the analysis of the *state* under a lens of transition and constant transformation. The state adapted in this way, not only to times of peace or war, but in order to fulfil particular objectives of the governors and the governed. It refracted the dynamics of what Appadurai termed the 'anxiety of incompleteness' as the idea and construction of a majority brought into question the primary identity of the nation, and by extension the question of who was entitled to become full citizens of that state (Appadurai 2006). The parallel state and its 'imagined community' (Anderson 1983) attempted to define Angola and Sudan through the representations of UNITA and the SPLM/A. It was in this state of incompleteness that the state and nation were reconceived and created. Both movements did this by layering state-making on several tangibles and intangibles through which the state was constructed, experienced and imagined. The parallel state challenged in this way the assumption of the fixed boundaries and a unified set of rules regardimg states, considering instead the shifting, procedural and spatial nature of state-making so that it was in the images and practices of the state where power and authority were generated in dynamic, integrated and contradictory ways. In this way, both state actors and rebels managed to 'see' and 'do' the state (Migdal and Schlichte 2005).[3]

The parallel states of UNITA and the SPLM/A provide two examples of the transient, paradoxical and contingent nature of nation- and state-making. It was in the very search for the state and the power of reconfigured sovereignty of different national communities that political orders were formed during wartime. These states were local in their character while simultaneously serving as examples of the dynamics and master cleavages of their wars, societies and governing organisations (rebel movements). The state in these two cases was born from the interests, strategies, values and interactions of the governors and the governed, continuously reconfiguring authority, legitimacy and contestation. The design, processes and structures of the parallel states were profoundly influenced by the internal characteristics of the movements, in particular by the leadership dynamics, the ideological formulations, the organisational strengths, the level of resources (human, material, logistical) and the function and symbolism attributed to certain structures and institutions. They took particular forms because of the very character and strategies of these movements. This sheds light on the influence of ruling parties, leadership and elite dynamics on the state itself. After all, institutions are people, and the individuals that create and operate them will influence their political culture.

The struggles of UNITA and the SPLM/A also revealed important aspects of the nationalisms produced by reformist rebel governments. The parallel state was a sub-nation state that '"extrude[d] blood" [by engaging] in acts of exclusion, cleansing and purification' (Appadurai 2006).[4] In order to understand the condition upon which the nation and the state were redefined under UNITA and the SPLM/A, it is necessary to delve deeply into the ideology of nationalism that both provided. The nationalism espoused by these two movements was 'governed by the properties of political fields, not by the properties of collectivities' (Brubaker 1996: 17). The nations produced by UNITA and the SPLM/A were rather a contingent event instead of a result of enduring and substantial collectivities (Brubaker 1996: 21). Yet the form and nature of the resulting state and sovereignty were intrinsically linked to the process of sub-nationalism and the symbols and beliefs that bound and divided communities that were redefining their collectivity at different stages of the war and socially reengineering a nation.

The nationalism of these two reform rebellions was derived at the sub-national level of divided societies, incorporating local grievances with national objectives. It was aimed not at seeking political independence but rather at seeking reform and asserting a new national identity that would integrate the excluded. This nationalism was very different from that experienced during the anti-colonial wars or during secessionist wars. It was aimed at creating a cohesive identity from fractured landscapes using these very cleavages to define the right and duty to rebel. Yet in order to justify war and mobilise constituents, a new concept of the state and society had to be proposed, becoming in essence a struggle for the soul of the nation. Those whom the rebel movements claimed as their constituents—the excluded and marginalised—had in this way experienced a form of segmented sovereignty where they had only partial rights, entitlements and access to services, making them the ideal group to proposition with another form of sovereignty (Migdal 2004). State-making therefore became the process of creating the bases upon which this new national community could be enacted and sustained through a myriad of structures, processes and practices.

The evolving nature of war and political contest, both local and transnational, will increasingly see the emergence of a different type of nationalism based on sub-national identities that attempt to mask their local nature and the paradoxical objective of un-making the existing nation. Sub-nationalism used the national platform to empower local society and attempted to bond the micro to the macro by fundamentally rejecting the macro-nationalist identity of the past. It used sub-nationalist identities, needs and values to form the micro-level solidarity necessary to connect it to the larger nationalist narratives of war. The nationalism of UNITA and the SPLM/A superimposed a set of grievances and multiple inequalities on each other, transforming them into political fault lines, posing the question of how they could be corrected and marginalised identities empowered. Both movements aimed to impose their versions of the nation, and its corresponding state–idea, in a heterogeneous setting that they could not unite. The legacy of this type of sub-nation nationalism is still felt in both countries; in Angola it has become an impediment to reintegration and reconciliation, and in South Sudan it has morphed and scaled down to the tribal sub-community level, driving different insurgencies in another cycle of war.

The rebel-systems

This book introduced the idea of a rebel-system as a form of separating the agentic elements of insurgencies from the externally dependent elements that impacted their strategies and choices. The aim was to highlight, through an analysis of change and transformation, the motivations and constraints faced by insurgent leaders as they progress along their chosen paths of war and order. The parallel states, as assessed in Jamba and Yambio, were established as a strategy to survive the critical junctures of 1976 and 1991, and they were deconstructed in the subsequent junctures as other strategies proved necessary to survive sequential, multipronged shocks for which the parallel state no longer provided a solution. These were determined by the form of the critical juncture but also by the shifting political, military and social conditions faced by each movement. This understanding helped explain the fragilities of the SPLM/A and UNITA and how they responded to the subsequent critical junctures; why the SPLM/A survived and achieved independence but subsequently disintegrated; and why UNITA was militarily defeated, losing its political definition and support of key constituencies, but was able to reinvent itself in peacetime.

Like each war, each society and each rebel movement is a transitory and everchanging ecosystem, and the parallel states that emerge from these elements are unique experiments. The parallel states and symbolic sovereignty of UNITA and the SPLM/A revealed the many ways governance could occur during wartime. The differences between them were a result of their rebel-systems and their conflict-systems. Each movement was a factor of the prevailing circumstances and elements of uncertainty of their wars, and each applied a different balance to the elements of consent, authority and repression. These cases point to a few larger dynamics that highlight how the different aspects of each internal element directly impacted the form of the parallel state. The rebel-systems of both movements revealed how they were powered and personalised by their founding leaders, but because UNITA had solid political organs and an ideology that resonated with its constituent base it was powered to an equal extent by these elements. In contrast, the SPLM/A sustained an ideology followed by its commanding elites but not by its social base, and it had weak party organs that could contain militarist tendencies. UNITA would derail when it lost its political direction in 1992–2002 and would rebuild when it repowered its political message in 2012–22. The SPLM/A similarly derailed with the death of its leader, Garang, and further imploded when its political elites and commanders disagreed over reforms. It had no ideology or political organs to contain this fallout, resulting in a genocidal war that further militarised ethnicities, bred sentiments which led to collective punishment and localised politics in irreversible ways. The obvious conclusion was that leadership in the SPLM/A was unrestrained by structures, despite the movement having a high level of organisation and military hierarchy. While leadership undid the SPLM/A, it was party structures that kept UNITA from following suit during its darkest years under Savimbi.

For the first two decades, and to bring about the success of their liberations, the leadership of Garang and Savimbi was instrumental. These highly complex and charismatic leaders brought together a diverse group of commanders, supporters and communities in violent political projects that carried great risk and relatively little reward. They used the tools they had available to manage the fault lines of their conflict-systems. Garang had entire units of military men willing to join his liberation from the onset, and a mobilised society angry at northern domination, but he had to struggle with a highly fragmented and stratified population that wanted independence (a far cry from New Sudan's unity) and sustained ethnic loyalties that trumped nationalist allegiance. Conversely, Savimbi had no army and little weaponry to begin his liberation. He had entire ethnic groups that lacked political representation but were not mobilised for war despite a widespread desire for independence. His political positioning had to find ground between two existing liberation movements – the MPLA and the FNLA—that were internationally and regionally recognised and backed up by strong ideologies. As a result, both Garang and Savimbi commanded their movements against a national landscape that was divided and detrimental to the success of their visions. They also fought many enemies from within that created severe impediments—ethnic militias and the Anyanya II for the SPLM/A and the MPLA during the anti-colonial war for UNITA. Yet both leaders overcame these constraints and sustained their movements through decades of war against stronger and better resourced armies. Their success was due to a combination of their leadership traits, their vision and their capacity to organise structures that brought diverse groups into a relatively coherent alignment of purpose. Garang had little choice but to do this militarily, while Savimbi understood that political mobilisation was the only way to garner the support he needed for a protracted people's war. These choices were reflected in their organisations. Ultimately, both leaders succeeded in persuading their fighters and cadres to defend the interests of the organisation and stay the course through long and difficult wars. For decades they never lost the political control of their liberations, building effective command and control systems that allowed them to survive multiple defeats. While many of these aspects related to resources, they were grounded in the effective planning and ability of leaders to devise chains of command, structures and management systems while orientating people and purpose. Collective leadership structures and a core group of loyal, politically coherent commanders and politicians were key in supporting Savimbi through his wars. However, mid-level leaders became just as important in running the parallel state and continuing the liberation. UNITA had them, the SPLM/A didn't. The SPLM/A did little to power its syndicated organisations and cadres to build structures for policy and coordination. UNITA instituted such rigid protocols and supported widespread training programmes that it built a parallel army of politicians, cadres and party members. In peacetime, these differences would become defining characteristics of the movements' capacity to transition successfully.

Leadership structures of the SPLM/A reflected the contradictory interests at the central command levels that utilised hegemonic control, negotiation and power-sharing formulas to stave off fragmentation. None of these dynamics affected local administration but rather allowed for power to be devolved to the local levels because of the absence of fully cohesive leadership structures within the party. Had the SPLM/A at the time been able to provide for collective decision-making structures, linking the central leadership to lower levels through effective mid-level commands, administration may have been different. Instead, Garang chose to unify commanders and leaders through the military hierarchy, placing political leaders below military commanders. This was due to the failings of the Anyanya I and Garang's own distrust of politicians, but also the schisms he inherited by having so many fractured and unaligned militia groups joining his liberation struggle. It was also a consequence of instituting a system that would level out ethnic considerations and the issue of representation, which was dealt with at lower leadership levels. The strategy of autonomous commands within the military leadership kept the movement relatively united, but it did not result in the cohesion of different leaders across liberated areas at the administrative level. Placing the 'sons and daughters' of each liberated area in command positions allowed the movement to gain legitimacy but did not overcome the problem of Dinka hegemony within the central commands and army. For collective leadership structures to work in the political bureau and the NLC, several SPLM/A leaders had to bring with them the unequivocal support of their communities. Many failed to do so, and this weakened the SPLM and the political strength of these organs to counter the president when he moved to govern without the party later on. Concentric circles of who could benefit through proximity to the leadership were underpinned by what they could deliver rather than their loyalty to the vision and the country.

At the leadership level, Savimbi understood from inception the need to take full political control of the movement and the liberation struggle. The first attempt to institute a power-sharing formula sustaining a coalition of associations in the first few years, giving vice president positions to different leaders of other ethnic groups, failed. The cohesion UNITA sought in the context of two more experienced and better-resourced movements, the MPLA and FNLA, and the tendencies to factionalise led Savimbi to structure the movement under his command. He divided the branches, in line with his Maoist training, and developed each by training leaders at all levels to manage the structures. This translated into centralised institutions in the liberated areas that standardised a division of labour into separate command structures, all of which were accountable to COPE and Savimbi. The administrative, military and party branches would as a result have rotation of leaders at all levels, never allowing them to entrench their influence or challenge Savimbi's stranglehold on the movement. Leaders and cadres were trained and educated into the political order of UNITA. This bound them to Savimbi's vision and created a critical mass of support. It also prepared a class of leaders and cadres who were politically capable of steering the difficult post-conflict transformation of the movement into a political party. These leaders succeeded in rebuilding a political project and mobilising support across peacetime Angola. Even when they faltered, the leadership structures around them proved capable of re-steering the party through two decades of adversarial partisanship by a hegemonic, securitised and powerful MPLA government.

In terms of ideology, both movements managed to organise and channel the interests of a large segment of their people—even if incoherently, as was the case of the SPLM/A. They built on a sense of exclusion and humiliation to forge a new form of nationalism that would unite communities behind a new liberation and quest for a reformed state and reconfigured society. The movements' founding leaders managed to align their pursuit for power and permanence with certain popular aspirations, which in turn provided them with a way to connect and redefine identities. The strength of the nationalist rhetoric and capacity to maintain engaged constituents and civilians more generally played a huge role in the form of the parallel state. While New Sudan failed to result in sustained mobilisation and integration of diverse constituents, its nationalist underpinnings and drive to empower marginalised people gave it tremendous popular strength. Southerners wanted liberation from the North, and the SPLM/A was the strongest armed group that could deliver this. This also gave the SPLM/A a false sense of support for its political projects, which would later unravel. UNITA also had natural constituents to take forward forms of nationalist and ideological fervour, including the disenfranchised and politically marginal Ovimbundu and other ethnic groups. UNITA's strict ideological and doctrinal discipline somewhat narrowed the forms of participation to allow for broader appeals to win over supporters of the MPLA. In this sense, the promise of power for the excluded was an insufficient political programme for populations that felt disgruntled with their governments but required more nuanced reforms. In this way, the nationalism of the SPLM/A and UNITA may have united the people of the South, whom the movements saw themselves as representing, but it failed to fully rally other communities, ethnic groups and demographics in urban centres and northern provinces (at least initially for UNITA). Part of this was the positioning of the identity of the other—in this case the MPLA in Angola and in Sudan the different northern parties that governed during the war—as intrinsically opposed to the identity of the reformed state, as mutually exclusive political projects. In this way, neither the SPLM/A and UNITA could have realistically represented all the Sudanese or the totality of Angolans.

Ideologically, the SPLM/A's establishment of the movement in Ethiopia and the imposition of socialism did not result in the movement adopting a vertical party hierarchy that linked mass popular horizontal organisations and a strong political party. Personal decisions and leadership contestations led Garang to sideline ideologues and intellectuals and delay the development of the party. The proposal of a unified Sudan, rather than a secessionist stance, meant that many groups would not follow the SPLM/A on an ideological level. The levels of mass anger allowed mobilisation to happen around opposition to northern domination. When the New Sudan programme took on more adaptive applications, as a reform programme for a unified or independent South, the movement lacked sufficient political commissars to begin explaining the vision in all the liberated areas. This was delegated to the local leaders that became the only link they had to the central command. There was a broad definition of the New Sudan, un-implementable resolutions and vague directives, which allowed for degrees of interpretation to occur at the local levels of governance. The result was different imaginings of the New Sudan at the local levels and within the leadership. When the SPLM/A was given the mandate to govern the South, it lacked the political structures to unite a social fabric divided by competing interests, identities and needs. Weak ideological definitions and localised governance experiences were engulfed and surpassed by the state-building exercise of the CPA and the external modes of peacebuilding, which weakened the SPLM's action and the possibility of redefining a new political order. The death of Garang, the discarding of the 2004 'Peace Through Development' plan and the dismissal of the lessons learnt from wartime misgovernance left the SPLM/A politically rudderless and unable to institute the reforms of its liberation. Inequalities prevailed, regionalism and tribalism outranked nationalism, state institutions became the property of leaders and militarisation deepened. In the absence of ideology and political structures, the narrow, personalised interests of elites took the forefront.

Ideologically, UNITA balanced several contradictory elements that joined Maoism with capitalism and Afro-populist principles to tailor a political programme that suited Angola's socio-economic conditions and satisfied external allies that were key to building the movement's military capacity and international political support. The movement was concerned with mobilising and uniting different communities behind an alternative idea of what it meant to be Angolan and to experience a 'real' independence. Yet it also mobilised sub-national grievances that were not fully experienced by all the constituencies it was trying to unite. UNITA's use of traditional authorities and respect for African culture contrasted with the perspectives of modernity espoused by the city elite and the MPLA. This led to UNITA being portrayed as a tribalistic and rural movement, which would make it even harder to propagate its nationalism to wider—and especially urban—constituencies. The controlled indoctrination programmes in the liberated areas were a response to this. They were meant to create legitimacy and a sense of political perpetuity for UNITA's world order, elevating the marginalised with education, skill and political indoctrination so that they would be capable of governing any city and municipality. The 1990s witnessed the 'exile' of UNITA's political project as it failed to reinvent itself after the MPLA had accepted multi-party democracy, a market economy and the withdrawal of the Cubans. Instead, events in the last decade of war led to a perpetuation of political revenge and fear for the future. Despite this, during peacetime UNITA re-styled its political rhetoric, mirroring concerns and grievances of the past and rallying collectivities over inequalities and exclusion, which gave it the strength to face the MPLA in elections in 2022. However, this was more a reflection of the MPLA's mistakes than UNITA's strong political programme and peacetime reform agenda. For two decades of peace, UNITA's rhetoric was reactive and used the negative example of the MPLA to project itself as a political alternative. It would capitalise on mass popular frustration in its election strategies, but to govern Angola would require much more.

Organisationally, both insurgencies operated using the triad of administration, military and party/ideological branches. It was their rapid and impressive military successes and military prowess, as well as the capacity of their armies to defeat conventional forces in asymmetrical terrains and battles, that provided these movements with support internally and externally. Their ability to conquer and hold territory through military means was what gave them the platform to run the parallel state. Their military organs were robust and functioned under tight command structures; they incorporated different fighting forces and were versatile enough to engage in combat in different fronts. The political/ideological organs would supplement these efforts in creating reinforcing dynamics among their triads. However, only UNITA carefully separated its leadership among the three branches, and it closely coordinated operations in reinforcing ways because of the procedures, regulations and careful bureaucracy it put in place. UNITA's capacity to secure a social contract with the population through the delivery of services, order and indoctrination was dependent on and influenced by these organisational and administrative shortcomings and strengths. The SPLM/A delivered order and justice at different stages of its governance but failed to effectively provide services, which remained outsourced to the international community. Structures for control and enforcement of procedures that provided political direction were crucial. This is how UNITA managed to create a functioning society and state that was linked to utopian ideals.

UNITA's central commands and the three branches functioned under a tightly controlled structure. Organisationally, the ambition to create a new political and social order led UNITA to institute widespread and standardised education, skills training and leadership programmes. All the cadres, fighters and followers were led by political commissars and the party structures that stood at the helm of the movement. Engagement with civilians was determined by these objectives. Savimbi believed that he and UNITA would only attain power by applying the theory of large numbers, which drove him to mobilise men and women for this state project and army. This implied that the movement had enough organisation to train these people and indoctrinate them to follow UNITA's party line and war strategy. It also meant that the movement had the necessary logistics to place fighters and cadres into structured commands throughout the liberated areas. All areas of operation had strict guidelines and operating procedures; communicated and delegated effectively; and supervised personnel through the different intelligence and party structures. There was no room for interpretation or doubt, true to the party's totalitarian form. After 1990, with the deaths of several of its most capable leaders and cadres, UNITA would struggle to sustain the same level of political organisation. Its ability for criticism and self-criticism was significantly reduced, and democratic centralism functioned in principle yet failed to shift strategy at the top. It became ridden with contradictions, as a partner in government and peacebuilding while fighting a war and delegitimising the same government's performance. Effort was funnelled towards sustaining the world's largest illegal diamond enterprise rather than towards political education, training cadres and mobilising civilians. The organisation veered towards the pursuit of war rather than building the human infrastructure for peace. In peacetime, UNITA would struggle organisationally to link its city leaders to those in the provinces. It would fail to build the necessary cadres to monitor elections and prepare safeguards against fraud. It would also struggle to resurrect its propaganda machine to rally support for its party and the country's main opposition party.

For the SPLM/A, defining power in military terms could have produced centralised structures to run the liberated areas if there was division of labour and sufficient cadres. Yet the SPLM/A lacked the supporting administrative and political branches to fully control governance of the liberated areas. The movement was also unable to institute regulations and practices that placed military commanders under the control of political and civilian leaders. By default, the movement devolved power to traditional authorities, community leaders and civilians. This same handicap led the movement to outsource service provision to relief agencies and NGOs, which allowed civilians and civil society the space to define their roles in the parallel state. This entrenched several of the 'localisms' Garang was attempting to avoid and did not fully bring the local areas into the main political frame of the revolution so that a Dinka from Bahr El Ghazal, for example, would connect with nationalistic appeals to a Kakwa in Yei. This was a consequence of the political programme, of the fact that the movement didn't have a rear base and rarely consulted its leaders, and of weak party structures at all levels. When positioned to govern, the SPLM/A lacked the human capital, the administrative capacity, the political consistency and a sufficient range of ethnically diverse nationalist leaders capable of steering state structures and development programmes. As a result, external interventions took over; services remained outsourced to NGOs and UN agencies; central government offices were disconnected from local state governments; and nepotism, corruption and tribalism permeated appointments.

The underlying principles that governed the command, control and organisation of the SPLM/A and UNITA, when tested by opposing forces from within, would generate deep schisms and contradictions. This partly explained the paths that led to UNITA's military defeat and SPLM/A's political implosion. The loss of political vision and grounding that characterised UNITA's performance during the 1992–2002 war meant that the leading strategy that had delivered success in the battlefield, in the rear, abroad and with civilians was no longer able to power the administrative and military wings. Because of this, there ensued defections, dissent, factionalism, loss of civilian support, international isolation and a disconnect with UNITA's core support base. For the SPLM/A, the military hierarchy that kept leaders united, appeased ethnic sentiments through balancing formulas at leadership levels, integrated militias and silenced difficult conversations around nation-building and diversity was challenged politically in peacetime. The organisation of an insurgency was ill-suited to the intricacies of governing a state, formulating policy and tolerating opposition. Political divisions became perceived as treason and threats to the organisation, which catapulted securitised responses in 2012. The SPLM/A's militarisation legacy invariably led it back to war from within its ranks, while UNITA's loss of political direction led it to prioritise military solutions. Simply put, both movements failed their supporters and the people they claimed to represent in both peace and wartime because they were politically indolent and ideologically weakened, which led otherwise nationalistic leaders down a path of narrow interests and personalised agendas. Military structures and procedures were ill-suited to negotiating difficult political issues, identities and agendas.

Post-1992 UNITA and post-2005 SPLM/A's leadership no longer subordinated their own interests to those of the organisation, and this derailed their liberation and their cause.

Their approach to civilians during their wartime states, however, differed. Both insurgencies (in the 1980s for UNITA and the 1990s for the SPLM/A) governed across large areas of land and over millions of people, which required decentralised structures for practical and logistical reasons. Traditional authorities of different communities were given prominent roles in their strategies towards civilians. They did this for pragmatic reasons, to fortify their territorial control and to avoid internal frontlines within the parallel state that could threaten their ability to govern. The levels of consent and legitimacy varied for each movement but were pillared on similar dynamics. The ability to provide security and some degree of predictability allowed for this. Yet the provision of justice was a major factor for the SPLM/A, while for UNITA it was the provision of services and training that allowed it to govern diverse populations. UNITA used decentralised structures at the political level to help perpetuate and extend their grip on populations, extending influence and structure within the politically defined order. In UNITA areas, civilians operated within a single rule system (Putzel 2007) and institutional centralisation, whereby the rule of the insurgency trumped any other rule system that civilians might have devised to survive. The SPLM/A didn't have this structuring force, which created a disconnect between the centre and the locality. This became a lost transformational opportunity. Local leaders began to appropriate the appeals of loyalty and even diffused the need to be linked to the central command, leaving a vacuum that would later cause problems for the movement's objective of longevity and legacy. The SPLM/A never truly factored in the role that civilians could play in the revolution. Civilian populations were towed behind a nationalistic drive for independence that was the only common denominator across regions. The SPLM/A failed to build a much-needed political coalition of diverse tribes that could realign identities and interests.

Despite this, there was a shift from the CMA to the CANS governing strategy. There was greater acceptance of SPLM/A governance when it became demilitarised with the CANS. This also translated into devolving power to local leaders. Harmony was achieved through the chiefs' courts and by aligning statutory and customary legal structures. The self-sufficiency drives meant that the SPLM/A interfered less with development and agricultural projects, but it also meant that education and health sectors would remain underdeveloped and under-resourced unless supported by NGOs. Within certain communities, civilians were only as loyal to the SPLM/A as its local representative was connected and respected by the community. Garang was known and respected, but few other senior leaders rallied acceptance across the South, existing rather in a parallel reality of power around Garang and possibly for their kinsmen which did not carry across different communities. The incomplete application of the New Sudan deepened the localisms in the everyday lives of civilians, even if it provided a roadmap of possibility and hope. In peacetime, and especially after the death of Garang, civilians were greatly demobilised by the SPLM, shifting their loyalties to the localisms and securing a social contract with international agencies that led the post-war recovery efforts. In peacetime, the SPLM/A became a vehicle used for elite power; when denied power, politicians would resurrect militias and begin small wars. Civilians would be caught in the middle of political and social calculations that never truly factored in their well-being or reflected their identities.

At the civilian level, UNITA's ambition of creating a new order implied having to alter civilians' experience of the state and politics. While it respected traditional authorities, it also inserted them into the structures of the movement and conditioned them to operate within established confines. Service provision and the development of health and education sectors in the liberated areas were how UNITA fulfilled its side of a social contract that ensured obedience, loyalty and reciprocity from civilians. This was in fact the main link that it had to several captured communities that did not feel represented by its political programme. The performance element of trying to project 'normality' was a phenomenon experienced in Jamba. The guerrilla democracy forums were applied in all the liberated areas and were meant to allow civilians and fighters moments of controlled freedom. UNITA was concerned that doubt and criticism would create an environment that could be exploited by enemy infiltration. Social order was therefore key in Jamba, but it was tightly regulated by the party and the intelligence services. Yet in the 1990s UNITA lost a significant amount of civilian support as it shifted strategy, and a war of attrition that lasted for a decade reduced its number of supporters as well as the role civilians played in this conflict. This last decade of war did not mobilise them. It was no longer a war to correct historical injustices but a war of punishment.

Those who experienced the legacy of these parallel states reflected differently on them. What the SPLM/A achieved in its liberated areas was a fragile, deeply flawed and incomplete parallel state that functioned in an unregulated and haphazard way. It still retained elements of militarism, violence and extortion. However, research conducted in South Sudan since 2008 and in 2011–12 revealed a political project that created legitimacy and acceptance of the movement by diverse communities. It generated support and succeeded in forging a form of southern nationalism. What the SPLM/A achieved in military terms in the 1980s was impressive, but all its victories were fatally reversed in 1991 and it suffered levels of defeat it had never before experienced. The impetus to rebuild itself politically and socially to survive was done without political infrastructure, human capital or ideological fervour. Neither was it done based on previous state organisation and existing administrative legacies, as these barely existed. It was done by rallying social structures of organisation and by motivating local leaders and civilians to take charge and build the state and the party. Despite not being built on a strong political party capable of overriding localisms, the New Sudan was probably the greatest unifying symbol the South Sudanese would experience until 2013. What the CANS in fact achieved for many was a means of communication and proximity between the movement and the civilians; it 'brought the people closer to the SPLM'.[5] This symbolic capital gave the movement significant credit of governance with the population, even when they failed to deliver. 'People were behind the SPLM as a revolutionary war and assisted in pushing the enemy out. This was the success of the CANS.'[6] One commissioner explained that 'there was a new political dispensation being created that allowed for the old, the paradigm of Arabism that denied us our rights, to be destroyed'.[7] It had delivered a government southerners could identify with, despite its shortcomings. Others highlighted the issue of consent from the population as necessary for the CANS to take root: 'after the vision was conceptualised it could only exist in an atmosphere conducive to its survival'.[8] There was space in conceptual and real terms to allow for the interpretation of this new SPLM/A state to factor in civilian organisation and their needs, which allowed them degrees of freedom to structure their participation. When the war restarted in 2013, all the intangibles of hope, national identity, symbolism, forged unity and greatness evaporated. The shortcomings of the SPLM/A revealed a failure of leadership but also a myopic and naïve intervention by external actors who championed a resolution and poured billions into supporting its implementation, but themselves failed to heed the lessons of the war. The international community today is as complicit in the implosion of the SPLM/A as are its leaders.

The Free Lands of Angola were for the UNITA cadres and the people it claimed to represent a symbol of strength, resistance, discipline, organisation, political indoctrination and a utopian society. It was also a highly controlled and regulated reality that would impact those who experienced it in very profound ways. In Jamba, those who experienced the parallel state would describe it in two ways: for some it was the closest they would come to taking part in building a future for Angola. For others, it was a prison that inserted them into a social order they were estranged from. Jamba today continues to exist in the memories of the people who lived under UNITA, in the imagination of younger generations that seek to understand a part of the war's history and as a small military outpost. When government forces overran Jamba in late 1999, they destroyed most of the structures and confiscated all the intelligence and administrative files. 'The memory of what was achieved in Jamba and UNITA areas is still dangerous for the MPLA. My files are no longer strategically relevant, but the intelligence chiefs will not hand them back to me … UNITA's history must be erased,' explained a UNITA general who integrated into the FAA in 1992.[9] Today, over 23,000 civilians remain in Jamba, having returned from their refugee camps in Zambia after 2002. Many speak of the past with some nostalgia, even the captured populations who resented Savimbi's authoritarian rule. 'He was a bandit, but he knew how to run a state and everything worked here.'[10] 'We were never hungry and had running water to drink and grow our crops. Today there is desertification, and we have nothing.'[11] What was achieved in Jamba—the training and literacy programmes—are still credited with preparing the current UNITA leadership, and many others who defected and joined the MPLA, with the necessary skills and work ethic. 'What was achieved in Jamba resonates deeply in society today. We prepared our leaders.'[12] While UNITA's parallel state was totalitarian, it was efficient and complex. It has also endured. For many, it was the only nation–state they experienced that served its people and was responsive to their needs. The social and political divisions that emerged post-war in 2002 became crystallised in the socio-economic conditions of several communities across Angola. For them, post-war reality continued to enhance the historical and social cleavages into which they had been indoctrinated of a clash of two states and two societies.

Today, Angola has experienced twenty-two years of peace and the SPLM/A ten years of a post-independence fratricidal war. While UNITA lost the war against Luanda, the SPLM/A won its war against Khartoum. Yet the SPLM/A lost the peace when it came to governing its new state, and UNITA won its peace as the MPLA perpetuated injustices, exclusion and a dividendless peace. UNITA's sub-nationalism was kept alive, and its identity as an opposition party gathered strength, because of the failings of the ruling MPLA. Conversely, the SPLM/A's sub-nationalism became redundant in peacetime and fragmented into multiple micro-state sub-nationalisms among tribal identities and communities that drifted apart because the SPLM/A lacked an integrative ideology. In pre-election polls in 2022, UNITA won all the urban areas as well as the youth vote, faring the highest among the educated, while the MPLA was better at rallying the rural communities, uneducated and the older generation. The splintered SPLM/A factions too were heading towards elections in 2024 as uncontrollable violence raged because of the way the militarised elites held political reforms hostage through violence, corruption and patronage to favour their own narrow interests. Voters were rallied through fear, tribal animosities and violence, not through policy and political ideas.

In looking to the future, both UNITA and the SPLM/A will need to go back to their roots. The SPLM/A will need to secure rural peace and justice while UNITA will need to advance its policy objectives of development and delivery of services. These areas were the tangibles that gave both movements legitimacy and a relatively wide following during their wars. Governing in peacetime requires much more than this, but the hallmark of their liberations must be resurrected to correct their pathways, so that the SPLM/A can move towards peace and UNITA into government. Their rebel-systems also show that without a political programme, collective leadership structures and party organs, the SPLM/A will never be able to govern adequately, while UNITA—without the formulation of a new political project and recalibrated organisational capacity—will continuously be outflanked by the MPLA.

In search of the state and nation …

As the conflict in Ukraine raged from 2022 and Russia's imperialistic war to reclaim historical greatness initiates a new era of rivalry and proxy wars between the great powers, the power of asymmetric warfare among highly committed and nationalistic warrior people crystallises the need for a strong defence of state and nation. While the war in Ukraine is an inter-state war, the vast differences between the two warring sides in terms of military might, fighting capability and available resources to fund campaigns places renewed importance on understanding the concept of the 'war of the flea' (Taber 2002 [1965]). Ukraine's legion of fighters resisting an invading army has brought together trained officers with inexperienced civilians, village militias and bands of supporters sustaining the logistics systems of weapons, food, medication and evacuations, and a transnational effort of lawfare, economic sanctions and cyber soldiers. Russia's military primacy has failed to produce the victory it assumed it would easily and rapidly achieve. This war, like the asymmetric wars in Angola and Sudan, despite clear and obvious differences, highlights the importance of a people's will to revolt against military giants, and the political victories they can achieve when fighting in wars of liberation.

Across the world today, several insurgencies hold and govern territory. In one form or another, they seek to define a new nation, society and state. In Africa alone, the crisis of the nation–state has led to the emergence of such groups as Al-Shabaab in Somalia, the Azawad movements in Mali, Boko Haram in Nigeria, the SPLM-North in Sudan, the ex-Seleka in the Central African Republic, among others. Elsewhere, the Houthis and Al-Qaeda in the Arabian peninsula in Yemen, the Kachin Independence Organisation and the Karen National Union in Myanmar, the Islamic State and the provinces under its control, the Kurdish Democratic Union Party/People's Defence Units in Syria, among others, lead sub-national, national or transnational wars aimed at installing fundamental change and reconstructing political orders. Territory-governing and nation-seeking insurgencies, on the increase globally, will progressively make the building of parallel states pivotal to their struggle. As rebellions they differ in many aspects, being a product of specific local and regional contexts, and have crucially distinct drivers of conflicts. Some emerged within a context of existing wars while others began their own wars. Some are secessionist, while several reject entirely the nation–state formulation. Others have strong ideological/religious or nationalist underpinnings, while some carry ill-defined programmes to rally constituencies. Some are transnational and fed by regional rivalries, while others are locally defined. Despite this, these groups carve out constituencies in need of liberation to correct the failings of past injustices and failed nation- and state-building projects. They mobilise around ideas and potential utopian outcomes that aim to transform existing social, political and territorial orders. They weave in diverse mobilising sentiments ranging from religion, sectarianism and sub-nationalism, to anti-imperialism, anti-establishment and revolution. When they prove organisationally resilient and ideologically persuasive, with the ability to consolidate constituency support and govern territory effectively, they can render insurgent wars intractable (Roque 2021b). These wars will continue as groups search for idealised representations of the state and nation.

Several factors will continue to favour the emergence of such groups. These include state fragility and the resurgence of sub-state nationalism because of deeply unintegrated countries and suppressed identities that have morphed over time. Linked to this is the masked weakness of governments upheld by a state-system that has done little to strengthen local governance and heterogenous representation. This has resulted in peripheral marginalisation and the creation of ungoverned territories where other forms of social authority thrive. The growing number of unemployed or disaffected cadres, civil servants and youths—a factor that contributed to the 2011 Arab Spring—has changed the political demography of some countries and positioned many in opposition to their governments. Their disillusionment is with the political establishment, breeding a complete lack of confidence in their governments' capacity to treat them fairly and equally. The combination of all of these factors results in the fusion of several distinct dynamics linking marginalisation with ethnic, cultural, educational and religious stagnation; corruption; and the loss of unifying national visions that feed new ways of thinking about the future. In addition to this is the ease with which some groups can access support and resources, bolstering their internal sustainability and logistics to supply sanctuary, recruits and funding because of globalisation, as well as the ease of communication systems to assist in propaganda and mobilisation.

International and regional responses, however, have failed to transform and de-escalate these crises and wars. The many tools used invariably aim to re-establish state authority and return the countries to their pre-war states. Because they have the *state* as the horizon, these tools become unresponsive to the local concerns of such movements that want to dislocate the state and reformulate the way constituencies have been governed in the past. When power has already become territorialised outside the national state through interactions with parallel states, new strategies must be explored. In the past, resolution of these conflicts has required the recognition of the different grievances of these armed groups and communities, most of which contested governments do not fully understand, nor deem legitimate, thus failing to acknowledge their own role in exacerbating their grievances. Solutions to these crises will invariably have to address the dispensation of power, emblems of identity and institutional changes guided by different forms justice. Thought and effort need to be directed towards political outcomes that restrain sectarian, ethnic and sub-national sentiments, while reconceiving nation- and state-building under new constructs, the shape of which will differ. Policies need to become more holistic, multi-layered, inclusive and localised. While there remains resistance to changing international borders due to fears of the instability it may unleash on a regional and global system predicated on the building blocks of sovereign states, many political, ethnic and religious communities 'seek to live in a political setting that matches their identity' (Guzansky and Kulick 2016: 24).[13] The result may be a more hybrid and complex form of government that emerges because of the erosion of state sovereignty and the need to balance different forms of sovereignty.

The residual impact of these wars, and the insurgencies fighting them, will place greater pressure on state sovereignty and the responses required of heterogenous nation–states in dealing with their diverse populations. Best practices and modular approaches to conflict resolution will no longer sufficiently address these wars. Narrow responses to these insurgencies will only increase the likelihood that they will become more extreme each time they resurge as either violent jihadism, separatist nationalism, reformist sub-nationalism or utopian extremism. Governance will need to take on different forms to adapt to the challenges and changing environment ahead, which may lead to more localised organic and transnational societies. Analysts and political leaders globally would do well to begin thinking flexibly about how to accommodate such shifts and what they will mean for the international order. The hybridisation of government, where key state functions are transferred to non-state actors, will increasingly challenge this order. Demands for devolution of power and assertive demands by minorities for control of their resources, political systems and regional engagements will increasingly elevate the local level and certain peripheries to the forefront of politics. Power will as a result be dispersed across borders, unconfined to existing nation–states and increasingly networked to compete with established internationally regulated systems. These insurgencies will not be responsible for catalysing these shifts, but they are influencing change and will increasingly benefit from the inability of states to shape this shift in the international order. The timing for such a recalibration may be difficult, as the formation of large antagonistic geopolitical blocs may renew the focus on the state system. However, the fragmentation that is looming due to the global economic aftershocks of the Ukraine war, the unprecedented risk of famine, climate change and the mass migration of populations will bring to the fore the need to rethink how to rebuild socio-political communities.

TIMELINE FOR SUBSEQUENT CRITICAL JUNCTURES

 UNITA

1992 ● **1st Critical Juncture: Election & Resumption of Hostilities**

The 1992 elections are the culmination of a process of political and security arrangements under the 1991 Bicesse Peace Agreement, monitored by the UN mission UNAVEM II. The results of the presidential polls reveal that a second round is necessary while the parliamentary polls reveal an MPLA win. Eight of the twelve opposition parties, including UNITA, contest the results and deem the process fraudulent. Savimbi sends a team to negotiate the situation while he prepares for war. On 31 October, the MPLA, armed supporters, paramilitary police and the army stage the Halloween Massacre. Over 30,000 UNITA supporters and some of its leaders are estimated to have been killed.

UNITA was already suffering from an internal crisis and political isolation before the 1992 elections. The killing of its representative in the US, Tito Chingunji, in 1991 creates the deepest fissure among the founding leaders of the movement. In the run-up to the 1992 elections, Miguel N'zau Puna and Tony da Costa Fernandes leave the party, initiating a period of fragmentation within UNITA that continues until the end of the war. In the aftermath of the 1992 elections, UNITA is left with severe internal weaknesses. It has lost key leaders (the VP, SG and other commanders in the massacre in Luanda) and has also lost several key commanders and military units to the national army in accordance with the Bicesse Peace Agreement's DDR process.

In a series of military victories, UNITA gains control of several provincial capitals including Huambo, M'Banza-Kongo, N'dalatando and Caxito, and several areas in the Lundas provinces that give it access to diamonds.

1993 In January, war breaks out in 10 of the 18 provincial capitals. By August, UNITA has conquered over 70% of the territory, though these are short-term gains as government forces begin to retake many areas, leading to new negotiations. In mid-1993, the US declares UNITA a threat to its interests in Angola, permanently damaging the alliance. Over 18 months, following the 1992 elections, 120,000 die (half the casualty rate of the previous 16 years), revealing the ferocity of the fighting on both sides. UNITA's governance of several cities in the Central Highlands is deemed an occupation by many, in a rejection of the movement. The first set of UN sanctions are applied in September against UNITA.

1994 The Lusaka Agreement is signed providing for a power-sharing formula and a new DDR process. Weak implementation and mistrust on both sides continues.

1997 The Government of National Unity takes office as per the Lusaka Protocol. UNITA takes three ministerial posts and several other positions within the executive as part of the power-sharing agreement. UNITA does not, however, allow the government to take residence in several cities. The movement begins to function both as a partner in government and an armed insurgency, leading to several inconsistencies. The second set of UN sanctions are applied against UNITA.

1998 In December, during the MPLA's Fourth Congress, Dos Santos rejects the Lusaka agreement, asks the UN to leave, and declares that peace will be achieved through war.

1999 UNITA loses its headquarters in the Central Highlands and returns to guerrilla warfare after successive military defeats. Following the loss of Bailundu in December 1998, the second of UNITA's HQs, Andulo, is captured in February 1999. By December, the government estimates that they had destroyed over 80% of UNITA's military capability. In late 2000, UNITA loses its access to the diamond areas. UNITA suffers a series of high-level military defections. The military wing is divided into five guerrilla zones.

2002 **2nd Critical Juncture: Death of Savimbi & Luena Peace Accords**

Following successive military defeats, increased isolation, logistical collapse, years of government scorched-earth policy and even famine, UNITA divides its leaders into different columns. Government forces begin advancing on Moxico towards Savimbi where they ambush and kill him. Despite the loss of territory, civilian support and internal purges, at the time of the ceasefire UNITA still has 90,000 troops that remain loyal, as well as over 450,000 family members— the majority of whom go either into IDP camps or quartering areas for demobilisation.

2003 Isaias Samakuva (diplomat and civilian) is elected as UNITA's president at the Ninth Party Congress where over 1,500 delegates take part. Samakuva is elected overwhelmingly, defeating General Paulo Lukamba Gato (former Sscretary general and lead commander). The country continues to experience a severe humanitarian crisis with over 5 million people in need of emergency relief. The DDR process, managed and overseen uniquely by the Angolan government, is badly mismanaged.

2008

The first post-war elections are held in September. UNITA becomes a residual political force. It loses 54 seats in parliament, managing to only get 10% of the national vote. This becomes the first of many procedural democracy exercises revealing the MPLA's unchallenged hegemony.

2012

UNITA splinters before the elections with the creation of CASA-CE but manages to increase it seats in Parliament. CASA-CE, a coalition of several parties is headed by Chivukuvuku, a UNITA senior leader, and presents itself as a bridge party able to remove support from both the MPLA and UNITA.

2017

The third post-war polls reveal the fragilities of the ruling parties and growing strength of UNITA and the opposition as they challenge MPLA hegemony.

Angola holds its third post-war elections on 23 August 2017. All the opposition parties reject the official results that attributed 61% of the vote to the MPLA, claiming that their parallel tabulation process revealed that the ruling party lost its majority, and the real result was closer to 54%. For the first time, the opposition, in particular UNITA, are believed to have won the vote in several provinces.

TIMELINE FOR SUBSEQUENT CRITICAL JUNCTURES

SPLM/A

2005 ● 1st **Critical Juncture: Death of Garang & CPA Transition**

Three weeks into his tenure as first vice president, Garang is killed in a helicopter crash.

Months before his death, several fault lines were emerging at the leadership level—most notable being the Rumbek crisis of 2004 before the signing of the CPA, which saw Salva Kiir threaten to oppose Garang in a similar manner to Riek Machar in 1991.

Although there is no obvious successor, Salva Kiir takes the leadership of the party in 2005. He abandons all of Garang's policies to direct the development of the South. Kiir stops working for unity and begins moving towards secession, creating a deep division with the 'Garangist' leaders of the party, including the Secretary General Pagan Amum. Developments during the six-year transitional period reveal a rudderless SPLM/A that reacts to crises and is torn by internal divisions. The SPLM continues to expect international donors and NGOs to fund key sectors—in particular service provision—losing an opportunity to gain legitimacy across the South.

2006 The 'big tent' strategy and Lafon Declaration integrates Paulino Matiep's militias and begins a process of absorbing several government-allied militias. Kiir's strategy replicates what Garang did during the war, with the exception that he fails to understand that in peacetime military alliances and the militarisation of politics dilutes political control and blocks the much-needed DDR process.

2008 The SPLM/A hold its Second Convention and the leadership crisis develops as several commanders position themselves to take the chairmanship, including Riek Machar (a Nuer). A solution is found to bring Machar in as Kiir's deputy followed by James Wani Igga (an Equatorian) and Malik Agar (a Nubian) below him. This is meant to ensure a balance across the different regions and different ethnic groups.

2010 The first post-war elections are held across the country which lead to several insurrections in the South. The SPLM/A and the NCP become entrenched as the ruling parties in the South and North, respectively. The SPLM mismanages its candidate nominations leading to several running as independents. Those that were side-lined by the SPLM's nomination process take up arms against it, including George Athore, David Yau Yau and Gatluak Gai, which lead to local uprisings—mainly in Greater Upper Nile. The party suffers a splintering before the elections as Lam Akol forms his own party—the SPLM/Democratic Change. The leadership begins to understand the level of dissatisfaction across constituencies yet is unable to organise itself to build strong bases for political representation. Several high-ranking national SPLM leaders fail to secure their constituent vote at the local level, revealing the key

APPENDIX 2

constraint of disengagement between central command
and local society that became evident during the war.

2011 The self-determination referendum as stipulated in the
CPA peace agreement is held in January. Southerners
vote overwhelmingly to separate from Sudan with 98%
in favour. Independence is declared in July in one of
the last moments of national unity the country would
experience.

2012 The South begins an oil shutdown following a dispute
with Khartoum. Amid difficult negotiations in Addis
between Sudan and South Sudan over several issues
resulting from secession, tensions reach breaking point
with the South accusing Sudan of stealing its oil. It
proceeds to shut down all oil operations. Over 90%
of Juba's revenues came from oil. Border disputes
(including the oil fields in Heglig) lead to military
confrontations.

2013 2nd Critical Juncture: SLPM/A Leadership
Dispute & Civil War

The divisions within the leadership of the SPLM/A,
made more pronounced after Garang's death, lead to
the party becoming increasingly divided. In Kiir's 'big
tent' approach, the composition of the government
and key positions in the army reflects the integration
of groups outside of the SPLM, further marginalising
key leaders and their constituencies. In mid-2013, the
entire cabinet, Riek Machar and the SG of the party are
dismissed by Kiir. Machar, Garang's widow Rebecca
Nyandeng and SG Pagan Amum openly criticise
Kiir and emerge as challengers to the chairmanship.
Overnight Kiir dismantles his 'big tent' approach and
divides the political and military elites, placing many
against the SPLM. Following a press conference where
these leaders and several other senior commanders

319

and cadres criticise Kiir and call for an NLC meeting, fighting erupts in Juba in December. House-to-house searches target Nuer civilians and Machar barely escapes Juba. The army splits along the Nuer-Dinka fault lines. Machar begins his rebellion and the Nuer seek revenge against the killing of their kinsmen and massacre Dinka in Bor. The party splits into three factions: one led by Kiir, one led by Machar and the non-armed group led by Pagan Amum.

2015 After months of negotiations in Addis Ababa and in Arusha, two agreements are signed: the SPLM Reunification Agreement and the ARCISS peace agreement. The Arusha agreement, signed six months before the IGAD-led accords, focused on party reform mediated by Tanzanian ruling party CM and the ANC of South Africa. President Kiir presents a list of reservations to the ARCISS agreement which he subsequently implements rather than the agreement itself.

2016 The ARCISS collapses after fighting erupts in Juba in July. Riek Machar escapes and crosses into the DRC and is exiled in South Africa. The war becomes more fractured and ethnicised with several other armed factions emerging. Almost two million seek refuge in neighbouring countries, with the majority in Uganda. The UN claims it is becoming a genocidal war.

2018 After a year of uncoordinated and misdirected international and regional efforts, the parties agree to sign the Revitalised ARCISS Agreement. A new power sharing arrangement is set to transition the country back to peace.

APPENDIX 3

LIST OF INTERVIEWS

Interviews conducted for the SPLM/A case study, South Sudan

Juba, Central Equatoria State

Name	Position
Mr BW (three interviews)	SPLM cadre; worked at the Council of States
Justice Deng Biong	Key legislator for the movement and customary law expert
Prof. Alfred Lukoji (three interviews)	Professor at Juba University; critic of the SPLM
Mrs MKK	Former head of women's organisation
General Daniel Awet Akot	Member of PMHC; third in command after Garang; former Minister of Interior and presidential advisor
General Edward Lino (two interviews)	Former Head of Military Intelligence; later in opposition
Gabriel Alaak Garang	Finance Director, SPLM
Timothy Tut Choul	Former local government officer in Greater Upper Nile; former MP
Dr Luka Biong Deng	Former Minister in Presidency; Professor at Juba University
Mr AN	Leading SPLM political commissar
Akol Paul	SPLM Youth leader; former Deputy Minister for Information
Elijah Malok (two interviews)	Former head of SRRA; former Governor of Central Bank

Name	Position
Dr Aleu Garang Aleu (two interviews)	Former State Prosecutor for Ministry of Justice; former CANS official in Rumbek
Ezekiel Lol Gatkuoth (two interviews)	Former Minister of Petroleum; formerly allied to Riek Machar
Gabriel Mathiang Rok	Former speaker of the NLC
Canon Clement Janda (three interviews)	Member of South Sudan Council of Churches; former member of Council of States; Equatorian leader/elder
Gabriel Gabriel Deng (two interviews)	Former Director General of the Ministry of Parliamentary Affairs; intellectual, in opposition
Atem Garang Atem (two interviews)	Former Chief Whip of SPLM during the CPA
James Wani Igga (two interviews)	Current vice president; member of PMHC in succession line for chairmanship
Dr Lual Deng	Former Head of Development Strategy for CANS; PhD in economics
Atem Yaak Atem (two interviews)	Founding member of SPLA radio; former Deputy Minister of Information
Dr Steven Abraham Yar	Formerly with Coordination Council-Khartoum civil service; joined Ministry of Cabinet Affairs
Dr James Okuk	Lecturer at Juba University; opposition member
Dr Peter Adwok Nyaba	Leader and intellectual, defected in 1991 and returned to movement; former Minister for Higher Education
Mr RT	Former head of local NGO; agronomist and development expert, Equatoria
Dr Steven Wondu	Former auditor general
Dr William Kon Bior	Former CANs legal expert; practising lawyer
Martin Okeruk	Former MP; former Minister of Housing; close aide to John Garang
Colonel LL	SPLA officer
Mr DM	Former SPLA officer; working with international NGOs

Name	Position
Peter Longole	Former commander in Eastern Equatoria; former MP
David Deng Athorbei	Former Minister of Finance; former CANS secretary
Kosti Manibe	Former Minister of Finance; former CANS Humanitarian Affairs Secretary; in opposition
Michael Makwei	Former Minister of Information and Minister of Parliamentary Affairs; former CANS legislator
Pagan Amum (three interviews)	Former SPLM secretary general; leader for an SPLM faction
General Majak D'Agoot	Former SPLA commander; former Deputy Defence Minister; in opposition
Philip Thon Leek	Former Head of FACE schools; former Governor of Jonglei
Dr Valerio Awoy	Leading member of CANS Health Ministry
Pascal Bandidi (two interviews)	Former MP; former CANS Agriculture Secretary
Dr Anne Itto	Former civil society leader; former deputy SPLM secretary general
General James Hoth Mai	Former SPLA Chief of Staff
Lt Colonel AM	Former aide to SPLA Chief of Staff; current governor of one of the 32 states
Gier Chuang	Former Head of Communications for the SPLM/A; former minister; in opposition
John Luk	Former Minister of Legal Affairs; key SPLM/A legislator; defected in 1991 and returned to movement; in opposition
General Oyay Deng Ajak	Former commander and former SPLA Chief of Staff under Garang; former Minister of National Security; in opposition
General Malual Ayom Dor	Current SPLA Deputy Chief of Staff for Administration; former commander and director of SPLA production

Yei, Central Equatoria State

Name	Position
Mr RLG	Local SPLM political officer
Ms RC	Women's association and civil society
Mr LC	Community development organiser
Mr EJG	Founder of local NGO
Mr PM	Leader of local NGO
Mr HJ	Former CANS bureaucrat
Rev Hilary Luate Adeba	Bishop of Yei
Mr AI	Former Yei payam administrator; former Coordination Council member
Mr AS	Former SRRA county secretary
Mr AD	Former Otogo payam deputy director
Mr VL	Civilian from Ombasi Boma
Mr CL	Former local CANS administrator

Yambio, Western Equatoria State

Name	Position
Mary Biba (two interviews)	First female commissioner in Yambio
Edward Bukulu (two interviews)	Former Commissioner of CANS in Maridi; former speaker for Yambio state legislator
Mr EA (three interviews)	Former CANS bureaucrat
Chief EE	Zande chief
Mr PK	Former Yambio local government official
Mr GOL	Former local SPLA officer
Chief EAP	Zande chief
Richard Noti	Former speaker of WES state legislator
Mr AE	Former Secretary General of YAFA
Mr LM	Former Chairperson of YAFA
Mr SJ	Former Treasurer of YAFA
Mr BD	Former land officer
Chief Wilson Hassen Peni	Zande paramount chief
Mr RZ	Civilian and former community leader Yambio
Colonel SB (two interviews)	Former SPLA officer; former radio expert

Name	Position
Mrs MS	Former head of local women's association
Executive Chief M	Zande chief
Mr X	Elder, civilian, 95 years old
Mr FF	Former local official with SRRC
Mr DW	Former local government official
Mrs NE	Member of women's association
Mr MDA	Former Yambio SPLM State Secretary
Mr SJ	Headman
Mrs LC	Leader of women's empowerment group
Mr ST	Former local SPLM Secretary for Youth
Mr DO	Former Deputy SPLM Secretary General for WES
Mr PK	Former Nzara SPLM secretary
Mrs L	Former teacher and county inspector during CANS
Mr PJ	Former Director for Documentation, WES State government

Interviews conducted in New Site, Chukudum, Nathinga and Torit, Eastern Equatoria State

Name	Position
Captain GA	Former Head of War Veterans
Captain JB	Former bodyguard for John Garang
Chief KM	Dinka chief
Mr MKG	EES state local government officer
Chief JA	Toposa chief
Chief RL	Didinga chief present at 1st national convention
Colonel F	Former SPLA officer

Interviews conducted for UNITA case study, Angola

Luanda

Name	Position
Brigadier Horacio Njunjuvili (two interviews)	Former *Chef de cabinet* for Savimbi; UNITA representative in electoral commission since 2008
General Peregrino Chindondo Wambu (two interviews)	Former Head of Military Intelligence; COPE member; integrated into FAA in the 1990s
General N	Former front commander; defected in 1990s and integrated into FAA
Lt Colonel A (two interviews)	Grew up in Jamba; stayed alongside Savimbi; integrated into FAA in 2002
Lt Colonel AS	Grew up in Jamba; integrated into FAA in 2002
Brigadier Marcial Dachala	Former Spokesperson for the Presidency (Savimbi); former Communication and Information Minister; sanctioned by the UN in 1998
General Samuel Chiwale	UNITA founder and only surviving member of the 'China 12'; COPE member
General Camalata Numa (two interviews)	UNITA Chief of Staff, integrating the FAA alongside MPLA counterpart in 1991; sanctioned by the UN in 1998
Alcides Sakala	Former UNITA representative in Germany and Belgium; former foreign minister, 1995
Eng Ernesto Mulato	Formerly with UPA/FNLA; former prime minister in Jamba, mid-1980s; former Vice President of UNITA
General Paulo Lukamba 'Gato' (two interviews)	Former director of Savimbi's office; former secretary general; negotiated 2002 peace agreement
Adalberto da Costa Junior	Former UNITA representative in Italy, Spain and Portugal; current President of UNITA since 2019
Chipindo Bonga (two interviews)	Former Director of CENFIN (school for orphans in Jamba); ideologue of the party
Isaias Samakuva (two interviews)	Former UNITA representative to UK and France; UNITA President, 2003–19

APPENDIX 3

Name	Position
Abel Chivukuvuku	Former UNITA representative in Africa; Head of the UNITA Parliamentary Group in 1998 (under the GURN); splintered in 2008 and formed CASA-CE
Tony da Costa Fernandes	UNITA founder; former secretary general; defected in 1991
General Carlos Kandanda	FALA commander; sanctioned by the UN in 1998; left UNITA and joined CASA-CE party in 2012
General Jacinto Bandua	Founding UNITA family, key commander that defected in 1999; current Head of Psychological Warfare for FAA
Isaias Chitombi	Former Governor of Jamba after 1992; UNITA representative in Electoral Commission
Dr Ruben Sikato	Former Health Minister; former Health Minister under Unity Government 1997
Miguel Nzau Puna	Former Interior Minister and COPE member; defected in 1991; joined MPLA
General Antonino Chyiolo	Commander during the first war; former current secretary of UNITA veterans
General A	Commander during the first war (1966), remained a military commander until the 1990s
General Vicente Vihemba	Commander during the first war (1966); former commander, Eastern Front; former MP in 1997 under Unity government
Rafael Massango Sakaita Savimbi	Savimbi's son; Deputy Secretary General of UNITA
General Demóstenes Chilingutila	Key commander and former Chief of Staff of FALA 1978–85 and 1986
Clarice Caputo	Women's Association and former MP
Etna Chindondo	LIMA member
Mrs GM	Daughter of UNITA hero; LIMA member
Nela Casote	Joined FALA aged 15; former member of Battalion 89
Colonel JK	Savimbi's key mapmaker; integrated into FAA in 2002

Name	Position
Jose Pedro Katchiungo	Former *Chef de cabinet* for Savimbi, 1994/5; member of external missions in Portugal
General Samuel Epalanga	Former Chief of Intelligence for BRINDE; UN sanctioned 1998; captured in 2002 by government forces
Jaka Jamba	Former Education Minister and historian of the movement
Eugenio Manuvakola	Former Education Minister; leader of breakaway group UNITA-Renovada 1997; re-joins UNITA 2002
Brigadier FC	Former leading political commissar, Propaganda Department
Armindo Kassesse	Former Head of Propaganda, 1978; former Secretary for Information; Director of CEKK Leadership school

Interviews in Jamba, province of Kuando Kubango

Those interviewed in Jamba lived in the base before in was captured in 1999 and returned to Jamba after 2003 from refugee camps in Zambia.

Name	Position
Mr D	Captured civilian; former military instructor, worked with the South African National Defence Force
Mr PP	Captured civilian, 1984; former teacher in Jamba High School
Mr EN	Recruited from Huambo, 1989; former nurse in Central Hospital
Mr DA	Captured civilian, 1983; former VORGAN radio operator
Captain C	Former military instructor; logistics unit and active UNITA supporter
Mrs M	LIMA member
Mrs K	LIMA member; came to Jamba in 1985
Mrs A	LIMA member; worked in agriculture organisation Agrupec
Mrs CC	Captured MPLA member; held prisoner in Jamba; current municipal administrator

Interviews in Huambo province (cities of Bailundo, Huambo, Dondo, Katchiungu)

Name	Position
Liberty Chiaka (two interviews)	Former youth leader, grew up in Jamba; provincial UNITA representative
Mr E	Civilian that joined UNITA in 1960s; elder from Jamba
Colonel AJC	Former military instructor in Jamba
Brigadier Menezes Sahepo	Former Director of MIRNA
Mr JM	Key communications operator in Bailundo and Andulo in 1990s and later in West Africa
Mr CMI	Key agronomist worked in Ministry of Agriculture in Jamba
Mr AH	Clandestine operations officer, later worked at the Housing Ministry in Bailundu
Colonel VV	Former Principal Operator of Military and Leadership Communications
Valeriana Bandua	Founding member of UNITA
Mr AS	Civilian, lived in Jamba
Father A	Priest who was forced to teach in Jamba, became a sympathiser
Brigadier Alvaro Mussili	Key commander; trained in China; sanctioned by the UN in 1998

Interviews in Bie province (cities of Angulo, Kuito)

Name	Position
General Eliote Ekolelo	Former FALA commander; former provincial representative UNITA in Bie
General Severino Sawenda	Commander during the first war; former Chief of Staff of FALA; retired in 2002
Mr ANL	Former National Secretary for Youth in Military (FALA)
Manuel Savihemba	Former clandestine operations officer; became MP for UNITA in 1997, Unity government

Name	Position
Vitorino Nhany	Former clandestine operations officer; worked in agricultural secretariat in 1995; former Secretary General
Mr M	Former Director General of Central Logistics in Jamba
Mr C	Civilian who lived in Jamba; considered an elder
Mr C	Former political commissar, 1980–90s
Mr ES	Former civilian mobiliser
Mrs T	Former member of Battalion 89
Father J	Priest who was captured and forced to teach in Jamba High School in 1982
Colonel VC	Former director of OFICENGUE, 1986; transferred to MIRNA in 1996; worked in diamond sector
Mr JC	Former communications officer in Jamba under DIVITAC

NOTES

INTRODUCTION

1. Allen 1994: 114–16, in Fukui and Markakis 1994.

1. ORIGINS, CHOICES AND EXPLANATIONS

1. Quoted in Weigert 2011: 10.
2. Clapham, in Boas and Dunn 2007.
3. Brittain 1998; Assis Malaquias in Boas and Dunn 2007, among others.
4. The NIF splintered in the 1990s. The NCP became its dominant faction between 1998 and 2019 following Sudan's popular revolution and subsequent military takeover.
5. John Young, in Kingston and Spears 2004; Alex de Waal and Africa Rights worked on Sudan in the 1990s, among others.
6. Zeller, in Korf and Raeymaekers 2013: 211.
7. Johnson (2003) identified these for the case of Sudan, but they can be equally applied to the case of Angola. Other factors identified were specific to Sudan. These include the militant brand of Islam and the weakened state of the economy in 1970s, pp. xvi–xvii.
8. Wakoson, in Daly and Sikainga 1993: 47.
9. Johnson and Prunier, in Daly and Sikainga 1993: 118.
10. The first civil war took place from 1963 until 1972.
11. 'God, oil and country', International Crisis Group, report number 39, 2002, p. 99.
12. 'South Sudan: The humanitarian toll of half a decade of war', *IRIN News*, 14 December 2018.
13. Messiant, in Birmingham and Martin 1983.
14. Newitt, in Chabal and Vidal 2008: 66.
15. Malyn, in Chabal and Vidal 2008: 77.

16. Ibid.
17. Messiant, in Birmingham and Martin 1983.
18. Johnson, in Clapham 1998: 55.
19. Johnson, in Clapham 1998: 70.
20. The National Democratic Alliance (NDA) was established in October 1986, bringing together several opposition parties from all over Sudan. It had the objective of overthrowing the military regime in Khartoum and restoring democracy. The SPLM/A established an alliance with the NDA in January 1990.
21. Model 1 became the transformed democratic Sudan, while Model 2 took the 'one country, two systems' approach (implemented during the CPA transition from 2005–11). Model 3 referred to an Islamic Arab Sudan that was dominant over the South, while Model 4 was a hypothetical scenario with an African indigenous secular state dominating northern Sudan. Model 5 referred to the final solution with the independence model of two separate countries (which happened in July 2011).
22. Author interview with UNITA's former secretary general, January 2013, Luanda.
23. Potgieter, in Cilliers and Dietrich 2000: 256.
24. Ibid.
25. Author interview with with SPLM's former secretary general, May 2012, Juba.

2. THE SPLM/A'S GOVERNANCE

1. 'The call for good governance in the Republic of South Sudan', delivered to SPLA military officers, Wel, PaanLuel (ed.), *The Genius of Dr John Garang: The Essential Writings and Speeches Volume I*, printed by Amazon.co.uk.
2. Author interview with former secretary general of the SPLM, May 2012, Juba.
3. Author interview with with SPLM youth leader, February 2012, Juba.
4. Johnson, in Clapham 1998.
5. Johnson and Prunier, in Daly and Sikainga 1993: 117.
6. Johnson, in Clapham 1998: 59.
7. Justice Africa 1997: 64.
8. Luk, John, 'Return to normalcy: Relief, rehabilitation and reconstruction in the SPLM/A administered areas', in Doornbos et al. 1992.
9. WES no longer exists as part of the 10-state division in South Sudan, yet will still be used in this study to reflect the territorial divisions at the time of research. In late 2015, President Salva Kirr divided the 10 states into 28 states, and in 2017 he divided these into 32 states.
10. Author interview, June 2012, Yambio; he is considered the most senior Zande traditional authority.
11. Author interview with former Commissioner of Maridi, April 2012, Yambio.

12. Author interview with CANS Humanitarian Affairs Secretary, April 2012, Juba.
13. Testimonies collected from April to October 2012 from interviews conducted with civil society and traditional authorities in Yambio and some Equatorian intellectuals in Juba all pointed to this distinction.
14. Payam is a subdivision of counties that brings together several bomas, a category created by the SPLM/A; it is also an old name of the Kushite Kingdoms.
15. Boma refers to a livestock enclosure or a collection of villages and was the smallest administrative unit of the SPLM/A. Boma was also the name of the first area the SPLM liberated in Jonglei in 1984.
16. Author interview with former Speaker of Parliament of Yambio, June 2012, Yambio.
17. Author interview with former MP, March 2012, Juba.
18. These military divisions are explained further in Chapter 4.
19. Author interview with key member of SPLM secretariat, former member of Economic Commission of CANS, March 2012, Juba.
20. Author interview with former commissioner of Yambio, April 2012, Yambio.
21. Figures given at the National Dialogue Conference on Peace held in Khartoum in 1989, in Luk 1992: 45.
22. Author interview with paramount chief, June 2012, Yambio.
23. Author interview with SPLM State Secretary for WES, October 2012, Yambio.
24. Author interview with former SPLM ambassador, March 2012, Juba.
25. Author interview with leading SPLM intellectual and former MP, March 2012, Juba.
26. A quote by Francis Mading Deng, in Jok et al. 2004: 25.
27. Author interview with legal authority that prepared laws of the New Sudan, March 2012, Juba.
28. 'A' courts referred to a chief's court (later Boma court), while 'B' courts were higher courts made up of several chiefs and a president (later Payam court).
29. Author interview with former commissioner of Yambio, June 2012, Yambio.
30. Author interview with civilian SPLM leader from Jonglei, March 2012, Juba.
31. See Johnson 1998, when referring to establishment of SPLA courts in Lakes and Bahr El Ghazal.
32. Author interview with former commissioner of Yambio, April 2012, Yambio.
33. Ibid.
34. Author interview with local government officer, April 2012, Yambio.
35. Author interview with paramount chief of Yambio, June 2012, Yambio.
36. 'The famine in Sudan', 1996, Human Rights Watch Report.
37. Author interview with senior SPLA commander leading military production, 10 November, London.
38. Africa Rights 1997.

39. Johnson, in Sharif and Tvedt 1994: 136–41.
40. See D'Silva and Sakinas, 1999, USAID report; the Bor massacre occurred in 1991 after the movement splintered when Riek Machar's faction targeted and killed Dinka Bor (Garang's community) in Jonglei.
41. Author interview with SPLM cadre, February 2012, Juba.
42. Ibid.
43. Author interview with former CANS officer, March 2012, Juba.
44. Author interview with former SPLA Chief of Staff, October 2012, Juba.
45. Author interview with senior SPLA commander from Jonglei, November 2012, London.
46. Fainsod 1962, in Hutchcroft 2001.
47. Author interview with local government state ministry, June 2012, Yambio.
48. Author interview with paramount chief, June 2012, Yambio.
49. Author interview with NEC member and one of Garang's aides, March 2012, Juba.
50. Author interview with key SPLM political commissar, February 2012, Juba.
51. Author interview with SPLM civilian leader, March 2012, Juba.
52. Author interview with CANS official from Upper Nile, March 2012, Juba.
53. These committees were divided as follows: peace and internal solidarity, members affairs, legal affairs, military and security, foreign affairs, finance and economic affairs, information and publicity, public administration and local governance, relief, rehabilitation and humanitarian affairs, social affairs and services, refugees and displaced, human rights, women's affairs and social welfare.
54. Author interview with former NLC chairperson, February 2012, Juba.
55. Author interview with executive chief of Yambio town payam, June 2012, Yambio.
56. Author interview with CSO leader from Yambio, March 2012, Juba.
57. Author interview with former Bangasu payam administrator, June 2012, Yambio.
58. A chief justice was appointed only in 1995 but was unable to serve given that the court of appeal couldn't function with merely one judge.
59. Author interview with executive chief of Yambio town payam, June 2012, Yambio.
60. Kasirbet means house trespassing; to explain how women in the family are considered part of the household and no breaches are allowed before formal proceedings of marriage or other arrangements are met.
61. Author interview with former Chairman of Land Committee, June 2012, Yambio.
62. Author interviews, June 2012, Yambio.
63. Author interview with former Yambio commissioner, June 2012, Yambio.
64. Author interview with SPLA colonel, June 2012, Yambio.
65. Author interview with former SPLM ambassador, March 2012, Juba.
66. Author interview with YAFA chairperson, June 2012, Yambio.

67. The IPCS was created with the support of General James Wanni Igga, one of the PMHC members.
68. Author interview with founder of IPCS, March 2012, Juba.
69. Author interview with CSO founder in Central Equatoria, March 2012, Juba.
70. Author interview with member of women's association, June 2012, Yambio.
71. Author interview with women's empowerment group, October 2012, Nzara.
72. Author interview with founder of this organisation, March 2012, Juba.
73. Author interview with CSO founder in Central Equatoria, March 2012, Juba.
74. Africa Rights 1997.
75. Duffield, Mark, 'Famine, conflict and internationalisation of public welfare', in Doornbos et al. 1992.
76. Quote by a former USAID field officer, in D'Silva and Sakinas 1999: 7.
77. Author interview with former CANS Secretary of SAFFAR, October 2012, Juba.
78. Ibid.
79. Ibid.
80. *Education Policy of the New Sudan and Implementation Guidelines*, SPLM Secretariat of Education, January 2002.
81. Johnson, in Sharif and Tvedt 1994.
82. Author interview with Deputy Chairperson of Social Welfare Committee, October 2012, Yambio.
83. Author interview with SPLM health policy advisor, October 2012, Juba.
84. Akbar, September–October 1995 Report, Progress Report Western Equatoria.
85. Author interview with SPLM health policy advisor, October 2012, Juba.
86. Ibid.
87. Gibana is a tax on goods transiting through the county.
88. Author interview with former Governor of Jonglei, October 2012, Juba.
89. Author interview, October 2012, Juba.
90. Author interview with former CANS Secretary/Minister for Agriculture and Livestock, 13 October 2012, Juba.
91. These commissions were divided into: Military, Political, External Relations, Judiciary and Law Enforcement, Economy, Social Services and Civil Society.
92. Author interview with former commissioner of Yambio, June 2012, Yambio.
93. Author interview with SPLM civilian leader from Jonglei, March 2012, Juba.
94. Author interview with former minister mandated by Garang to begin the viability study, April 2012, Juba.
95. Author interview with minister and former advisor to Garang, March 2012, Juba.
96. The chairman therefore nominated Riek Machar (from Upper Nile) to be the Governor of Western Equatoria, Wanni Igga (from Central Equatoria)

as Governor of Upper Nile; Daniel Awet (from Lakes state) to Eastern Equatoria; Lam Akol (from Upper Nile) to Western Bahr El Ghazal; Kuol Manyang (from Jonglei) to Northern Bahr El Ghazal; Deng Alor (from Abyei) to Jongeli state; Pagan Amum (from Upper Nile) to Lakes state and so forth.

3. UNITA'S GOVERNANCE

1. Roque et al. 1988: 49 (author's translation).
2. Author interview with UNITA colonel, January 2013, Luanda.
3. Author interview with the Chief of Intelligence Services for BRINDE, February 2013, Luanda.
4. Marcum 1983.
5. Author interview with former Governor of Jamba, January 2013, Luanda. After 1992, when UNITA's shadow government moved to the cities, Jamba was run by a governor.
6. Author interview with former military instructor and current teacher, September 2012, Jamba.
7. Author interview with administrator of the commune, September 2012, Jamba.
8. Informal conversations with young FAA sergeants in Menongue, the provincial capital of Kuando Kubango, on the route to visit Jamba in 2012, portrayed the military outpost as an area where soldiers and officers would be sent to be punished. Their punishment in this case was the area's lack of comfort, complete isolation and harsh weather and infrastructure conditions. Soldiers there would be supplied once a month by plane and would otherwise have to ration all their supplies. Agriculture was impossible due to the lack of irrigation and the presence of wild animals. Nothing in Jamba was easy, and the military made sure that what was once a haven of organisation and functionality under UNITA was now merely a military outpost that would one day be forgotten.
9. Mitchell, Timothy, 'Society, economy and the state effect', in Steinmetz 1999.
10. Strayer 1970, in Meierhenrich 2004: 155.
11. Author interview with commander of the first war 1966–75, September 2012, Luanda.
12. As the war progressed in the 1980s, these military regions (RMs) would grow exponentially in number and the extent of their organisation. While the MPLA divided Angola into 10 military regions, UNITA divided the country into over 22 politico-military regions that overlapped with the number of strategic fronts.
13. UNITA Bulleting 1/74, Published by the Chief Representative of UNITA in the United States.
14. Alberts 1980: 252, in O'Neill et al. 1990.
15. Author interview with political mobiliser, January 2013, Andulo.

16. Author interview with commander, first war, September 2012, Luanda.
17. Savimbi, Jonas, 1986, *Por um Futuro Melhor*, Lisbon: Nova Nordica, p. 40.
18. *Ocibandas* were the local witch figures; the *sobas* and *sekulus* were authority figures (ranking below the king—a figure that remained important after the fall of the Ovimbundu and Bakongo kingdoms) who managed disputes, distributed land and presided over traditional courts.
19. Messiant 1998: 133, in Birmingham and Martin 1983.
20 Author interview with former logistics captain, September 2012, Jamba.
21. Author interviews with commanders of the first war, retired generals and UNITA MPs, January 2013, Luanda.
22. Author interview with UNITA founder, January 2013, Luanda.
23. Sitte, Franz, 'Angola's guerrilla republic', *Observer*, London, 9 April 1972.
24. Ibid.
25. Described in Bridgland 1987: 120–6.
26. Sitte, 'Angola's guerrilla republic'.
27. 'Rebel bands roam at will in Portuguese territory', *Washington Post*, 23 December 1973.
28. Bender 1978, 'Angola, the Cubans and American anxieties', Carnegie Endowment for International Peace.
29. 'UNITA six years of struggle', March 1972, Freeland of Angola, Central Base of Region Number 2.
30. Author interview with retired brigadier, January 2013, Huambo.
31. Author interview with general, first war, January 2013, Luanda.
32. Author interview with senior UNITA leader who defected in 1991, January 2013, Luanda.
33. Author interview with former governor of Jamba, January 2014, Luanda.
34. Author interview with former FALA Chief of Staff, September 2012, Luanda.
35. Author interview with former FALA Chief of Staff and leading commander, January 2013, Luanda.
36. Author interview with FALA colonel and former military instructor, January 2013, Luanda.
37. UNITA, River Cuanza Manifesto, 17 June 1976.
38. The team tasked to produce this manual included Savimbi for the political and strategic section, Nzau Puna for the economy and Samuel Chiwale for the military side. *The Cartilha* (The Warriors Manual) would be published in 1977. Chiwale 2011: 226.
39. River Cuanza Manifesto.
40. Author interview with UNITA general, January 2013, Luanda.
41. Author interview with Savimbi's former *chef de cabinet*, January 2013, Luanda.
42. Messiant, in Birmingham and Martin 1983: 155.
43. 'If UNITA ruled Angola' report, US Library of Congress, June 1986.
44. Adam 1983: 379–80, in Banton 1998: 207.
45. Quoted in Pearce 2015: 104.

46. Author interview with UNITA general, September 2012, Bie.
47. Ibid.
48. Author interview with former health minister, September 2012, Luanda.
49. Author interview with UNITA general, September 2012, Bie.
50. Author interview with Isaias Samakuva, January 2013, Luanda.
51. Author interview with military instructor, January 2013, Huambo.
52. Author interview with colonel, January 2013, Huambo.
53. Author interview with Savimbi's former *chef de cabinet*, January 2013, Luanda.
54. Author interview with UNITA brigadier, January 2013, Katchiungo.
55. Ibid.
56. Author interview with former military instructor, January 2013, Huambo.
57. Ibid.
58. At the annual meeting, held at the Delta base between May and June 1979, several issues were discussed to recalibrate the struggle and reorder it to suit changing circumstances. Chiwale 2011: 254.
59. Author interview with former military instructor, September 2012, Jamba.
60. Author interview with military instructors and captured civilians, September 2012, Jamba.
61. Esoteric appeals are one of Bard O'Neill's six identified methods to gain popular support. They 'seek to clarify the situation by placing it in an ideological or theoretical context that orders and integrates political complexities' (O'Neill et al.: 1980: 7).
62. Author interview with former nurse, September 2012, Jamba.
63. Author interview with former general, September 2012, Luanda.
64. Author interview with former general, February 2013, Luanda.
65. Author interview with former FALA Chief of Staff, January 2013, Luanda.
66. Author interview with ideologue of the party, January 2013, Luanda.
67. Skari, Tala, 'Inside the camps of UNITA's stubborn rebels', *US News & World Report*, 1 October 1984.
68. Author interviews with logistics personnel, September 2012, Huambo.
69. Author interview with logistics officer, January 2013, Huambo.
70. Author interview with LIMA member, September 2012, Luanda.
71. *The Angolan Road to National Recovery: Defining the Principles and the Objectives*, UNITA, December 1983, Jamba, p. 22.
72. Ibid, pp. 30–1.
73. Author interview with UNITA Minister for Agriculture, September 2012, Luanda
74. The Angolan Road to National Recovery, p. 35.
75. Author interview with party ideologue, January 2013, Luanda.
76. Luis de Camões and Gil Vicente are a leading part of the Portuguese literary canon.
77. Author interview with Education Minister, January 2013, Luanda.
78. Author interview with captured teacher, September 2012, Jamba.

79. The Dondi Mission was a leading institution that taught many of the anti-colonial liberation leaders and formed the backbone of UNITA's leadership schooling.

80. Author interview with Catholic priest, January 2013, Katchiungo.

81. Author interview with pastor who taught in Jamba, January 2013, Huambo.

82. Author interview with UNITA official, September 2012, Huambo.

83. Author interview with Catholic priest, January 2013, Katchiungo.

84. Author interview with UNITA general, September 2012, Bie.

85. Author interview with CENFIN student, current colonel, January 2013, Luanda.

86. Author interview with CENFIN director, January 2013, Luanda.

87. Author interview with UNITA general, September 2012, Luanda.

88. In the 1980s, UNITA is reported to have made between $3 and $12 million a year with the export of hardwoods. Minter, William, 'Accounts from Angola. UNITA as described by ex-participants and foreign visitors', 15 June 1990, Leon Dash Archives, p. 9.

89. Author interview with nurse, September 2012, Jamba.

90. Author interview with Director of OFICENGUE, January 2013, Huambo.

91. Author interview with former craftsman and current colonel, September 2012, Luanda.

92. Author interview with former secretary general, January 2013, Andulo.

93. Author interview with captain, September 2012, Jamba.

94. This was a result of the New York Agreement of 1989 that led to the withdrawal of Cuban troops and the independence of Namibia in 1990.

95. Author interview with agricultural technician, January 2013, Huambo.

96. Ibid.

97. Ibid.

98. Author interview with secretary general, January 2013, Andulo.

99. Author interview with Savimbi's *chef de cabinet*, January 2013, Luanda.

100. Roque et al. 1988: 43 (author's translation).

101. Author interview with former member of external mission in Portugal, January 2008, Lisbon.

102. Author interview with former member of external missions, January 2013, Luanda.

103. The extent of UNITA's revenue from its diamond trade is difficult to ascertain. However, there are estimates that it was managing an annual output of $300 million in 1993, reaching its production peak in 1996 with $600 million annually, which reduced to $100–300 million between 1998 and 2000. Sources quoted in Stuvoy 2002: 77.

104. Reported by *Expresso* Journalist Paulo Camacho, in Minter 1990: 9.

105. Dietrich, Christian, 'UNITA's diamond mining and exporting capacity', in Cilliers and Dietrich 2000: 277.

106. Author interview with former Health Minister, January 2013, Luanda.

107. Ibid.

108. Ibid.
109. Author interview with nurse, September 2012, Jamba.
110. Author interview with former military instructor, September 2012, Jamba.
111. Propaganda was a priority for UNITA as early as the late 1960s, when the movement began producing written briefings and publications explaining its vision and cause, and its battlefield successes.
112. Author interview with political commissar, February 2013, Luanda.
113. Ibid.
114. Author interview with former VORGAN technician, September 2012, Jamba.
115. Ibid.
116. Ibid.
117. Author interview with officer from presidential communications, January 2013, Huambo.
118. Ibid.
119. Author interview with UNITA colonel, January 2013, Luanda.
120. Author interview with former Chief of Staff, January 2013, Luanda.
121. Author interview with political commissar, February 2013, Luanda.
122. Ibid.
123. Author interview with BRINDE Director, February 2013, Luanda.
124. Nzau Puna's defection in 1991, following the death of UNITA Representative to the United States Tito Chingunji, cost Savimbi his international image and US support. The question of who ordered and killed Tito is debated secretly among UNITA leading members, none of whom explicitly state or deny that the order came from Savimbi.
125. Author interview with BRINDE Director, February 2013, Luanda.
126. Author interviews with numerous UNITA leaders, Lisbon and Luanda, 2019–23.
127. Author interview with UNITA general, Luanda, January 2013.
128. Author interview with colonel who stayed with Savimbi until 2002, January 2012, Andulo.
129. Author interview with party ideologue, January 2013, Luanda.
130. Ibid.
131. Author interview with general from first war, January 2013, Luanda.
132. Author interview with former secretary general, January 2013, Luanda.
133. Author interview with UNITA general, September 2012, Bie.
134. Author interview with party ideologue, January 2013, Luanda.
135. Girardet, Edward, 'Angola's UNITA: Guerillas … or shadow government?', *Christian Science Monitor*, 1 June 1983.
136. Author interview with UNITA commander, September 2012, Luanda.
137. Author interview with Vice Governor of Jamba, February 2013, Luanda.
138. 'Ending the Angolan conflict: Our time has come to be heard', *National Society for Human Rights (NSHR)*, 29 March 2000.
139. Author interview with senior UNITA general, a member of core negotiating team in 1992, May 2023, Lisbon.

140. 'A rough trade: The role of companies and governments in the Angolan conflict', Global Witness Report, December 1998.

4. COMPARATIVE STRATEGIES, DILEMMAS AND RESPONSES

1. Letter to General Ulysses S. Grant, referenced in 'Army leadership: Competent, confident, and agile', US Department of the Army publication, October 2006.
2. Tyler, Tom, 'Psychological perspectives on legitimacy and legitimation', *Annual Review of Psychology* 57, 2006, in Duyvesteyn 2019: 11.
3. Worrall, James, '(Re)Emergent orders: Understanding the negotiation(s) of rebel governance', in Duyvesteyn 2019.
4. Burns 1978, *Leadership*, Harper, p. 4, in Conger and Kanungo 2012.
5. These testimonies were gathered in Sudan, South Africa and Kenya by diplomats and SPLM/A leaders, from 2008 to 2012, in the context of prior work and during my research.
6. US House Committee on Foreign Affairs report, 1993.
7. The term 'genocide' was used to describe the war of July 2016 by the UN Human Rights Commission.
8. Interviews with numerous Portuguese and Angolan intellectuals and politicians who were core supporters of UNITA, 2004–08, Lisbon and Luanda.
9. US journalist Leon Dash, quoted in Burke 1984.
10. Quote by John Stockwell, former top CIA agent in Angola, in Bridgland 1987: 15.
11. Author interview with former UNITA general, January 2013, Luanda.
12. Author interview with US diplomat stationed in Angola in the 1990s, April 2015, Washington.
13. Roberts, N. and Bradley, R., 1988, 'Limits of charisma', referenced in Conger and Kanungo 2012.
14. From Garang's letter to Lagu, 'Captain John Garang's January 1972 letter to Gen. Joseph Lagu of Anyanya One', January 1972.
15. 'UNITA the people's struggle until victory', published by Norman Bethune Institute.
16. These included the National Action Movement (NAM), led by Akwot Atem de Mayen, Joseph Oduho and Samual Gai Tut, the Anyanya Absorbed Forces Underground Movement, the Juwama African People's Organisation, the Council for the Unity of Southern Sudan and the Movement for the Total Liberation of South Sudan led by Equatorian dissidents.
17. The Amigos do Manifesto Angolano (Amangola) called upon Angolans to return to the country and mobilise for guerrilla warfare.
18. These included Joao Jose Liahuka, Tony da Costa Fernandes, David Jonatao Chingunji, Miguel Nzau Puna, Ernesto Joaquim Mulato, Alexandre Magno Chinguto, Pedro Paulino Moises, Jose Kalundungu, Jacob Hossi Inacio, Nicolau Biago Tchiuka, Isaias Mussumba, Mateus Bandua, Samuel

Chivava Muanangola, Tiago Sachilombo and Jeremis Kussia Nundu, the commanders of region 5 Smanuel Chiwale and region 6 Kolungu. Chiwale 2008: 99–101.

19. Author interview with key commander and COPE member, September 2012, Luanda.
20. These included Nyachugak Nyachiluk, Riek Machar Teny, James Wanni Igga, Yusif Kuwa Mekki, Kuol Manyang, Martin Manyiel Ayeul, Lual Ding Wuol, Daniel Awet, Gordon Koang Chol and Gelario Modi.
21. Author interviews with commanders that liberated Yambio, February 2012, Juba.
22. Author interview with UNITA general from first war, January 2013, Luanda.
23. Author interview with UNITA founder, January 2013, Luanda.
24. This expression was used by several defecting commanders in 1991 and repeated in author's interviews with numerous SPLM/A leaders, 2011–12, Juba.
25. Johnson 2002, 'The final struggle is to stay in power', Focus, No. 25, Helen Suzman Foundation, in Melber 2010.
26. Collins, Randall, 'Does nationalist sentiment increase fighting efficacy?', in Hall and Malesevic 2013.
27. Author interview with UNITA general, January 2013, Luanda.
28. Jonas Savimbi, 1986, 'The war against Soviet colonialism: The strategy and tactics of anti-communist resistance', Policy Review 35.
29. Author interview with UNITA general, January 2013, Luanda.
30. Author interview with ideologue of the movement, January 2013, Luanda.
31. Author interviews with UNITA leaders, 2012, Luanda.
32. UNITA: Identity of a Free Angola, 1985, Jamba Press, p. 25.
33. Ibid., p. 26.
34. Author interview, October 2012, Juba.
35. Justice Africa 1997: 65.
36. Ignatieff, Michael, 1998, The Warrior's Honor: Ethnic War and the Modern Conscience, quoted in Waihenya 2006: 68.
37. Speech by Garang, 3 March 1984, in Khalid, Mansour (ed.), 1987, John Garang Speaks, KPI Limited, p. 19.
38. Quoted in James 2011: 133.
39. Free Angola UNITA publication 1986, in James 2011: 102.
40. Author interview with President of UNITA, January 2013, Luanda.
41. SPLM 1998 Constitution.
42. Author interview with former secretary general, May 2012, Juba.
43. Justice Africa, 1997: 84.
44. Johnson 1998: 72, in Clapham 1998.
45. Author interview with political commissar, February 2013, Luanda.
46. Author interview with SPLA colonel in communications, May 2012, Yambio.
47. Author interview with former Chief of Military Intelligence, May 2012, Juba.

48. Author interview, January 2013, Luanda.
49. Final Communique XII Annual Conference UNITA.
50. Author interviews with Savimbi's close aides and his son, January 2013, Luanda.
51. Author interview with former SPLA Head of Communications and former minister, October 2012, Juba.
52. Africa Rights 1997: 65.
53. There were five axis commands: Axis 1 was commanded by Garang and covered the areas east of the Nile, including parts of Eastern, Central and Western Equatoria; Axis 2 was commanded by Kerubino and covered southern Blue Nile; Axis 3 was led by Willian Nyuon, covering eastern and western Upper Nile; Axis 4 was commanded by Salva Kiir and covered southern Upper Nile; Axis 5 was led by Arok Thon Arok and covered Akobo, Waat, Ayod and Panjak, but was also there to support Axis 3 and 4. Arop 2006: 196.
54. The Bentiu Independent Military Area was under Riek Machar; the Bahr El Ghazal independent military area was under Daniel Awet; the Nuba mountains were under Abdel Azziz, and the Darfur independent military areas was under Duad Balad. Arop 2006: 197–8.
55. Warner, Lesley, 2012, 'Lasting solutions elusive for South Sudan's militia problem', *World Politics Review*.
56. Author interview with NLC member and former advisor to Garang, May 2017.
57. Author interview with former brigadier, January 2013, Huambo.
58. Samuel Chingunji (known as Kapesi Kafundanga), Severino Sawenda, Waldemar Pires Chindondo, Alberto Joaquim Vinama (known as Chendovava), Arlkindo Chenda Pena (known as Ben Ben), Demóstenes Chilingutila, General Ben Ben served for a second time, Altino Bango Sapalalo (known as Bock), Geraldo Ukwatchitembo Muendo (known as Kamorteiro).
59. The first deputy chiefs of staff were General Oyay Deng Ajak (for Operations), Anthony Bol Madut (for Logistics) and Peter Was Athiu (for Administrations). Directors were appointed to assist them in their branches but also in different areas like military intelligence, military training and research.
60. Opening Address to SPLM Conference on Civil Society and Organisation of Civil Authority, New Kush, April–May 1996.

5. RISE AND FALL

1. 'Angola's secret bloodbath', *Washington Post*, 29 March 1992.
2. Author interview with UNITA senior politician, January 2013, Luanda.
3. Author interview with UNITA general, October 2012, Luanda.
4. Author interview with former South African military intelligence officer present in Luanda at the time, September 2022, online.

5. Author interview with UNITA election campaign manager, May 2023, Lisbon.
6. 'Angola's balloting ballots', *Washington Times*, 30 October 1992.
7. 'Report on observation of the elections in Angola', prepared by Dietrich Kantel, Team Chief of the German election observation team.
8. Author interview with UNITA election campaign manager, May 2023, Lisbon.
9. Jolliffe, Jill, 'Angola: The big cover-up', 26 November 1992, NCN.
10. Author interview with UNITA election campaign manager, May 2023, Lisbon.
11. Schmults, Robert, 'Bloodshed and blame in Angola', *Insight*, 14 February 1993, in Heywood 2000.
12. 'Audi et alteram partem. It is necessary to listen to the other side: UNITA's December 1993 "Bill of Particulars" regarding the elections of 1992', publication of Marek Enterprise NCN, 4 August 1999.
13. 'Et tu Butros', *O Independente*, 27 November 1992.
14. Author interview with senior Portuguese diplomat, May 2023, Lisbon.
15. 'Don't abandon Jonas Savimbi', *Washington Post*, 26 January 1993.
16. Report by Margaret Hemenway, who was an officially accredited observer to the 1992 elections, House Republican Study Committee, US House of Representatives, with portions published by NCN opinion, in 'Angola: Salvaging another UN peacekeeping fiasco', 13 September 1993.
17. Author interview with former UNITA secretary general, September 2012, Luanda.
18. Author interview with UNITA general, October 2012, Luanda.
19. Ibid.
20. Dietrich, Christian, 'UNITA's diamond mining and exporting capacity', in Cillers and Dietrich 2000.
21. 'A rough trade. The role of companies and governments in the Angolan conflict', Global Witness, 1998.
22. Author interview with UNITA general, October 2012, Luanda.
23. Author interview with UNITA leader and Savimbi's nephew, January 2013, Luanda.
24. Referenced in Global Witness report, 1998.
25. Fowler Report of the UN Panel of Experts on Violations of Security Council Sanctions against UNITA, February 2000.
26. Addendum to the Report of the Monitoring Mechanism on Sanctions against UNITA, UN Security Council Committee Report established pursuant to resolution 864 (1993), 12 October 2001.
27. Ibid.
28. Ibid.
29. 'Savimbi's last stand', *Africa Confidential* 39:5, 6 March 1998.
30. Author interview with with leading commander that defected and integrated into the General FAA Headquarters, January 2012, Luanda.

31. Author interview with UNITA colonel who was in Andulo at the time, January 2013, Andulo.

32. 'Later rather than sooner', *Africa Confidential* 42:24, 7 December 2001.

33. Author interview with member of all-female Battalion 89, January 2013, Bie.

34. Addendum to the Report of the Monitoring Mechanism on Sanctions against UNITA UN Security Council Committee Report established pursuant to resolution 864 (1993), 12 October 2001.

35. Author interview with UNITA leader present at the meeting, October 2012, Luanda.

36. As per Law 10/12 of March 2012; cf. Pearce 2020.

37. Author interview with member UNITA's top leadership, January 2013, Luanda.

38. Samakuva's opening speech at Third Political Commission meeting, Portal Angola 24 horas, 8 November 2013.

39. Author interview with former UNITA army officers and soldiers, January 2015–October 2019, Luanda.

40. 'Angolan opposition chiefs hope for election success as he steps down', *France24*, 13 November 2019.

41. Phone conversation, August 2021.

42. Results tweeted on 17 February 2022.

43. 'Sondagem indica victoria do MPLA mas sem maioria absoluta', *VOA Portugues*, 11 May 2022.

44. Author interview with retired UNITA general, September 2022, online.

45. Author interview with Dinka intellectual and Garang's family member, February 2012, Juba.

46. Author interview with with NLC member who would in 2013 defect with Riek and return to Kiir's camp in 2016, February 2012, Juba.

47. *Kokora* is a Bari word for division/decentralisation but carries negative connotations for historical reasons. Although it carries different meanings for different audiences, the term is used here to mean 'divisionism'.

48. Interview with a member of the Council of States and an SPLM elder, February 2012, Juba.

49. Interview with an old SPLM cadre and member of government, February 2012, Juba.

50. As argued in Schomerus and Allen 2010.

51. Interview with former member of the SPLM Leadership Council, March 2012, Juba.

52. Interview with five NLC members, February and March 2012, Juba.

53. Interview with minister and former SPLM leader mandated by Garang to begin the viability study, April 2012, Juba.

54. Author interview with SPLA colonel, February 2012, Juba.

55. Author interview with member of Council of States and NLC, March 2012, Juba.

56. UN Panel of Experts on South Sudan report 2015; HSBA report: 'The conflict in Upper Nile State', Small Arms Survey, March 2016.

57. Unpublished report on corruption in South Sudan, prepared for a Western aid agency, November 2013.

58. Author interview with with senior UN official, January 2011, Juba.

59. Young, John, HSBA Working Paper 1, 'The South Sudan defence forces in the wake of the Juba Declaration', Small Arms Survey, November 2006.

60. UNOCHA, 'Humanitarian action in Southern Sudan bulletin', Issue 39, December 2009.

61. African Union (AU) Commission of Inquiry on South Sudan, *Final Report of the African Union Commission of Inquiry on South Sudan—Executive* Summary. Addis Ababa: AU Commission of Inquiry on South Sudan, 15 October 2014.

62. 'Overview of corruption and anti-corruption in South Sudan', Transparency International, March 2013.

63. Yoh, John Gai, 'The CPA: An embodiment of the New Sudan vision?', in Deng 2009.

64. Author interview with with member of NLC, February 2012, Juba.

65. Author interview, February 2012, Juba.

66. Author interview with with NLC observer and SPLM cadre, April 2012, Juba.

67. 'South Sudan's crisis: Its drivers, key players, and post-conflict prospects', Special Report, August 2014, Sudd Institute.

68. *Africa Confidential*, 'From power struggle to uprising', 10 January 2014.

69. United Nations Panel of Experts on South Sudan report, S/2022/359.

70. Author interviews 2004–12 in several areas of Luanda, and the provinces of Huambo and Moxico with ex-combatants and cadres who felt that the UNITA leadership after 2003 had focused on building their credibility in Luanda and forgot 'their people' in the rural areas.

71. Author interview with former Education Minister, February 2016, Juba.

CONCLUSION

1. Tilly, Charles, 'War making and state making as organised crime', in Evans et al. 1985.

2. Leander, Anna, 2004, 'War and the un-making of states: Taking Tilly seriously in the contemporary world', in Guzzini and Jung 2004.

3. Migdal, Joel and Schlichte, Klaus, 2005, 'Rethinking the state', in Schlichte 2005.

4. Appadurai 2006, in Korf and Raeymaekers 2013: 254.

5. Author interview with Payam administrator, March 2012, Yei.

6. Author interview with commissioner in Central Equatoria state, March 2012, Yei.

7. Author interview with former commissioner of Maridi, April 2012, Yambio.

8. Ibid.

9. Author interview with former UNITA general, September 2008, Luanda.

10. Author interview with former radio technician, September 2012, Jamba.

11. Author interview with captured teacher, September 2012, Jamba.

12. Author interview with FAA colonel, August 2012, Luanda.

13. Guzansky, Yoel and Kulick, Amir, 2016, 'The failed state: Ramifications for Israel's strategic environment', *Strategic Assessment* 13:2, in Schweitzer and Einav 2016.

REFERENCES

Abrams, Philip, 1988, 'Notes on the difficulty of studying the state', *Journal of Historical Sociology* 1:1, pp. 58–89.

Africa Rights, 1997, *Food and Power in Sudan: A Critique of Humanitarianism*, www.justiceafrica.org.

Akol, Lam, 2003, *The Nasir Declaration*, Nairobi: iUniverse.

Albuquerque, Carlos, 2002, *Angola: A Cultura do Medo*, Lisbon: Livros do Brasil.

Anderson, Benedict, 1991 [1983], *Imagined Communities: Reflections on the Origins and Spread of Nationalism*, London: New Left Books.

Andreski, Stanislav, 1971 [1954], *Military Organization and Society*, Berkeley, CA: University of California Press.

Andresen Guimarães, Fernando, 2001, *The Origins of the Angolan Civil War: Foreign Intervention and Domestic Political Conflict, 1961–76*, London: Palgrave Macmillan.

Appadurai, Arjun, 2006, *Fear of Small Numbers: An Essay on the Geography of Anger*, Durham, NC: Duke University Press.

Arjona, Ana, 2009, 'Armed groups' governance in civil war: A synthesis', Ralph Bunche Institute for International Studies.

Arjona, Ana, 2016, *Rebelocracy: Social Order in the Colombian Civil War*, Cambridge: Cambridge University Press.

Arjona, Ana, Kasfir, Nelson and Mampilly, Zachariah (eds), 2015, *Rebel Governance in Civil War*, Cambridge: Cambridge University Press.

Arop, Madut-Arop, 2006, *Sudan's Painful Road to Peace*, Nairobi: Book Surge.

Bahcheli, Tozun, Bartmann, Barry and Srebrnik, Henry, 2004, *De Facto States: The Quest for Sovereignty*, London: Routledge.

Banton, Michael, 1998, *Racial Theories*, Cambridge: Cambridge University Press.

Barata-Feyo, José Manuel, 1985, 'Angola: A Terra dos Robinsons', *Grandes Reportagens*, Lisbon: Amigos do Livros Editores.

Bayissa, Regassa, 2007, 'The Derg-SPLM/A cooperation: An analysis of Ethio-Sudan proxy wars', *EJOSSAH* V:2, December, pp. 20–44.

Beck, Teresa Koloma, 2009, 'Staging society: Sources of loyalty in the Angolan UNITA', *Contemporary Security Policy* 30:2, pp. 343–55.

Beck, Teresa Koloma, 2012, *The Normality of Civil War: Armed Groups and Everyday Life in Angola*, New York: Campus Verlag.

Bender, Gerald, 1972, 'The limits of counterinsurgency: An African case', *Comparative Politics* 4:3, April, pp. 331–60.

Bender, Gerald J., 1978, 'Angola, the Cubans, and American anxieties', *Foreign Policy* 31, pp. 3–30.

Birmingham, David, 2015, *A Short History of Modern Angola*, London: Hurst.

Birmingham, David and Martin, Phyllis (eds), 1983, *History of Central Africa Vol. 2*, London: Longman.

Boas, Morten and Dunn, Kevin (eds), 2007, *African Guerrillas Raging Against the Machine*, Boulder, CO: Lynne Rienner.

Borzel, Tanja and Risse, Thomas, 2010, 'Governance without a state: Can it work?', *Regulation and Government* 4, pp. 113–260.

Breidlid, Anders, 2013, 'The role of education in South Sudan's civil war', *Prospects* 43:1, pp. 35–47.

Bridgland, Fred, 1987, *Jonas Savimbi A Key to Africa*, New York: Paragon House Publishers.

Brittain, Victoria, 1998, *Death of Dignity: Angola's Civil War*, London: Pluto Press.

Brubaker, Rogers, 1996, *Nationalism Reframed: Nationalism and the National Question in the New Europe*, Cambridge: Cambridge University Press.

Burke, Robert, 1984, 'UNITA—a case study in modern insurgency', US Marine Corps Command and Staff College, April.

Chabal, Patrick, 2002 (1983), *Amilcar Cabral Revolutionary Leadership and People's War*, London: Hurst.

Chabal, Patrick and Vidal, Nuno (eds), 2008, *Angola: The Weight of History*, New York: Columbia University Press.

Chiwale, Samuel, 2008, *Cruzei-me com a Historia*, Lisbon: Sextante Editora.

Chol, Timothy Tot, 1996, 'Civil authority in the New Sudan: Organisation, functions and problems', presentation at the Conference on Civil Society and the Organisation of Civil Authority in New Sudan, SPLM/A.

Cilliers, Jakkie and Dietrich, Christian (eds), 2000, *Angola's War Economy*, Pretoria: Institute for Security Studies.

Clapham, Christopher, 1976, *Liberia and Sierra Leone: An Essay in Comparative Politics*, Cambridge: Cambridge University Press.

Clapham, Christopher (ed.), 1998, *African Guerrillas*, Oxford: James Currey.

Cleary, Sean, 2001, 'Understanding Angola's conflict and the way forward for future stability', Angola Development Forum.

Collier, Ruth and Collier, David, 2002, *Shaping the Political Arena: Critical Junctures, the Labour Movements, and Regime Dynamics in Latin America*, Notre Dame, IN: University of Notre Dame.

Conger, J. and Kanungo, R. (eds), 2012, *Charismatic Leadership: The Elusive Factor in Organisational Effectiveness*, San Francisco, CA: Jossey Bass.

Connable, Ben and Libicki, Martin, 2010, 'How insurgencies end', Santa Monica, CA: RAND Corporation.

Cooper, Frederick, 2002, *Africa Since 1940: The Past of the Present*, Cambridge: Cambridge University Press.

Cramer, Christopher, 2006, *War Is Not a Stupid Thing*, London: Hurst.

Cunningham, Kathleen Gallagher, Huang, Reyko and Sawyer, Katherine M., 2021, 'Voting for militants: Rebel elections in civil war', *Journal of Conflict Resolution* 65:1, pp. 81–107.

Dak, Samuek Ater, 1996, 'Experiences and problems in the organization of local authorities', paper presented at the Conference on Civil Society and the Organization of Civil Authority in New Sudan, SPLM/A.

Daly, M.W. and Sikainga, A.A (eds), 1993, *Civil War in the Sudan*, London: British Academic Press.

Das, Veena and Poole, Deborah (eds), 2004, *Anthropology in the Margins of the State*, Santa Fe, NM: School of American Research Press.

Deng, Francis, 1995, *War of Visions Conflict of Identities in the Sudan*, Washington, DC: Brookings Institution.

Deng, Francis (ed.), 2009, *New Sudan in the Making?*, Trenton, NJ: Red Sea Press.

Deng, Biong Hot, Eli Achol Deng and Leonardi, Cherry, 2005, 'Report on traditional authority in Western and Central Equatoria', unpublished UNDP report.

Deng, Lual, 2013, *The Power of Creative Reasoning: The Ideas and Vision of John Garang*, Nairobi: iUniverse.

Deng, Luka Biong, 2003, 'Education in southern Sudan: War, status and challenges of achieving Education for All goals', Monitoring report, UNESCO.

De Simone, Sara, 2018, 'Playing the fragile state card: The SPLM and state extraversion in South Sudan', *Journal of Modern African Studies* 56:3, pp. 395–420.

De Waal, Alex, 2014, 'When kleptocracy becomes insolvent: Brute causes of the civil war in South Sudan', *African Affairs* 11/452, pp. 231–50.

De Waal, Alex, 2015, *The Real Politics of the Horn of Africa*, Cambridge: Polity.

DeVore, Marc, 2012, 'Armed forces, states and threats: Institutions and the British and French responses to the 1991 Gulf War', *Comparative Strategy* 31:1, pp. 56–83.

Diamond, Larry, 1992, 'The second liberation', *Africa Report* 37:6, pp. 38–42.

Doornbos, Martin, Cliffe, Lionel, Ahmed, Abdel and Markakais, John (eds), 1992, *Beyond Conflict in the Horn*, Oxford: James Currey.

D'Silva, Brian and Sakinas, Anne, 1999, 'Evolution of a transition strategy and lessons learnt', USAID report.

Duyvesteyn, Isabelle (ed.), 2019, *Rebels and Legitimacy: Processes and Practices*, London: Routledge.

ElHussein, Ahmed Mustafa, 1989, 'The revival of "native administration" in Sudan: A pragmatic view', *Public Administration and Development*, Vol. 9.

Evans, Peter, Rueschemeyer, Dietrich and Skocpol, Theda (eds), 1985, *Bringing Back the State*, Cambridge: Cambridge University Press.

Fall, Bernard, 1965, 'The theory and practice of insurgency and counterinsurgency', *Naval College Review* 18:3, pp. 21–37.

Farrell, Theo, 1996, 'Figuring out fighting organisations: The new organisational analysis in strategic studies', *Journal of Strategic Studies* 19:1, pp. 122–35.

Fearon, James and Laitin, David, 2003, 'Ethnicity, insurgency and civil war', *American Political Science Review* 97:1, pp. 75–90.

Freeman, Michael, 2014, 'A theory of terrorist leadership (and its consequences for leadership targeting)', *Terrorism and Political Violence* 26, pp. 666–87.

Frisch, Ethan, 2011, 'Insurgencies are organisations too: Organisational structure and the effectiveness of insurgent strategy', *Peace & Conflict Review* 6:1.

Fukui, Katsuyoshi and Markakis, John (eds), 1994, *Ethnicity and Conflict in the Horn of Africa*, Oxford: James Currey.

Furlan, Marta, 2020, 'Understanding governance by insurgent non-state actors: A multi-dimentional approach', *Civil Wars* 22:4.

Gallo, Giorgio, 2012, 'Conflict theory, complexity and systems approach', *Systems Research and Behavioral Science* 30, pp. 493–512.

Geldenhuys, Leon, 2009, *Contested States in World Politics*, London: Palgrave Macmillan.

Gellner, Ernest, 1983, *Nations and Nationalism*, London: Blackwell.

Grynkewish, Alexus, 2008, 'Welfare as warfare: How violent non-state groups use social services to attack the state', *Studies in Conflict and Terrorism* 31:4, pp. 350–70.

Gupta, Akhil and Ferguson, James, 1997, *Culture, Power, Place. Explorations in Cultural Anthropology*, Durham, NC: Duke University Press.

Gurr, Ted, 1970, *Why Men Rebel*, London: Routledge.

Guzzini, Stefano and Jung, Dietrich (eds), 2004, *Contemporary Security Analysis and Copenhagen Peace Research*, London: Routledge.

Hall, John and Malesevic, Sinisa (eds), 2013, *Nationalism and War*, Cambridge: Cambridge University Press.

Hansen, Thomas Blom and Stepputat, Finn (eds), 2001, *States of Imagination: Ethnographic Explorations of the Post-Colonial State*, Durham, NC: Duke University Press.

Hansen, Thomas Blom and Stepputat, Finn (eds), 2005, *Sovereign Bodies*, Princeton, NJ: Princeton University Press.

Herzog, Herbert, 1998, 'Report on mission on governance to Western Equatoria, Southern Sudan', Liebefeld, Switzerland: Herzog Consult.

Heywood, Linda, 1998, 'Towards an understanding of modern political ideology in Africa: The case of the Ovimbundu of Angola', *Journal of Modern African Studies* 36:1, pp. 139–67.

Heywood, Linda, 2000, *Contested Power in Angola 1984 to the Present*, New York: University of Rochester Press.

Hobsbawm, Eric and Ranger, Terence, 1983, *The Invention of Tradition*, Cambridge: Cambridge University Press.

REFERENCES

Hodges, Tony, 2004, *Angola Anatomy of an Oil State*, Oxford: James Currey.

Huang, Reyko, 2016, 'Rebel diplomacy in civil war', *International Security* 40:4, pp. 89–126.

Human Rights Watch, 1996, *The Famine in Sudan*, https://www.hrw.org/legacy/worldreport99/africa/sudan.html

Humphreys, Macartan and Weinstein, Jeremy, 2006, 'Handling and mishandling civilians in civil war', *American Political Science Review* 100:3, pp. 429–47.

Huntington, Samuel, 1957 [1995], *The Soldier and the State: The Theory and Politics of Civil Military Relations*, Cambridge, MA: Harvard University Press.

Huntington, Samuel, 1968, *Political Order in Changing Societies*, New Haven, CT: Yale University Press.

Hutchcroft, Paul, 2001, 'Centralisation and decentralisation in administration and politics: Assessing territorial dimensions of authority and power', *Governance: An International Journal of Policy and Administration* 14:1, pp. 23–53.

Ignatieff, Michael, 1994, *Blood and Belonging, Journeys into the New Nationalism*, London: Vintage.

James, Martin, 2011, *A Political History of the Civil War in Angola, 1974–1990*, New Brunswick, NJ: Transaction Publishers.

Johnson, Douglas, 2003, *The Root Causes of Sudan's Civil War*, Oxford: James Currey.

Johnson, Douglas, 2014, 'Briefing: The crisis in South Sudan', *African Affairs* 113/451, pp. 300–9.

Johnson, Patrick, 2008, 'The geography of insurgent organization and its consequences for civil wars: Evidence from Liberia and Sierra Leone', *Security Studies* 17:1, pp. 107–37.

Jok, Aleu Akechak, Leitch, Robert A. and Vandewint, Carrie, 2004, 'A Study of Customary Law in Contemporary Southern Sudan', Monrovia, CA: World Vision International and Juba, South Sudan: The South Sudan Secretariat of Legal and Constitutional Affairs.

Jok, Jok Madut, 2007, *Sudan Religion, Race and Violence*, Oxford: One World Publications.

Jones, Seth, 2017, *Waging Insurgent Warfare Lessons From the Vietcong to the Islamic State*, New York: Oxford University Press.

Justice Africa, 1997, 'Food and the abuse of power in Sudan. Learning from the past to face the future', held by Durham University Library, Archives and Special Collections.

Kalyvas, Stathis, 2003, 'The ontology of political violence: Action and identity in civil wars', *American Political Science Review* 1–3, pp. 715–35.

Kalyvas, Stathis, 2006, *The Logic of Violence in Civil War*, Cambridge: Cambridge University Press.

Kalyvas, Stathis, 2012, 'Micro-level studies of violence in civil war: Refining and extending the control-collaboration model', *Terrorism and Political Violence*, 24, pp. 658–68.

Kalyvas, Stathis, Shapiro, Ian and Masoud, Tarek (eds), 2008, *Order, Conflict and Violence*, Cambridge: Cambridge University Press.

REFERENCES

Kalyvas, Stathis and Balcells, Laia, 2010, 'Did Marxism make a difference? Marxist rebellions and national liberation movements', paper prepared for the Annual Meeting of American Political Science Association, Washington, https://digital.csic.es/bitstream/10261/58669/1/Did%20Marxism.pdf

Kanyane, Modimowabarwa Hendrick, Mai, James Hoth and Deng, Abot Kuol, 2013, *Liberation Struggle in South Sudan*, Amman: Reach Publishers.

Kasfir, Nelson, 2002, 'Dilemmas of popular support in guerrilla war: The National Resistance Army in Uganda, 1981–86', paper presented at Laboratory in Comparative Ethnic Processes, UCLA.

Kasfir, Nelson, 2005, 'Guerillas and civilian participation. The National Resistance Army in Uganda, 1981–86', *Journal of Modern African Studies* 43:2, pp. 271–6.

Kasfir, Nelson, Frerks, Georg and Terpstra, Niels, 2017, 'Introduction: Armed groups and multi-layered governance', *Civil Wars* 19:3, pp. 257–78.

Keister, Jennifer and Slantchev, Branislav, 2014, 'Statemakers to statebreakers: stretegies of rebel governance', Working Paper, University of San Diego.

Khalid, Mansour (ed.), 1989, *The Call for Democracy in Sudan*, London: Kegan Paul International.

Kilcullen, David, 2004, 'Countering global insurgency', *Small Wars Journal*, (extended online version).

Kilcullen, David, 2005, 'Countering global insurgency', *Journal of Strategic Studies* 28:4, pp. 597–617.

Kilcullen, David, 2006, 'Counterinsurgency redux', *Survival* 48:4.

Kingston, Paul and Spears, Ian (eds), 2004, *States Within States: Incipient Political Entities in the Post-Cold War Era*, New York: Palgrave Macmillan.

Kok, Peter, 1996, 'Sudan: Between radical restructuring and deconstruction of state systems', *Review of African Political Economy* 23:70, pp. 555–62.

Korf, Benedikt and Raeymaekers, Timothy (eds), 2013, *Violence on the Margins*, New York: Palgrave Macmillan.

Kuol, Kuol Deng-Abot, 2008, 'An Investigation of the Roles of Traditional Leadership in the Liberation Struggle in Southern Sudan from 1983–2004', MA thesis, University of Fort Hare.

Kuol, Monyluak Alor, 1997, *Administration of Justice in SPLA/M Liberated Areas: Court Cases in War-Torn Southern Sudan*, Refugee Studies Program, Oxford University.

Latham, R., 2000, 'Social sovereignty', *Theory, Culture and Society* 17:4.

LeRiche, Matthew and Arnold, Matthew, 2012, *South Sudan From Revolution to Independence*, London: Hurst.

Lichbach, Mark, 1995, *The Rebels Dilemma*, Ann Arbor: University of Michigan Press.

Lidow, Nicholai, 2010, 'Rebel governance and civilian abuse: Comparing Liberia's rebels using satellite data', paper prepared for WGAPE, University of Berkeley.

Lidow, Nicholai, 2016, *Violent Order: Understanding Rebel Governance Through Liberia's Civil War*, Cambridge: Cambridge University Press.

Lijphart, Arend, 1977, *Democracy in Plural Societies: A Comparative Exploration*, New Haven, CT: Yale University Press.

Linz, Juan, 2000, *Totalitarian and Authoritarian Regimes*, London: Lynne Rienner.

Luttwak, Edward, 1987, *Strategy:The Logic of War and Peace*, Harvard, MA: Belknap.

Mach Guarak, Mawut, 2011, *Integration and Fragmentation of the Sudan*, Bloomington, IN: Author House.

Mai, James Hoth, 2008, 'Political reconciliation between SPLM, SPLA and Anyanya: A negotiation tool for national reconciliation and peace in post-war Sudan', thesis, University of Fort Hare.

Mampilly, Z. and Stewart, M.A., 2021, 'A typology of rebel political institutional arrangements', *Journal of Conflict Resolution* 65:1, pp. 15–45.

Mao Tse-Tung, 1961, *On Guerrilla Warfare*, Urbana, IL: University of Illinois Press.

Mao Tse-Tung and Guevara, Che, 1961, *Guerrilla Warfare*, London: Cassell.

McChrystal, Stan, 2014, 'Operational leadership', *RUSI Journal* 159:2, pp. 38–42.

MacKinlay, John, 2005, *Globalisation and Insurgency*, The Adelphi Papers Series, International Institute for Strategic Studies.

Mai, James Hoth, Kuol, Deng and Kanyane, Modimowabarwa, 2009, *Liberation Struggle in South Sudan*, Pinetown Printers.

Malkki, Liisa, 1995, *Purity and Exile*, Chicago, IL: University of Chicago Press.

Malok, Elijah, 2009, *The Southern Sudan Struggle for Liberty*, Nairobi: East African Educational Publishers.

Mamdani, Mahmoud, 1996, *Citizens and Subject. Contemporary Africa and the Legacy of Late Colonialism*, Oxford: James Currey.

Mampilly, Zachariah, 2008, 'Bandits, warlord, embryonic state or anti-state sovereign: What is a rebel government?', Order, Conflict and Violence Seminar Series, Yale University.

Mampilly, Zachariah, 2011, *Rebel Rulers, Insurgent Governance and Civilian Life During War*, New York: Cornell University Press.

Marcum, James, 1983, 'The politics of survival: UNITA in Angola', *Africa Notes* 8, CSIS.

Marcum, John, 1978, *The Angolan Revolution: Exile Politics and Guerrilla Warfare, 1962–1976*, Cambridge, MA: MIT Press.

Martell, Peter, 2018, *First Raise a Flag*, London: Hurst.

Meierhenrich, J., 2004, 'Forming states after failure', in Rotberg, R.I. (ed.), *When States Fail: Causes and Consequences*, Princeton, NJ: Princeton University Press.

Melber, Henning, 2010, 'The legacy of anti-colonial struggles in Southern Africa: Liberation movements as governments', conference paper.

Mennen, Tiernan, 2010, 'Lessons from Yambio: Legal pluralism and customary justice reform in Southern Sudan', *Hague Journal on the Rule of Law* 2, pp. 218–52.

Metelis, Claire, 2010, *Inside Insurgency*, New York: New York University Press.

Metz, Steven, 1993, 'The future of insurgency', Carlisle, PA: United States Army War College Press.

Metz, Steven, 2007, 'Rethinking insurgency', Carlisle, PA: United States Army War College Press, Strategic Studies Institute.

REFERENCES

Migdal, Joel, 1988, *Strong Societies and Weak States: State–Society Relations and State Capabilities in the Third World*, Princeton, NJ: Princeton University Press.

Migdal, Joel, 2004, 'State building and the non-nation–state', *Journal of International Affairs* 58:1, pp. 17–47.

Minter, William, 1990, 'Accounts from Angola. UNITA as described by ex-participants and foreign visitors', 15 June 1990, Leon Dash Archives, p. 9.

Minter, William, 1994, *Apartheid's Contras*, Johannesburg: Witwatersrand University Press.

Muekalia, Anabela Chipeio, 2015, *Angola: Quando o impossivel se torna Possivel*, Lisbon: Porto Editora.

Muekalia, Jardo, 2010, *Angola a Segunda Revolução*, Lisbon: Sextante Editora.

Munro, William A, 1996, 'Power, peasants and political development: Reconsidering state reconstruction in Africa', *Comparative Studies in Society and History* 38:1, pp. 112–48.

Neto, Maria da Conceição, 2012, 'In town and out of town: A social history of Huambo (Angola), 1902–1961', PhD thesis, SOAS, University of London.

Nyaba, Peter Adwok, 1997, *The Politics of Liberation in South Sudan*, Kampala: Fountain.

Nyang'oro, Julius, 1989, 'The state of politics in Africa: The corporatist factor', in *Comparative International Development* 24:1, pp. 5–19.

Nyang'oro, Julius and Shaw, Timothy, 1998, *Corporatism in Africa*, London: Routledge.

Obadare, Ebenezer and Adebanwi, Wale (eds), 2016, *Governance and the Crisis of Rule in Contemporary Africa*, New York: Palgrave Macmillan.

Ohm, Manfred, 2014, *War and Statehood in South Sudan*, London: Bloomsbury.

Olson, Mancur, 1993, 'Dictatorship, democracy and development', *American Political Science Review* 87:3, pp. 567–76.

O'Neill, Bard, 1990, *Insurgency & Terrorism: Inside Modern Revolutionary Warfare*, Washington, DC: Brasseys.

O'Neill, Bard, Heaton, William and Alberts, Donald (eds), 1980, *Insurgency in the Modern World*, Boulder, CO: Westview Press.

Paret, Peter, 1989, 'Military power', *Journal of Military History* 53:3, pp. 239–56.

Pearce, Justin, 2015, *Political Identity and Conflict in Central Angola, 1975–2002*, Cambridge: Cambridge University Press.

Pearce, Justin, 2020, 'From rebellion to opposition: UNITA's social engagement in post-war Angola', *Government and Opposition* 55, pp. 478–89.

Péclard, Didier, 2021, 'Nationalism, liberation, and decolonization in Angola', in *Oxford Research Encyclopedia of African History*, Oxford: Oxford University Press.

Péclard, Didier and Mechoulan, Delphine, 2015, 'Rebel Governance and the Politics of Civil War', Working Paper Swiss Peace. https://www.swisspeace.ch/assets/publications/downloads/Working-Papers/3b4a3caa24/Rebel-Governance-and-the-Politics-of-Civil-War-Working-Paper-15-swisspeace-didier_peclard.pdf.

Pegg, Scott, 1998, *International Society and the De Facto Society*, Abingdon, UK: Routledge.

Pereira, Anthony, 1994, 'The neglected tragedy: The return to war in Angola, 1992–94', *Journal of Modern African History* 2:1, pp. 1–28.

Pinaud, Clémence, 2021, *War and Genocide in South Sudan*, Ithaca, NY: Cornell University Press.

Pincus, Steve and Robinson, James, 2013, 'Wars and state-making reconsidered: The rise of the interventionist state', www.law.nyu (online version).

Pool, David, 2001, *From Guerrillas to Government: The Eritrean People's Liberation Front*, Oxford: James Currey.

Putzel, J, 2007, 'Governance challenges in post-war states: Security, democratic politics and economic management', Crisis States Research Centre, LSE.

Raeymaekers, Timothy, Menkhaus, Ken and Vlassenroot, Koen, 2008, 'State and non-state regulation in African protracted crises: Governance without government?', *Afrika Focus* 21:2, pp. 7–21.

Reno, William, 2011, *Warfare in Independent Africa*, Cambridge: Cambridge University Press.

Riehl, Volker, 1994, 'Who rules in South Sudan?', in Sharif, Harir and Tvedt, Terje (eds), *Short-Cut to Decay – The Case of Sudan*, Uppsala, Sweden: Nordiska Afrikainstitutet.

Riehl, Volker, 2001, 'Who is ruling South Sudan? The role of NGOs in rebuilding socio-political order', Report No. 9, Uppsala, Sweden: Nordiska Afrikainstitutet.

Rohn, Helge, Nyaba, Peter Adwok and Benjamin, George, 1997, 'Report of the study on local administrative structures in Maridi, Mundri, and Yei counties, West Bank Equatoria, South Sudan', Nairobi: Aktion Afrika Hilfe.

Rolandsen, Oystein, 2005, *Guerilla Government, Political Changes in the Southern Sudan during the 1990s*, Uppsala, Sweden: Nordiska Afrikainstitutet.

Roque, Fatima, Vaz da Silva, Helena, Manoel de Vilhena, Luiza, Avilez, Maria João, Nogueira Pinto and Maria José, 1988, *Seis Portuguesas em Terras da UNITA*, Lisbon: Bertrand Editora.

Roque, Paula Cristina, 2008, 'Angolan legislative elections: Analysing the MPLA's triumph', Situation Report, Institute for Security Studies.

Roque, Paula Cristina, 2012, 'The SPLM: Political transformation or strategic adaptation?', in Heinrich Böll Foundation and Weis, Toni (eds), *Sudan After Separation – New Approaches to a New Region* 28, pp. 68–80.

Roque, Paula Cristina, 2014, 'Reforming the SPLM: A requisite for peace and nation-building', *Policy Brief* 63, Institute for Security Studies.

Roque, Paula and Miamingi, Remember, 2017, 'Beyond ARCISS: New fault lines in South Sudan', Situation Report, Institute for Security Studies.

Roque, Paula Cristina, 2021a, *Governing in the Shadows: Angola's Securitised State*, London: Hurst.

Roque, Paula Cristina, 2021b, 'The challenge of territory-governing insurgencies on war and peace strategies', in Johnson, Rob, Kitzen, Martijn and Sweijs, Tim (eds), *The Conduct of War in the 21st Century*, London: Routledge.

Rotberg, Robert (ed.), 2004, *When States Fail: Causes and Consequences*, Princeton, NJ: Princeton University Press.

Rothchild, Donald and Olorunsola, Victor (eds), 1983, *State Versus Ethnic Claims: African Policy Dilemmas*, Boulder, CO: Westview Press.

Salih, Mohamed, 1989, 'Tribal militias, SPLA/M and the Sudanese state: New wine in old bottles', paper delivered at the Management of the Crisis in Sudan Conference, Bergen Forum, www.fou.uib.no/fd/1996/f/712001/backevid.htm

Sambanis, Nicolas, 'Do ethnic and nonethnic civil wars have the same causes?: A theoretical and empirical inquiry', *Journal of Conflict Resolution* 45:3, pp. 259–82.

Sanin, Francisco Gutierrez and Wood, Elisabeth Jean, 2014, 'Ideology in civil war, instrumental adoption and beyond', *Journal of Peace Research* 51:2, pp. 259–82.

Savimbi, Jonas, 1986, *Por um Futuro Melhor*, Lisbon: Nova Nordica.

Scharpf, Fritz W., 1998, 'Interdependence and democratic legitimation', MPIfG Working Paper, No. 98/2, Max Planck Institute for the Study of Societies.

Schlichte, Klaus (ed.), 2005, *The Dynamics of States: The Formation and Crises of State Domination*, London: Routledge.

Schomerus, Mareike and T. Allen, 2010, *Sudan at Odds With Itself: Dynamics of Conflict and Predicaments of Peace*, DESTIN report, LSE.

Schweitzer, Yoram and Einav, Omer (eds), 2016, 'The Islamic State: How Viable is it?', Tel Aviv: Institue for National Security Studies.

Scott, Philippa, 1985, 'The Sudan People's Liberation Movement and Liberation Army', *Review of African Political Economy* 33, pp. 69–82.

Sharif, Harir and Tvedt, Terje (eds), 1994, *Short-Cut to Decay – The Case of Sudan*, Uppsala, Sweden: Nordiska Afrikainstitutet.

Sharma, Aradhana and Gupta, Akhil (eds), 2006, *The Anthropology of the State: A Reader*, Oxford: Blackwell.

Simpkins, Gregory B., 1996, *Angola: A Chronology of Major Political Developments, February 1961–September 1996*, Alexandria, VA: Institute for Democratic Strategies.

Skocpol, Theda, 1979, *States and Social Revolutions: A Comparative Analysis of France, Russia and China,* Cambridge: Cambridge University Press.

Smith, Anthony D., 1986, *The Ethnic Origins of Nations*, Oxford: Blackwell.

Snow, David, Soule, Sarah and Kriesi, Hanspeter (eds), 2004, *The Blackwell Companion to Social Movements*, Wiley-Blackwell (online paper version).

Staniland, Paul, 2014, *Networks of Rebellion: Explaining Insurgent Cohesion and Collapse,* Ithaca, NY: Cornell University Press.

Stearns, Jason, 2012, *Dancing in the Glory of Monsters: The Collapse of the Congo and the Great War of Africa*, New York: Public Affairs.

Steinmetz, George, 1999, *State/Culture: State-Formation After the Cultural Turn*, Ithaca, NY: Cornell University Press.

Stewart, Megan, 2020, 'Rebel governance: Military boon or military bust?', *Conflict Management and Peace Science* 37:1, pp. 16–38.

REFERENCES

Stewart, Megan, 2021, *Governing for Revolution: Social Transformation in Civil War*, Cambridge: Cambridge University Press.

Stuvoy, Kirsti, 2002, 'The UNITA social order in Angola', in War Economy and the Social Order of Insurgencies. Analysis of UNITA's war economy, Paper N3, University of Hamburg.

Taber, Robert, 2002 [1965], *War of the Flea*, Dulles, VA: Potomac Books.

Thomson J.E., 1995, 'State sovereignty in international relations: Bridging the gap between theory and empirical research', *International Studies Quarterly* 39(2), pp. 213–33.

Toussie, Sam, 1989, 'War and survival in southern Angola: The UNITA assessment mission', International Rescue Committee, US State Department.

Tuori, Kaius, 2011, 'The disputed roots of legal pluralism', *Law, Culture, and the Humanities* 9:2 pp. 330–52.

Turbiville, Graham, 2005, 'Logistic Support and Insurgency. Guerilla Sustainment and Applied Lessons of Soviet Insurgent Warfare: Why it Should Still Be Studied', Joint Special Operations University Report.

Valentim, Jorge, 2011, *Caminho para a Paz e a Reconciliação Nacional*, Luanda: Mayamba.

Villalon, Leonardo and Huxtable, Phillip (eds), 1998, *The African State at a Critical Juncture: Between Disintegration and Reconfiguration*, Boulder, CO: Lynne Rienner.

Vlasak, Marian, 2007, 'The paradox of logistics in insurgencies and counterinsurgencies', *Military Review* 89:1, pp. 89–95.

Waihenya, Waitaka, 2006, *The Mediator*, Nairobi: East African Educational Publishers.

Weigert, Stephen, 2011, *Angola: A Modern Military History, 1961–2002*, New York: Palgrave Macmillan.

Weinstein, Jeremy, 2007, *Inside Rebellion: The Politics of Insurgent Violence*, Cambridge: Cambridge University Press.

Wickham-Crowley, Timothy, 1987, 'The rise (and sometimes fall) of guerrilla governments in Latin America', *Sociological Forum* 2:3, pp. 473–99.

Wondu, Steven, 2011, *From Bush to Bush: Journey to Liberty in South Sudan*, Nairobi: East African Educational Publishers.

Yihun, Belete Belachew, 2013, 'Ethiopia's role in South Sudan's March to Independence 1955–1991', *African Studies Quarterly* 14:1, pp. 35–54.

Young, John, 2003, 'Sudan: Liberation movements, regional armies, ethnic militias and peace', *Review of African Political Economy* 97, pp. 423–34.

Young, John, 2012, *The Fate of Sudan: The Origins and Consequences of a Flawed Peace Process*, London: Zed Books.

Young, John, 2019, *South Sudan's Civil War: Violence, Insurgency and Failed Peace-Making*, London: Zed Books.

Zartman, I.W., Knudsen, C. and Mundt, A., 2000, 'Peace agreements: The case of Angola', African Centre for the Constructive Resolution of Disputes, www.reliefweb.int

INDEX

Note:
Page numbers followed by 't' refer to tables, 'f' refer to figures.

INDEX

91, 96, 103, 104, 205, 206,
231, 263, 264, 265, 303,
305, 306
Civil–Military Administration
(CMA), 25–6, 52, 56, 61–5,
64f, 70, 71, 205, 206, 303
critical juncture (1991) and the
impetus to transform, 72–6
economic activities and relief,
69–72
elections (2010), 57
ethnic tensions, 59–61
justice system, 66–8, 85–90
limitations in, 37
militarisation of society, 65–9,
104

military farms, 70
military units, creating, 55
relative peace, 58
return to militarisation, 103
service delivery and economic
development, 90–102
trade, 70
WES riots (1956), 59
See also SPLM/A (Sudan
People's Liberation
Movement/Army)

Zambia, 1, 109, 113, 131, 134,
166, 179, 182, 196, 243, 247,
306